Whereas it has been *Industriously* and **Maliciously** reported, That Mr. *John Jones* (now a Candidate for the Place of ORGANIST to the United Parishes of *Alhallows Bread-Street*, and St. *John* the Evangelist) is a BUNGLER, *&c.*

This *False Report* having already been a very great Prejudice to Mr. *Jones*'s Interest, in relation to his being elected *Organist* to the said Parishes; Therefore (in Justice to the said Mr. *Jones*) 'tis thought fit to undeceive those Gentlemen who have been thus impos'd on, by such *False* and *Base Insinuations*; That the said Mr. *Jones* is a Person *fitly Qualified*, and *Capable* of playing on *any Organ*, being very well recommended and approv'd; as appears by a Certificate of several undeniable MASTERS, who have given it under their own Hands, and did it before an Organ was put up (or design'd so to be) in the said Parish-Church.

Any Gentlemen desirous of seeing the *Original* of the following *Certificate*, may do it at *Steel*'s Coffeehouse in *Bread-street*.

WE whose Names are under written, do certifie, That Mr. John Jones, *brought up in the Cathedral Church of St.* Paul's, *is Capable of Playing (in any Parish-Church in* England*) on the Organ. As witness Our Hands:*

† Richard Brind, *Organist of St.* Paul's.
Cha. King, *B. M. Master of the Boys of St.* Paul's, *and Organist of St.* Bennet Fink.
† Daniel Purcell, *Organist of St.* Dunstan's *in the East, and St.* Andrew's, Holborn.
Charles Young, *Organist of* Alhallows Barkin.
Peter Horwood, *Organist of* Christ-Church.
Benj. Short, *Organist of St.* Sepulchres, *and St.* Dunstan Stepney.
Geo. Hayden, *Organist of St.* Mary Magdalen Bermondsey.
Mau. Greene, *Organist of St.* Paul's, *St.* Andrew's Holborn, *aud St.* Dunstan's *in the West.*
Edw. Hen. Purcell, *Organist of St.* Martin Orgars.

Gentlemen,

YOur Vote and Interest is earnestly Desir'd in favour of the said Mr. JONES, who has given full Assurance of a Constant Attendance.

NB. Those Persons against whose Names this mark † is plac'd, are since dead; And the two last sign'd some Time after the rest.

Election broadside of John Jones for the post of organist at All Hallows, Bread Street, 1718.

British Library

ORGANISTS OF THE CITY OF LONDON 1666–1850

A RECORD OF ONE THOUSAND ORGANISTS WITH AN ANNOTATED INDEX

by

DONOVAN DAWE

DONOVAN DAWE
1983

First published 1983 by the Author

Production and Distribution by
Quill Printing Services Ltd.,
6 Cross Street, Padstow, Cornwall PL28 8AT

ISBN 0 9509064 0 9

Typeset by Inforum Ltd, Portsmouth
Printed and bound in Great Britain by A. Wheaton & Co. London & Exeter

Contents

Introduction

This account of the organists of the City of London covers the period between the rebuilding of the churches after the Great Fire of 1666 and 1850. Unsuccessful candidates for organists' posts are included and a small number of organists who lived in the City but appear to have been employed outside are incorporated in the Annotated Index.

The book is in three parts. The first is a series of essays on various aspects of the organists and their work, their salaries, long serving organists, women organists and so on. This is followed by the lists of organists and candidates arranged under churches and other institutions giving details about dates of appointment and vacation, votes cast, salaries paid and other information.

The third and most substantial section is an Annotated Index of organists and candidates. The entries are not intended to be biographical but to record miscellaneous facts drawn almost entirely from original sources. Much of the newly discovered material adds to or corrects information about composers or musicians who feature in standard works of reference. Dates of death are sometimes corrected or revealed for the first time and miscellaneous details are given when they have presented themselves in the course of the investigations. These have covered the original records of all the parishes in the City of London (mostly housed in Guildhall Library), the records of many City livery companies, contemporary newspapers, wills in various repositories, London directories, assessments in the Guildhall Library and Guildhall Records Office, subscribers' lists etc.

Among nearly a thousand organists included in this survey are found some of the most significant figures in two hundred years of English music. Of the more eminent, William Boyce can claim the closest ties with the City having been born, baptised and buried within its boundaries and it is a matter of regret that he was dismissed from both his City posts. Maurice Greene, also born and buried in the City, John Stanley, Daniel Purcell, Charles Burney and R.J.S. Stevens were all City organists while John Blow, Jeremiah Clarke and Michael Wise held office at St. Paul's. There are probably three hundred more who could claim to have left musical compositions behind them and an increasing number of them are asserting themselves in the current trend for reviving the works of minor eighteenth century English composers.

Selection from these is somewhat invidious but composers such as Thomas Attwood, William Babell, John Barrett, Jonathan Battishill, Sir John Goss, Philip Hart, Henry Heron, Samuel Howard, Robert Hudson, Samuel Long,

George Monro, J.C. Pepusch, William Reeve, John Weldon, Abiell Whichello and John Worgan all held office in the City and were among the most prolific.

The only previous attempt in book form to put on record the City organists was by C.W. Pearce, himself a City organist, whose *Notes on old London city churches, their organs, organists, and musical associations* was published in 1909. Valuable though this work is, Pearce regretted that he had "found it impossible to *complete* the lists of organists in *every* parish, for the reason that in some cases the records of organ appointments no longer exist". In fact the lists are so incomplete that they amount to little more than random selections for which the unavailability of records was not by any means entirely responsible. Pearce was assisted by his fellow organists, the incumbents of City churches and the manuscript work of J.H. Leffler, organist of St. Katherine by the Tower around 1800.

Apart from Pearce, lists of organists of many individual City of London churches have appeared in print, notably those included in a series of articles on London church organs by the Rev. Andrew Freeman which appeared regularly in *The Organ*. Although limited in their coverage of City churches and not entirely reliable, they represent a considerable advance on Pearce both in accuracy and completeness. Church histories either in book or pamphlet form sometimes include the names of the organists and a few churches have issued authoritative pamphlets on their organs with lists of varying quality.

Before describing the main sources of information used in compiling the church lists, a word of explanation is necessary on the organisation of the churches and parishes within the City of London. Before the Great Fire of 1666 there were 107 churches each ministering to the needs of a separate parish. Of the 86 destroyed in the Fire only 51 were rebuilt so that the City then had 72 churches. The original 107 parishes continued to operate as separate entities, many of the churches serving as the parish church for two or, in a few cases, three parishes. Each united parish held its own vestry meetings and maintained its own accounts and registers of baptisms, marriages and burials. Each appointed its own church officers but the organist was elected by the combined parishes and the payment of his salary shared between them.

The 72 parish churches which emerged from the ruins of the Great Fire in 1666 remained until 1781 when, as a result of the Gordon riots, St. Christopher le Stocks had to be demolished. St. Michael Crooked Lane was removed for the formation of the approaches to a new London Bridge in 1831 and ten years later St. Bartholomew by the Exchange was taken down to make room for the new Royal Exchange. Two new churches were built about the same time; Holy Trinity Gough Square in 1838 and St. Bartholomew Moor Lane in 1850.

Although all these 74 churches are included in the lists there is no evidence of an organ at St. Christopher le Stocks and an early nineteenth century allusion to an organ in All Hallows Staining finds no corroboration in the parish records. The 74 lists are brought up to 84 by the addition of St. Paul's Cathedral, for which both organists and almoners are given, the collegiate churches of Holy Trinity Minories and St. Katherine by the Tower (removed from the City to Regent's Park in 1825), the Temple Church (with separate lists for organists supplied by the Inner and Middle Temples), the Dutch Church Austin Friars, the organists of Charterhouse, Crosby Hall and the

Parish Clerks' Company and the music masters of Christ's Hospital.

The main sources of information for the church lists are the vestry minute books of the individual parishes which ideally contain details of the elections of the organists, the names of the unsuccessful candidates, the votes cast and the salaries paid. The organist was usually re-elected each April and other matters relating to him appeared irregularly. His death, resignation or dismissal was put on record and his death was sometimes followed by a plea for financial aid to his widow. Ostensibly, then, the compilation of the church lists should present no problems but unfortunately, for a variety of reasons, only a small minority fail to do so.

Many series of vestry minute books are incomplete and in a few cases, such as St. Peter le Poer and Christ Church Newgate Street, they are virtually non-existent. Gaps can sometimes be filled from the churchwardens' accounts which normally reveal at least the surname of the organist, his salary and the approximate date of his appointment and replacement. They do not give the names of the unsuccessful candidates and other details of the election.

Sometimes neither vestry minute books nor churchwardens' accounts have survived and it is then that the equivalent series of a united parish as indicated above can provide the key. The salary as entered in the churchwardens' accounts of a united parish can be misleading as each united parish paid only its allotted proportion of the whole.

In many instances the vestry minute books and churchwardens' accounts are non-productive. This arises when the organist was paid by voluntary subscription and neither his election nor the payments to him feature in surviving records. No doubt a separate account of organ expenditure was kept but no surviving example has been found. Sometimes for no apparent reason the record of an organist's appointment is not found in the minutes or, as in the case of St. Andrew Holborn, some elections are given and others pass unnoticed. The explanation can only be that a secondary series of minutes was maintained giving details of such matters.

The introduction of the "annuity organ" in the mid eighteenth century (see pp. 13–17) poses additional problems. The "annuity organ" was installed by an organ builder or an organ supplier through an annuity agreement with the parish which included the supply of an organist. Details of the transactions are found in the vestry minute books but for the most part they fail to reveal the name of the organist, the responsibility for whose appointment rested with the annuitant. The churchwardens' accounts can produce misleading payments such as to "John Smith, organist" which means in effect that the payments were made to the annuitant John Smith for paying the organist.

As they often undertook to play themselves, the organ providers have been included in the Annotated Index. It is improbable that all of them did or indeed that many were competent to do so. There are instances, however, when the children of an organ annuitant undoubtedly played and Hugh Russell's son William was a talented example.

When no parish records are available, information can occasionally be found in contemporary newspapers. Reporting of such news was sporadic and a few successive years of very selective election results are followed too often by a longer succession of lean years. An obituary notice can sometimes be helpful but newspapers tended to lose interest in organists' deaths for long periods at a time. For the most part, even in the most informative years, only the most eminent are recognised and selection is frequently haphazard.

It is therefore inevitable that the church lists can never be complete. Gaps can sometimes be tentatively filled from secondary sources and such intrusions are clearly indicated in both lists and index.

It would be folly to ignore this secondary material entirely, for earlier authorities had access to records no longer available. This applies to Pearce's work and, where no alternative sources survive, his findings have been used to fill gaps. In view of the many established inaccuracies in his work, however, they must be accepted with reservation. Grove, too, gives details of some City organists' appointments which cannot now be authenticated.

Much of such information has been copied and its inaccuracies perpetuated by successive authorities and it is not always possible to establish its origin. Later writers, whose authority on the organ is unchallenged, are frequently less qualified in the location and interpretation of eighteenth century records and tend to use suspect printed material unquestioningly.

Among other secondary sources referred to is the monumental eighteenth century *General history of music* by Sir John Hawkins. Only occasionally helpful, he supplies the only evidence for Peter Prelleur's appointment to St. Alban Wood Street in 1728. In an entirely different category is the work of established London historians of repute such as William Herbert. His history of St. Michael Crooked Lane published around 1833 quoted verbatim and doubtlessly with a high degree of accuracy from records which no longer survive. His extracts relating to the election of organists before that date can therefore be accepted with reasonable confidence.

Altogether nearly a thousand organists appear in the Annotated Index of whom rather less than half held appointments in the City of London. The remainder appeared as unsuccessful candidates or lived in the City without contesting City posts. About 140 appear either in *The new Grove dictionary of music and musicians*, 20 vol. 1980 or in the 5th edition of Grove, 9 vol. 1954–61. Considerably more than this are found in the *British union-catalogue of early music printed before 1801*, 2 vol. 1957 which includes all composers whose scores have been identified in print before 1801. Many more of them than this composed music – possibly the number is over 200 – a discrepancy only partly accounted for by the British union-catalogue's terminal date of 1801.

The symbols B, G and G(5) will be seen to follow many of the entries in the Annotated Index. B indicates that the organist's name appears in *the British union-catalogue of early music*, although it must be emphasised that there is no necessary guarantee of the common identity of the organist and composer of the same name. G refers to *The new Grove dictionary of music and musicians* and G(5) to the 5th edition of Grove for details of appointments outside the City of London and for other biographical information. In many cases however the Annotated Index will be found to supply facts not given in Grove nor elsewhere and to correct existing entries.

Purley, 1980 — Donovan Dawe.

Acknowledgements

I acknowledge with gratitude the encouragement and help given to me over many years in the compilation of this book. The bulk of the material has come from Guildhall Library and it is to that institution that I owe my greatest debt. My thanks, then, to the Librarian, Mr. Godfrey Thompson, to his successive archivists Dr. A.E.J. Hollaender and Mr. C.R.H. Cooper and to many other members of the staff past and present including the past Librarian Mr. Arthur Hall and his successive deputies Mr. John Bromley and Mr. E.W. Padwick. Miss Betty Masters has helped me with the resources of the Guildhall Records Office as have the late Mr. J.F.V. Woodman and his successor Mr. J.H. Dermit with the freedom records in the Chamberlain's Court at Guildhall.

I have had assistance from many other institutions including the British Library, the Bodleian Library, the Pendlebury Library at Cambridge, the Public Records Office, the libraries of St. Paul's Cathedral, the Royal College of Music, the Royal College of Organists and the Greater London Record office, the Central Music Library and the reference libraries of Southwark and Tower Hamlets and from the authorities at Charterhouse and St. Bartholomew's Hospital. The records of the Royal Society of Musicians have been used extensively and I am grateful to Mrs. Gleed for making them readily available to me. Of the City livery companies my thanks to the Merchant Taylors', the Stationers' and the Mercers' for giving me access to their records and to the many other companies whose records I have freely used at Guildhall.

On a more personal note I am particularly indebted to Dr. H. Diack Johnstone with his extensive knowledge of eighteenth century musicians. Many other musicologists have been of great practical assistance including Dr. Stanley Sadie, C.B.E., Prof. Nicholas Temperley, the late Mr. Charles Cudworth and Mr. Timothy Rishton who at the last moment drew my attention to William Smethergell's apprenticeship to Thomas Curtis in the Weavers' Company. Mr. A.W. Rolfe kindly put at my disposal the results of his researches into the Rolfe family. The late Miss Kathleen Garrett helped me extensively with the text and with the information derived from her researches into the life of Maria Hackett, the champion of choirboys.

On the production side I have had valuable assistance from Mr. George Nullis who has so generously and efficiently handled the complexities of publication.

The publication of this book, however, would never have been possible without the tireless energy and enthusiasm of Lady Jeans and my gratitude to her is boundless. My wife has been of immense help throughout, bearing the brunt of the discouragements which have delayed its publication for so long and undertaking the typing and re-typing of the MS with characteristic cheerfulness. My daughters Sarah and Elizabeth have also been of great assistance to me with their practical help, advice and encouragement.

Part One
Introductory Essays

Long Serving Organists

Although no City organist occupied a post for as long as sixty years, John Stanley at St. Andrew Holborn came within three months of it and his death brought an end to 62 years 7 months continuous service in the City. This latter achievement was equalled by Ann Mounsey (afterwards Mrs. Bartholomew) almost exactly a century later. Ann Mounsey might easily have done her 62 years 7 months at a single church if the electors of St. Vedast Foster Lane had voted her in in 1828. As it was she was runner-up out of seventeen candidates and returned to win the next election nine years later with a big majority. Both John Stanley and Ann Mounsey could attribute their length of service to early success. Stanley of course was a prodigy, ostensibly beating Maurice Greene and Obadiah Shuttleworth to win All Hallows Bread Street at the age of ten. Ann Mounsey was seven years older when she was elected to St. Michael Wood Street but at their deaths, both still in possession of City posts, Ann Mounsey had made up for her later start by living seven years longer.

If John Stanley's 59 years 9 months at St. Andrew Holborn was the longest at a single church, several organists came within striking distance of it. Edward Griffes served St. Dunstan in the East for 58 years 2 months, E. J. Hopkins was 55 years at the Temple Church and William Duncombe 54 years at St. Dunstan in the West. James Heseltine was nominally organist of St. Katherine by the Tower for 53 years 9 months but as he was organist of Durham Cathedral at the same time, London probably saw little but his deputy. Ann Mounsey's 53 years 7 months at St. Vedast came next to lead the women and in fact the only other woman to exceed fifty years was Sarah Morrice. Altogether sixteen City organists served their churches for more than fifty years and another thirty-six, including nine women, for between forty and fifty years.

Although some churches enjoyed a succession of long serving organists many more changed them frequently. It was not only a matter of salary: luck seemed to play at least an equal part. The three George Coopers successively served St. Sepulchre for a combined total of ninety-two years and between 1736 and 1870 St. Antholin had only three organists, each staying more than forty years.

Salaries

As the post-Fire churches were completed and their organs installed, the first salaries paid to their organists were mostly of the order of £12 to £18 per annum. St. Giles Cripplegate in 1674 and St. Sepulchre in 1676 both started with annual salaries of £20 but St. Giles reduced it within a few years to £16 to come into line with the majority. St. Sepulchre alone maintained it and by the later sixteen eighties many parishes had increased their organists' salaries to the same figure. Although there were some exceptions, £20 remained the standard rate for the next few decades. St. Lawrence Jewry was probably the first to raise it with £30 paid to John Robinson in 1710 and St. Dionis Backchurch at the inauguration of its organ in 1724 offered the same. Within the next twenty years the salaries of several organists were increased to £30 and this seems to have been the accepted level until the end of the century.

The mid eighteenth century norm of £20 to £30 compares with the £40 earned by instrumentalists in the King's band of musicians and £73 by the sixteen gentleman of the Chapel Royal, both salaries remaining unchanged between 1750 and 1800. There were several organists playing different instruments in the King's band, others singing in the Chapel Royal and a few drawing salaries from each. Both Maurice Greene and William Boyce who succeeded him were paid £200 per year as master of the King's band and £116 (raised to £146) as organist and composer of the Chapel Royal. No wonder William Boyce could afford to give short shrift to the vestries of the two City churches in which his playing had become little more than nominal.

By 1816 some City churches were beginning to pay £40 and the organists who fell far short of it petitioned for more. The organist of St. Margaret Lothbury brought out a long report listing, sometimes inaccurately, salaries paid elsewhere and was awarded a 40% increase to his £25. Although £40 became the standard rate for the wealthier parishes, few exceeded it and the £60 paid by All Hallows Bread Street in 1852 was exceptional.

At the other end of the scale were St. James Duke's Place which was paying its organist only £8 in 1839, St. Ethelburga £15 in 1812, Holy Trinity Gough Square the same amount in 1850, and St. Mary Somerset the unbelievable figure of £5 in 1847.

Generally speaking the quality of the organist depended on the amount the church was prepared to pay. Low salaries attracted few candidates and it was in these kinds of circumstances that the parish clerks' daughters were appointed without opposition. Where a church stipulated that no other post was to be held and that the successful candidate must attend regularly in person, a higher rate of pay was not unnaturally expected.

Cuts in salary, less common than increases, usually resulted from inefficiency or neglect of duty and those suffering this indignity included William Boyce. Salary reductions or even dismissals occasionally arose through lack of funds. Ann Mounsey had her salary reduced at St. Michael Wood Street and accepted it gracefully, and James Rolfe, the father of the famous "Baron Corvo", had to vacate St. Mildred Bread Street because there were no funds available to pay him. Rebuilding the church made the organist redundant at St.

Mary Woolnoth in 1716 and at St. Dunstan in the West in 1829, and in 1776 the money for the payment of the organist of St. Peter Cornhill was unavailable because it had been "seized" by the Rector.

A full and accurate survey of City organists' salaries is impossible to compile. Often the vestry minute books, when they survive, are silent on the subject, sometimes because the organist's salary was paid for by public subscription. The churchwardens' accounts in these circumstances are equally uninformative. The accounts, too, can be misleading in giving only the contribution towards the salary paid by one of a number of united parishes. Frequently the accounts of the others have failed to survive and the total salary paid is therefore unobtainable. The "annuity organ" (see pp. 13–17) poses additional problems, for the organist was given an unrevealed salary paid by the annuitant himself.

Women Organists

"Let your women keep silence in the churches" enjoined St. Paul in his first letter to the Corinthians, and the women organists of the City before 1750 held to the letter of the law. Until then all the organ posts had been filled by men and no woman had dared to challenge their authority.

In 1753 Mary Worgan, daughter of a City carpenter, broke their monopoly. She could scarcely have been better placed to do so for her two brothers James and John had already acquired reputations as organists. James, the older brother, died in possession of the organs of the two churches of St. Botolph Aldgate and St. Dunstan in the East. The electors of St. Botolph lost little time in electing his brother John to fill the vacancy while St. Dunstan chose his sister. Although the loss of church records obscures the event it was probably on May 10th that Mary Worgan was appointed. Her service ended prematurely, for the Gentleman's Magazine reported the marriage on May 19th of "Miss Mary Worgan, who was lately chosen organist of St. Dunstan in the East. Since her marriage she has resigned". There is no evidence that she ever took another post.

Another decade passed before the next woman candidate presented herself, this time at the church of St. Peter le Poer in 1764. Loss of records again obscures the details of the election but according to a newspaper report "Miss Hardin of the Old Jewry was elected by a great majority". This is all the more remarkable in that evidence suggests her identity as Elizabeth Hardin age fourteen. She may also have been the Miss Hardin named as the composer of harpsichord music and other minor works. Elizabeth Hardin probably stayed at St. Peter until her death at the early age of twenty-nine in January 1780.

Within the next few years Hannah Benson unsuccessfully offered herself as candidate at three City churches and Frances Paxton and Elizabeth Smith each at two before the unhappy appointment of Ann Kitchingman to St. Mildred Poultry in 1778. In 1790, by which time she had become Mrs. Beverley, it was blandly admitted that she had "for many years neglected to play" and two months later was traced, "confined by indisposition", to Hull. At least she made no attempt to apply for her salary and at the end of 1792 it was accepted by the vestry that their organist would never play again. Undeterred by the failure of their previous appointment, another woman, Catherine Linton, was elected and served for forty-five trouble-free years.

The election of Mary Hudson, the third woman organist, to St. Olave Hart Street in 1781 marked the beginning of a series of female appointments and before 1790 six other women had replaced men. Mary Hudson, daughter of Dr. Robert Hudson, almoner of St. Paul's and music master of Christ's Hospital, was a professional and provided the earliest example of a woman holding two City posts at the same time.

If there is no doubt about the professionalism of Mary Hudson, the same cannot be said of the seventy-five women organists who filled over eighty City posts between them and even less so of the eighty-five other discovered candidates who unsuccessfully applied for 143 vacancies before 1850. The local voters too often elected a local girl or the daughter of the parish clerk, frequently in the face of professional opposition and against the advice of the appointed umpire. This was to happen time and time again often ending in complaints, recriminations, resignations and, less frequently, dismissals. Of the seventy-five women organists before 1850 at least eight, and probably many more, were daughters of parish clerks and others were local girls whose skill was not of a high order to say the least.

There were of course plenty of professionals besides Mary Hudson: Eliza and Thomasine Wesley, the Mounsey sisters, Esther Fleet, Mary Horth, Maria Naish, Ann Blewitt and Eliza Silverlock to name but a few. Many of them were daughters of organists, related to them or came of musical families. Several of them married organists and in some cases were succeeded by their children.

Some of the women organists were blind, at least eight were dismissed or resigned under pressure. Still more distinguished themselves in other ways. Lisetta Rist of All Hallows Barking by the Tower earned a reputation for scattering ashes on Tower Hill to help the horses in frosty weather. The blind Elizabeth Holland spent nearly half of her thirty years at St. Augustine Watling Street in a state of feud with the Rector and half the vestry. Mary Le Cren, unsuccessful candidate at St. Stephen Coleman Street, brought an action against the church for alleged irregularity at the election.

Although many women organists married after their appointments, most of them continued at their posts. Marriage, however, ended Henrietta Lockhart's career when she was forbidden by her husband "to play at all in public".

The youthfulness of Elizabeth Hardin has already been alluded to. Elizabeth Mounsey was also fourteen when elected to St. Peter Cornhill in 1834 and Esther Fleet, placed in the top four of twenty-three candidates at St. Bride Fleet Street in 1821, was disqualified because her age was found "not to exceed 14".

In the six decades between 1790 and 1850 the number of women appointed increased from six to twenty-four and by 1850 only a quarter of the parish churches of the City had never had a woman organist. St. Olave Hart Street, from the opening of its organ in 1781, had employed only women. St. Bartholomew by the Exchange had no men after 1784 and most of the several churches which installed organs for the first time after 1800 employed only women, largely because they were prepared to pay so little for the organists' services. By 1850 in the sixty-nine parish churches with organs there were forty-one men and twenty-eight women.

The "Singing Boys of Paul's"

The choir of ten singing boys of Paul's are listed in a City assessment of 1698 as "Samuel Marshall, William Chocke, George Heydon, Thomas Carter, Peter Horwood, Charles Younge, Oliver Bowden, Charles Christian, Charles King and George Treavers". Exactly half of these became organists, four at City churches. Samuel Marshall, "the exquisite" organist of St. Katherine Cree and composer died before he reached the age of twenty-seven. Peter Horwood became music master of Christ's Hospital and organist of Christ Church. Charles Young, organist of All Hallows Barking by the Tower for forty-five years and a composer, begat three well-known singing daughters, two of whom married Thomas Arne and J.F. Lampe. Charles King, besides holding a City organ post, returned to St. Paul's as almoner and vicar choral. George Hayden, unsuccessfully competing with Charles Young at St. Andrew Holborn on Maurice Greene's appointment to St. Paul's, became organist of St. Mary Magdalen Bermondsey.

The ten singing boys, reduced to eight by the mid eighteenth century, still continued to contribute towards the supply of organists both within the City and outside it. Between 1698 and 1830, a period which includes most of the organ appointments in this survey, it is estimated that between 200 and 250 choirboys passed through St. Paul's. No complete record of them appears to exist and the nineteenth century list compiled by Maria Hackett, the reformer and choirboys' champion, lists only 132 in that period. (An additional 39 are accorded no dates but many of them are after 1830). Out of Miss Hackett's 132 no fewer than forty are known to have been City organists or candidates who found posts elsewhere. A further eight City organists not listed by Maria Hackett have been identified from other sources. It therefore seems reasonable to suppose that St. Paul's choir supplied the City with at least fifty organists or candidates during this period and probably many more.

The number is impressive but the quality is even more so. If William Boyce and Maurice Greene are outstanding as composers, Robert Hudson, Charles King, Samuel Long, R.J.S. Stevens, Joseph Baildon and Jonathan Battishill are by no means negligible and the list could be extended.

Not surprisingly some of the ex-choirboy organists were also professional singers and Robert Hudson, John Soaper, James Chelsum and Thomas Baildon became gentlemen of the Chapel Royal. Hudson, also music master of Christ's Hospital, and Chelsum both returned to St. Paul's as vicars-choral and Hudson served as almoner for twenty years. Other professional singing organists from St. Paul's included Edward Frith (also a viola player), Henry Smith,

Samuel Kemm and J.C. Pring and there were probably many others.

It would be interesting to know the family backgrounds of the St. Paul's boys in the eighteenth century, their social strata, whether their parents were musical and above all how they were recognised as potential choirboys at such an early age. How were they selected and what was the driving force that led them to St. Paul's? There is very little information available, for none of them appears to have revealed it. None that is except the Elizabethan Thomas Tusser, nearly two hundred years earlier. His musical experiences at the Chapel Royal, St. Paul's and later at Norwich Cathedral produced not an organist but an agricultural writer and poet and, unlike most organists, he ended his days in a debtors' prison, the Poultry Compter in the City of London. In his *Five hundred pointes of good husbandrie*, after a harrowing description of his life as a chorister and impressment for the Chapel Royal, his relief on his admission to the choir of St. Paul's is shared by the reader:

But marke the chance, my self to vance,
By friendships lot, to Paules I got,
So found I grace, a certaine space
still to remaine:
With Redford there, the like no where,
For cunning such, and vertue much,
By whom some part of Musicke art,
so did I gaine.

So the practice of impressing boys into the choir of the Chapel Royal was clearly not followed at St. Paul's. It has been suggested that in later years St. Paul's adopted this system of recruitment but not a shred of evidence has been found to support it. Indeed by the time Maria Hackett began to write about the recruitment of boys in 1818 it all sounds rather colourless. "The selection of the choristers", she says, "is principally left to the Music Master (i.e. the almoner) subject of course to the approbation of the Dean and Chapter. They are usually admitted between 7 & 9 years of age. A good voice and a taste for music will be found the best recommendations to introduce a boy into this very desirable situation".

So much for the introduction of the singing boys. The other questions for the most part remain unanswered. Secondary sources provide at least the family background of the more eminent names and the list of choirboys compiled by Maria Hackett supplies a few more. William Boyce and Maurice Greene both came from the City at different levels of society, the first the son of the beadle of a City livery company, the second the son of the vicar of St. Olave Jewry. The few fathers mentioned by Miss Hackett could scarcely be more varied and although the singing man from Windsor, the almoner of St. Paul's and the parish clerk are predictable, the butcher and the artificial flower maker provide interesting contrasts.

The evidence suggests that the musical successes of the St. Paul's boys were the outcome not of parental or pre-choir environment but the external influence of music upon them in impressionable years. The musical stature of the almoners, men like Blow, Jeremiah Clark, Charles King and Robert Hudson, and of the organists Maurice Greene and John Jones who between them spent all but twenty years of the eighteenth century at St. Paul's, is unquestionable.

Although the boys of St. Paul's were primarily intended to make music and to learn about it, it is probable that they received a good general education as well, at least through the greater part of the eighteenth century. The decline in choir schools' educational standards at a later period was one of the factors that concerned Maria Hackett deeply and one which she strove so bravely to reverse.

It is probably true to say that a boy who can sing and who has a good ear has at least some degree of inborn musical ability. But if the few who were chosen for St. Paul's displayed it there must have been many more who were equally equipped or in whom the same talents were dormant and never had a chance to reveal them.

Nevertheless the singing boys of Paul's, small in number though they were, made an outstanding contribution to the musical life of eighteenth century England.

SOURCES. Maria Hackett's list has been translated and annotated by Miss K.I. Garrett (bibliography item 342). Other sources appear in the bibliography numbered 164, 102, 103, 106, 166 and 167.

The Custom of London

The customs of the City of London or the "Custom of London", to give it its official title, is the generic term for the common laws which have existed since time immemorial and been confirmed by royal charters to the City of London which date back to William the Conqueror. Over the centuries the Custom of London has been crystallised in the form of orders, ordinances and acts, for the successive charters confirmed the City's unique right to develop its own constitution by means of acts passed by its own Common Council.

This may sound irrelevant to the subject of this book, but the organists of the City of London were in many cases inhabitants too, and, even if they lived outside, the churches in which they played lay within its boundaries.

The inhabitants of London and those who had their business there were subject to regulations imposed upon them by the City fathers and in return they enjoyed certain privileges. One of the rules concerned the freedom of the City of London without which no inhabitant could consider himself a citizen of London. An act of Common Council of 1606 declaratory of the Custom of London prohibited non-freemen from using any art, trade, occupation, mistery, or handicraft within the City and imposed a penalty of £5 for every offence, the prosecution to be brought in the name of the Chamberlain of London.

The freedom of the City could be obtained only by first joining one of the livery companies, the ancient trade or craft guilds of the City. There were three methods. The applicant could receive the freedom of a company after serving an apprenticeship of at least seven years to a freeman. He could acquire it by simple purchase, i.e. he became a freeman by redemption. Thirdly, the sons or daughters of freemen had the right to claim the freedom by patrimony. In all cases the would-be freeman had to have reached the age of twenty-one and, following the granting to him of the company's freedom, he had to receive the freedom of the City at Guildhall from the hands of the City Chamberlain.

For the historian the value of the granting of a freedom lies in the fact that the records of both the livery company and the City Chamberlain throw light upon the applicant, frequently revealing at least his parentage, his address and the nature of his occupation. From a biographical point of view it is therefore a matter of regret that so few organists became freemen of London.

Essentially mercantile in its effect, the act of 1606 cited above would seem to exclude the church organist as in fact it excluded the dignitaries of church and law and, at the other end of the scale, domestics and labourers.

For the few organists who became freemen of the City reasons can usually be found. Some like Joseph Dale and the Rolfes had other occupations in the City which necessitated it, others such as James Worgan and Thomas Curtis became free by patrimony because their fathers were freemen. Very few became freemen by their own inclination although a few, like William Smethergell, became free after serving an apprenticeship to a freeman organist.

Only once did the City attempt to force an organist to become free and that was in 1724. The target was Henry Green, the blind organist of St. Giles Cripplegate, but the complaint that prompted the action was not because he was a church organist but because he played for the Festival of the Sons of the Clergy and other concerts and this presumably encroached upon the performing rights of City musicians who had had to become free. Henry Green in short was regarded not as a church organist but as a professional secular musician by the initiators of the action, the City waits. (The City waits were the Lord Mayor of London's equivalent of the King's Band).

The British Gazetteer newspaper described it as "the trial between the City Waits and Mr. Green Organist of St. Giles Cripplegate, for his exercising the Science of Musick in the City without being free thereof . . . It was insisted in his Defence, that Musick was a Liberal Science, and therefore not restrain'd by that Law (i.e. the Act of 1606 referred to above), but a Distinction being made by the Plaintiff's Council, between the Scientifical Part, and the Manual Part, a Verdict was given in Favour of the Plaintiff".

The official report of the case, though wordy, sheds additional light upon it. Described officially as "The Company of Musicians in London or the Chamberlain of London against Green" it would seem that the City musicians who were freemen were not employed by the stewards of the Festival of the Sons of the Clergy whereas Green, a non-freeman, was. The City musicians wanted to see the act extended to cover music "which is a *science* and not a *trade*; and if this should be allowed, they may extend it to *lawyers* who are not freemen . . . for the law is a science, and so is music . . . The arguing of a lawyer is wind-music, and no handicraft trade".

". . . at the trial a difference was taken between exercising such handicrafts for lucre and gain (which was the defendant's case) and exercising them for diversion and amusement, and that the one was within the bye-law, and the other not. And thereupon the plaintiff had a verdict and judgement, and afterwards the defendant took up his freedom, and acquiesced".

It will be noted that not a word was said about Henry Green's exercising "his handicraft for lucre and gain" in the church of St. Giles, as he undoubtedly did. Nor on this or on any other occasion was a church organist made to take up the freedom because he was a church organist. There is no doubt that the church and all associated with it were exempt from the Custom of the City and the lawyers, too, enjoyed an immunity that was never challenged.

Henry Green's acquiescence to the verdict of the court followed three days later when, cocking a snook at the Musicians' Company, he "was admitted a Member of the Company of Leathersellers, and made a freeman of the City of London, which Freedom he has purchas'd, that he may continue his Business of Musick in the City, where he has practis'd these 21 years" (the length of his service at St. Giles Cripplegate). Although there seems to be no reasonable link between leatherselling and organ playing Henry Green acted within his rights by joining the Leathersellers' Company. To become a freeman of the City he had first to become a freeman of a company and the Custom of London was not concerned with what art, craft or trade the company represented. Some of the companies, on the contrary, admitted only those representative of their interests but the Leathersellers were clearly not so disposed.

It has been shown already how the task of identifying the church organists of the City would be simplified if they had been required to be freemen. The simplification would have extended to the identification of their pupils who would have been apprentices according to the Custom of London. In consequence information about them would be found in the records of the appropriate livery company and in the records of the Chamberlain of London. At the end of their apprenticeship they too would have become freemen and in turn taken apprentices of their own. As it is, few "free" organists seem to have taken apprentices according to the Custom of London.

The non-free organists were of course immune from the Custom of London. But they were not exempt from the provisions of the Stamp Act of 1710 which imposed a duty on any sum of money paid in consideration of the placing of a clerk, apprentice or servant to learn a profession, trade or employment. As a result the records of the Stamp Office in the Public Record Office include entries for non-livery company apprenticeships or contracts of service entered into between organists and their pupils. The returns, which are unfortunately incomplete, cover the period 1710 to 1774 and are much more productive in revealing organists' pupils than are the City records.

NOTE. The case of Henry Green is fully reported in vol. 88 of the English reports 1724 p. 152 and in Modern reports vol. 8 p. 211.

The Musicians' Company

Ordinances dated 1350 show that a Fellowship of Minstrels of London was in existence in the fourteenth century. In 1500 they obtained from the Mayor and Aldermen of the City authority to govern their own affairs and later acts of Common Council confirmed it. It was not until 1604 however that the authority of "the Master, Wardens and Commonalty of the Art or Science of the Musicians of London" over all minstrels and musicians within the City and three miles around it was recognised by Royal Charter.

Unfortunately control over all musicians including those of the City had already been granted by a royal charter of 1469 to the King's Minstrels attached to the court at Westminster. The inevitable conflict led to the revocation of the City company's charter in 1634 and the granting of a new one to the King's Minstrels. Nevertheless the City company, though charterless, continued to exercise control within the City by acts of Common Council and, apart from a loss of prestige, probably suffered no disadvantages.

The rules and regulations the Musicians' Company devised with the authority of the Custom of London were stringent and far-reaching. The categories of musicians over whom their control extended included all those who exercised the art or science of music for gain. They specifically included dancing masters and even laid down the fees and regulations for the teaching of dancing. But the church organist, who was never mentioned, was clearly excluded. While the City authorities' main concern was that musicians should be free, the Musicians' Company did all within their limited powers to see that City musicians became free through them.

Unfortunately the surviving records of the Company for the first half of the 18th century are fragmentary and before 1700 non-existent. In the early seventeen hundreds the musical freemen were small fry and, apart from the City waits and dancing masters who formed the backbone, are for the most part unidentifiable. Although the number of freemen cannot be discovered, in 1710 there were only twenty-five liverymen. (A liveryman was a freeman of higher status who paid an additional fee to wear the livery of the company). This was small by comparison with many other City companies and, as a further indication of their numerical inferiority, betwen 1715 and 1733 only two or three new freemen were admitted each year.

Before 1733 the names of three City church organists are found in the Musicians' Company but their common identity cannot be proved. Walter Holt was organist of St. Michael Cornhill from 1699 to 1704. In May 1699 a Walter Holt became a freeman of the Company by patrimony, which means that having reached the age of twenty-one he was entitled to the freedom because his father was already free. According to the freedom certificate he was the son of Walter Holt, a freeman of the Musicians' Company since 1670, and was born in Bishopsgate. Both Walter Holts were dancing masters and it seems likely that one of them, probably the elder, was also the organist of St. Michael.

Both Thomas Low(e), organist of St. Martin Ludgate 1685, and his son Richard who succeeded him there on his death in 1690 were freemen of the Musicians' Company. Richard was apprenticed to his father and, on his death, to Walter Holt. Richard became free in 1695 and his name occurs in a list of the Company's liverymen which also includes James Vincent, the name of the Middle Temple organist of the Temple Church between 1737 and 1749. But the organist is more likely to have been the James Vincent who was apprenticed to an unnamed member of the Company in 1732 and whose freedom cannot be traced.

It seems clear that before 1733 the organists of the City had little or nothing to do with the Musicians' Company and that for their part the Company was equally disinterested in the City organists. The mutual feeling has already been illustrated by the case of Henry Green in 1724 (see pp. 8–9).

The significance of the year 1733 is that it appears to have marked a turning point in the Company's fortunes. With its small membership and annual intake of three or less its very existence must have been in jeopardy. No court minutes of the period survive to explain the metamorphosis that followed. Between May and December 1734 thirty-two new freemen were admitted and in 1735 more than fifty. But on analysis few if any had any association with music.

Whereas the majority of the few surviving members were practising musicians, after 1734 they were swamped by new members of a diversity of trades and occupations, from drysalters to staymakers and from glovers to tobacconists. Within a few years the proportion of musicians had sunk so low that the Company could scarcely justify its name.

Brigadier Crewdson in his *Short history* of the Company recognises that ". . . in the middle of the century there had been some radical change in policy within the Company leading to membership being thrown open to all comers. No doubt the westward migration of the professions had reduced the functions of the Guild to an anachronism".

There is no doubt that in the mid eighteenth century increase in mercantile activity within the City induced a corresponding increase in applications for the City freedom. To most the freedom alone was the essential goal, the company through which it was obtained was of no importance. Not only were the Musicians' fees lower than those of many other companies and their need for new members vital but the Company's clerk drew a guinea for each new member he introduced. Between 1727 and 1750 the livery increased from 28 to 101 and by 1790 it numbered 245. Brigadier Crewdson reveals that between 1743 and 1769 only nineteen out of the 700 freemen admitted described themselves as musicians and by 1794 the 600 members of the Company included only sixteen.

In view of this, it is surprising that the most eminent organist members of the Company are found after the transformation of 1733–4. It is perhaps less surprising when it is realised that most of them joined the Company virtually by accident.

Starling Goodwin was the first. On January 15, 1727/8 he was apprenticed to his father Michael Goodwin in the Bakers' Company. It can be assumed that the purpose of the apprenticeship was not to learn to bake but to play the organ and it is probable therefore that Michael Goodwin himself was an organist. In March 1735 at the end of his apprenticeship he was granted his freedom by servitude in the Musicians' Company, no doubt considered somewhat more appropriate than the Bakers'. Starling was later organist at Southwark and at Ranelagh Gardens and author of the *Organist's pocket companion*. The common date of death of Starling Goodwin of Southwark and William Goodwin, organist of St. Bartholomew by the Exchange, raises the interesting but not altogether likely possibility that they were one and the same person. More probably they were father and son or brothers dying from an unidentified common cause.

The next City organist-Musician was James Worgan admitted by patrimony on March 13 1740/1 by virtue of his father's freedom in the Carpenters' Company. His younger and more eminent brother John did not avail himself of the opportunity.

John Young's freedom in 1748 may have been necessary through participation in his father's business as musical-instrument seller in St. Paul's Churchyard or because, as an outstanding violinist, he almost certainly played in the City for gain.

In the following year the Musicians' Company admitted its most eminent, or perhaps its only, musical notability of the eighteenth century, Charles Burney. R.H. Lonsdale in his splendid biography suggests no reason for Burney's freedom in the Musicians' Company, by then musically devalued and discredited and containing an overwhelming preponderance of merchants of all kinds. Neither does he nor Burney's other biographer, Dr. Scholes, attempt to identify his first wife Esther Sleep, beyond the assertion by Dr. Scholes that she was the granddaughter of one Dubois, a Huguenot.

The identification of Esther Sleep, however, provides the reason for Burney's freedom in the Musicians' Company. Three generations of the Sleep family are to be found as members of the Company during the first half of the eighteenth century, two of whom, Richard and his son Francis, were players in the City waits, the Lord Mayor's band. Among the daughters of Richard Sleep, Esther and Martha in 1747 took the rather unusual step for women of claiming their freedom in the Company by patrimony on presentation by their father, then a warden of the Company. Richard Sleep appears to have been in charge of the waits at this time. In 1739 he was "paid £4 for the City musick at laying of foundation stone of Mansion House 25 Oct." and "Mr. Sleep, one of the light wayts of this City" was ordered to "add two trumpets to his band of music". His official position in the City Corporation as leader of its music and his high rank in the Company must have enhanced his musical status and Burney, on his marriage to Esther Sleep at St. George's Chapel Hyde Park Corner on 25th June 1749, would have been confronted with a wife who was free of the Company and a father-in-law who was by then in all probability its master.

No doubt this formidable partnership provided an irresistible incentive to Burney who was enrolled into the freedom eight days later. Oddly enough Esther would have lost it, for the Custom of London ordained that on her marriage a spinster's freedom was suspended.

In view of Burney's membership of the Musicians' Company it is curious that he should have thought fit to attack it so bitterly in his *General history of music*. If of course his membership stemmed from wifely persuasion and pressure from his father-in-law, the death of Esther Burney in 1762 many years before the publication of the history would in some degree have absolved him.

After some introductory jibes he goes on ". . . this company has ever been held in derision by real professors, who have regarded it as an institution as foreign to the cultivation and prosperity of good Music, as the Train-bands to the art of war. Indeed the only uses that have hitherto been made of this charter seem the affording to aliens an easy and cheap expedient of acquiring the freedom of the city, and enabling them to pursue some more profitable and respectable trade than that of fidling; as well as empowering the company to keep out of processions and city-feasts every street and country-dance player of superior abilities, to those who have the honour of being styled the *waits of the corporation*."

Although Burney had clearly interpreted the word "foreigners" in the ordinances as "aliens" whereas it meant those who were not of the City of London, there was considerable truth in his words. The views of Hawkins were of much the same order.

After Burney only one other possible eighteenth century organist-Musician can be identified. William Selby, a distinguished organist and harpsichordist, was at All Hallows Bread Street and St. Sepulchre Holborn until emigrating to America in 1773. His identity with William Selby, son of Joseph Selby of the Fishmongers' Company, who was made free by patrimony in the Musicians' Company in February 1766 cannot however be proved. Apart from this handful of organist-Musicians, the names of five candidates who held no City posts are also found among the freemen: Richard Stanton (1705), John Lestrange (1741), John Salmon (1734), Thomas Scott (1765) and Timothy Smart (1761). Again positive identification is impossible.

Not only did the Company start the nineteenth century almost entirely divorced from music but it failed to maintain the large membership which had earlier saved it from extinction. William Chappell's election to the Court in 1870, however, paved the way for an influx of musicians and the Company, for the first time for a century and a half, began to return to the art to which it was dedicated. Two of the leading organists of the day came on to the Court, Sir Frederick Bridge in 1885 and, a few years later, Sir John Stainer, who was elected a City organist at the age of fourteen. With royal patronage the much publicised and outstandingly successful tercentenary celebrations of 1904 further enhanced the Company's revived musical stature. A belated royal charter was granted in 1950 and in recent years the Company has made a valuable contribution to English music with competitions, grants and scholarships.

NOTE. For the history of the Company see H.A.F. Crewdson's *Short history*, 1971 (Bibliography item 291). For the Company's records see items 124–129.

Annuity Organs

The introduction of the annuity organ in the mid eighteenth century enabled a parish to acquire an organ without raising the capital for its purchase. In return for an annuity payment from the parish on his life or on the lives of his dependants an organ provider would instal an organ and supply an organist to play it. As the annual payment amounted to little if anything more than an organist's normal salary, the terms were attractive to the many churches still without organs in 1740. Within five years four parishes had taken steps to acquire an annuity organ and by 1814, when the last was installed in St. Olave Jewry, the number had risen to eleven.

The initiator of the annuity organ in the City was the versatile Thomas Griffin. In 1741 he offered to the church of St. Katherine Coleman a set of proposals on lines which were soon to become familiar but which at that time were new, at least in the City. It is possible that Griffin had had previous experience elsewhere or that the idea was not originally his, but there is no evidence to support either suggestion.

The son of a City wharfinger, he was apprenticed to a barber in the Barber Surgeon's Company and thereafter appears to have followed the trade of either a barber, a peruke maker or both. He was in his mid thirties when in 1741 he offered to instal an organ in the church of St. Katherine Coleman and to play it himself or supply an organist in exchange for an annuity.

The course of events which led him to this apparently unique proposition remains a puzzle. Did he continue as a peruke maker or barber? Did he himself build organs? The latter is generally discounted but in agreements of 1746–9 for supplying St. Margaret Pattens with an organ and in a manuscript list of the Barber Surgeons' Company of about the same date he is described as "organ builder of Fenchurch Street", a description which could have come only from Griffin himself. In a similar printed list of 1750 however he is entered as a barber while in the 1741 agreement with St. Katherine Coleman, surely the most likely to credit him with organ building, he is a peruke maker. It is doubtful if the enigma of Thomas Griffin will ever be solved or whether it will be established if he played the organs he supplied. His nephew George Griffin was an organist of some repute and certainly played some if not all of his uncle's annuity organs.

The opportunism of Thomas Griffin is reflected in other aspects of his City life. He sat on the City's Court of Common Council from 1752 until 1763 and no doubt used this as a lever to his remarkable appointment as Gresham Professor of Music in 1763. This position, for which John Potter was the only other candidate, carried with it a free apartment at Mercers' Hall and an allowance of £100 a year. He held it until his death nine years later. It is true that the Gresham professorship had sunk to a sinecure prior to Griffin's appointment but by all accounts he made a dismal showing and appears to have been openly derided on the occasion of his inaugural address in January 1763:

> On Saturday afternoon there was a large audience assembled at Gresham College, to hear Mr. Griffin read his first lecture on Music, but were disappointed, on account of Mr. Griffin having engaged Mr. Potter to read for him; as soon as Mr. Potter went into [sic] the rostrum, a great disturbance began, and after much noise and confusion, the whole company departed, seemingly much displeased.

Contemporary opinion seems to have agreed that Griffin's knowledge of music was rudimentary.

John Potter, who read Griffin's inaugural address after being defeated by him in the election for the professorship, was a musician and song writer for Vauxhall Gardens. He was also a student of physics, a novelist, a poet and a writer on subjects as varied as music, medicine and topography. His *Observations on the present state of music and musicians* was based on lectures delivered at Gresham College in 1762 but even these qualifications proved insufficient to stave off defeat by the City-sponsored Thomas Griffin.

In his proposals to St. Katherine Coleman in September 1741 Thomas Griffin undertook to erect an organ in the church "which in the opinion of such masters of musick as he the said Thomas Griffin and the parishes should agree on as to the tone should be valued at £300 and the workmanship to be approved on by organ builders and would keep the same in repair and perform on it or cause to be performed." In return he would be paid "£25 per annum during his life, and his present wife Mary Griffin during the time she may survive him, £10 per annum".

For his next annuity organ Thomas Griffin had to face competition, for in 1742 a committee of St. Helen Bishopsgate met to decide on the relative merits of proposals from "Abraham Jordan, organ builder, John Harris & Co. of Budge Row" and Thomas Griffin. The straightforward offer of an organ for £350 by Abraham Jordan was considered less attractive than Griffin's proposal "to build at my own proper cost and charge . . ." a new organ value £500 of new materials "to tune and perform on it or cause to be performed during the time of my natural life" for a payment of £250 and £25 per annum. After Thomas Griffin's death in 1771 his nephew George continued to play the St. Helen organ for nearly forty years.

Although St. Mildred Bread Street acquired an annuity organ in 1745, Thomas Griffin's involvement is not clear. In 1744 Richard Hussey contracted to provide an instrument which he agreed to build at his own charge and to play in exchange for an annuity of £20 per annum. "Mr. Griffin" was paid separately for repairing, cleaning and tuning it. Unfortunately the parish records provide an inadequate picture of the circumstances, and entries in the accounts such as "paid Hussey pp. Griffith" [i.e. Griffin] hardly help. Richard Hussey appears to have died a few years later and whether "paid Mr. Griffin for Mrs. Hussey for one year playing the organ" means that Richard Hussey's widow succeeded him as organist is possible but unlikely. Such entries are soon followed by "paid Mr. Griffin for playing and tuning" but in 1751 the combined parishes using St. Mildred appear to have pensioned George Griffin (Thomas's nephew) and the 1753 accounts show a payment to Thomas Griffin of 1¼ years annuity due to George Griffin. By then an organist elected by the parishes was playing in St. Mildred for an annual salary of £20.

The last annuity organ installed by Thomas Griffin in the City was at St. Margaret Pattens in 1749. The agreement was reached after protracted negotiations and its most interesting feature is that for the first and only time Griffin is described as "organ builder". His offer of an organ for 200 guineas to St. Michael Bassishaw in 1762 was accepted without any question of annuity. The identity of the builder is not disclosed but Pearce quoting Leffler, who saw the organ around 1800, unquestioningly ascribed it to Griffin.

There is little indication whether the annuity organ system as instituted by Griffin gave general satisfaction to the participating parishes. Evidence suggests that the supplied organists were not always up to the standards hoped for and the fact that the vestries had no say in their appointment doubtless led to friction. This may account for the fact that Griffin supplied no further annuity organs in the last twenty years of his life. Derogatory reports from participating parishes could have influenced the uncommitted parishes unfavourably.

It is significant that with the exception of St. Vedast in 1773 and St. Mary Aldermary in 1781 no annuity organs were installed between 1749 and 1794 when the idea again found favour. St. Augustine Watling Street turned down an annuity offer by James Lewer of Cheshunt in 1766 and bought the organ instead.

The idea of the annuity organ was later taken up by several London organ builders: Hugh Russell at St. Mary Aldermary in 1781, John Byfield the younger at St. Bartholomew the Less in 1794, William Gray at St. Michael Paternoster Royal in 1797, George Pike England at St. Martin Outwich in 1805 and William Warrell at St. Olave Jewry in 1814.

At St. Mary Aldermary, Hugh Russell was paid an annuity of 44 guineas during his lifetime and the lives of his children William then aged six and Ann aged four. William was in due time to become the appointed organist of the church of St. Mary and one of the most talented performers of his day. Dying in his late thirties, twelve years before his father, it was left to Ann to keep the annuity going until her death in 1854.

John Byfield the younger named himself and his sister in his annuity agreement with St. Bartholomew the Less in 1794 by which he undertook to instal an organ in conjunction with his father "and play the same" for an astonishingly low annuity payment of £20 per annum. Although there is no doubt that John Byfield himself played until 1800 and again a few years later, the fact that he failed to secure a single vote out of the 91 cast at St. Martin Ludgate in 1786 is perhaps a measure of his ability as an organist. If this was in fact below the standard expected by the parishioners so perhaps was the organ, for thirty years later it was replaced by a new instrument built by John Gray.

The parish of St. Michael Paternoster Royal having accepted in principle the idea of an annuity organ in 1797 organised a public competition in which a number of unnamed organ builders and others participated. "Mr. Phillips" and "Mr. Howard" offered the lowest terms and at first these were the only ones considered. Phillips was possibly William Phillips, musical-instrument dealer of Little Tower Hill, and Howard probably Thomas Howard of Camberwell who later supplied an annuity organ to St. Mary le Bow. On examination both organs were considered too small and Howard's alternative offer of a £300 instrument with an organist for £40 per annum was rejected in favour of a three manual organ and an organist for £38 per annum from the organ builder William Gray. The supplied organist was later William Gray's son John who was persuaded by the parish to continue after his father's death in 1821.

Although it is not clear whether George Pike England played the annuity organ he built and installed in St. Martin Outwich in 1805, there is little doubt that members of his family were among those he supplied as organists. The annuity was still held by the family in the eighteen seventies.

William Warrell of Lambeth, probably the "– Warrell" listed in Doane's *Musical directory* of 1794 as a music seller and organ builder, had installed an annuity organ in St. Mary le Strand twenty four years before submitting his proposals to St. Olave Jewry in 1814. For 36 guineas per annum he undertook to provide an organ "which had been for several years in the King's Chapel in the Savoy now at Mr. Allen's organ builder" and believed by Warrell to have been built originally by "Parker". The agreement was unusual in that although the annuity was on Warrell's own life, his supply organist Ralph Kinkee was also involved and succeeded to the annuity. It was not until twenty years later that the vestry gave voice to their disapproval of his playing and it was "resolved that Mr. Ralph Kinkee being willing to forego his contract for an annuity of £20 . . ." an organist of the parish's own choosing should be appointed at a salary equivalent to the difference between 36 guineas and £20.

Only two annuity organs remain unaccounted for: those at St. Vedast Foster Lane and St. Mary le Bow. The annuitant at St. Vedast was William Duncombe whose identity with the organist of the same name at St. Dunstan in the West cannot be substantiated. He and George England were competitors for the annuity organ contract at St. Vedast in 1773 and it seems likely that after winning it Duncombe himself played at least until 1783. Again there is no contemporary information as to who built the organ which cost Duncombe £240. Pearce asserts that it was Crang and Hancock, an attribution that is almost certainly correct in that Hancock was tuning it in 1790 when he reported to the vestry that it would cost £4 "to repair the damage done by Abbé Vogler" (G.J. Vogler, 1749–1814, German organist and composer who was in London in 1790). By that time Thomas Jones was being paid £10 per annum to play and was succeeded by Catherine Jones, probably his daughter, neither of whom appears to have impressed the parish as an organist. By 1807 the vestry decided that it had had enough and that the annuity to Duncombe should be brought to an end. Catherine Jones was allowed £10 per annum until after the repair and overhaul of the organ when the parish would elect its own organist at an annual salary of £30.

It is surprising that such an outstanding church as St. Mary le Bow should have been without an organ for so long. The idea had been put forward and rejected on three occasions during the eighteenth century and it was not until 1801 that the vestry of the combined parishes accepted the proposals of Thomas Howard. Thomas Howard of Camberwell, who described himself as a professor of music, offered to have a two manual organ valued at £300 made at his expense and to supply "a qualified performer" in exchange for an annuity on his life of 40 guineas per annum. The organ builder was unnamed but credence is given to Leffler's assertion that it was Hugh Russell by the fact that in 1852 Timothy Russell was employed to enlarge it. After twenty years Howard sold his interest in the organ to the pianoforte-making firm of Rolfe in Cheapside which numbered among its family some able organists of whom one was the father of the illustrious Baron Corvo.

So much for annuity organs and the personalities associated with them. Advantageous though they undoubtedly were to the eleven churches which installed them, the unfortunate fact remains that information as to who actually played them is fragmentary and uncertain.

Rogue Organists

"On Monday evening a watchmaker in Clerkenwell catched an organist of this City too familiar with his wife, on which a quarrel ensued, when the latter beat and abused the watchmaker very grossly, who had him and his wife both taken up, and being carried before a Magistrate, he committed them both to Bridewell; and the husband is bound over to prosecute."

This lamentable episode occurred on August 30th 1762 and was reported in the London Evening Post. The identity of the City organist and the outcome are undiscovered and the church lists show no resignations or dismissals at the appropriate date.

On the whole the organists of the City appear to have been law abiding. Their dismissals, and there were plenty of them, arose largely from dissatisfaction over their playing, the supply of unsatisfactory deputies or their continued absence from the keyboard. More serious offences were rare but in the case of the music masters of Christ's Hospital and the organists of St. Bartholomew the Great followed one another in succession.

The troubles at Christ's Hospital began with the appointment of John Curtis on February 4th 1675/6 after "declaring his skill in playing upon the organ and other instruments of musick". Nine years later it was reported that he had been negligent in teaching the children and it was decided to make a new appointment. Despite further complaints and protracted discussions regarding a suitable successor nothing further was done until March 13th 1687/8 when matters were brought to a head with a complaint that "he had frequently used the children with inhumane and barbarous severities". Richard Browne was appointed as his successor.

John Curtis took his dismissal badly. The Hospital court minutes described the aftermath on March 29th 1687/8 when he went off with three violins and all the books and refused to give them to Richard Browne. He "had soe misbehaved himselfe when Mr. Browne now Music Mr. came to receive possession that he utterly refused to give him quiet possession retireing from one roome to another locking himselfe up, till a smith being sent for, broak open all the doores, and out of the last roome he fled and hath not since appeared. The Com[mittee] in the first place gave order noe sallery shall be paid to him, till he comes and restores all the bookes and instruments he hath taken away and given the courte satisfaction. Secondly ordered that his rude behaviour shall be reported to the next Court, and if the Court shall soe think fit, the same to be made knowne to the Lord Mayor and Court of Aldermen".

Unhappily Richard Browne, his successor, proved little better. Admonished for his treatment of the children in 1689, he was dismissed for negligence in 1697 but fortunately refrained from histrionics. Instead he unsuccessfully applied for reinstatment.

At the end of the eighteenth century St. Bartholomew the Great successively appointed two music sellers as organists. The first was Thomas Ball who, after eight years divided between the organ and his business in Clerkenwell, went bankrupt and deserted not only the organ but his wife as well. He was replaced by John Whitaker of the firm of Button & Whitaker of St. Paul's Churchyard who had played while Thomas Ball was being unsuccessfully sought for. He was discharged after twelve years for "gross neglect of duty" and failing to apologise for his shortcomings. As an inhabitant of the parish he immediately became liable to serve one of the numerous parish offices, from which his occupation as organist had exempted him. No time was lost in appointing him a parish constable and his refusal to accept it sent him to the Court of King's Bench. John Whitaker pleaded unfitness for office "having lost an eye and being subject to spitting of blood" and unsuccessfully argued that his election had been deliberately designed to extract from him the non-serving fine of £10.

There seems little doubt that Samuel Showell was a bad lot. He first appeared as a City candidate in 1784 and four months later appeared on the list of candidates at St. Botolph Bishopsgate. But according to a report given to the vestry he "was thrown down by a horse in Bishopsgate St." on his way to the election "and received a wound on his head and was obliged to be carried to the Hospital where he now is with very little hopes of a recovery". He was nevertheless not too ill to suggest that the vestry pay him £10 "if and when recovered" or, if he failed to survive, £10 should be paid to his father for and towards his son's expenses "he was at during the election and in the hospital". Perhaps the £10 the vestry agreed to pay was worth it in the long run for not employing him. After four more attempts Showell was appointed to St. Stephen Walbrook in 1793 but was frequently in trouble for "great neglect of duties" and "inattention". Despite this he had the audacity to put up for the post of music master at Christ's Hospital in 1810 and to apply for increases in salary at St. Stephen. His salary was at last raised to £42, high by City standards in 1814, but it was coupled with a stipulation as to his future conduct. At his death in 1825 he left his wife and family almost destitute but the parish generously raised a subscription for their relief.

Occasional instances are found of trouble in the organ loft as at St. Andrew Undershaft in 1756: "On the Vestry being acquainted that one Mr. Lowe (who was formerly Deputy to Mr. John Worgan, Organist of this Parish) has frequently on a Sunday gone into the Organ Loft or Gallery and there Intermeddled and interfered with the Deputy at present sent by Mr. Worgan and interrupts him in the playing the Organ. Whereupon it was ordered that the said Mr. Lowe be forbid to intermeddle with the said Organ . . ." and so on.

At the church of St. Augustine Watling Street in the eighteen thirties it was a case of a rogue rector and vestry rather than of a rogue organist which led to a highly undignified scene in the organ loft. The parish of St. Faith, without a church since the Great Fire, was united to St. Augustine but all signs of unity vanished over a difference of opinion regarding the efficiency of their blind organist Mrs. Carter. St. Augustine re-elected Mrs. Carter while St. Faith elected their own candidate John Peck. As there was only one organ there was considerable friction, the rector and St. Faith supporting Peck, the churchwardens and vestry of St. Augustine Mrs. Carter. After a series of ultimatums the churchwardens were informed that Peck would attend as organist and, if he was obstructed, action would be taken against them. On the following Sunday Mrs. Carter supported by the churchwardens took her seat at the organ and John Peck was physically obstructed from entering the organ loft. The rector brought a charge against his churchwardens in the Consistory Court of London which ruled that the charge did not amount to a violation of ecclesiastical law. For many years both organists were paid, complaints were made against each and the issue was finally settled only by the Rector's removal and the death of Mrs. Carter three weeks later.

Although women organists caused more minor troubles than men they provided scarcely any examples of roguery. The already mentioned (pp. 3–4) failings of Ann Kitchingman were scarcely less than gay abandon and Mrs. Carter of St. Augustine, however inefficient, was always on the receiving end. Even Esther Fleet hardly qualifies. A very talented organist whose age at her first City candidature "was found not to exceed 14", she settled in at St. Botolph Bishopsgate for thirteen trouble-free years. But ambition led her to compete for and win St. Saviour Southwark in 1838, on condition that she resigned from the City church. Instead she installed a deputy at St. Botolph and presumably hoped that nobody would miss her. Not until the deputy had collected her salary for nearly a year was anything found to be amiss and then the storm broke. An official enquiry was quickly followed by her resignation.

No instance has been found of a City organist committing murder but in his *Recollections* R.J.S. Stevens recalls that Charles Hullatt once "secreted a knife to murder me when I was asleep". The circumstances are unrevealed but the incident presumably occurred when they were boys together in St. Paul's choir and was probably nothing more than a childish prank.

The most distasteful of the rogue organists perhaps was T.S. Grady whose thirty years service at Holy Trinity Minories ended in disgrace in 1838. The vestry minutes give the first hint of scandal when "Mr. Evitt laid the subject of poor Izod's daughter before the vestry" and Grady was suspended and banned from the church until "he clears his character from the charges made against him". When "Mr. Kelly, a very old inhabitant and treasurer of the parish" completed a report on the matter the vestry took "further consideration of Mr. Grady and Letitia Izod" but disregarded Grady's plea of innocence. They resolved that his services were "not to be retained in consequence of his conduct not being in accordance with the performance of that sacred duty and that his future services as organist of this church be discontinued".

One instance of a rogue organ builder (none other than the great Renatus Harris himself) is perhaps not inappropriate. The evidence is found in the churchwardens' accounts of St. Clement Eastcheap of 1704: "Pd. for a lock for the organ 1/6. Expended on Mr. Smith the organ maker to show him the Cheat Mr. Harris putt into the Organ in order to putt the Organ out of order 5/-".

Part Two

THE CHURCHES AND OTHER INSTITUTIONS OF THE CITY OF LONDON RECORDING THE ELECTIONS OF ORGANISTS TOGETHER WITH THE NAMES OF THE UNSUCCESSFUL CANDIDATES AND BRIEF NOTES ON THE ORGANS.

In the numbered lists which follow, appointments of organists and the names of unsuccessful candidates (indicated by the letter U or u) are given for each of 76 City parish and collegiate churches and for St. Paul's Cathedral, Charterhouse, Crosby Hall, the Inner and Middle Temples, the Dutch Church Austin Friars and the Parish Clerks' Company. A further list gives the appointments of music masters of Christ's Hospital, a post invariably held by an organist.

The number in round brackets following an applicant's name indicates the number of votes cast for him. Fuller information about both organists and candidates can be found in the Annotated Index forming part three of this work.

Subsidiary information includes brief notes on the organs (which are not intended to be definitive) gathered from the parish records, the manuscript notes by J.H. Sperling[188], the anonymous manuscript *Organographia*[180], C.W. Pearce's *Notes on old London city churches*[323] and the articles in *The organ* and elsewhere by the Rev. Andrew Freeman.

Most of the information in these numbered lists comes from the vestry minute books (indicated by the letter V) and churchwardens' accounts (C) of the parishes concerned. These are set out in the first 77 entries in the bibliography where each entry is numbered according to the number of the list to which it refers. As explained in the introduction (p. ix), the records of a "united parish" have sometimes supplied information and these appear as an indented "a" entry in the bibliography.

Other sources are indicated by numbers which refer to the bibliography. For convenience G refers to *The New Grove Dictionary of music and musicians*[302] and G(5) to the 5th edition of Grove[302a]. L followed by a number indicates the page number in *Lloyd's Evening Post*[234] of the appropriate date.

Apart from such obvious abbreviations as b – born, d – died, mar – married, bur – buried etc. the following are also used:

e. elected	est. estimated	sal. salary
el. election	maj. majority	u. or U. unsuccessful candidate(s).

1. ALL HALLOWS BARKING BY THE TOWER

Sources: V. and C.[1]. See also[315 403].

Organ c. 1674–5 T. & R. Harris. 1720 new case by Gerard Smith. 1813 improvements by George Pike England[323]. (Church destroyed 1940. Rebuilt with Harrison & Harrison organ).

1675 May 4 Plans for receiving organ. No record found of appointment of organist but organ expense a/c in 1678 has "paid Mr. Bryne the organist 2½ yrs. sal. ending Michaelmas 1678," so it may be concluded that:-

1676 c.Mar. BRYNE (later given as BRYAN) appointed. (The C. which around 1675–6 are badly damaged never give his christian name. Probably Albertus Bryan, son of a St. Paul's organist of same name).

1713 Aug.21 BRYAN death reported.

1713 Aug.21 CHARLES YOUNG (7) e. u. Orbell (6), Crowfoot (0), Milborne (3).

1758 Dec.22 CHARLES YOUNG death reported (bur.1758 Dec.16). Candidates named as Archer, Aylward, Bagley, Blackbeard (appeared), Curtis (appeared), Chickley [sic], Davidge (appeared), Daves (appeared), L.Heureux, James (appeared), King (appeared), James Frederick Lampe (appeared), Parker, Patch, Raymond, Selbey (appeared). King, Parker and Selbey "declined playing".

1758 Dec.29 CHARLES [JAMES] FREDERICK LAMPE (15) e. u. Bagley (0), Chickley (0), Davidge (7), L.Heureux (0), Patch (0).

1767 Sep.15 CHARLES JAMES FREDERICK LAMPE death reported (died Sep. 10 bur. Sep.15).

1767 Sep.23 SAMUEL BOWYER [i.e. BOWER] (7) e. u. Thomas Curtis (2), John Davidge (7), Edward Griffiths ("declined standing"), William Lewis (5), James Moore, William Yeates.

1770 Sep.14 SAMUEL BOWYER [i.e. BOWER] resigns.

1770 Nov.22 Clemetshaw (sic) (4), Yarnold (6), Knyvett (9), Jackson (0), Davidge (refused, as organist of another church), Moore (0), Smethergell (7). Final poll gives Knyvett & Smethergell 13 votes each.

1770 Nov.22 CHARLES KNYVETT & WILLIAM SMETHERGELL jointly appointed.

1782 Apr.4 Annual el. still confirms this, but

1783 Apr.24 WILLIAM SMETHERGELL only, so KNYVETT vacates.

1823 May 1 WILLIAM SMETHERGELL superannuated.

1823 June 10 Miss [MARY] MORRICE (117) e. All other candidates, Miss Esther Fleet, Miss Howe, Messrs. Limming, Robinson, Perry, Sturges, Cope, all poll nil but a tribute paid to high abilities of Esther E. Fleet.

1840 MARY MORRICE vacates. V. for 1840 missing but other authorities[315] confirm appointment of Miss Lisetta Rist in 1840.

1840 Miss LISETTA RIST appointed. She appears annually in C. in this form, also in later V.

1880 LISETTA RIST vacates.

2. ALL HALLOWS BREAD STREET

Sources: V. and C.[2]. See also[404].

Organ 1718 no documentary evidence of builder. Rimbault and Sumner say Gerard Smith[309 330], others Christopher Schreider[188 323]. (Church demolished 1877).

1718 Nov.4 "Organ lately set up in parish church".

1718 Nov.12 WILLIAM BABELL (36) e. u. John Jones (34) (voting list gives William Jones). Sal. £20.

1723 Oct.10 WILLIAM BABELL death reported (bur. Sep.26).

1723 Oct.23 JOHN STANLEY e. u. Maurice Greene, Obadiah Shuttleworth.

1726/7 Mar.8 JOHN STANLEY to leave next Lady Day.

1726/7 Mar.15 EDWARD SALISBURY e. u. Phineas Cooper, Richard Low, Samuel Manwaring, John James, Joseph Jones.

1727/8 Mar.22 EDWARD SALISBURY to vacate next Lady Day. Vestry suggest as candidates Digard, Neale, Phineas Cooper, John James, Henry Duncalfe, Jones, Miller, Samuel Manwaring, Tanfield Hawks, Harrison, Dolman, John Silvester.

1728 Apr.17 JOHN SILVESTER e. u. Capt. Neale.

1729 Dec.5 Void: JOHN SILVESTER gone. Greene, Robinson & Hart to hear candidates.

1729 Dec.31 TALBOT YOUNG[E] e. u. John James, Peter Lewis, Samuel Mainwaring [sic], Richard Lowe, William Markham.

1756 Mar.30 TALBOT YOUNG resigns.

1756 May William Selby (23), Jonathan Battershall [i.e. Battishill] (26), Joseph Bryan (10), John Gray (0), Burton Hudson (9). Poll for top two:-

1756 May WILLIAM SELBY (40) e. u. John Battershall (30).

1773 Oct.14 WILLIAM SELBY resigns. Miss Frances Paxton (25), George Cooper, jun. (24), Charles Griffes (6). New election held:-

1773 Nov.11 GEORGE COOPER, jun. (39) e. u. Frances Paxton (35), Charles Griffes (2).

1799 Sep.26 GEORGE COOPER death reported.

1799 Oct.30 E.H. DAVIS [i.e. HENRY EDWARD DAVIS] (42) e. u. Joseph Major (20), Margaret Jones (1), Lowndes (1), Nicholls (0). (DAVIS is sometimes H.E. DAVIS or EDWARD DAVIS).

1852 June 15 New organist to be appointed at sal. of £60 of which £25 to go to DAVIS during his lifetime.

3. ALL HALLOWS LOMBARD STREET

Sources: V. and C. (gap 1694–1741)[3].

Organ 1700–1 Renatus Harris. (Church demolished 1939).

1700 Apr.1 Proposal for organ. Mr. Harris named as builder.

1701 Sep.9 Payment for organist to commence from Michaelmas next.

1701 Sep.24 Payment for organist confirmed. The gap in C. obscures the name of the organist but the absence of subsequent elections in V. suggests that Renatus Harris, the son of the builder, held the post. So:-

1701 Sep.29 RENATUS HARRIS, jun. appointed. £22 p.a. for maintaining organ and paying organist.

1702 Mar.31 £22 for annual maintenance of organ & pay of organist not sufficient – £2 p.a. added. Confirmation that organist had been paid since last Michaelmas.

1737 May 25 RENATUS HARRIS, organist, death reported. No election until

1737/8 Mar.1 Candidates: William Jackson, John L'Estrange, James Cappar, William Collins, (Young, Worgan, Hawkes withdraw names). Final ballot between:-

1737/8 Mar.1 WILLIAM JACKSON (44) e. u. John L'Estrange (22).

1780 May 24 WILLIAM JACKSON death reported.

1780 June 2 Candidates: Charles Bennett, Jonas Blewitt, James Wade (20), Charles Cross (4), Thomas Curtis (1), Edward Davis (9), John Webb (1), Alexander Edmonds (18), Griffith Jones, Mary Lock (5), Lewis Pearse (5), John Shuckford (6), Cornelius Keith withdraws name. William Beverley & John Shute fail to attend audition. Second ballot:-

1780 June 2 ALEXANDER EDMONDS (34) e. u. Davis (14), Wade (26), Shuckford (2).

1812 Feb.6 ALEXANDER EDMONDS death reported. Sal. for new appointment raised to £30.

1812 Feb.13 ELIZABETH RODD (45) e. u. John Cash (25), Henry Giles (14), Mary Morrice (0), J.C. Nightingale (0), Jonathan Rush (1).
1842 Mar.30 ELIZABETH RODD retires.
1842 Mar.30 Miss MARIAN HILDYARD e. (? only candidate). In 1844 the C. payments are to Mrs. ARCHER (? née HILDYARD).
1849 Aug.1 Mrs ARCHER death reported.
1849 Aug.10 Miss HARRIS (41) e. u. Miss Cowtan (37), Miss Bates, Mary Ann Boughey, James Baines. Miss Harris, who probably became Mrs. GEORGE GRESHAM in 1861, served until
1867 Apr.23 Mrs. GEORGE GRESHAM resigns.

4. ALL HALLOWS LONDON WALL

Sources: V. and C. (gaps in both series)[4].

Organ 1783 installed by John England but original maker unknown (see below). George England[180 188], John England & Hugh Russell suggested[330]. (Replaced after damage in 1940).

1782 Feb.11 "Pd, Mr. Ivers 6 weeks performing on the bassoon 13s/1½."
1783 Aug.6 Organ to be bought by voluntary subscription.
1783 Aug.14 With the assistance of Mr. Soaper of King's Chapel and Mr. England, organ examined in French Chapel in St. John St., Spitalfields and bought for £42. [John] England to fit additional stop and instal for £20.
1784 Jan.21 JOSEPH HENSHAW (57) e. u. Sarah Bonwick (43), Alexander Edmonds (declines). Sal. 12 guineas.
1824 Sep.23 JOSEPH HENSHAW resigns.
1825 Apr.21 20 candidates listed (names included in Annotated Index).
1825 May 3 Miss ELIZABETH ANN BARBER (46) e. u. Miss Shower (or Shervers) (39), Miss Kirby (or Kerby) (2).
1833 Apr.4 Miss E.A. BARBER not re-elected at annual election but
1833 Apr.11 re-elected.
1834 Mar.27 Mrs. ELIZABETH ANN SMITH née BARBER re-elected.
1837 Mar.28 Mrs. ELIZABETH ANN SMITH resigns.
1837 Apr.13 Candidates James Whitaker [sic], Alfred Bobbett, Octavia Bradfield, Benvici (?) Parker. Octavia Bradfield e. but poll demanded:
1837 Apr.13 ALFRED BOBBETT (51) e. u. Bradfield (31), Whitaker (21).
1844 Aug.8 ALFRED BOBBETT dismissed.
1844 Sep.4 Miss ELIZA JAMES e. u. Miss Duglas [sic]. Miss Eliza James becomes Mrs. ELIZA WRIGHT between 1857 Apr. & 1858 Apr.
1858 Apr.6 Mrs. ELIZA WRIGHT last appearance at annual election.

5. ALL HALLOWS STAINING

Sources: V. very incomplete, C lost before 1841[5].

No evidence of organ from either. It appears that the statement in George Godwin's *Churches of London*, 1838–9[299] that an organ was erected in 1777 is incorrect. Pearce asserts there was a harmonium but no organ at the time of the church's demolition in 1870 and that J.W. Billinghurst "found no organ there" in 1855[323]. Mackeson's *Guide to the churches of London*, 1866 & 1867 both have "organist – Lady amateur"[209 210].

6. ALL HALLOWS THE GREAT

Source: V.[6]. See also[405].

Organ 1748–9 no documentary evidence of builder. Perhaps Parker[180 188] or Glyn &

Parker[323]. 1836 enlarged by James Butler[323]. (Church demolished 1894).

1748 Oct.10 Committee for erecting organ.

1749 Jul.28 WILLIAM BOYCE e. sal. £30.

1758 Jan.5 Sal. reduced to £20. To change Mr. Bullbrick his deputy.

1764 Mar.21 WILLIAM BOYCE dismissed. Sal. to be £30 for new appointment. Mr. Bullbrick not to apply.

1764 Apr.6 JAMES EVANCE e. u. Robert Rowe, John Turner (declined to stand).

1811 Dec.11 JAMES EVANCE death reported.

1811 Dec.30 RICHARD EVANCE (75) e. u. Elizabeth Rodd (2), John Cash (2).

1817 May 27 RICHARD EVANCE resigns.

1817 June 3 WALTER AUGUSTUS LORD e. (no other candidates).

1833 Mar.26 WALTER AUGUSTUS LORD resigns to succeed his late father as parish clerk.

1833 Feb.27 Elizabeth (or Eliza) Elsden of 18 Bush Lane asks for post.

1833 Apr.10 Miss Eliza (or ELIZABETH) ELSDEN appointed.

1868 Apr.17 Miss ELIZA ELSDEN services not required after June 24 next.

7. CHRIST CHURCH NEWGATE STREET

Sources: (V. and C. destroyed in 1940). V. 1814–1913 survive for the united parish of St. Leonard Foster Lane from which the later organists are derived[7a]. Pearce[323] gives no information before 1800 and very inaccurate information thereafter. At some periods there is little doubt that the organist was also music master of Christ's Hospital (see list 81) and the intention of the parishioners of Christ Church to appoint the music master of Christ's Hospital as their first post-Fire organist is noted in the Court minute books of Christ's Hospital[156].

Organ 1690? Renatus Harris (secondary sources). 1835 rebuilt by Hill[280]. (Destroyed 1940).

1682 June 23 Parishioners of Christ Church acquainted Christ's Hospital that it was the desire of that parish that JOHN CURTIS the singing school mr. of this hospitall might be settled as organist of the said church & to have £10 p.a. for his said service[156].

1687/8 Mar.13 JOHN CURTIS successor appointed at Christ's Hospital 3 years before installation of Christ Church organ. As John Curtis did not die until early in 1704 he may have played at Christ Church from 1690 to 1704. Between John Curtis and Peter Horwood in 1720 the music masters at Christ's Hospital were Richard Browne (1688) and John Barrett (1697) who died between Dec. 1719 and Jan. 1719/20 (not c.1735 as in G.). As Peter Horwood was at Christ Church as early as 1718 (see Annotated Index) i.e. before his appointment to Christ's Hospital, there seems to be at least a possibility that neither Browne nor Barrett served Christ Church and that Horwood succeeded Curtis in 1704 (Horwood was a "singing boy at Paul's" in 1698).

1689 Jul.24 Court of Christ's Hospital informed that "some of the parishioners of Christ Church doe intend with all convenient speed to set up an Organ in the said Church".

1690 Alleged date of installation of organ by Renatus Harris[380].

1718 or before PETER HORWOOD appointed.

1739 Dec. PETER HORWOOD died.

1740 c.Feb. ?JOHN YOUNG appointed (John Young, jun., appointed music master Christ's Hospital 1740 Feb.12).

1767 Apr.30 JOHN YOUNG "organist of Christ Church, Newgate St." died[242].

1767 May 20 JONATHAN BATTISHILL e. (maj.94) u. Heron, Levingstone, Yates, Griffiths, Bamber[L481]. (Robert Hudson elected to Christ's Hospital in 1767).

1801 Dec.10 JONATHAN BATTISHILL died. There is no further source until the V. of the amalgamated parish of St. Leonard Foster begin in 1814[7a].

1802–1814 (probably 1802 Jan.) GEORGE MACQUISTIN[E] e.

1817 Nov.21 GEORGE MACQUISTIN[E] resigns "because he has come into a fortune" (letter to vestry from 34 Burton St., Burton Crescent).

1817 Dec.16 CHRISTOPHER DAVIES (84) e. u. Robert Glenn (48), Miss Mary Ann Thompson (41), James Hook (1), Mrs. Harriet Page withdraws.

1836–46 HENRY JOHN GAUNTLETT evening organist according to G. The information may have come from V. before destruction in 1940. H.J. Gauntlett is so described in a list of subscribers in Cherubini's *Course of Counterpoint*[256] (no evidence in V. of St. Leonard) and he referred to himself as "lay-minister of the great metropolitan organ of Christ Church, London"[280].

1849 Apr.12 (annual election) Christopher Davies e. "pro tem.".

1850 Apr.4 (annual election) Christopher Davies e. "pro tem.".

1850 Apr.30 JOHN BOYER to undertake duties now performed by Christopher Davies. To cooperate with teacher of singing at Christ's Hospital.

1850 Jul.3 John Boyer to allow Christopher Davies regular allotment out of his salary.

1850 Sep.12 £50 p.a. to be allowed to John Boyer for playing morning & afternoon upon his allowing the present organist Mr. Christopher Davies such yearly annuity as is satisfactory to the parish officers.

1866 Apr.5 JOHN BOYER resigns.

8. HOLY TRINITY, GOUGH SQUARE

Sources: V. 1845–98 (no separate C.) and Committee for building new church minutes 1836–8[8].

Organ 1838 T.C. Bates. (Church demolished 1913).

1838 Apr.10 Mr. Bates's organ to be hired at £15 p.a.

1838 June 21 Church consecrated. No. V. available so no record of organist although on June 13 "temporary arrangement" to be made for organist.

1845–53 Payment of "organist" (unnamed) in C. which are included in V.

1852 ALFRED MOLSON appointed (see below).

1854 Jul.5 ALFRED MOLSON first named as organist in C. Sal. £15.

1883 Apr.19 Vote of sympathy to Alfred Molson, more than 30 years organist, on death of wife.

1900 Apr.26 ALFRED MOLSON death reported (died 1900 Jan.7). "Organist for 48 years". This is confirmed by Mackeson 1889, who gives date of appointment as 1852[210].

9. HOLY TRINITY MINORIES

Sources: V. (at Tower Hamlets Central Library)[9].

Organ 1808? no documentary evidence of builder. Sperling described it as small chamber organ of 6 stops by H.C. Lincoln[188]. (Church destroyed 1940).

1808 Jul.25 THOMAS S. GRADY (32) e. u. James Hyatt Little (9).

1838 Jul.9 THOMAS S. GRADY dismissed following suspension 1838 May 10. (Details of his disgrace in Annotated Index).

1840 Mar.20 Miss HARRIET BROWN re-elected (no previous record of appointment). Sal. £20.

1844 Apr.9 – 1845 Mar.17 (between) Miss Brown becomes Mrs. OXLEE.

1846 Mar.19 Mrs. HARRIET OXLEE resigns.

1846 Mar.19 Miss SARAH SOPHIA ANN AUSTIN appointed unanimously. Still in office in 1850.

After the unfortunate affair of T.S. Grady the parish appears to have played for safety and appointed female members of the parish.

10. ST. ALBAN WOOD STREET

Sources: V. 1731–1790 only but V. of united parish of St. Olave Silver Street continue from 1790 until 1862. These are not well kept and no annual elections given. C. commence 1767. C. of St. Olave offer no information for period before 1736[10] [10a].

Organ: no documentary evidence of date or builder. Given variously as Richard Bridge[188] or, more likely, John Harris and John Byfield, sen.[323]. (Destroyed with church 1940).

1728? Organ installed.
1728? PETER PRELLEUR appointed. (Hawkins gives this date but absence of V. and C. make confirmation impossible. No record of his resignation in 1735 or 1736 but date seems reasonable as he was appointed to Christ Church Spitalfields in 1735/6 Mar.)
1735–6? PETER PRELLEUR resigns.
1736 Apr.28 MATTHEW HUSSEY e. u. L'Estrange, Cappar.
1766 Apr.8 MATTHEW HUSSEY death reported.
1766 Apr.15 BENJAMIN WAYNE (40) e. u. Miss Benson (2), Ayrton (24), Rowe (7), Scott (3), Kirkshaw (or Kirshaw) (16), Davidge (21). Sal. £24.
1774 Dec.2 BENJAMIN WAYNE death reported.
1774 Dec.2 GEORGE JACKSON (82) e. u. John Jee (26).
1790 Oct.7 GEORGE JACKSON resigns.
1790 Nov.4 JONATHAN PERKINS (54) e. u. Frederick Augustus Smallshaw (21), Samuel Showell (20), Thomas Lester (41).
1835 Mar.24 JONATHAN PERKINS resigns.
1835 Mar.24 Miss ELIZABETH HEATHER (69) e. u. Miss Louisa Smith (1), J. Reynolds (1).
1839 c.Feb. Miss ELIZABETH HEATHER vacates (last payment made 1839 Jan.).
1839 c.Apr. J. GOSS appointed. (Paid ¾ year 1840 Feb.11).
1840 Jan.26 J. GOSS resignation reported.
1840 Jan.26 Miss HULL e. u. Norman, Miss Payton, Creeger.
1841 c.Aug. Miss HULL vacates (no evidence of this).
1841 Aug.23 Miss ELIZABETH GURRY e. (No candidates mentioned).
1846 Mar.31–Jul.7 (between) Miss ELIZABETH GURRY replaced by Mrs. GALE (?the same).
1846 Jul.7–Oct.24 (between) Mrs. GALE vacates.
1846 Jul.7–Oct.24 (between) JOSHUA STONE appointed.
1849 Jul.6–Oct.5 (between) JOSHUA STONE leaves.
1849 Jul.6–Oct.5 (between) WALTER GOSS appointed.

Walter Goss's end not established from surviving records.

11. ST. ALPHAGE LONDON WALL

Sources: V.[11]. See also[406].

Organ 1843 Grover of Hackney Road[188]. (Later replaced. Church demolished 1924).

1843 Aug.31 Gift from Rector, Rev. J. Hutchins of "a little organ".
1845 Mar.25 Election of organist deferred until midsummer.
1845 June 27 Miss KEARNES e. No evidence of other candidates.
1854 Mar.30 Miss KEARNES resigns.

12. ST. ANDREW BY THE WARDROBE

Sources: (V. nil before 1875, C. nil between 1704 & 1835). Information from V. & C. of united parish of St. Anne, Blackfriars[12 12a].

Organ 1808 no documentary evidence of builder probably William Gray[180] or Robert Gray[323]. No evidence found of earlier organ which, according to Pearce, was presented in 1774[323]. (Destroyed 1940 and replaced).

1808 May 20 Faculty for organ granted[178]. It appears from this that organ & organist's salary would be paid from fund already in existence. Nothing found in V. of St. Anne about organ. However, positive evidence exists that organist in

1811 JOHN JEREMIAH JONES. Probably voluntary (see Annotated Index).

1815 Apr.19 Agreement to pay organist. (First reference to organist in V.)

1816 Jan.9 Organist to have £40 p.a.

1816 Apr.17 ROBERT WILLIAMS e. No other candidates proposed.

1842 Oct.6 ROBERT WILLIAMS resignation reported.

1842 Oct.25 About 50 applicants (names included in Annotated Index). Four candidates selected:-

1842 Nov.10 Miss Wesley e. on show of hands, u. Miss Carrey, Cornish, May. Ballot on following day:-

1842 Nov.11 Miss [THOMASINE] WESLEY (137) e. u. Cornish (108), May & Miss Carrey withdraw. Election of Miss Thomasine Wesley reported in Times[250].

1858 May 6 Mrs. THOMASINE MARTIN (née Wesley) resigns.

13. ST. ANDREW HOLBORN

Sources: V. 1624–1797 which are inconsistent as suppliers of information. None survives after 1797 (C. 1683–91 only)[13]. See also[407].

Organ 1699? Renatus Harris (part of organ intended for Temple). According to Hawkins erected in 1699 but "shut up" until 1713. (Destroyed 1940 and replaced by Renatus Harris organ from Foundling Hospital).

c.1713 (definitely before 1715) DANIEL PURCELL voluntary organist without election[308]. (Details in Annotated Index).

1717 Nov. DANIEL PURCELL died (buried St. Andrew Nov. 26 "from Fetter Lane").

1717/18 Feb. 19 [MAURICE] GREEN[E] (6) e. u. Short, Isham, Young, Pursill [i.e. Edward Purcell], Haydon, Harris, Hart, all of whom fail to get a vote. (The first entry in V. relating to organists).

1718 Apr.3 MAURICE GREEN[E]resigns on appointment to St. Paul's.

1718 Apr.3 JOHN ISHAM (11) e. u. George Haydon (1) (runner-up), Charles Young (0), Edward Pursil [i.e. Purcell] (0). Sal. £50.

1726 June JOHN ISHAM died (bur. June 12 St. Margaret Westminster). The V. after 1718 are completely uninformative about the comings and goings of the organists. Nevertheless the continuity can be established from extraneous sources (but not the u.)

1726 Aug.15–17 JOHN STANLEY e. u. (inter alia) Short after 3 day ballot reversing the choice of Short on a show of hands[241].

1786 May 19 JOHN STANLEY died (contemp. obits. describe him as organist of St. Andrew's for nearly 60 years).

1786 c.June JAMES EVANCE e. (pupil of Stanley).

1811 Nov. JAMES EVANCE died (death announced All Hallows the Great Dec.11). The evidence for the organists between 1811 and the appointment of James Higgs in 1867 is scanty. Pearce[323] quoting G.M. Ogbourne (organist 1903) gives a fuller list than usual and the general accuracy of it up to 1811 is confirmed by primary evidence. Thereafter he gives John Grosvenor (1811–14), J. Reynolds (no dates) and —— Boyer (to 1867).

The City Press of 1867 Oct. 12[217] announced that "the organist of St. Andrew Holborn (Mr. Reynolds) has resigned" and that Mr. Higgs had been appointed from 150 candidates. Two earlier entries asserted that "the office of organist and choirmaster is vacant" (Jul.20)[215] and that "the organist who has been with them nearly 40 years has been pensioned" (Aug.31)[216]. Reynolds was thus the immediate predecessor of Higgs and probably the organist with "nearly 40 years" service. Such an interpretation leaves no room for Boyer and it is possible that Pearce mistakenly assigned him to St. Andrew Holborn instead of Christ Church Newgate Street. (He was in fact at Christ Church between 1850 and 1866, a fact not recorded by Pearce).

The J. Reynolds at St. Andrew was probably Joshua Reynolds (see Annotated Index) and as suggested above it is likely that he served from c.1828 until 1867. Pearce's John Grosvenor seems a likely successor to Evance as he had been an unsuccessful candidate at St. Anne and St. Agnes in 1809. No confirmation of his terminal date of 1814 has been found nor the name of his immediate successor. The tentative succession can therefore be given as

1811 Dec. JOHN GROSVENOR e. (evidence of Pearce only).
1814? JOHN GROSVENOR vacates (evidence of Pearce only).
c.1828 J. REYNOLDS e. [216].
1867 Jul. J. REYNOLDS pensioned[216].

14. ST. ANDREW UNDERSHAFT

Sources V. and C.[14]. See also[408].

Organ 1695–6 Renatus Harris. 1749–50 swell and other additions by John Byfield, sen. 1799 repairs and extensions by John Byfield (the third?). 1810–11 repairs by George Pike England [180 188].

1696 May 31 Organ opened.
1696 Jul.30 WILLIAM GOODGROOME e. PHILIP HART unan. e. for assistant. To work alternate weeks.
1697 Oct.19 PHILIP HART "unan. e. & chosen organist". (No mention of fate of WILLIAM GOODGROOME). First C. of 1711 gives Hart's sal. as £20.
1720 Apr.18 Mr HART e. (first annual election recorded).
1749 Jul.26 PHILIP HART death reported (died Jul.17). Sal. to be £30 in future.
1749 Sep.14 Election. Attfield (4), Berg (0), Curtis (3), Duncalf (36), Gates (0), Hart (0), Peirce (20), Relfe (2), Salmon (1), Whittle (0), John Worgan (45). New ballot: JOHN WORGAN (70) e. u. Duncalf (44), Peirce (5).
1749 Sep.25 [JOHN] SALMON mentioned as having been Hart's deputy.
1750 Apr.16 Completion of work by John Byfield sen. including new swell.
1790 Sep.8 JOHN WORGAN's death reported (died Aug.24). Candidates named. Richard Worgan, son of John, should be allowed to offer himself as candidate. Sal. to be £30.
1790 Oct.13 Miss MARY ALLEN (64) e. u. John McKerroll (or McKirroll) (1), Rayner Taylor (59), Richard Worgan (1), Alexander Edmonds withdraws. Frequent complaints during Mary Allen's long tenure.
1836 Apr.7 MARY ALLEN to be permitted to retire on pension of £25.
1834–36 Miss ELIZA HARVEY assistant organist.
1836 May 26 JOHN SMITH e. (only candidate). (A contemp. subscribers' list gives Frank A. Smith). Sal. £30 raised to £40 in 1839.
1847? JOHN SMITH vacates? (no record of fate).
1847 Apr.8 RICHARD LIMPUS e. (annual election only).
1847 Jul.8 RICHARD LIMPUS resigns.
1847 Jul.8 WILLIAM REA e. (sole candidate). Sal. £50.
1858 Aug.12 WILLIAM REA resigns for "more advantageous appointment".

15. ST. ANNE AND ST. AGNES

Sources: V. and C. supplemented by V. of St. John Zachary[15 15a].

Organ 1782 no documentary evidence of builder reputedly Robert Gray[188 323]. (Destroyed with church 1940 and replaced).

1763 Apr.6 Proposal for organ rejected.

1781 May 1 Organ to be built. Organ & organist's sal. to be paid for by voluntary subscriptions.

1782 Oct.29 Miss SMALLSHAWE (106) e. u. Poole (22). By 1783 Apr. Miss Smallshawe becomes Mrs. MILWARD.

1790 Oct.20 Mrs. MILWARD to be allowed £25 p.a. in lieu of voluntary subscriptions.

1804 Oct.17 Vacancy declared. Fate of Mrs. MILWARD unknown.

1804 Nov.1 WILLIAM TAYLOR (66) e. u. John Banner (30), Charles Dupuis (withdraws), Samuel John Ferry, William Harding (20), Joseph Major (withdraws), John Frederick Milward (28).

1809 Apr.19 WILLIAM TAYLOR re-election suspended.

1809 May 5 WILLIAM TAYLOR (89) e. u. Joseph Nightingale (22), Grosvenor withdraws.

1809 Sep.14 WILLIAM TAYLOR vacates (no information as to why).

1809 Sep.21 JOSEPH GOODMAN (30) e. u. Elizabeth Rodd (27), J. Grosvenor (15), Maria Nash (13), Jonathan Rush (10), S.J. Ferry (0), Sal. £25.

1836 Sep.16 JOSEPH GOODMAN death reported.

1836 Sep.16–30 Candidates: W. Wrede, James Whittaker, George Cooper, jun., J.W. Lowes, Josiah Pittman, Joshua Reynolds, J.T. Cooper, John Strickland, J.H. Howard, Wilkinson, Henry Culham, Edward West, J.F.T. Adams, W.F. Robinson, Mrs. Elizabeth Barchard, Miss Fleet, Cornish, Batt, Cupit. Umpires (John Banner, John Goss & James Turle) select 4 candidates for election:-

1836 Oct.26 GEORGE COOPER, jun. (37) e. u. Henry Cullum (23), Cornish (2), Cupit (0).

1844 Jan.12 GEORGE COOPER resigns.

1844 Jan.19 Candidates: Miss Caroline Mary Wood, Miss S. Waller, Miss H. Maria Arnott, Miss M. Edmonds, Miss R. Schnergant (?Schnerganer), Miss M.A. Johnson, Algernon Sidney Lumley, William White, Henry Wylde, John Joseph Strickland. Umpire (Mr. Goss) selects candidates for election.

1844 Feb.23 Henry Wylde, J.J. Strickland, William White, Miss S. Waller poll equal votes. Chairman (Rev. J.V. Povah) casting vote in favour of HENRY WYLDE e.

1847 Oct.14 HENRY WYLDE resigns.

1847 Oct.22 Candidates Miss Mary Jane Boughey, William Baley (or Baly), Miss Sellman, E.J. Westrop, Miss E. Trufley (or Tufley), Miss Senior (or Simon) (withdraws), Miss Emily Cope, Foord, J.H. Deane (Dean), Miss Arnott, W.H. Essex, Miss Agatha Cowtan. (The variants arise from differences in V. of St. Anne & St. Agnes and V. of St. John Zachary).

1847 Nov.4 Mr. Turle selects 4 for election (J.H. Deane greatly superior to others and Miss Arnott "much inferior to Westrop and Bailey"):-

1847 Dec.2 EAST JOHN WESTROP (35) e. u. Miss Arnott (0), William Baley (27), J.H. Deane (0).

1856 Nov.13 EAST JOHN WESTROP death reported (died Oct.27).

16. ST. ANTHOLIN BUDGE ROW

Source: V. & C.[16]. See also[409].

Organ 1735 Abraham Jordan. Swell added by John England & Hugh Russell[180 188].

(Church demolished 1875–6).
1734/5 Feb.14 Mr. Jordan to erect an organ £315.
1735/6 Feb.25 RICHARD WARD (54) e. u. John Allcock (18), Salary £20.
1777 Feb.13 RICHARD WARD death reported.
1777 Feb.28 JOSEPH DALE (72) e. u. Keith (1), Webb (9).
1821 Sep.3 JOSEPH DALE death reported.
1821 Sep.12 ANDREW CASH (43) e. u. William Knowles (42), William Bradley, Miss Jane Howe.
1870 Apr.21 ANDREW CASH not re-elected. No money available for paying officers. (Church demolished 1875).

17. ST. AUGUSTINE WATLING STREET

Sources: V. Gap between 1800 and 1826 filled by V. of St. Faith[17 17a] and Lloyd's Evening Post.

Organ 1766 no documentary evidence of builder generally believed to be Rawlings & Pether[180 188]. 1808 swell added by Hugh Russell[180 323]. (Destroyed 1941).
1766 Sep.16 Organ to be bought from James Lewer of Cheshunt.
1766 Sep.23 Organ committee reports on visit to Cheshunt. James Lewer's offer to erect organ, find organist and tune it for £30 p.a. during lives of his 2 daughters aged 32 & 16 not accepted. Lewer will sell organ for £240. Vestry suggests £210 plus 5%. Organist to have £15 p.a. To be a ballot for organist but no record appears in V. and no C. survive. However Timothy Smart advertised his candidature 1766 Nov.[226] (see Annotated Index). Otherwise all that is known is that
1767 Feb.12 [GEORGE] LEVINGSTONE e.[149]. Levingstone sometimes appears in V. subsequently as Livingstone.
1808 Apr.22 [GEORGE] LEVINGSTONE death reported (bur. Apr.24).
1808 May 5 GEORGE PRICE (71) e. u. Miss Maria Naish (37), Thomas Martin Platts (19). George Price appears in annual elections but 1812 election postponed for no apparent reason, so
1812 Apr.? GEORGE PRICE vacates.
1812 Apr.23 Miss ELIZABETH HOLLAND e. u. Miss Margaret Jones, John Cash, Miss Maria Nash [sic].
1831 Easter Mrs. CARTER (née HOLLAND) suspended after much dissatisfaction.
1832 Apr.27 JOHN PECK (12) e. u. Mrs. E. Carter (6). But Mrs. Carter continues to be re-elected by St. Augustine while the united parish of St. Faith continues to re-elect John Peck. During the next few years Mrs. Carter, John Peck and Henry Michelmore play at St. Augustine while an inter-parish feud leads to intervention by the Bishop and a hearing in the Consistory Court. The battle not finally settled until
1842 Oct.31 Mrs. ELIZABETH CARTER died and JOHN PECK, previously elected only by St. Faith, now elected by St. Augustine also.
1851 Feb.26 JOHN PECK death reported.

18. ST. BARTHOLOMEW BY THE EXCHANGE

Sources: V.[18]. See also[410].

Organ 1731–2 John Harris & John Byfield, sen. Although secondary sources except Clutton and Nyland[289] unanimous in naming "Byfield 1740", Harris & Byfield elected organ keepers 1732. Organ removed to St. Bartholomew Moor Lane q.v. on demolition of church. After 50 years at Fulham restored by Noel Mander and re-erected in St. Vedast.
1730 Nov.11 Organ proposed.

1732 Apr. Mr. Shuttleworth . . . gave fine performance on new organ[221].
1732 June 21 Organ "lately erected". Harris and Byfield elected organ keepers.
1732 June 21 HENRY DUNCALF e. u. Arnold Powers. Sal. £20. These two appear at each annual election in April until 1745. Duncalf's unsuccessful opponent in 1746 given as Bennett, 1747 to 1750 Samuel Jenkinson and 1751 to 1756 John Byfield. John Byfield as organ keeper opposed by Jenkinson at each annual election. The opposition would appear to be theoretical. Byfield followed as nominal u. by Thomas Jackson.
1762 June 10 HENRY DUNCALF died[L558].
1762 June 18 JOHN ATFIELD (41) e. u. Burton Hudson (2), Samuel Jarvis (14), John Scott (13), John Selby (2), Thomas Curtis (1). Sal. £20.
1766 Mar.20 JOHN ATFIELD death reported (bur. Mar.13). Post in future not to be in plurality. Sal. 30 guineas.
1766 Mar.27 WILLIAM GOODWIN e. u. Hannah Benson, Walter Bamber, Edward Davis, Samuel Bower.
1784 Mar.16 WILLIAM GOODWIN death reported. Single post clause again for new appointment.
1784 Mar.25 SARAH BONWICK e. u. Sarah Ormes, Thomas Devoy, Thomas Howard, Thomas Huddon [sic], Cornelius Keith, John McKerrell, Samuel Showell.
1819 Oct.28 SARAH BONWICK death reported.
1819 Nov.3 Miss GRACE CHAPMAN (33) e. u. Miss Marian England (20), William Knowles (6), William Blackman (0), William Hill (0), F. Lemare (0).
1841 Church demolished and GRACE CHAPMAN drafted to the united parish of St. Margaret Lothbury to be "weekday organist".

19. ST. BARTHOLOMEW MOOR LANE

Source: Cash book 1850–89[19]. See also[412].

Organ from St. Bartholomew by the Exchange, q.v. (Church demolished 1862–5. Organ stored at Fulham until re-erected St. Vedast, q.v.).

1850 Apr. Church consecrated.
1851 Jan.2 Mr. PALLET organist (first mention). He does not appear again and it seems likely that PALLET served from 1850 Apr.? until 1851.
1851 Oct.29 CURTIS appears in cash book.

20. ST. BARTHOLOMEW THE GREAT

Sources: V. & C.[20]. See also[411].

Organ 1715 John Knopple*. 1731 new organ by Richard Bridge[220]. (Replaced by England organ from St. Stephen Walbrook 1886).

1715 Apr.5 Ordered that Mr Canoble's [sic] organ is brought into the church.
1715 Jul.6 Mr. Kanople [sic] to be paid £20 as part of the sum agreed for the organ.
1715 Dec.7 [ADRIAN] VAN HELSDING appointed. Sal. £18. (The organist's name is subject to the wildest variations. At his appointment he is entered as Venallson and at his departure he is Vanghelsden. The C. entries also include Vanhelsding and, once, Adrian Vanhelsden. He can probably be identified with the Adrian van Helsdingen who was buried at the Dutch church 1721 Nov.3).
1720 Nov.3 Organist to be continued as organist with proviso "that he provide one to do his business".

* John Knopple either built organ or altered and installed Bernard Smith organ St. James Garlickhythe 1718 and altered and maintained organ St. John Hackney c.1714–24.

1721 c.June [ADRIAN] VAN HELSDING vacates.
1721 Aug.16 ISAAC ORBELL appointed.
1721 Dec.6 Ordered that nothing be paid for playing from midsummer to Michaelmas last, that quarter being supplied by candidates playing for place.
1731 autumn? ISAAC ORBELL vacates.
1731 Oct.31 New organ by Richard Bridge opened[220].
1731 Nov.3 Organist to be elected. Sal. £20.
1731 Dec.14 ROWLAND EVANS e. u. James, Preluer (? Peter Prelleur), Markham, Middlebrook, Powers. "Rowland Evans to play at all times as before".
1739/40 Jan.13 ROWLAND EVANS death reported.
1740 Mar.26 RICHARD WARD e. u. Worgan, Hilburn, Smith, Carey. Sal. £20.
1777 Feb.12 RICHARD WARD death reported.
1777 Feb.14 NICHOLAS STEELE e. u. Lewis Pearce, Richard Bride, Henry Heron, jun., John Scott, Edward Griffes, Jonas Blewitt. Sal. £20. To attend at all times.
1785 Aug.17 NICHOLAS STEELE death reported.
1785 Aug.17 THOMAS BALL[IS] e. u. Negus (?) (4).
1793 June 26 THOMAS BALL discharged for non-attendance.
1793 Jul.3 Quarter's sal. to be divided between JOHN WHITAKER who has performed this duty and Mrs. Ball who has been deserted by her husband. JOHN WHITAKER appointed.
1805 June 25 JOHN WHITAKER dismissed for inefficiency.
1805 Jul.10 WILLIAM BRADLEY (18) e. u. Joseph Major (7), John Hammond, Hugh Josiah Ferry.
1819 Sep.3 WILLIAM BRADLEY death reported.
1819 Oct.27 JOHN MONRO (14) e. u. Fr. LeMare (or Lemare) (9), G. Mather (2), William Lowndes (1), Joseph John Harris (0), Joseph Haycock (0), C. Smith (withdraws).
1827 Jan.26 JOHN MONRO resigns.
1827 Apr.19 Miss WAFFORNE e. u. Robinson (runner-up), Cleland, Miss Dowling, Pyne, Miss Warne, Snell, Miss Tookey, Michelmore.
1834 Apr.3 Miss WAFFORNE "has retired into country". Not to seek re-election.
1834 May 22 Umpire selects 4 candidates including, surprisingly, Miss Wafforne (presumably a sister).
1834 June 26 JOLLY, jun. (15) e. u. Miss Wafforne (15), Miss Sinderby (4), Cornish (0). (Chairman exercised casting vote).
1836 Apr.7 JOLLY vacates (?dismissed).
1836 May 25 MISS ELIZABETH ELLEN WAFFORNE (22) e. u. Jolly (20) (runner-up), Miss Pescott, Miss Boulton?, Adams, Ingram, Cooper, Roe, Crabb, Cornish, Barrett, Tidmarsh, Foster, Perry, Miss Brown, Fagg, Pole.
1842 Mar.–1843 Mar. Miss WAFFORNE becomes Mrs. WILLIAMS between these dates.
1849 Apr.12 Mrs. ELIZABETH ELLEN WILLIAMS resigns "after 13 years service".
1849 June 13 Miss MARY ANN WILLIAMS appointed without election. (Dau. of Rev. D. Williams, lecturer of this parish).
1867 Apr.24 Position of organist abolished until church reopens.

21. ST. BARTHOLOMEW THE LESS

Sources: V., C. and records of Board of Governors (at St. Bartholomew's Hospital)[21]. See also[459].

Organ 1794–5 "annuity organ" by John Byfield the third with his father John Byfield, jun. (see p.16). 1825 new organ by John Gray. (Replaced 1930[459]).

1794 Feb.24 Agreed to erect organ.

1794 Mar.20 Acceptance of proposal by John Byfield the younger, age 28, son of John Byfield of Constitution Row, Grays Inn Rd., St. Pancras that he and father would erect organ "and play the same". J.B. the younger would "play or cause to be played" and to be paid £20 p.a. during lives of himself & sister Mary Frances Byfield now age 24. It is frequently impossible to identify the actual organist with these annuity organs. But the payments in C. are as follows:-
1796 Jan. onwards JOHN BYFIELD organist.
1800 Jul.16 JOHN BYFIELD last payment.
1800 Oct.22 [WILLIAM] SHRUBSOLE first payment.
1806 Jan.18 [WILLIAM] SHRUBSOLE died.
1806 first 3 quarters JOHN BYFIELD.
1806 last quarter [GEORGE?] MACQUISTIN first payment.
1822 Mar.25 MACQUISTIN last payment.
1823 Aug.20 Organ to be given up and removed.
1824 Aug.17 Proposal to provide organ.
1825 Jan.21 Sir George Smart to superintend building by Gray.
1825 May 4 Miss PROBYN (9) e. u. Nichols (0), West (8). Sal. 25 guineas.
1863 Mrs. COOPER (née Probyn) retires.

22. ST. BENET FINK

Sources: V. and C.[22]. See also[390 413].
Organ 1714 Abraham Jordan from £400 bequeathed by Mrs. Sarah Gregory.
1713 Jul.9 Madam Gregory's executors are about to provide an organ.
1714/15 Jan.6 CHARLES KING chosen from June 24 next. Sal. £20. Abraham Jordan, senior, and in case of his death his son, elected to keep organ in repair.
1746 Jul.3 CHARLES KING to be continued until vestry makes order for discontinuing him. Sal. reduced to £15.
1747 Sep.9 CHARLES KING dismissed at Michaelmas next.
1747 Oct.15 BURTON HUDSON (34) e. u. John Cary (9), Joseph Baildon (14), John Keene (0), William Curtis (0), John Whittell (1).
1765 Aug. BURTON HUDSON died (bur. St. Benet under the organ loft Aug. 12).
1765 Aug.22 HENRY BREWSTER (48) e. u. William Courtney (3), Charles Lockhart (24), John Casson (4), Timothy Smart (0).
1788 Dec.17 HENRY BREWSTER death reported.
1789 Feb.11 THOMAS NAISH (42) e. u. Woodthorpe (7), Edmonds (4), Showell (2), Platts (0), Clapton (1).
1818 Mar.26 THOMAS NAISH resigns. "Long and faithful service". Gratuity of £10.
1818 Apr.3 Miss MARIA NAISH (only candidate) e.
1834 Apr.3 Miss MARIA NAISH resigns.
1834 Apr.3 JOHN HALLIDAY e. u. Miss Ether (?Miss Elizabeth Heather), Norman, Whittaker.
c.1842–6 Church demolished and parish united to St. Peter le Poer. Organist latterly entered as Edward Halliday.

23. ST. BENET GRACECHURCH

Sources: V. and C. & V. and C. of united parish of St. Leonard Eastcheap, both incomplete[23 23a]. See also[414].

Organ probably from St. Michael Crooked Lane (q.v.) following its demolition in 1831. (Church demolished 1867).

Although Pearce asserts that there was no organ[323], V. of St. Leonard give clear indication of the decision to acquire the unwanted organ of St. Michael Crooked Lane in

1831. Engravings of St. Benet's a few years later show the organ in a gallery at the rear of the church. Mackeson in 1866[209] asserts "no organ" but the church was demolished in the following year. V. of both churches show no elections for organists and C. no entries for payments. However there *are* payments to an unnamed organ blower and to a Mr. Hill for salaries of church choir.

24. ST. BENET PAUL'S WHARF

Sources: V. and C.[24].

Organ 1833 no documentary evidence of builder but apparently J.C. Bishop cost £157.10[188 323]. (Damaged 1971).

1823 May 15 Proposal for organ. Nothing came of this.
1834 Feb.13 GEORGE COOPER, jun. appointed. (Paid from Christmas 1833). Sal. £21.
1844 Sep. GEORGE COOPER vacates.
1844 Sep.26 JAMES HIGGS appointed. Sal. increased 1847 Dec.30 to £30.
1852 Apr.15 JAMES HIGGS resigns.

25. ST. BOTOLPH ALDERSGATE

Source: V.[25]. See also[393].

Organ 1772 no documentary evidence of builder believed to be Samuel Green[180 188 323]. (Subsequently rebuilt).

1772 Oct.13 Motion to erect organ.
1773 Jan.14 JOSEPH OLIVE (56) e. u. Benjamin Wayn (26), Moore (9). Sal. by voluntary subscription.
1786 Nov.14 JOSEPH OLIVE death reported (died Nov.8). Next organist shall do duty himself and not by substitute. Also to instruct charity children of ward to sing.
1786 Nov.23 Miss Elizabeth Goadby (117), Jacob Cubitt Pring (116), u. Miss Elizabeth Anne Shute (?) (19), Henry Chitterly [? Chicheley] (16), Samuel Showell (9), Alexander Edmonds (0), John Immyns (0), Miss Steele (?) & Miss Smith also in list of candidates.
1787 Jan.2 Debate on whether organist should be Miss Goadby (117) or Pring (116). Selection of Pring leads to more trouble.
1787 Jan.16 Miss ELIZABETH GOADBY (to play aftn. & evng.) and JACOB CUBITT PRING (to play mng. & teach children) jointly elected. Sal. to be divided between them.
1789 Apr.15 & 1790 Apr.7 (between) Miss ELIZABETH GOADBY vacates.
1799 Jul.10 JACOB CUBITT PRING death reported.
1799 Jul.25 [HENRY] VOKES e. u. Scott, Williams, Simpson, Perks, Barry, Kemm, Taylor, Whitaker, Major, Wilson, Busby, Clifton.
1800 Apr.16 Extra £10 to Vokes for instructing charity children.
1820 Jul.26 [HENRY] VOKES death reported (died Jul. 17?).
1820 Sep.7 Miss MARY WARNE (167) e. u. Munroe [?Monroe] (127), Miss Thompson (5), Harris (2), Mr. [?or Mrs.] Wilkins (2).
1826 Mar.29 Mary Warne "very ill from diseased state of lungs". Hopes to return to duty. PERRY acting as substitute. Mary Warne to have £10 gratuity.
1826 Aug.23 Miss MARY WARNE e. "during pleasure".
1826 Oct.18 Miss MARY WARNE death reported.
1826 Oct.26 Candidates: Crathorn, Munroe [i.e. Monroe], Miss Warne [sic], Topliss [sic i.e. Topliff], Done, Hoar, Morpheti, Mackenzie, Adams, Miss Dowling, Blackman, Stone, D.C. Hewitt, B. Curzens, J.E. Goodson, Blockley, A.C. Whitcombe, Miss Tookey, Vinnacomb.
1827 Jan.18 JOHN MONRO[E] (151) e. u. Miss Warne (90), Topliff (60), Miss Dowling (4), Morpheti (2).

1846 Apr.14, Nov.19 John Monroe "very ill", W. Essex acting as substitute.
1847 Mar. JOHN MONRO[E] vacates (?died).
1847 Mar.25 63 (unnamed) applicants from whom 22 candidates selected. Following attend audition: Miss Arnott, Batt, Beale, Chipp, Mrs. Day, Deane, Foord, Mrs. Lindley, Miss Martindale, Mellish, Miss Morris, Rockstro, Miss Sellman, Westlake, Wilson. "Declined playing": Baker, Blackbee, Hoskins, Pickering. Absent hurt: Essex. Price & Temple not wanted as blind & therefore not suitable for teaching. James Turle selects Beale, Chipp, Deane, Mrs. Lindley, Miss Morris, Rockstro for poll.
1847 Mar.25, 26, 27 Poll: Mrs. LUCY LINDLEY e. Chipp runner-up.
1864 Aug.11 Mrs. LUCY GARRETT (formerly Mrs. LUCY LINDLEY) resigns.

26. ST. BOTOLPH ALDGATE

Sources: V. gap between 1771 and 1807. C. gap 1691 to 1720 and incomplete series of "renter churchwardens' accounts" etc.[26]. See also[400 460].

Organ 1676 no documentary evidence of builder of organ presented by Thomas Whiting 1676. Attributed to T. & R. Harris by Sumner[330], Pearce[323] and C.M. Houghton[400] but Organographia asserts "great part of full organ by Schmidt [i.e. Bernard Smith] rest by Byfield"[180], and Sperling "Schmidt 1676, swell Byfield"[188]. 1744 John Byfield, sen. repaired and installed in new church after rebuilding.

1677–80 Organist & blowbellows sal. £20 between them.
1681 Entries under June 6 & 26, Jul. 19 indicate organ in poor condition & out of tune. [James] White employed to repair and tune (V.)
1681 Mar.? EDWARD BARRON appointed.
1681 Aug.28 Agreed with Edward Barran [sic] organist to pay him £12 from Lady Day last.
1691 Edward Barron last named as organist in C., subsequent entries referring only to "the organist". His tenure of office *could* have extended from 1677 to 1702 but this is uncertain.
1702 or earlier EDWARD BARRON vacates.
1702 Oct.22 WILLIAM LUD[D]INGTON chosen. £20 from Michaelmas last.
1724 June 30 WILLIAM LUDDINGTON death reported.
1724 June 30 WILLIAM STROLOGER [sic i.e. STROLGER?] e. maj. of 29. u. John Crawfoot [sic i.e. Crofoot].
1732 Nov.10 WILLIAM STROLGER resigns ("gone to reside in to the country").
1732 Nov.10 [JAMES] WORGAN e. u. Sandford, Scott, Shackleton, Vincent. Sal. £20.
1741–1744 Church rebuilt.
1741 June 4 John Harris and John Byfield employed to dismantle organ.
1743/4 Mar.13 John Byfield to repair, make additions to and reinstal organ for £30.
1753 May 7 JAMES WORGAN death reported.
1753 May 14 JOHN WORGAN (59) e. u. Richard Lowe (33), Thomas Curtis, John Gates.
1790 Aug.24 JOHN WORGAN died.
1790 Oct.6 (?) Miss MARY CHRISTY appointed. Between 1791 Oct. 4 and 1792 Mar. 28 the organist becomes Mrs. MARY EDMONDS (by marriage).
1805 Sep.30 & Nov.22 (between) Mrs. MARY EDMONDS vacates.
1805 Sep.–Oct. RUSH & EDMONDS play (during Mrs. Edmonds's illness).
1805 Nov. ROLFE plays first 3 Sundays.
1805 Nov.22 HENRY SMITH e.
1818 Jan.2 HENRY SMITH resigns.
1818 Feb.27 JOSHUA CASH (348) e. u. George Savage (244), Robert Beale (9).

1822 Sept.19 JOSHUA CASH death reported.
1822 Oct.5 HENRY GILES (439) e. u. Andrew Cash (330), Miss Elizabeth Mary Taylor (9).
1847 Jan.14 HENRY GILES vacates.
1847 Mar.25–27 JOHN BARNES (160) e. u. Thomas Mellish (61).
1866 Aug.23 JOHN BARNES resigns because of "extreme debility".

27. ST. BOTOLPH BISHOPSGATE

Source: V.[27]. See also[415].

Organ 1763–4 John Byfield, jun., George Wilcox and Thomas Knight.

1763 Mar.2 Committee considers choice of organ: John Byfield & George Wilcox est. £450 accepted, Geo. England est. £410 not accepted.
1763 Mar.17 Agreement with Byfield, Wilcox & Thomas Knight, organ builders. £410.
1764 Oct.12 New organ opened by John Stanley[L365].
1764 Nov.7 SAMUEL JARVIS e. u. Thomas Curtis. Sal. 30 guineas.
1784 Jul.22 SAMUEL JARVIS death reported (died June 21).
1784 Jul.27 Candidates: Thomas Curtis, Charles Cross, Alexander Edmonds, James Thomas Field, Showell (absent). Ballot:
1784 Jul.27 JAMES THOMAS FIELD (223) e. u. Charles Cross (149), Alexander Edmonds (118).
1805 June 13 JAMES THOMAS FIELD death reported. Sal. to continue at £30.
1805 June 20 GEORGE EUGENE GRIFFIN e. u. Alexander Edmonds.
1815 Mar.30 GEORGE EUGENE GRIFFIN vacates.
1815 Apr.27 Candidates: Corpe, Galot, Godwin, Jolly, Nicholls, Nightingale, Warne, Richardson, White, Yarrow.
1815 Apr.27 WILLIAM WHITE (247) e. u. Corpe (111), Warne (2), Nightingale (11).
1821 Apr.25 Annual election postponed pending arrangement for performance of duty by deputy.
1822 Apr.4 WILLIAM WHITE re-elected subject to approval of deputy by vestry.
1825 Feb.24 WILLIAM WHITE death reported.
1825 Feb.24 Committee had examined candidates: "Mr. Godwin most eligible, Miss Probyn next". Apprehension that female organist would not have command over boys while teaching to sing. Other nominations (ex-committee) G.Godwin, Miss E.E. Fleet. Ballot:
1825 Apr.7 Miss ESTHER ELIZABETH FLEET (264) e. u. Godwin (119).
1830 Apr.13–1831 Apr.7 (between) Miss FLEET becomes Mrs. COPE.
1839 Apr.4 Mrs. ESTHER ELIZABETH COPE resigns. On May 2 the V. reports result of an enquiry into Mrs. Cope. (For details see Annotated Index under FLEET). W.H. KEARNES deputy to Mrs. Cope.
1839 May 2 CHARLES WRIGHT e. (u. not named).
1863 Dec.30 CHARLES WRIGHT retires (unable to perform the duties of organist).

28. ST. BRIDE FLEET STREET

Sources: V.[28]. See also[387 388 416].

Organ 1692? Renatus Harris after rejection of presentation organ by Sir Fairmead Penistone on Harris's advice. 1784 enlarged by William Gray £120. (Destroyed 1940).

1692/3 Feb.10 Ordered & voted that Mr. Fra: Forser [sic], Mr. Philip Hart junior & Mr. Eagles junior shall play upon the organ . . . no other to bee putt in competition.
1693 May 11 Mr. Fran: fforcer [sic], Mr. Hart & Mr. Eagles shall play . . . (etc.) as

above. All those who have subscribed to pay the organist for 3 years shall have liberty of choosing one of the three. (This is the last reference to these three. The subscribers presumably had their election outside the vestry & no record exists). So all that can be deduced is that on

1693 May 11 FRANCIS FORCER or PHILIP HART junior or EAGLES [or ECCLES] (see Annotated Index) e.
1696 Mar.27 (before) FORCER, HART or EAGLES vacates.
1696 Mar.27 HENRY LIGHTINDOLLAR appointed. Sal. £20.
1702 June 3 HENRY LIGHTINDOLLAR death reported (buried 1702 June 3).
1702 June 18 JOHN WELDON e. u. Purcell, Gorton, Foster [sic], Isaac [sic].
1736 May 7 JOHN WELDON died.
1736 Aug.10 [SAMUEL] HOWARD (45) e. u. Lowe (15), Keeble (3).
1782 Jul.26 SAMUEL HOWARD death reported.
1782 Jul.30 [RICHARD HUDDLESTON] POTTER (185) e. u. Warrell [sic] (149), Thomson (41), Lowndes (6). No other post permitted.
1821 June 13 RICHARD HUDDLESTON POTTER death reported.
1821 Aug.21 Organ committee select 4 candidates from 23 applicants (not named). The 6 "found competent" reduced to 4 by ballot. Of these Miss Esther Fleet disqualified as age found "not to exceed 14".
1821 Aug.28 GEORGE MATHER (159) e. u. Thomas Platts (96), G. Harris (86).
1854 Jul.20 GEORGE MATHER death reported.

29. ST. CHRISTOPHER LE STOCKS

Sources: V. and C.[29].
No evidence of any post-1666 organ in this church which was demolished 1781.

30. ST. CLEMENT EASTCHEAP

Sources: V. and C., although complete, provide no information[30]. V. and C., church ledgers and annual accounts of united parish of St. Martin Orgar supply the names of the organists but the unsuccessful candidates are not revealed[30a].

Organ 1695–6 no documentary evidence of builder but apparently Renatus Harris[180 188 323].

1696? HENRY LIGHTINDOLLAR appointed. (First evidence in C. 1699). Sal. £20.
1702 June 3 HENRY LIGHTINDOLLAR buried in St. Bride Fleet Street.
1702 June? WILLIAM GORTON appointed. (First evidence in C. 1703–4).
1704 Irrelevant extract from C.: "Pd. for a lock for the organ 1/6. Expended on Mr. Smith the organ maker to show him the Cheat Mr. Harris putt into the Organ in order to putt the Organ out of order 5/-".
1711 Oct. WILLIAM GORTON died (bur. Oct.21). (1711/12 Jan. 31, £30 to be paid to Mrs. Gorton, widow to Mr. Gorton our late organist).
1711 end [EDWARD] PURCELL (Pd. Mr. Pursill the organist one quarter's sal. £5 in C. 1711). Pursill and variants continue with no christian name up to 1738. Gap in 1739 and then E.H. Purcell, occasionally Henry Purcell, up to 1765. That the 1711 appointment was Edward (son of Henry Purcell) is borne out by the entry in the burial reg. of St. Clement's dated 1740 Jul. 4: "Edward Purcell, organist, buried near the organ gallery door". So,
1740 Jul.1 EDWARD PURCELL died.
1740 Jul.? EDWARD HENRY PURCELL (son of above) appointed.
1764 Aug.22 Purcell asks for rise (£20 "not sufficient for him and payment of a deputy"). Sal. raised to £30.

1765 c.Aug.1 EDWARD HENRY PURCELL died (bur. St. Clement 1765 Aug. 5, "by the organ galary").
1765 Aug.21 JONATHAN BATTISHILL appointed[L185].
1801 Dec.10 JONATHAN BATTISHILL died.
1802 Jan.? THOMAS BARTHOLOMEW appointed. Sal. £30.
1819 May (end) THOMAS BARTHOLOMEW died (bur. St. Clement June 2). (C. June 30 quarter's sal. to Mrs. Bartholomew for late husband).
1819 June & Aug. (between) [WILLIAM] BRADLEY appointed. (Appears only as Mr. Bradley in C. Identified as William in Hackett papers which give date of appointment as Aug.)[102].
1828 end WILLIAM BRADLEY vacates.
1828 end JOHN WHITAKER appointed.
1847 Dec.4 JOHN WHITAKER died.
1847 Dec.16 JOHN ALEXANDER JOPP, assistant to the late organist for more than 2 years appointed without election.
1885 Mar.24 JOHN ALEXANDER JOPP death reported.

31. ST. DIONIS BACKCHURCH

Sources: V.[31]. See also[417].
Organ 1723–24 Renatus Harris. (Church demolished 1878).
1722 Jul.26 Committee appointed to treat with organ builder.
1722 Nov.13 Renatus Harris named as builder.
1723 June 24 Assignment by Renatus Harris of Bristol[86].
1724 May 28 PHILIP HART e. (no other candidates). Sal. £30. Organ to be opened 2nd Sunday in June.
1749 Jul.27 PHILIP HART death reported (died Jul.17).
1749 Jul.–Oct. JOHN SALMON (temporary).
1749 Oct.26 CHARLES BURNEY e. u. Edmund Gilding, Edward Griffes, Burton Hudson, Edmund Larkin, Lupton Relfe, John Salmon. No deputy to be permitted leads to withdrawal of William Jackson and Philip Markham. Sal. £30.
1752 Jan.23 CHARLES BURNEY resigns.
1752 Apr.3 JOHN BENNET[T] e. u. Atfield, Gigleir [sic] name given as Juliere in General Advertiser[227]. For reason given under 1749, Worgan, Gates, Hudson & Scott withdraw. Sal. £30.
1784 Oct.1 JOHN BENNETT death reported (bur. Sep.24).
1784 Jan.–Oct. CORNELIUS KEITH (temporary during Bennett's illness).
1784 Oct.7 Miss SARAH ORMES (70) e. u. Alexander Edmonds (0), Cornelius Keith (52). For reason given under 1749, Henry Chicheley, Richard Evance & Francis Pool withdraw.
1832 Dec.13 Miss SARAH ORMES to resign next Easter.
1833 Apr.22 Miss SARAH ORMES resigns.
1833 Apr.23 JONATHAN RUSH (49) e. (dep. for Sarah Ormes for 23 years). u. Mrs. Maria Bonsor (28).
1849 Nov.8 JONATHAN RUSH death reported.
1849 Nov.22 Miss MARY ARCHER (30) e. (after voluntarily doing Rush's duty for 8 years). u. Miss Mary Jane Boughey (2), Miss A. Cowtan (2), Miss Bates plus 23 unnamed.
1861 Apr.–1862 Apr. (between) Miss Mary Archer becomes Mrs. MARY MOORCROFT.
1862 Aug.8 Mrs. MARY MOORCROFT resigns.

32. ST. DUNSTAN IN THE EAST

Sources: V. (none before 1779) yield no information. C., which are complete, reveal neither the precise dates of appointment nor candidates[32].

Organ 1669? Bernard Smith unanimously accepted by secondary sources[180 188]. Byfield swell and choir organ. 1819 William or Robert Gray new organ during church rebuilding[180 188]. (Destroyed 1941).

1669 or 1669/70 Jan. WILLIAM THATCHER appointed. Sal. £12.
1680 Oct.? WILLIAM THATCHER vacates.
1680 or 1681 THOMAS BEEDAM appointed.
1683? THOMAS BEEDAM vacates.
1683 Mar.? JOHN MOSS appointed.
1696 JOHN MOSS vacates.
1696? DANIEL PURCELL. C. give no payment to an organist in 1696 and 1697. In 1698 "organist" is paid £20 and first referred to as "Mr. Purcell" Nov. 3. Did Daniel Purcell play for no reward from 1696 to 1698 as he apparently did at St. Andrew Holborn? Identity first established in C. 1700 Aug. 15 with entry for "Mr. Danl. Purcell".
1717 Nov.11 DANIEL PURCELL last payment of salary. Died Nov. (Bur. Nov. 26 St. Andrew Holborn).
1718 c.Jan. JAMES SCOTT appointed. Sal. £20.
1738 end JAMES SCOTT died (payment to widow Mary 1738/9 Feb. 9).
1738 Dec.22? JAMES WORGAN appointed.
1753 before May 10 JAMES WORGAN died.
1753 May Miss MARY WORGAN resigns on marriage after holding post briefly (?since May 10 when C. entry "blowing organ for candidates").
1753 June 1 EDWARD GRIFFES appointed (C. entry "expences for choosing organist").
1811 Aug.? EDWARD GRIFFES vacates.
1811 Aug.29 Miss MARIA STIMSON e. Sal. £30.
1821 Feb.14 Miss Maria Stimson becomes Mrs. MARIA BAYLIS.
1830 Dec.? Mrs. MARIA BAYLIS vacates. Last payment Dec. 15. She seems to have been overlapped since 1828 by Job Austin.
1828 (end) or 1829 JOB AUSTIN appointed.
1866 end JOB AUSTIN vacates.

33. ST. DUNSTAN IN THE WEST

Sources: V. and C.[33].

Organ c.1672–4 builder not revealed in parish records but George Dallam appointed organ keeper 1677. Secondary sources unanimously give Abraham Jordan and Sperling adds the date 1705[188]. 1702 additions by "Harris". 1736 new organ by Jordan (V.). 1805 Hugh Russell enlargement[180 188 323]. 1834 new organ by Robson in rebuilt church[188]. (Damaged 1940).

1671 Dec.5 First ref. to organ: application for licence.
1674 Dec. ISAAC BLACKWELL appointed. (1674 Dec. 14 "Mr. Blackwell or some other to be organist". C. for 1675 Apr. 1: Mr. Blackwell the organist £3.15.0 for quarter's sal.)
1675 Nov.10 Sal. to be £18 from Xmas next.
1676/7 Jan.22 Mr. George Dallam the organ maker shall have 40/- a year to keep the organ in repair.
1699 May 4 ISAAC BLACKWELL death reported.
1699 May 4 —— FOSTER appointed. Sal. £18.
1702 June 9, Aug. 4 etc. Dispute with "Mr. Harris the organ maker" over payment

for enlargement of organ.

1713/14 Mar.19 —— FOSTER death reported. (Thomas Forster bur. St. Dunstan in the West 1713/14 Feb.9 from Bell Yard in Fleet Street. The same?)

1713/14 Mar.19 MAURICE GREENE e. u. Bowman, Solter [?i.e. Salter], Foster, Miller. Sal. £18.

1718 Apr.1 MAURICE GREENE resigns on appointment to St. Paul's. Petitions for post of organist from John Salter & Clement Magnus for his son William Edmund Magnus.

1718 Apr.8 JOHN SALTER e.

1724/5 Jan.15 Salter called to vestry to answer complaints. Promises to take more care.

1729 Apr.25 JOHN SALTER vacates ("gone beyond the seas").

1729 May 9 STEPHEN HARRISON e. u. Richard Low, Joseph Jones.

1730/31 Mar.4 STEPHEN HARRISON resigns.

1731 Apr.9 JOHN READING e. u. Richard Neal, Joseph Jones.

1736 Oct.20 Agreement with Abraham Jordan for new organ.

1764 Nov. 8 JOHN READING death reported (died Sep.2).

1764 Dec.24 to 1765 Jan.2 WILLIAM DUNCOMBE (133) e. u. John Selby (108) (after poll demanded by Selby), George Scrivener.

1814 May 26 William Duncombe in "a state of embarrassment: 76 years old, 49 years organist at St. D." Gratuity of £20 given.

1819 Feb.5 WILLIAM DUNCOMBE death reported.

1819 Feb.5 WILLIAM LING (155) e. u. Woodthorpe (115).

1824 Apr.20 William Ling asks for sal. increase. Granted.

1829 Apr.22 WILLIAM LING vacates. "In consequence of rebuilding the church resolved that situation of organist remains vacant". Ling given £30 gratuity.

1832 Sep.28 Judges to be appointed for selection of organist.

1832 Oct.12 "Trial of skill abandoned". Judges not required.

1832 Oct.24 Thomas Adams(9), Miss Catherine Rogers(38), William Jones(41). Poll demanded:

1832 Oct.25 THOMAS ADAMS (89) e. u. William Jones (35).

1858 Oct.8 THOMAS ADAMS death reported. Great tribute paid to him (died Sep.15).

34. ST. EDMUND, KING AND MARTYR

Sources: V. and C. also for united parish of St. Nicholas Acons[34 34a]. See also[418]. Organ 1701–2 no documentary evidence of builder but attributed to Renatus Harris [323etc.]. 1833 rebuilt by J.C. Bishop[188].

1702 Sep.28 Organ erected. Sal. to be £20.

1702 Dec. JOHN PIGOTT appointed (V. of 1703 Apr.12 "to be paid from Xmas day last").

1709 Apr.25 JOHN PIGOTT vacates.

1709 Apr.25 JOHN CLAXTON appointed ("appeared and desired to be admitted in room of John Piggott . . . is now employed as deputy to said Piggott") Sal. £20.

1712 Aug.19 JOHN CLAXTON vacates.

1712 Aug.19 Candidates Abel Wichello [i.e. Abiell Whichello] and Charles King. Election adjourned.

1712 Aug.28 ABIELL WHICHELLOW (66) e. u. John Bashan (33). ?What happened to Charles King.

1747 Aug. ABIELL WHICHELLO died (bur. St. Giles Cripplegate Aug.16).

1747 Sep.10 EDWARD HENRY PURCELL (39) e. u. Gilding (37), Goodwin (34), Gates (4), Baildon(2), Wheatley(0).

1753 Oct.10 EDWARD HENRY PURCELL resigns.

1753 Nov.23 EDMUND GILDING (58) e. u. Burton Hudson (36), L'Heureux (0), Willam Selby (0), Thompson (0), John Henry Moze (4), William Goodwin (9).
1782 Aug.21 EDMUND GILDING death reported (died Aug. 5 or 4?)
1782 Aug.21 CHARLES BENNETT (80) e. u. William Cope (4), Thomas Hudden (18), Jackson.
1790 Apr.14 CHARLES BENNETT death reported.
1790 Apr.14 Miss ELIZABETH GOADBY (42) e. u. Miss Mary Christy (27), Alexander Edmonds (4), William Cope (31), Thomas Hudden (20). Shortly before her resignation Miss Elizabeth Goadby becomes Mrs. ELIZABETH ATKINSON.
1797 May 19 Mrs. ELIZABETH ATKINSON vacates.
1797 May 31 HENRY EDWARD DAVIS (79) e. u. Miss Mary Ann Barry (3), Miss Elizabeth Bullock (1), Thomas Tripcony (0).
1832 Oct.? HENRY EDWARD DAVIS vacates. V. are not informative. Although some authorities give Henry Westrop's date of appointment as 1834 Apr.3, it is likely that this date originates from the fact that at the 1834 Apr.3 annual election Henry Westrop is named. It is probable that he followed Davis at the end of 1833. Davis given pension of £5 p.a. until 1859–60.
1833 end HENRY WESTROP appointed.
1879 Sep.23 HENRY WESTROP died.

35. ST. ETHELBURGA BISHOPSGATE

Sources: V. and C.[35].

Organ 1812 possibly Thomas Elliot although built c.1790 according to Sperling and Pearce[188 323]. 1845 new organ by William Hill & Son cost £210[188].

1812 June 18 Organ suggested. Agreed Jul.2.
1812 Nov.12 Miss MARY MORRICE e. (only candidate). Sal. £15.
1823 June 23 Miss MARY MORRICE resigns.
1823 Jul.9 [JOHN] VINNICOMBE, jun. e. Probably the eldest son of the parish clerk of the same name. The only other candidate, Miss Wesley, withdraws.
1827 Feb.1 [JOHN] VINNICOMBE resigns.
1827 Feb.1 Miss [M.E.?] HALSEY (24) e. u. Halliday (21).
1844 June 20 Miss [M.E.?] HALSEY resigns.
1844 June 20 Mrs. INGRAM appointed (no election).
1845 Feb.13 Permission to remove organ & instal new one value £210.
1853 Apr.4 Last record of Mrs. INGRAM.

36. ST. GEORGE BOTOLPH LANE

Sources: V. and C.[36]. See also[419].

Organ 1723 Abraham Jordan. (Church demolished 1904).

1723 Oct.17 JAMES WILLIAMS e. Other candidates not listed. Sal. £20. Next vestry (undated) authorises £300 to be paid to Abraham Jordan on account of organ.
1739 Aug.29 James Williams's father presents petition on behalf of son. Deputy to be appointed, deputy to receive £12 and James Williams £8 during lifetime.
1739 Sep.26 SAMUEL MANWARING e. deputy. u. Simon Stubly, John Worgan.
1745 Oct.31 JAMES WILLIAMS voted out.
1745 Oct.31 SAMUEL MANWARING appointed. Sal. £20.
1780 Jul.19 SAMUEL MANWARING death reported.
1780 Jul.19 JAMES WADE appointed (no candidates).
1831 Apr.12 JAMES WADE superannuated: pension £20 p.a.
1831 Apr.12 FRANCIS BELL unan. e. (no candidates).

1848 Jan.18 FRANCIS BELL resigns.
1848 Feb.21 Miss Isabella Harris, R.A. Harson(?), J.H. Deane selected for election from 18 unnamed candidates.
1848 Mar.13 Miss ISABELLA HARRIS unan. e.
1852 Apr.14–1853 Mar.30 (between) Miss Isabella Harris becomes Mrs. ISABELLA WRIGHTSON.
1861 Apr.26 Mrs. ISABELLA WRIGHTSON resigns. (Miss Boughey, her deputy, appointed).

37. ST. GILES CRIPPLEGATE

Sources: V. (gap 1818–40), C. (fragmentary)[37]. See also[320 420].

Organ 1672 builder unknown. 1704 new organ by Renatus Harris cost £400. 1735 enlargement by Richard Bridge. 1840 rebuilt by Gray & Davison and in 1899 by J.W. Walker & Sons. Destroyed 1940. (Replaced by Jordan and Bridge organ from St. Luke Old Street[420]).

1672 Mrs. Charnock shall have thanks given her for her affection in bestowing a faire Organ upon the parish church of St. Giles . . . and that the Vicar and vestrymen find out some way and means for the maintenance of the organist.
1672/3 Feb.28 JAMES BROOKES chosen sexton & organist "by the King's Majesties Letter". Either to play himself or provide organist at own cost.
1673 Oct.25 New sexton to pay £20 p.a. to organist.
c.1673–4 FRANCIS FORCER appointed (1674 May 21 & Nov.3, 1674/5 Feb.1: payment to Mr. Forser [sic] for playing). Sal. £20.
1676 FRANCIS FORCER vacates.
1676 JOHN CURTIS appointed (first referred to by name with payment of £3, 1676/7 Feb.20 "to pay Mr. Curtis the organist").
1681 Jul.1 Sal. £16.
1703/4 Feb.25 JOHN CURTIS death reported.
1703/4 Feb.25 HENRY GREEN appointed. A blind man. In the 1730s his playing causes discontent.
1704 Jul.19 Old organ to be replaced by a new.
1705 May 31 Mr. Harris to be paid £400 and the old organ for new organ.
1734 May 14 New organist to be chosen. Green to be paid £20 p.a. until successor appointed then £10 p.a. for life.
1734 Aug.22 Sal. of new organist to be £30 p.a. out of which Green to be allowed £10 p.a. until death.
1734/5 Mar.10 HENRY GREEN discharged. "Mr. Green have notice that the organ shall be shut up [for repairs] on Lady Day next and that he be then discharged". £10 pension confirmed.
1735 Apr.14 Richard Bridge to repair organ and add new stops for £170. (Jordan's tender for £190 rejected).
1736 Apr.26 New organist to have £20 p.a. till Green's death, then £30.
1736 May 25 CHARLES FROUD e. "by a large majority". u. Thomas Wood, John Alcock.
1737 Aug.4 Salary to be raised to £30 but no mention of Green's death, which does not appear to have occurred until 1741 Sep.25[232].
1770 Nov.7 CHARLES FROUD death reported.
1770 Nov.14 EDMUND GILDING e. "by a great majority". u. William Courtney, James Moore.
1782 Aug.9 EDMUND GILDING death reported (died Aug.5).
1782 Aug.12 WILLIAM COURTNEY e. unanimously (no other candidates mentioned).
1785 June 29 WILLIAM COURTNEY death reported (bur. June 30).

1785 June 29 Miss MARY WORSLEY BICKERTON e. u. Mrs. Johanna Lowe, George Bruin, Charles Bennett, Rayner Taylor, John Junnings [sic].

1795 Mar.12 Miss MARY WORSLEY BICKERTON death reported.

1795 Mar.30 JOHN IMMYNS e. No details of election or candidates. Election result reported to vestry Apr.6.

1818 Apr.2 JOHN IMMYNS resigns. For events leading up to resignation see Annotated Index.

1818 May 1 Six candidates for election selected from 12 (unnamed) applicants.

1818 May 1 Miss MARY HORTH (34) e. u. J. Harvey, jun.(1), George Mather(2), C.E. Powis(0), Henry Giles(0), William Crathorn [?Crathern] (1).

1819 Apr.(before) Mary Horth becomes Mrs. MARY DEANE.

1832 Jan. Mrs MARY DEANE resigns. No surviving records to confirm this or the following entry for which the only authority is William Miller, (*London before the fire of 1666: with an historical account of . . . St. Giles Without Cripplegate*, 1867). Is the author the organist appointed in 1832?

1832 Feb.17 WILLIAM MILLER appointed from 19 candidates reduced to 3.

1873 Apr.18 WILLIAM MILLER joined by son William, his assistant for several years. Then WILLIAM MILLER, sen. retires.

38. ST. HELEN BISHOPSGATE

Sources: V. (to 1842 only), C.[38]. See also[421].

Organ 1742–4 "annuity organ" by Thomas Griffin (see pp. 13–15 and Annotated Index).

1741/2 Mar.11 Vestry committee consider proposals for new organ. The proposal of "Abraham Jordan, organ builder, John Harris & Co. [sic] of Budge Row" to supply organ for £350 not accepted. Thomas Griffin proposed "to build at my own proper cost and charge . . ." a new organ value £500. All materials new. "To tune and perform on it or cause to be performed during time of my natural life" for a payment of £250 and £25 per annum until his death.

1742 Apr.22 Contract for new organ on Griffin's terms. Faculty for opening Nov.3.

1744 summer THOMAS GRIFFIN commences as nominal organist.

1771 May 16 THOMAS GRIFFIN death reported (died Apr. 29).

1771 May 16 GEORGE GRIFFIN (nephew of above) "offered himself" and accepted.

1809 Apr.27 GEORGE GRIFFIN death reported (died Apr.19). Described in obituary as "many years organist of St. Helen Bishopsgate"[232].

1809 May 12 WILLIAM HENRY CUTLER ("Master W.H. Cutler") (36) e. u. Miss Rodd (29), Miss Naish (1). Sal. 20 guineas.

1819 Feb.25 WILLIAM HENRY CUTLER resigns. 6 candidates selected.

1819 Mar.18 GEORGE WARNE (28) e. u. William Crathern (16), J. Nightingale (8), J.J. Harris (4), William Bradley (3), Robert Beale withdraws.

1820 Jul.17 GEORGE WARNE resigns owing to another appointment.

1820 Sep.20 JOSEPH NIGHTINGALE (30) e. u. Robert Beale (9). (William Crathern organ tuner at this time).

1842 Apr. Last evidence of Joseph Nightingale owing to gap in V. Did he continue until his death in 1847?

1848 Feb.? WILLIAM RICHARD BEXFIELD appointed [G]. No contemporary confirmation found.

1853 Oct.29 WILLIAM RICHARD BEXFIELD died.

39. ST. JAMES DUKE'S PLACE

Sources: V. and C. (both with gaps)[39]. See also[422].

Organ. Although an organ is alleged to have been erected in 1815[323], V. and C. provide no evidence of organ until 1824, builder unknown. "A little second hand organ put up 1847, one row of keys and 5 stops"[188]. (Church demolished 1874).

1824 Apr. 19 Miss [M.E.] HALSEY "unanimously appointed". Sal. 10 guineas.
1831 Mar.31 Miss Halsey's request for increment rejected.
1838 Apr.16 Miss [M.E.] HALSEY resigns.
1838 Apr.16 Miss [ELIZABETH] MINTON (dau. of parish clerk) e. u. Mrs. Pritchard. Corpe withdraws. Miss Minton organist a year later. A gap in surviving records obscures the date of her vacating and also the appointment of
1839–1847 (between) SAMUEL KING HALES e. Sal. £8 (later raised to 10 guineas).
1853 Apr.18 SAMUEL KING HALES vacates.

40. ST. JAMES GARLICKHYTHE

Sources: V.[40].

Organ 1718–19 no clear evidence of builder in parish records (see below). Given as Bernard Smith by most authorities but Smith died 1708. Did John Knopple alter and instal a Smith organ? (Damaged 1941 and restored).

1718 Dec.18 Mr. John Knopple the organ builder to be given £100.
1718/19 Mar.21 "Whereas an organ has been lately erected and set up", Further sum of £36 to Knopple for the full discharge of the organ builder's account and £6 p.a. for keeping in repair and cleaning Mar. 25.
1719 Mar.25 TALBOT YOUNG e. u. unnamed. Sal. £20.
1719 May 14 JOHN JONES e. u. Talbot Young, Edward Henry Purcell [sic. i.e. Edward Purcell?]
1722 Mar.26 JOHN JONES death reported.
1722 Mar.26 RICHARD NEALE e. u. Lowe, Markham, Moore, Hart, Greene.
1723 Apr.15–Apr.1744 Nominal annual contest between Richard Neale (always e.) and "Mr. Hart" (? his deputy).
1744/5 Jan.16 RICHARD NEALE death reported.
1744/5 Mar.14 JOHN GATES e. u. Baildon (runner up), Carter (3rd), Hudson, Markham, Grey, Bennett, Carey, Fearon.
1746 Apr.–1750 Apr. Nominal annual contest between John Gates and "Mr. Hart" (? his deputy).
1751 Apr.–1781 Apr. Nominal annual contest between John Gates and Joseph Baildon (? his deputy).
1782 Apr.1 Nominal annual election between John Gates and John Short (? his deputy).
1783 Apr.21–1784 Apr.12 Nominal annual election between John Gates and Richard Short (? his deputy).
1785 Mar.28–1788 Mar.24 Nominal annual election between John Gates and Edward Frith (? his deputy).
1789 Apr.13–1792 Apr.9 Nominal annual election between John Gates and Joseph Frith (? his deputy) (? mistake for Edward Frith).
1793 Mar.21 JOHN GATES death reported.
1793 Mar.28 EDWARD FRITH (19) e. u. Thomas Lester (3), John Norman (0), William Bride (0), Alexander Glenny (17).
1793 Apr.1–1805 Apr.15 Edward Frith contests annually Alexander Glenny (? his deputy). After 1805 no annual contests are recorded.
1831 June 29 EDWARD FRITH death reported (bur. June 30).
1831 Jul.6 WILLIAM WILSON appointed (no election).
1867 Apr.24 WILLIAM WILSON retires (pensioned).

41. ST. KATHERINE BY THE TOWER

Sources: Chapter minutes, miscellaneous accounts[41].

Organ c. 1698 builder unknown. 1777–8 new organ by Samuel Green. The chapter minutes began in 1698 and the first relevant entry is

1698 Dec.14 "Mr. Barcas the organist to receive ½ years salary due to him", so
1698 June (or before) —— BARCAS appointed.
1703 June 16 —— BARCAS death reported.
1703 June 16 CHARLES ROGERS appointed. The volume of chapter minutes is badly damaged and no ref. to the organist can be found until the following entry in 1709. It seems likely therefore that
1709 Sep.? CHARLES ROGERS vacates.
1709 Sep.22 JAMES HESLETINE [i.e. HESELTINE] admitted. (Elected organist of Durham Cathedral in 1711)[339].
1714 Apr.1 John Crofoot "acts as deputy for Mr. Hasletine [sic] . . . during his absence allowed of by the Master & to be paid eight pounds per ann. to be paid out of Mr. Hasletine's salary".
1763 Nov.17 JAMES HESELTINE death reported (died June 20).
1763 Nov.17 JOHN HENRY MOZE appointed by Chapter unanimously. (Patent of appointment read & executed in Chapter 1763 Nov.29).
1777 Feb.13 Proposals from Samuel Green for building new organ. Paid £100 on account 1777 Jul. 10 and again 1778 Jan. 16.
1787 Dec.21 or 27 JOHN HENRY MOZE died[222 232] but death not reported by Chapter until
1788 Feb.14 JAMES HENRY LEFFLER to succeed. (Patent executed & registered Mar.27).
1819 JAMES HENRY LEFFLER died. There are no Chapter minutes after 1806 and no alternative sources are available. Pearce, who based his work on a MS by J.H. Leffler, gives the following successors:
1819 HENRY LEFFLER appointed. (Son of J.H. Leffler).
1825 Church (with organ) moved to Regent's Park.
1848 HENRY LEFFLER vacates.
1848 WILLIAM LOVELL PHILLIPS appointed.
1860 Mar.19 WILLIAM LOVELL PHILLIPS died.

42. ST. KATHERINE COLEMAN

Sources: V. (gap 1727–1801 & after 1843), C., parish officers' elections 1626–1841[42]. See also[423].

Organ 1741–2 "annuity organ" by Thomas Griffin (see pp.13–15 and Annotated Index under Griffin). (Church demolished 1926).

1741 Sep.10 Agreement with Thomas Griffin, peruke maker [sic] to install organ on annuity basis and to play himself or supply an organist. Organ to be valued at £300 and "the workmanship to be approved on by organ builders". Griffin to be paid £25 p.a. during his life and his present wife Mary Griffin during the time she may survive him £10 p.a.
1742 THOMAS GRIFFIN commences as nominal organist.
1771 Apr.29 THOMAS GRIFFIN died[232].
1771 May? —— REDHEAD appointed.
1772? —— REDHEAD vacates.
1772 JOHN PRINTER e. First evidence in parish officers' elections 1773 Apr.13 when John Printer to continue as organist.

1777 Nov.? JOHN PRINTER vacates to devote whole Sunday time to Foundling Hospital.
1777 Nov.? JONAS BLEWITT e. u. R.J.S. Stevens?[190].
1805 Apr.16 JONAS BLEWITT death reported.
1805 May 14 Miss ANN BLEWITT (dau. of above) (16) e. u. Nash (0), Margaret Jones (0), Thomas Grady (0), Anthony Smith (15), Terryll (15), Archibald Nichols (1).
1817 Mar.–1818 Mar. (between) Ann Blewitt becomes Mrs. ANN BARKER.
1833 Apr.11 Mrs. ANN BARKER not re-elected.
1833 May 21 LANCELOT SHARPE (34) e. u. Benson (0), Miss Hale (2), Porter (1), Peterson (0), Miss Rist (21).
1837 Dec.6 LANCELOT SHARPE resigns.
1837 Dec.13 Miss ELIZABETH [i.e. ELIZA] WESLEY(40) e. u. Miss Willsdon (0), Porter (0), Miss Halsey (22).
1844 Apr.? Miss ELIZA WESLEY resigns.
1844 May? Miss [M.E.] HALSEY appointed.
1868 Dec. Miss M.E. HALSEY vacates.

43. ST. KATHERINE CREE

Sources: V. (gaps 1719–32, 1740–59), C. (which fill the gap between 1740 & 1759), Annual accounts 1796–1842[43].

Organ 1685–6 Bernard Smith. 1755 Additional organ (?) by Jordan (see below).

1685 Nov.5 Agreement with "Mr Smith, the organ maker", (money to be raised by subscription Sep. 30).
1686 Sep.28 Organ finished. Joseph Cox to procure Mr. Purcell, Mr. Backwell [sic] & Mr. Mosse masters in music & Mr. White organ maker to give judgement.
1686 Sep.28 Beach, Niccolls, Snow & Heath apply for organist's post.
1686 Sep.30 Dr. Blow, Mr. Purcell, Mr. Mosse & Mr. Forcell [sic] pass judgement that organ good. Purcell plays. Same group listen to candidates & decide Mr. Snow played best & most skilfully. Mr. Niccolls second best. Sal. £20. MOSES SNOW (8) e. u. Beach (5), Niccolls (1), Heath (1). The church records only once give Snow's christian name (C.).
1700 June 19 Snow's sal. reduced to £16.
1702/3 Mar.9 MOSES SNOW death reported. New organist to play regularly & not to employ deputy on Sundays.
1702/3 Mar.9 SAMUEL MARSHALL e. u. Haines.
1713/14 Mar.18 SAMUEL MARSHALL death reported. Vestry suggest 6 candidates of whom Short & Luddington decline.
1714 Mar.25 —— MILBOURNE (14) e. u. Smith (0), Shuttleworth (7), Stanton (0).
1743 end? —— MILBOURNE vacates. Last payment of ½ year's salary (£10) made Aug.16.
1743 end? JOHN WORGAN appointed. First payment of 1 year's salary made 1744 June 25.
1753? JOHN WORGAN vacates. Last payment of ½ year's salary made 1752 June 5.
1753? JOHN ATFIELD appointed. First payment of 1 year's salary to Lady Day 1753 Jul.6.
1755 May 16 Payment to Mrs. Lucy Jordan of £100 "for a new organ". Lucy Jordan (née Gooddjerd mar. Abraham Jordan 1730/1 Jan.7 St. Stephen Walbrook) succeeded her late husband as organ keeper.
1766 Mar.17 JOHN ATFIELD death reported (died Mar.8).
1766 Mar.24 CHARLES LOCKHART (30) e. u. William Courtney (19), John Davidge (21), George Griffin (16), John Kewell (28).
1813 Apr.20 Charles Lockhart given sal. increase of £15.

c.1814 WILLIAM JOSEPH CASTELL deputy organist[182].
1815 Feb.9 CHARLES LOCKHART died.
1815 Mar.28 JOHN CASH e. (annual election. No record of other candidates).
1865 JOHN CASH pensioned.

44. ST. LAWRENCE JEWRY

Sources: V.[44]. See also[424 461].
Organ 1684–5 Renatus Harris. Additions by Byfield[188]. Largely rebuilt by [?Hugh] Russell[323]. (Replaced by Gray & Davison 1875 and later rebuilt. Destroyed 1940 and replaced by Noel Mander[461]).
1683/4 Mar.14 Proposals of Renatus Harris and Bernard Smith considered. Harris chosen.
1685 Dec. RICHARD BROWNE appointed (evidence below).
1685/6 Mar.16 "Mr. Browne shall proceed in playing the organ . . . and be organist for one whole year from the time he began to play the same he having for his satisfaction left himself to the goodwill and kindness of the parish."
1686 Apr.21 Dr. Blow, Mr. Purcell and Mr. Browne to view organ "and try the same".
1686 June 4 Mr. Browne . . . to be paid from Xmas last. Sal. £20.
1710 May 24 RICHARD BROWNE death reported (bur. Lambeth May 21).
1710 May 24 JOHN ROBINSON e. u. Shickelworth [i.e. Shuttleworth], King. Sal. £30.
1762 May 12 JOHN ROBINSON death reported (died Apr. 30).
1762 May 21 Candidates (not named) reduced to 4.
1762 May 21 THEODORE AYLWARD (54) e. u. Jervis (41), Cox (40), Atfield (37).
1788 June 12 THEODORE AYLWARD resigns.
1788 June 26 HENRY RICHARD CHICHELEY (109) e. u. Miss Lockhart (31) (testimonial from father Charles Lockhart, organist), William Thom[p]son (0), Alexander Edmonds (0), Sal. £30 "to regularly do church duty".
1805 Apr.18 HENRY RICHARD CHICHELEY death reported (bur. Apr. 13).
1805 May 7 JOHN BANNER (79) e. u. Jonathan Rush (39), Henry Smith (0).
1821 June 8 JOHN BANNER resigns: "No longer able to perform to our mutual satisfaction".
1821 June 26 ROBERT TURLE (84) e. u. Ansell (6), Andrew Cash (14), Mather (3), Harris (15).
1822 Dec.31 ROBERT TURLE resigns.
1823 Jan.7–17 GEORGE FREDERICK HARRIS(82) e. u. Samuel Wesley (7), Hainworth (40), Miss Hester Elizabeth Fleet (18), Henry Cope, George Phineas Hollocombe, J. Vinnicombe, Andrew Cash.
1867 Nov.21 GEORGE FREDERICK HARRIS died.

45. ST. MAGNUS THE MARTYR

Sources: V. and C., Committee of united parishes minute books[45]. See also [385 425].
Organ 1712 Abraham Jordan, sen. & jun.[248].
1712? JOHN ROBINSON appointed. Earliest ref. in C. 1712–13. Sal. £12. (This £12 may have been augmented by a salary subscribed by united parish of St. Margaret New Fish Street).
1762 May 3 JOHN ROBINSON death reported (died Apr.30).
1762 May 28 HENRY HERON e. unan. (no mention of other candidates).
1768 Apr.7 Sal. increased to £30 and given extra 10 guineas in 1791.
1795 June 23 HENRY HERON death reported. No charge to be made for funeral. New

appointment "not to play by deputy".
1795 Aug.24 THOMAS PHIPPEN COOK[E] (47) e. u. Joseph Major (27), Alexander Edmonds (0), John Purkis (1). Sal. 1796 £30.
1820 Jul.21 THOMAS PHIPPEN COOK[E] death reported.
1820 Aug.7 GEORGE WARNE (45) e. u. G.F. Harris (30), Henry Giles (18), John Blackburn (2).
1826 Nov.20 GEORGE WARNE resigns.
1826 Dec.6 29 applicants (names included in Annotated Index) from whom 4 selected for election.
1826 Dec.14 WILLIAM CRATHERN (48) e. u. William Bradley (36), Joseph Stone (0), Edward Sturges (1).
1840 Nov.27 WILLIAM CRATHERN resigns.
1840 Dec.29 Applicants: W.H. Adams, A.E. Blackburn, George Forster Cooke, Ann Crossthwaite, Edward Clare, Esther Cowtan, Edward Cruse, Alfred Deraux, John Hobson, George John Hills, John Larkin Hopkins, Caroline Orger, Sarah Day Payton, William Rackstraw, Joseph Stone, William Brand Wilson, Yarrow. 4 candidates selected.
1841 Jan.5 Edward Clare (22), Miss Esther Cowtan (30), Miss Sarah Day Payton (13), William S. Rackstraw (16).
1841 Jan.7 Miss ESTHER COWTAN (68) e. u. Payton (2), Clare (0), Rackstraw (0).
1854 Apr.17–1855 Apr. Esther Cowtan becomes Mrs. ESTHER HENNIKER.
1861 Apr.18 Mrs. ESTHER HENNIKER not unan. approved as organist. To become sextoness in place of Mrs. Mary Cowtan (her mother?) not re-elected to that post because of age and infirmity.

46. ST. MARGARET LOTHBURY

Sources: V. (also of united parish of St. Christopher le Stocks)[46 46a]. Trustees minutes & accounts. See also[394]

Organ 1800–1 George Pike England enlarged J.C. Bishop[188].
1800 Apr.4 Trust fund to be used for erection of organ.
1801 Mar. or Apr. JONATHAN PERKINS e. Sal. £25. (First appears in accounts Oct.1801). Organ opened Easter Day (Apr.5).
1816 Apr.19 Jonathan Perkins petitions for increase in sal. His sal. of £25 compares with £40 at St. Bartholomew by the Exchange, £40 St. Michael Cornhill, £37.16.0 St. Stephen Coleman Street, £40 St. Olave Jewry, £40 St. Mary le Bow, £40 St. James Garlickhythe, £80 St. Paul Covent Garden. Sal. increase to £35.
1831 Mar.25 JONATHAN PERKINS vacates.
1831 Mar.25 WILLIAM LIGHT appointed (? deputy before this).
1842 Mar.29 Miss GRACE CHAPMAN organist for weekdays.
1847 Apr.26 WILLIAM LIGHT resigns. Annuity of £20 paid until 1853 Apr. 16.
1847 Apr. Miss GRACE CHAPMAN vacates.
1847 c.May CHARLES BATT appointed.
1858 May 27 CHARLES BATT death reported.

47. ST. MARGARET PATTENS

Sources: V., C., V. of united parish of St. Gabriel Fenchurch Street, St. Margaret churchwardens' instructions 1840 which supply entries for 1746, 1805 May 1 and 1844 Mar.[47 47a]. See also[324].

Organ 1746–9? "annuity organ" by Thomas Griffin (see pp.13–15 and Annotated Index).
1746 June 6 Thomas Griffin "organ builder" offers to erect organ for annuity.

1749 Organ erected.
1749 THOMAS GRIFFIN commences as nominal organist. He seems to have been paid £35 p.a. C. refer to him as "organist" and paid "for playing the organ".
1771 May 15 THOMAS GRIFFIN death reported (died Apr. 29).
1771 May 24 THOMAS BROWN the younger e. u. George Berg, George Coopers[sic].
1777 Mar.? THOMAS BROWN vacates.
1777 Mar.? JOHN KEWELL appointed. No election recorded but appears in annual Easter election 1777 Apr. 1.
1783 Apr.? JOHN KEWELL vacates (last C. payment 1783 Apr. 4. V. give no annual elections at this date).
1783 Apr.? JONAS BLEWITT appointed (first payment June 28 "one quarter").
1805 Apr.10 JONAS BLEWITT death reported.
1805 May 1 ROBERT GLENN e. u. Miss Elderton, Messrs. Melward [sic i.e. Milward?], Nichols, Pyne.
1843 Apr.19 ROBERT GLENN reprimanded. If not efficient a substitute will be found next year.
1844 Mar.8 ROBERT GLENN death reported (died Feb.25).
1844 Mar. Miss ELIZA WESLEY (49) e. u. Miss Eliza A. Silverlock (18), Francis G. Halley (2). Sal. £40.
1887 Miss ELIZA WESLEY vacates.

48. ST. MARTIN LUDGATE

Sources: V. and C.[48]. See also[426].

Organ 1683–4 no documentary evidence of builder. Generally attributed to Bernard Smith[180 188etc] 1847 new organ by T.C. Bates & Son opened Feb. 20[188].

1684 Mar.31 JOHN PALMER appointed. Sal. £14.
1685 Apr.21 JOHN PALMER death reported. £4 to widow.
1685 Apr.21 THOMAS LOW appointed. Sal. £14.
1690 Oct.31 THOMAS LOW death reported.
1690 Oct.31 RICHARD LOW e. u. Hopsen (?) Swift.
1702 Apr.6 Churchwardens to speak to Richard Low about his playing on the organ.
1703 Apr.7 RICHARD LOW vacates (? dismissed).
1703 Apr.7 —— SMITH e. u. Tapley. Smith's christian name is unrecorded in V. & C.
1704 Apr.17 —— Smith re-elected u. Pigott, Tapley.
1706 Mar.25 —— Smith contested by Ezekiel Brathett "during pleasure only". It would appear to be a nominal opposition by the sexton.
1706 Oct.8 —— SMITH death reported.
1706 Oct.8 (HENRY) SYMONDS e. u. Claxton, Horwood, Miller.
1707 Apr.14 Mr. Symonds chosen "so [long] as he plays on holly dayes & behaves himself like a christian". u. Meaco.
1708–1721 Henry Symonds contested annually by Ezekiel Brathett. After 1738 SYMONDS is spelt SIMMONDS.
1740 Apr.7 HENRY SIMMONDS (i.e. SYMONDS) death reported. (? died Jan.6 – see Annotated Index).
1740 Apr.25 DAVID DIGARD (80) e. u. Benjamin Cooke (33).
1745 Apr.10 DAVID DIGARD death reported (died Feb.6).
1745 Apr.17 EDMUND GILDING (66) e. u. Joseph Baildon (9), Burton Hudson (8), John Bennett (8), Simon Stubley (3).
1782 Aug.14 EDMUND GILDING death reported (died Aug.5).
1782 Aug.21 TIMOTHY NEEVES (48) e. u. John Cadman (0), Thomas Ball (28), Peter Evans (12).

1786 Apr.21 TIMOTHY NEEVES vacates (no reason given).
1786 May 18 Miss MARY DORRELL (56) e. u. William Reeve (35), John Byfield (0).
1792 Feb.28 Miss MARY DORRELL death reported.
1792 Mar.15 WILLIAM REEVE (34) e. u. Samuel Showell (10), John Perkis (12), Miss Ann Beresford (25), Joseph Pring (7).
1805 Apr.17 WILLIAM REEVE resigns.
1805 May 16 JOHN PRINCE (49) e. u. F.H. Bond (withdraws), W. Bradley (2), T. Grady (withdraws), T. Tripcony & W.H. Meyer (absent), Eliza Immyns (1), Harriet Pain (3), Margaret Jones (1), John Warner (3). Sal. £20.
1834 Nov.13 JOHN PRINCE death reported.
1834 Nov.20 REES ELDRIDGE HARRIS (51) e. u. Alfred Bobbitt age 15, blind (2), Thomas E.Cripps (0), George Green (2), John L.Hopkins (absent), John Mills, blind (1), Miss Jane C. Webb (11).
1850 Jan.4 REES ELDRIDGE HARRIS resigns.
1850 Apr.2 Candidates Miss Morris, G.H. Tilbury, Stone.
1850 Apr.4 Election: G.H. Tilbury (9), Miss Morris (8). Ballot: GEORGE HAYWARD TILBURY (41), e. u. Miss Morris (35).
1852 June GEORGE HAYWARD TILBURY resigns.

49. ST. MARTIN OUTWICH

Sources: No V. after 1786 and C. are only source[49]. See also[427].

Organ 1805 "annuity organ" by George Pike England (see p.16). (Church demolished 1874). The C. payments beginning in 1805 are to "Mr England organist" and continue as under:-

1805–1814 Apr.5 [GEORGE PIKE] ENGLAND. Bur. 1815 Feb. 25 St. Andrew Holborn.
1815 Apr.27–1823 Mrs. ANN ENGLAND "organist" (widow of G.P. England). Bur. 1823 Mar. 5 St. Andrew Holborn.
1823–1866 Mrs. JANE ANN NICHOLLS (daughter of G.P. & Ann England). Subsequent entries refer only to "annuity on organ" until 1871 Oct. 19 "Louisa England annuity on organ". It is not known if these people played. An organist was probably paid by them out of the annuity but no record of their names has been found. It is significant that Pearce, quoting the contemporary Leffler[323], says that "the first organist in 1805 was Miss ENGLAND, a daughter of the builder (?)". This could possibly have been Jane Ann England (later Mrs. Nicholls). It is likely that for a few years before her death age 21 in 1819 Marian England was organist (see Annotated Index).

50. ST. MARY ABCHURCH

Sources: joint V. and rough V. St. Mary Abchurch & St. Lawrence Pountney. (Separate V. and C. St. Mary Abchurch give no information)[50 50a].

Organ 1822–3 J.C. Bishop cost 270 guineas. (Destroyed 1940 and replaced).

1821 Nov.21 Subscription to be opened for organ.
1823 Feb.20 Organ cost 270 guineas. Builder's name given as Bishop.
1823 Feb.20 Miss LINTOTT & Miss [EMMA] SMITH "to be allowed use of organ on alternate Sundays for next 2 months".
1823 Apr.17 above "to be put in nomination", Sal. £25.
1823 Apr.24 (reported in V. Dec. 23) Miss [EMMA] SMITH (58) e. u. Miss Lintott (48).
1858 Apr.30 Mrs EMMA THOMAS (née SMITH) resigns through failing health.

51. ST. MARY ALDERMANBURY

Sources: V.[51].

Organ 1825 no documentary evidence of builder (see below). J.C. Bishop suggested[188 323]. (Destroyed 1940).

1777 June 18 Offer of an organ turned down.

1824 June 10 Committee to consider erection of organ.

1825 June 9 Committee reports that Flight & Robson consulted. Organ to be acquired for between £200 & £400. No builder named.

1826 Jan.20 Miss ELIZABETH HEATHER (49) e. u. Miss Barnard (31), Hoar (0), Master Donne (0). Sal. £20.

1829 Jan.8 Miss ELIZABETH HEATHER dismissed for inefficiency.

1829 Jan.8 HORATIO ROWLAND MICHELMORE (21) e. u. Jones (9), Reynolds (0).

Although the new organist is referred to only as Mr. Michelmore and subsequent references are made to Henry and H.R. Michelmore there is little doubt about the above identification (see Annotated Index).

1840 Feb.19 HORATIO ROWLAND MICHELMORE death reported.

1840 Feb.19 WILLIAM THOMAS HALL e. (only candidate).

1855 Aug. 9, Nov. 1 Complaints about organist.

1855 Nov.1 WILLIAM THOMAS HALL resigns.

52. ST. MARY ALDERMARY

Sources: V. and C.[52]. (V. & C. of united parish of St. Thomas Apostle completely uninformative on organists), London parochial charity deeds of St. Mary Aldermary[88 92].

Organ 1781 "annuity organ" by Hugh Russell (see p.16) and entry for Russell in Annotated Index).

1781 Jan.8 Organ proposal considered. Hugh Russell to instal organ and find "proper person to play" for annuity of £46.4.0. during his life and lives of his children, William age 6 and Ann age 4. Agreement signed Mar.26. The payments to "the organist" in C. are in fact annuity payments. Hugh Russell may have played from 1783 Jan.2 and there is little doubt that his son WILLIAM RUSSELL, a very competent organist, did for some time before his death 1813 Nov. 21. Grove asserts that he was deputy organist of St. Mary Aldermanbury [sic i.e. Aldermary] 1789–93 and for 3 months to 1798 Sep.

1813 Nov.21 WILLIAM RUSSELL died.

1825 Oct.10 HUGH RUSSELL died and annuity passes to daughter Ann Russell who marries Philip Reilly, surgeon, 1828 Aug.2. Annuity ceases with her death 1854 June 17 and organ becomes property of parish. Hugh Russell's son Timothy continues to maintain organ for 4 guineas p.a.

1834 CHARLES GEORGE PLATTS (according to Pearce only[323]. No confirmation found).

1854 June 17 Annuity ceases on death of Ann Reilly.

53. ST. MARY AT HILL

Sources: V. and C., V. of united parish of St. Andrew Hubbard[53 53a]. See also[428].

Organ 1693 no documentary evidence of builder generally accepted to be Bernard Smith, 1788 new organ by Samuel Green for £320 plus old organ. 1849 new organ by William Hill & Son[188].

1692/3 Mar.3 Faculty for organ. No builder named.

1693 Aug.25 JOHN BARRETT chosen.

1720 Apr.18 JOHN BARRETT death reported.

1720 May 9 THEOPHILUS COLE e. u. William Miller who played since Barrett's death.
1730 May 7 THEOPHILUS COLE death reported (died Apr.20). Sal. to be paid to mother.
1730 June 24 HENRY DUNCALF e. u. Burgess, Husse, Low, Manwaring, West. Sal. £20.
1762 June 18 HENRY DUNCALF death reported (died June 10). Widow granted £10.
1762 Jul.2 GEORGE BERGE [i.e. BERG] e. u. Gates, Goodwin, jun., Jarvis, Griffies [sic], King, Selby.
1775 May 12 GEORGE BERG death reported.
1775 May 26 WILLIAM SMETHERGELL e. u. John Shuckford, Thomas Brown, John Webb, Richard Short, William Waterhouse, Elizabeth Smith.
1787 Jul.3 Proposal of Samuel Green to repair or rebuild old organ for £300 or build new organ for £320. Agreed to have new organ.
1788 Mar. 13 Samuel Green produces plan of new organ.
1826 Mar.30 WILLIAM SMETHERGELL pensioned: "advanced age & long service". To receive his sal. of £30 p.a. as pension plus £6 p.a. paid to him for teaching the children. Pension continues to Christmas 1835 (not March 1836).
1826 May 30 Miss HANNAH FORGE e. u. John Goodson jun., Edward Sturges, Samuel Wesley, jun., William Foster, Miss Clark, Miss Caroline Kerby, Henry John Don, Miss Tookey. W. Crathern withdraws. Sal. £45.
1845 Mar.26 – 1846 Apr.29 (between) Hannah Forge becomes Mrs. HALLEY.
1846 Apr.29 Complaints about her playing.
1847 Apr.9 Mrs. HANNAH HALLEY (née FORGE) resigns under pressure. Given £6.5.0 p.a. relief 1848 Mar.9.
1847 Dec.2 JOHN T. BURROWS e. u. T.G. Baines, A.J.S. Beale, J.H. Deane, James Higgs, C.F. Howell (withdraws), J.A. Jopp, J.S. Major (withdraws), J. Westlake. In view of Mr. Horsley (umpire), Burrows, Deane & Higgs best.
1848 Mar.16 Messrs. Hill to provide new organ.
1852 June 7 JOHN T. BURROWS resigns.

54. ST. MARY LE BOW

Sources: (V. give no information until 1822). Other details V. of united parish of St. Pancras Soper Lane[54 54a].

Organ 1802 "annuity" organ by Thomas Howard of Camberwell. (For annuity organs see pp.13–17). Contemporary Leffler, quoted by Pearce[323], gives builder as Hugh Russell, 1802. But he says "organist Mr. Howard" which is open to doubt. (Church burnt out 1941 and restored).

Proposals for an organ in 1747, 1773, & 1785 but nothing until:
1801 May 27 Proposals of Thomas Howard of Camberwell considered. A two manual organ value £300 to be made at his expense and played by "a qualified performer" in exchange for annuity on his life of 40 guineas per annum. Thomas Howard, of Union Row Camberwell, then aged 33.
1801 Dec.23 Howard's proposals accepted. Agreement 1802 Feb.24[93].
1802 Apr.18 Organ opened.
c.1817 ROBERT BEALE deputy organist[182].
1822 Jan.14 THOMAS HOWARD sells interest in organ and annuity arising therefrom amounting to £42 p.a. to Messrs. Rolfe of Cheapside.
1822 Jan. —— Rolfe commences duty. The firm of Rolfe, music sellers and publishers and pianoforte makers, included at least two organists in the family of whom T.H. Rolfe (see Annotated Index) served St. Mildred Bread Street from 1809 to 1847. William (jun.) was u. St. Vedast 1828.

1838 Dec.? —— ROLFE vacates.
1838 Dec.? JOHN JOSEPH STRICKLAND appointed.
1866 end JOHN JOSEPH STRICKLAND vacates.

55. ST. MARY MAGDALEN OLD FISH STREET

Sources: V. (to 1802 only), C. of united parish of St. Gregory by St. Paul[55 55a]. See also[392 429].

Organ 1785 no documentary evidence of builder. Pearce says Samuel Green[323] and Sperling "Longman [i.e. James Longman] – very inferior organ" to which "?Green" added in another hand[188]. (Church burnt 1886, demolished 1890).

1785 Mar.30 Organ proposed.
1785 June 15 Resolution passed & faculty to be applied for.
1785 Dec.29 Miss MARY HUDSON appointed (no other candidates).
1801 Mar.28 Miss MARY HUDSON died.
No record of her successor. All that is known is that:-
1801–1815 (between) WILLIAM ADAMS appointed (first ref. found in C. of St. Greogory 1815 Apr. 7).
1834 c. June WILLIAM ADAMS died (death reported St. Peter Cornhill June 19).
1834 June 18 FREDERICK MICHELMORE temporary until
1834 Sep. Miss CAROLINA TOWNSEND appointed.
1855 Apr.13 Miss CAROLINA TOWNSEND retires ill.

56. ST. MARY SOMERSET

Sources: V. give no information, C. information unsatisfactory[56]. See also[430].

Organ c.1830 no builder recorded. Sperling says "probably Green 1790"[188] but according to Godwin[299] "erected by present rector" (who served 1823–57). J.W. Billinghurst in 1855 described it as "a very insignificant looking organ"[323]. (Church demolished 1871). No record of organist until:-

1843? [WILLIAM HENRY] LANDERGAN appointed, (first record in C. 1844 Oct. 23 Landergan, organist 18 months £5).
1845 [WILLIAM HENRY] LANDERGAN vacates.
1845 before Apr. SAMUEL J. FOSTER appointed.
1846 SAMUEL J. FOSTER vacates.
1846 Mar.? Miss —— SMITH (pd. £5 for 1 year to Lady Day 1847).
1847 Miss SMITH vacates.
1847 R. SMITH appointed.
1853 R. SMITH vacates. Pearce notes that sal. in 1866 still only £10[323].

57. ST. MARY WOOLNOTH

Sources: V. and C. also V. and C. of united parish of St. Mary Wollchurch Haw[57 57a]. See also[386].

Organ c. 1678 no documentary evidence of builder allegedly Bernard Smith utilising some old Dallam pipework[330]. Inscription on old organ gallery "built by Father [sic] Smith 1681" obviously not contemporary. 1727 reinstalled after rebuilding church by Gerard Smith (see below under 1727 Jul. 25). 1805 or 6[323] or 1808[330] new swell by George Pike England.

1678 Dec.? JOHN MOSS appointed. The date of this appointment is doubtful: he is not named until 1681/2 Jan. 10. The following entries are relevant:
1678/9 Jan.8 £6 to be allowed organist from Xmas last.

1681 June 7 (inset) Difficulties about paying organist.
1681/2 Jan.10 Mr. Moss should be paid for his attendance as to the organ what shall be justly due to him & afterwards to be paid quarterly. (The £6 p.a. paid to Moss in C. of St. Mary Woolchurch represents only the contribution of the united parish).
1705/6 Mar.1 JOHN MOSS resigns from Lady Day next.
1705/6 Mar.1 —— WIN[D]SOR e. u. Robinson, King.
1716 —— WIN[D]SOR vacates on demolition of church.
1725 Sep.9 Decision to retain old organ.
1727 Apr.2 Church reopened after rebuilding.
1727 June 2 Agreed that the place of organist became vacant from the first pulling down of the old church. Future sal. to be £20.
1727 June 30 JOHN READING e. u. Samuel Manwaring, Henry Duncalfe.
1727 Jul.25 Payment to "Gerard Smith the organ maker" £112.
1764 Sep.14 JOHN READING death reported (died Sep. 2).
1764 Sep.14 JOHN SELBY e. u. Keith.
1772 Jan.3 JOHN SELBY resigns.
1772 Jan.3 RICHARD LOWE, jun. (89) e. u. William Crouch (11), James Moore (4).
1798 Mar.6 RICHARD LOWE death reported.
1798 Mar.15 THOMAS BUSBY nominated and unanimously e. No other candidates. Sal. £30.
1829 Apr.1 Annual election suspended. John Stone, late deputy, to officiate until next election.
1829 May5 THOMAS BUSBY dismissed.
1829 May5 JOHN STONE appointed without election.
1851 Apr. JOHN STONE resigns.

58. ST. MATTHEW FRIDAY STREET

Sources: V. and C. also V. and C. of united parish of St. Peter Westcheap[58 58a]. See also[431].

Organ 1735 no documentary evidence of builder allegedly Dr. Morse* of Barnet[395]. 1762 new organ by George England[180 188 323]. (Church demolished 1885).

1735 June 24 2 doors to be made for organ. Persons to be appointed judges of organ.
1735 Aug.29 JOHN YOUNG appointed. No record of election in V. which prior to 1735 are very inadequate. The date is deduced from entries in C.
1762 Mar.23 New organ proposed.
1767 May 6 JOHN YOUNG death reported (died Apr. 30).
1767 May 21 MARTIN RENNOLDSON (42) e. u. Smart (2), Miss Benson (1), Davis (0), Hooke (21), Cooper (5), Curtis (13), Moore (2).
1802 Mar.11 MARTIN RENNOLDSON death reported (bur. Jan. 20).
1802 Mar.11 WILLIAM BOYCE e. No other candidates mentioned.
1812 Oct.21 WILLIAM BOYCE resigns after taking offence (see Annotated Index).
1812 Nov.3 JOHN CASH e. unanimously.
1815 Mar.22 JOHN CASH resigns.
1815 Apr.5 [THOMAS?] GRADY e.
1817 Nov.11 [THOMAS]GRADY resigns. In consideration of his accident & infirmity £5 to be given to him by each parish. Sal. for next appointment to rise from £20 to £30.
1818 Feb.24 J.C. Webb, William Bradley, Lemare, Whittaker named as candidates.
1818 Mar.6 J.C. WEBB (45) e. u. William Bradley (33). "Very improper letter

* Dr. Morse builder of organs at Foundling Hospital, St. James Clerkenwell etc.

written by Mr. Lemare sen. & jun. to churchwardens". Payment usually given to u. withheld from Lemare.

1830 Oct.12 J.C. WEBB death reported.

1830 Oct.19 Creswick (blind), Miss Boult, Miss Webb, Cash (blind), Webb, Miss Sinderby, Mills, Miss Lea, Done named as candidates.

1830 Nov.10 Miss —— LEA (36) e. u. C.J.Webb (22), Miss Webb (7), Miss Sinderby (1), Mills (1).

1835 Apr.23 Complaints about Miss Lea.

1835 May 14 Miss —— LEA resigns.

1835 June 10 Four candidates selected from 28 (unnamed) applicants: John Cash, Thomas Erard Cripps, J.T. Cooper, Miss Lucy Richardson. John Cash, as holder of another post, disqualified. Mr. Slater in his place but Vestry substitute Miss Webb for him.

1835 June 16 Miss JANE C. WEBB (37) e. u. Miss Lucy Richardson (20), Miss Sinderby (6). Protest made about mode of election.

1836 Apr. Mrs. ANDREWS re-elected, so presumably née Webb.

1878 Apr.24 Mrs. ANDREWS vacates.

59. ST. MICHAEL BASSISHAW

Sources: V. and C.[59]. See also[432].

Organ 1762–3 installed by Thomas Griffin but apparently not on his usual annuity basis (see pp.13–15). (Church demolished 1900).

1762 June 16 Thomas Griffin's proposals accepted. Specification given. 200 guineas fee.

1763 June 15 Organ to be examined and T.G. not to be paid until favourable report.

1763 Sep.27 Balance to be paid.

1764 Feb.2 "Mr. English" to inspect organ.

1764 Feb.17 Thomas Griffin to be paid. Organist's sal. to be 20 guineas. Advt. for candidates in Daily Advertiser.

1764 Apr.12 John Raymond (24), Morgan (27), Keith (2), Golding (3), Jarvis (3), Rowe (1) and seven other unnamed candidates poll nil. Ballot to be held for Raymond and Morgan (who had acted as temporary organist).

1764 Apr.14 JOHN RAYMOND (46) e. u. Morgan (26).

1807 June 9 JOHN RAYMOND death reported.

1807 June 22 Miss SOPHIA POOLE (26) e. u. Coulden (24), Jonathan Rush (13), Woodthorpe (3), Grady (2), Herring (0), Gay (0).

1840 Jan.11 Miss SOPHIA POOLE resigns. Letter dated 1840 Jan. 27 from T.A. Adams implying that vestry had turned down "his proposal".

1840 Jan.27 27 applicants (names included in Annotated Index).

1840 Jan.31 THOMAS GEORGE BUCKLAND e.

1843 Jan.5 THOMAS GEORGE BUCKLAND resigns through ill health.

1843 C.H. Buckland plays temporarily Wednesday evenings & J. Salisbury on Sundays.

1843 Jan. 43 applicants (names included in Annotated Index) reduced by umpire to 3 candidates:

1843 Feb.23 GEORGE FIELDHOUSE (41) e. u. William Cupitt (0), Edmund T. Chipp (7).

1856 June 19 GEORGE FIELDHOUSE dismissed.

60. ST. MICHAEL CORNHILL

Sources: V. and C.[60]. See also[433].

Organ 1683–4 Renatus Harris. 1790 repaired and enlarged by Samuel Green[180 188]. 1849 reconstructed by Robson[188 323]. Additions 1920, 1949 and 1976 (rebuilt).

1682 Oct.10 Organ proposed: 5 models submitted.
1683 Oct.9 Subscription to be raised for organ.
1684 May 16 Blackall [i.e. ISAAC BLACKWELL] e. u. Bannister. Sal. £16.
1684 Jul.22 "Mr Harris the organ maker" requests to be paid £80 of £250 for the organ.
1685 "Paid Mr. Isaac Blackwell organist 1 year's sal. ending at Lady Day 1685".
1685 Paid to John Roberts for inviting Dr. Blow & other eminent musick masters to a Dinner & to try the organs 2/6 (from C.)
1685 Paid Anthony Gregory the charge of that Dinner (from C. which refer to annual general a/c ending Lady Day 1685).
1699 ISAAC BLACKWELL died.
1699 Dec.11 WALTER HOLT appointed. His "application to be organist from Xmas next" accepted. Widow Blackwell to have sal. till Lady Day next.
1703/4 Feb.25 WALTER HOLT "discharged".
1703/4 Feb.25 PHILIP HART appointed from Lady Day next. Sal. £20. In 1715 the steeple becomes unsafe & rebuilt. The organ apparently out of action for some years as
1719 Nov.10 ". . . whether feazable to putt the church & place the organ in the same condition as before the pulling down the tower".
1722/3 Feb.22 Committee "to treat with person or persons for putting up the organ". Renatus Harris "who made it" to have preference.
1723/4 Mar. Paid John Pape for setting up the organ & taking care of it before it was set up £60.
1723/4 Jan.1 PHILIP HART resigns.
1723 Dec.25 OBADIAH SHUTTLEWORTH commences duty. (1723/4 Jan. 1 Obadiah Shuttleworth "nominated & chosen" from Xmas last).
1734 June 20 OBADIAH SHUTTLEWORTH death reported (died May 2).
1734 June 20 JOSEPH KELWAY e. u. Froude, Boyce (runner-up), Young, Worgan.
1736 June 2 JOSEPH KELWAY resigns on appointment to St. Martin in the Fields.
1736 June 2 WILLIAM BOYCE e. u. Cooke, Young (runner-up), Manwaring.
1768 Apr.7 WILLIAM BOYCE resigns.
1768 Apr.29 THEODORE AYLWARD (61) e. u. James Evance (47) and many unnamed.
1781 Apr.19 THEODORE AYLWARD resigns.
1781 May 21 RICHARD JOHN SAMUEL STEVENS (77) e. u. Dr. Benjamin Cooke (20) in ballot after elimination of Burbridge, Jackson, Smith, Turene. Sal. £20.
1790 Samuel Green paid £300 for organ.
1810 Feb.20 RICHARD JOHN SAMUEL STEVENS resigns.
1810 May 11 GEORGE WILLIAM ARNULL (29) e. u. Henry Dale (26), Miss Elizabeth Rodd (18), Nightingale (1), Nicholls (0). In 1825 Apr. Arnull not to be re-elected but order rescinded a month later.
1849 May 29 GEORGE WILLIAM ARNULL retires. £30 pension.
1849 Jul.9 Miss Agatha Cowtan has acted as assistant during last 10 months.
1849 Jul.9 Many unnamed applicants reduced to 6 unnamed candidates.
1849 Jul.9 RICHARD LIMPUS appointed on umpire's recommendation.
1861 Resigns and re-elected[243].
1875 Apr.1 RICHARD LIMPUS death reported (died Mar. 15).

61. ST. MICHAEL CROOKED LANE

Sources: V. (none before 1791) and C.[61]. William Herbert in his *St. Michael Crooked*

Lane, 1833? must have had access to V. prior to 1791[306]. Information prior to 1791 from Herbert & C.

Organ 1731 no documentary evidence of builder. 1816 new organ, builder not known. (Church demolished 1831).

1730 Dec.17 Church to have organ, the rector having "acquainted the vestry that he had an opportunity of purchasing an organ at the sole expense & voluntary subscription of his own friends without putting parish to any charge".
1731 Jul.29 WILLIAM MARKHAM e. Sal. £16[306].
1749 Jul.6 WILLIAM MARKHAM, "many years organist of St. Michael's Crooked Lane", died[242].
1749 Jul. JOHN SCOTT appointed (evidence of C.).
1792 Jan.31 JOHN SCOTT death reported (buried Jan.25). No new appointment and the organ does not appear to have been used again.
1794 May 17 Organ "badly decayed and incapable of repair". To be pulled down.
1816 Dec.11 John Garratt to present organ. The election of organist constantly postponed.
1818 Mar.27 Organ is deficient: to be repaired.
1818 Dec.4 Decision to elect organist, but further delays.
1819 Jul.7 THOMAS HODSON (31) e. u. William Crathern (26), William Hill (0), Robert Beale (0), C. Smith (0). William Bradley withdraws.
1826 Jan.11 THOMAS HODSON death reported. New organist to perform personally. Sal. £20 plus £10 gratuity subject to his conduct being approved.
1826 Feb.8 JOHN GEORGE E[M]METT (22) e. u. Thomas Henry Hawker (0), Miss Showers (7), Henry John Don (5), J.W. Hoar (1), Miss Howe withdraws.
1830 Mar.8 JOHN GEORGE EMMETT vacates on election as organist of Bermondsey. Emmett to provide competent substitute.
1831 Church demolished. Organ probably removed to St. Benet Gracechurch (q.v.)

62. ST. MICHAEL PATERNOSTER ROYAL

Sources: V., C. and C. for joint parishes of St. Michael & St. Martin Vintry[62 62a]. See also[434].

Organ 1797 "annuity organ" by William Gray. (For annuity organs see pp.13–17). This organ allegedly by Renatus Harris c.1690 removed from St. Anne Soho and enlarged by Gray[180 188]. (Destroyed 1944). There is no evidence for W.L. Sumner's statement that a Jordan organ was installed in 1700 and removed in 1798. Curiously, though, an Abraham Jordan probably presented a font to the church in 1700 (V).

1797 Sep.11 Proposal that organ be installed by means of a life annuity by public competition.
1797 Sep.26 Organ builders attend. Terms offered by Mr. Phillips and Mr. Howard found to be lowest and each has organ available.
1797 Oct.2 Both organs seen by committee and rejected as too small. Howard offers to supply suitable organ which would cost him £300, keep in repair and supply organist for £40 per annum during natural life.
1797 Oct.6 William Gray, organ builder, of New Road, Fitzroy Square to be allowed annuity of 38 guineas p.a. for erecting 3 manual organ and finding suitable person to play. No information as to who played although probably JOHN GRAY who succeeded to annuity on death of William Gray.
1797 Dec.23 Agreement with William Gray completed.
1810 Apr.9 Organist to be appointed for evening service.
1810 May 9 THOMAS MARTIN PLATTS appointed evening organist. Sal. 10 guineas.
1820 Nov.16 William Gray's proposals as to enlargement of organ and alteration in annuity.

1820 Nov.25 Annuity increased to 46 guineas for alterations and additional supply of organist. So THOMAS MARTIN PLATTS evening services to be discontinued next Xmas.
1821 Jul.12 William Gray died.
1821 Jul.20 "An account of the respect in which the memory of Mr. William Gray is held" that JOHN GRAY to be paid 46 guineas annuity until Xmas next and to continue as organist.
1821 Jul.20 Canvas begun by THOMAS MARTIN PLATTS for office of organist in consequence of death of William Gray, but
1822 Jan.24 JOHN GRAY'S letter and proposition read. To continue as organist pro. tem.
1829 Apr.9 JOHN GRAY resigns.
1829 Apr.9 Miss SARAH FISHER, daughter of parish clerk, appointed (no candidates). In 1830 marries Thomas Plummer appointed parish clerk in 1836 (died 1838).
1870 Apr.19 Mrs. SARAH PLUMMER resigns through age and infirmity & succeeded by dau. Sarah.

63. ST. MICHAEL QUEENHITHE

Sources: V. and C.[63]. See also[435].

Organ 1731 no evidence of builder of "Isaac Orbell's organ" (see below) but possibly Richard Bridge. 1779 new organ by John England and Hugh Russell cost £300. 1837 additions by John Gray[323]. (Church demolished 1876).
1730 Dec.15 Committee appointed to view & inspect & to consider of Mr. Isaac Orbell's proposal relating to the organ.
1730/1 Jan.7 Organ offered by Mr. Isaac Orbell approved. To be set up.
1731 ISAAC ORBELL apppointed. (Evidence provided only by C.).
1748 Apr.3 ISAAC ORBELL death reported.
1748? —— ORBELL appointed. The V. entries are puzzling. 1748 Apr. 3 "Organ to be locked up until—— Orbell son of Isaac Orbell . . . shall apply to this parish in order to play the same" and 1748 Dec.9 "ordered that the organ shall be kept shut till Xmas next & then opened. Not played since last midsummer". But C.1749 May 9 pays "Mr. Orbell for ½ year & 1 month to Lady Day. £14.11.8" i.e. £25 p.a.
1754 Dec.13 —— ORBELL death reported. "Place not to be supplied & organ shut up unless Holy Trinity (united parish) shares the cost". Nothing further appears to have been done about it and the organ subsequently sold.
1778 Jul.10 Meeting called to consider erection of organ.
1778 Sep.21 Organ to be erected for £300 by England & Russell.
1779 Mar.9 Candidates (unnamed) reduced to Hartley, Olive & Short. Sal. £21. Organist to attend mng. & evng. in person.
1779 Mar.30 RICHARD SHORT (44) e. u. Olive (33).
1817 Apr.9 Annual re-election of Short postponed "till the churchwardens have an opportunity of conveying to him the sentiments of this vestry concerning his methods of playing the psalm tunes".
1824 Sep.15 RICHARD SHORT resigns.
1824 Nov.18 THOMAS CASH (46) e. u. T.M. Platts (12) (a better player than Cash in the view of the umpire, Thomas Attwood).
1831 Apr.5 Thomas Cash given 6 months notice (not proceeded with).
1837 Mar.1 THOMAS CASH resigns.
1837 Mar.8 JOHN THOMAS COOPER e. unan. u. James Howe (these two selected from unnamed applicants for election).
1844 Nov.29 JOHN THOMAS COOPER resigns.
1844 Dec.9 35 applicants (names included in Annotated Index) from which H.J.

Gauntlett, the umpire, selects 6 candidates to play before parishioners: Charles Batt, Miss Douglas, Lissant, W.H. Monk, H. May, Wesley.

1844 Dec.18 Miss Douglas (18), Lissant (12), Monk (0). A ballot results in Miss Douglas (23), Lissant (23).

1844 Dec.19 Miss CLARISSA DOUGLAS (41) e. u. Lissant (34) (2nd ballot).

1858 Oct.14 Miss CLARISSA DOUGLAS resigns.

64. ST. MICHAEL WOOD STREET

Sources: V.[64]. See also[436].

Organ 1818 Thomas Elliot £330. (Church demolished 1897).

1818 June 17 Advice sought from Mr. Nicholls who had succeeded to the business of the late Mr. England, organ builder, Mr. Elliot, organ builder, and Mr. Banner, organist of St. Lawrence Jewry. Proposal by Elliot of organ to cost £330 accepted.

1818 June 17 JOHN BANNER appointed. Sal. £30.

1822 Apr.22 John Banner petitions for increase of £10 (granted). Relinquishes St. Lawrence Jewry to give all attention to St. Michael (but see St. Lawrence Jewry).

1828 Nov.26 JOHN BANNER resigns from Xmas next.

1828 Nov.26 Miss ANN MOUNSEY e. u. Elizabeth Heather, Ann Burnham.

1834 June 5 Ann Mounsey's sal. reduced for economy reasons. Her reaction friendly & co-operative.

1837 Nov.22 Miss ANN MOUNSEY resigns on appointment to St. Vedast.

1837 Dec.7 3 candidates selected by umpire from George Godwin, Miss M.A. Pyne, Miss Lucy Richardson, Miss A.E. Tookey, Miss Williams, Miss Eliza Westley [sic].

1837 Dec.7 Miss M.A. PYNE (26) e. u. George Godwin (0), Miss Lucy Richardson (18).

c.1840 Miss Pyne becomes Mrs. GALTON.

1859 May 11 Mrs. GALTON resigns following dissatisfaction.

65. ST. MILDRED BREAD STREET

Sources: V. and C., also V. and C. for united parish of St. Margaret Moses which provide the only information for the earlier years[65, 65a].

Organ 1744–5 "annuity organ" by Richard Hussey and Thomas Griffin (see below and pp.13–17). (Destroyed with church 1941. Not rebuilt).

1743 Apr.27 Committee appointed for acquiring organ. Sal. of organist not to exceed £25.

1744 Oct.11 Annuity agreement (see p.15) with Richard Hussey to build and instal organ and to play for £20 per annum. "—— Griffin" to be paid £5 per annum to repair, clean and tune.

1745 Apr.21 Organ opened by Mr. Worgan, so presumably

1745 Apr.21 RICHARD HUSSEY commences.

The circumstances surrounding this annuity arrangement in which both Thomas and George Griffin appear to be involved are puzzling. The C. have entries for payments to "Hussey pp. Griffith" [sic i.e. Griffin?] until 1747/8 Jan.1 "Pd. Mr. Griffin for Mrs. Hussey for 1 years performing organ to Xmas" and 1748/9 Mar.7 "Pd. Mr. Griffin for Mrs. Hussey for one year playing the organ". But from 1750 to 1752 "Pd. Mr. Griffin organist" and "Pd. Mr. Griffin for playing and tuning." 1751 Sep. 26 "Parishes to allow George Griffin £8 per annum during his natural life and parishes to furnish themselves with an organist for salary of £20".

So the possible succession of organists could be:-

1747 end RICHARD HUSSEY? died?
1747 Dec. Mrs. HUSSEY? commences (very doubtful).
1749 Mrs. HUSSEY? vacates or died (very doubtful).
1749 GEORGE GRIFFIN? commences. (See Annotated Index).
1751 GEORGE GRIFFIN? vacates.
George Griffin continues to be paid annuity according to C. with sometimes "Thomas Griffin annuity due to George Griffin". After this the succession of organists is clear:-
1751 Sep.26 BENJAMIN YARNALD (also entered as YARNOLD, YARNELL) e. u. Purcell. Sal. £20.
1753 Aug.8 BENJAMIN YARNALD vacates.
1753 Sep.12 THOMAS CURTIS (34) e. u. Hudson (25), Wafler (0).
1806 May 21 THOMAS CURTIS death reported.
1806 May 21 Miss MARGARET JONES (28) e. u. T.H. Rolfe (21), William Adams (0), H.I. Ferry (0).
1809 May 17 Miss Margaret Jones suspended.
1809 June 6 Miss MARGARET JONES resigns in favour of
1809 June 6 T.H. ROLFE e. (no other candidates).
1847 Jul.1 T.H. ROLFE death reported.
1847 Jul.1 JAMES ROLFE e. unanimously (no other candidates).
1869 Apr.1 JAMES ROLFE vacates, i.e. not re-elected as no funds available to pay parish officers.

66. ST. MILDRED POULTRY

Sources: V. and C. of united parish of St. Mary Colechurch[66a]. See also [319] [437].

Organ 1778 George England, according to inscription "this organ was built by George England and was presented to the church A.D. 1778 by Mrs. Wylde"[319]. 1849 enlarged by J.W. Walker[323]. (Church demolished 1872).

1778 Feb.24 Gift of organ accepted.
1778 Feb.24 Miss ANN KITCHINGMAN appointed. Sal. £20. Miss A.K. caused much trouble as shown by frequent entries in V. Some relate to her deputy.
1790 Feb.8 Mrs. ANN BEVERLEY, formerly Ann Kitchingman, has for many years neglected to play.
1790 Apr.21 Mrs. Ann Beverley "confined at Hull by indisposition".
1790 June 30 JOHN [sic i.e. WILLIAM] BRIDE her deputy to be paid £10 p.a.
1791 Dec.23 Mrs. Ann Beverley not applied for sal. for considerable time. Present deputy John [i.e. William] Bride, who has played since June 1790, has sal. increased from £10 to £15. Adverts. for Ann Beverley's whereabouts.
1792 Sep.25 William [sic] Bride to be paid sal. to Xmas whether elected or not.
1792 Nov.12 Miss CATHERINE FRANCES LINTON (28) e. u. Miss Sophia Bonwick (27), Miss Catherine Jeyes (4), William [sic] Bride (19), Henry Vokes (0). Miss Linton to play at all services without deputy. Sal. £20.
1838 Jul. Miss CATHERINE FRANCES LINTON retires. Evidence from C. of St. Mary Colechurch which is also the only source for the following information. No V. available for either parish between 1818 and 1859.
1838 c.Aug. [HENRY] CULLUM e.
1840 c.Apr. [HENRY] CULLUM vacates.
1840 c.May Miss ALICE SOWARD e.
1847 late or 1848 early Miss Soward becomes Mrs. PAWSEY.
1872 Mrs. ALICE PAWSEY vacates on demolition of church.

67. ST. NICHOLAS COLE ABBEY

Sources: V. and V. of united parish of St. Nicholas Olave. No C. survive for either parish[67 67a].

Organ 1823–4 no documentary evidence of builder allegedly John Bunting[188 323]. (Destroyed 1941. Church restored).

1823 Oct. 3 Decision to buy organ.

1824 or 1825 Miss ANN WELCH appointed. Information from V. is sparse but by 1838 her position far from secure and an election called for:

1839 Jan.25 Miss ANN WELCH e. u. Miss Cooper, Mrs. E. Davis.

1850 Oct.10 Miss ANN WELCH resigns. The very inadequate V. give no information about an election.

68. ST. OLAVE HART STREET

Sources: V.[68]. See also[438].

Organ 1781 Samuel Green. (Destroyed 1941. Church rebuilt with Harrison & Harrison organ).

1781 June 7 Sal. to be 25 guineas. No other post allowed and not to employ deputy.

1781 Dec. 5 Mr. Green, organ builder, to keep organ in tune.

1781 Dec.20 Miss MARY HUDSON (131) e. u. William Shrubsole (0), John Turene (0), John Herring (1), Cornelius Keith (1).

1801 Apr.2 Miss MARY HUDSON death reported (died Mar.28).

1801 Apr.9 Miss LOUISA LINTON (48) e. u. John Wilkins (42), J. Blewitt, jun. (16).

1805 Dec.12 Miss LOUISA LINTON resigns.

1806 Jan.24 Miss SARAH MORRICE (64) e. u. Miss Hannah Bacon (6), Thomas Grady (15), James Hanson (3).

1810 Apr.–1811 Apr. (between) Miss Sarah Morrice becomes Mrs. SARAH WOOD.

1845 Apr.28 Miss ELIZA ANN SILVERLOCK (41) e. assistant organist. u. Miss Isabella Harris (34), John Horth Dean (2).

1857 Apr.16 Mrs. SARAH WOOD death reported. Succeeded by Miss E.A. Silverlock who served until 1885.

69. ST. OLAVE JEWRY

Sources: "C. with sundry V." which are more informative than the series of V. and C.[69].

Organ 1814 "annuity organ" installed by William Warrell (see pp.16–17) built by Parker? originally in Savoy Chapel, restored by William Allen (see below). 1848 new organ by J.W. Walker cost £200 plus old organ valued at £60[188]. (Church demolished 1887).

1814 Aug.9 Proposal by [William] Warrell of 53 Carlisle Place, Lambeth to provide organ for annuity of 36 guineas on his own life.

1814 Aug.12 Organ which had been for several years in King's Chapel in Savoy now at Mr. Allen's, organ builder, Sutton St., Soho Square. He believes originally built by Parker. Warrell engaged in same manner by deed of 1790 at St. Mary le Strand. Ralph Kinkee age 22 in Nov. 1814 also to be named in deed.

1814 Aug.24 Warrell's proposals adopted. Subsequent payments in C. are to Warrell and Kinkee organists.

1814 WILLIAM WARRELL (?nominal) and RALPH KINKEE organists.

1834 Aug.28 Resolved that Mr. Ralph Kinkee being willing to forego his contract for annuity of £20 p.a. & his playing being disapproved of, organist to be found to be paid difference between £20 and £37.16.0.

1834 Aug.28 RALPH KINKEE vacates.
1834 Oct.30 W.F. ROBINSON appointed.
1874 Jul.? W.F. ROBINSON vacates. 1874 is the last payment to him in C. Mackeson (1867) records him as F. Robinson[210].

70. ST. PAUL'S CATHEDRAL

Sources: St. Paul's Cathedral records[96 to 105]. See also [331 439].
Organ. See bibliog. nos. 331, 439.
1638? ALBERTUS BRYAN appointed (secondary sources only).
c.1671 ALBERTUS BRYAN died. No new appointment until
1686/7 Feb.7 ISAAC BLACKWELL appointed.
1699 ISAAC BLACKWELL died.
1699 June 6 JEREMIAH CLARKE appointed.
1707 Dec.1? JEREMIAH CLARKE died.
1707/8 Mar.14 RICHARD BRIND appointed.
1717/18 Mar. RICHARD BRIND died.
1717/18 Mar.20 MAURICE GREENE appointed.
1755 Dec.1 MAURICE GREENE died.
1755 Dec.25 JOHN JONES appointed.
1796 Feb.17 JOHN JONES died.
1796 THOMAS ATTWOOD appointed.
1838 Mar.24 THOMAS ATTWOOD died.
1838 Apr.26 JOHN GOSS appointed. u. include John Blackbourn.
1872 Sir JOHN GOSS vacates.

Almoners

1687–1687 died Michael Wise.
1687–1693 resigns John Blow.
1693–1707 died Jeremiah Clarke.
1707–1748 died Charles King.
1748–1773 removed William Savage.
1773–1793 resigns Robert Hudson.
1793–1799 resigns Richard Bellamy.
1799–1812 resigns John Sale.
1812 Dec.–1846 died William Hawes.
1846–1858 died William Bayley (styled music master).

71. ST. PETER CORNHILL

Sources: V. and C. (incomplete)[71].
Organ 1681–2 Bernard Smith. 1840 new organ designed by H.J. Gauntlett built by William Hill & Son cost £465 plus £44.16.0 extra work (some Smith pipework retained).[71V 280].
1681 Nov.15 Agreement upon erection of organ by Bernard Smith for £210 including painting, gilding & setting up.
1682/3 Mar.5 Ref. to payment of organist when appointed.
1683 Easter – 1684 Easter accounts: "Pd. Mr. Smith the organist £30 (C.). The inference could be that the organist is BERNARD SMITH himself but the following entry from V. suggests the possibility that it is a payment to the organ builder and that C. incorrectly describes him as organist.
1683 Nov.21 Money to be collected for "the compleate payment for the organ and what shall then be wanting of the thirty pounds now due for the same shall be paid". (See Annotated Index under Smith, Bernard).

1684/5 Jan.26 "Dr. Beveridge, Alderman Thorowgood and Mr. Dawes shall from henceforthward have the choyce and privilege of putting in and nameing of an organist". But no further reference to an organist until 1720/1 (in V.) and 1724, June 16 (C.) which is the first entry for his payment. Is it possible that the organ was not used for 40 years? The following entries suggest something was amiss.

1720/1 Jan.12 Organist to advise with makers what is to be done with organ.

1721 Sep.13 John Pape paid £150 for mending organ (C.).

1724 Apr.9 William Goodgroom the organist shall be discharged at Michaelmas next. So,

? WILLIAM GOODGROOM appointed.

1724 Apr.9 WILLIAM GOODGROOM dismissed from Michaelmas next.

1724 Jul.15 GEORGE MONRO e. "Spent when Mr. Monroe was chosen organist 3s./4d." (C.) but 1724 Sep.30 "Mr. Munro chose in room of William Goodgroom" (V.). After 1724 the annual re-elections of organist are not given regularly. Monro is given in C. up to 1730/1 Mar.6. Next ref. in V. 1731 Apr.28 when Thomas Pierce (or Peirce) e. (annual election). So,

1731 c.Mar. GEORGE MONRO vacates (?died).

1731 c.Mar. THOMAS PEIRCE [or PIERCE] e. His election appears annually until 1775 Apr. 20.

1776 THOMAS PEIRCE vacates (probably died, see Annotated Index).

1776 Apr.10 No organist in annual election because "the money by which he was paid is seized by Dr. Thomas the Rector".

c.1780 WILLIAM LEWIS appointed (1781 Apr.9 William Lewis paid £20 for playing organ last year).

1786 Apr.20 WILLIAM LEWIS retires. "Incapacitated by infirmities". Pension of £15 p.a.

1786 May 18 CORNELIUS KEITH (94) e. u. Miss Katherine Jeyes (8).

1800 Aug.22 CORNELIUS KEITH death reported (died Aug.7).

1800 Aug.22 GEORGE URLING (43) e. u. Hugh Ferry (5), Thomas D. Halley (4), William Mountain (4), John Simpson (0), Tripconey (6).

1807 Apr.10 GEORGE URLING resigns.

1807 Apr.28 WILLIAM ADAMS appointed without election.

1834 June 19 WILLIAM ADAMS death reported.

1834 June 19 Miss ELIZABETH MOUNSEY (36) e. u. Miss Lissetta Rist (6), George Smith (12). After a poll votes were 52, 1, 13.

1834 Aug.22 Gratuity of £10 awarded to above George Smith who had served "so long as deputy".

1840 Jul.12 New organ opened.

1882 May 26 Miss ELIZABETH MOUNSEY retires owing to "increasing infirmity". A letter from Rector to Miss Mounsey refers to her 48 years service and awards her pension of ⅔ of late stipend of £35. To have use of organ for teaching & opportunity of playing entrance voluntaries on Sundays.

72. ST. PETER LE POER

Sources: no V., C. or alternative sources available before 1843[72]. Information is therefore very limited. After 1846 V. of united parish of St. Benet Fink[72a]. See also[440].

Organ 1718 builder unknown. 1792? new organ by Samuel Green after rebuilding of church[188 323]. (Church demolished 1908).

1718 Nov.16 Organ opened by Philip Hart[253].

? SAMUEL LONG appointed. Pearce says 1745[323]. Earliest evidence of his being there 1763 Feb.22[L198].

1764 Aug.7 SAMUEL LONG died [L142].

1764 Nov.29 Miss HARDIN of the Old Jewry e. by a great majority[L525]. Probably Elizabeth Hardin who was bur. in churchyard of St. Olave Jewry 1780 Jan. 28 age 29. No further information until annual election in first available V. of 1843.
before 1843 Mar.30 Miss MATILDA ANN WILLSDON e.
1844 Oct.28 Miss MATILDA ANN WILLSDON died (bur.Nov.5).
1844 Nov.? WILLIAM FOSTER appointed. No evidence of election found.
1880 Dec.25 WILLIAM FOSTER retires with presentation of £150.

73. ST. SEPULCHRE HOLBORN

Sources: V. and C.[73]. See also[441].

Organ 1675–6 Renatus Harris. c.1730 swell by John Byfield, sen.[323]. 1817 enlarged by James Hancock & 1828, 1835 enlarged by John Gray[323]. Rebuilt 1932.

1676 May 4 "Mr. Harris the organ maker" to be paid £50 on account till subscription money ready.
1676 June 12 FRANCIS FORCER appointed. The first entry relating to an organist. Sal. to be £20.
1704/5 Feb.1 FRANCIS FORCER death reported (bur. Jan.26).
1705 Mar.27 THOMAS DEAN[E] e. u. Harris, Short, Shuttleworth, Isham, Harwood, Isaac. "Only those who have not more than one organist's place in the church" accepted as candidates. Sal. £20.
1712 June 12 THOMAS DEAN[E] dismissed "having neglected attendance for $\frac{3}{4}$ of a year".
1712 June 20 BENJAMIN SHORT appointed (no election).
1760 Mar.12 BENJAMIN SHORT died.
1760 Mar.20 WILLIAM SELBY & SAMUEL JARVIS jointly appointed during their good behaviour. Sal. £40 between them. At decease of either, survivor to get £30.
1773 Oct.27 WILLIAM SELBY resigns, SAMUEL JARVIS sole organist.
1784 June 24 SAMUEL JARVIS death reported (died June 21).
1784 Jul.1 GEORGE COOPER, jun. [sic] (89) e. u. Miss Ormes (54).
1799 Sep.25 GEORGE COOPER death reported.
1799 Oct.1 GEORGE COOPER (70) e. u. W. Lowndes (1), Jonathan Perkins, jun. (48).
1843 Dec.4 GEORGE COOPER death reported.
1843 Dec.11 GEORGE COOPER e. unanimously (no candidates called for).
1876 Oct.2 GEORGE COOPER died.

74. ST. STEPHEN COLEMAN STREET

Sources: V.[74]. See also[442].

Organ 1774–5 no documentary evidence of builder allegedly John Avery[180 188]. (Church and organ wrecked 1940).

1774 May 12 Vestry agree to erect organ by voluntary subscription. Design submitted.
1774 June 1 Licence (faculty) to be obtained.
1775 Apr.4 Sal. to be £30. Candidates to have no other Sunday post.
1775 May 2 Charles Rousseau Burney (77), Thomas Busbey (6), John Day (53), John Groombridge (63), H.S. Heron, jun. (4), Elizabeth Smith (0). Final ballot between 2 leaders:-
1775 May 2 JOHN GROOMBRIDGE (133) e. u. Charles Rousseau Burney (97).
1827 Oct.3 JOHN GROOMBRIDGE death reported (bur. Aug.8).
1827 Oct.23 Judges select 6 from 15 unnamed applicants: Gauntlet, Nicholls, Goodson, Michelmore, Rutland, Samuel Westley [sic], jun. But the candidates at election on Nov.1 show differences:-

1827 Nov.1 Miss SARAH ALDER BRADFIELD (217) e. u. Michelmore (23), Hall (18), Gauntlet, Nicholls, Wesley, jun.

1844 Apr.19 Miss SARAH ALDER BRADFIELD resigns through ill health; "severe affliction". £20 pension for life. Samuel J. Foster had been deputy.

1844 June 20 60 applicants (listed in Annotated Index). 35 play publicly, 25 decline to come forward. Vincent Novello as judge selects 6 best for election. Sal. £42.

1844 June 20 ALFRED BOBBETT (76) e. u. William Rea (0), Charles Batt (17), Miss Eliza Ann Silverlock (22), Mrs. Lucy Lindley (37). Miss Clarissa Douglas withdraws. The vestry also vote for Miss LeCren who secures 84 votes. Her disqualification leads to much strife, fully recorded in V. with letter from her father.

1865 before Jul. ALFRED BOBBETT vacates.

75. ST. STEPHEN WALBROOK

Sources: V. (gap 1734–1775)[75], MS report on building organ[95], V. of united parish of St. Benet Sherehog[75a]. See also [379 443].

Organ 1765 George England cost £750. 1825 enlarged by John Gray[323]. (Sold to St. Bartholomew the Great 1886. New organ by Hill badly damaged 1941).

1765 June 9 Organ opened by Dr. Worgan.

1765 June 16 Sal. to be £30. Constant attendance demanded.

1765 June 26 RICHARD LOWE e. u. Tremain, Casson, Evane [?Evance].

1793 Mar.1 RICHARD LOWE death reported.

1793 Mar.8 SAMUEL SHOWELL (58) e. u. Lowe, son of above (0), John Norman (22), John Purkis (0).

1825 Nov.16 SAMUEL SHOWELL death reported.

1825 Dec.5 25 applicants named (in Annotated Index). Of these, 11 selected as candidates: Edward Sturgess, J.H. Vinnecomb, George Tolkien, William Blackman, Miss Eliza Kingston Probyn, Joseph Stone, John George Emmett, Theodore Showell, Edward May, M.B. Miller, Miss Jane Howe. Of these Miller, Stone & May do not attend audition.

1825 Dec.16 [sic, ?26]. Miss ELIZA KINGSTON PROBYN (45) e. u. John George Emmett (10), Edward Sturgess (1). Miss Probyn later becomes Mrs. COOPER.

1868 Mrs. COOPER (née PROBYN) retires.

76. ST. SWITHIN LONDON STONE

Sources: V.[76].

Organ 1809 Robert or William Gray cost £304.10.0. (Wrecked with church 1941).

1809 May 21 Organ opened. Built Gray cost £304.10.0 according to organ committee's report of 1810 Apr. 11.

1809 Jul.4 Miss ELIZABETH MORREL e. Miss Nash, Crouch & Staples withdraw. Miss Morrel appears to have become Mrs. STYLES in 1826. Sal. £30, but no other posts.

1843 Oct.13 Mrs. ELIZABETH STYLES (née MORREL) death reported (died Oct. 3).

1843 Oct.24 39 applicants reduced by excluding those under age of 17 as "teaching the children" is involved. Thomas Adams selects 3 candidates for election.

1843 Nov.29 HENRY LAHEE (67) e. u. Septimus Parker (8), Edmund Thomas Chipp. Other u. named as Miss Johnson, Miss Silverlock, Miss Fuller, Miss Morris, Miss Douglas, Griffiths, Higgs, Hills, Major, Norman.

1847 Sep.1 HENRY LAHEE resigns. Edward White, jun. writes offering service without sal. till Easter. Has been organist at early Thurs. mng. service etc. for 3 years without reward. Also did whole duty from May last to closing of church in Jul.

1847 Sep.15 57 applicants reduced to 18 and then to 8: John Carter, J.H. Deane,

Miss Selman, Miss Cope, Charles F. Howell, John Weslake, John Lloyd, Edward White, jun. Lloyd withdraws & replaced by Thomas Westrop.

1847 Sep.24 Umpire John Goss selects 3 for election.

1847 Oct.14 Thomas Westrop (5), J.H. Deane (3), John Weslake (3) followed by a poll: THOMAS WESTROP (39) e. u. J.H. Deane (29), John Weslake (6).

1881 Dec.28 THOMAS WESTROP death reported (died Dec.17).

77. ST. VEDAST FOSTER LANE

Sources: V., C. and joint V. with St. Michael le Querne[77] [77]a. See also[444].

Organ 1773 "annuity organ" through William Duncombe (see p.17) built by Crang & Hancock for £240. (Burnt 1940. Replaced by organ originally in St. Bartholomew by the Exchange, q.v.).

1773 Jul.21 Proposal with William Duncombe for annuity of £37.16.0 for self & wife whoever lives longer. To supply organ valued at £240 and to play himself or find able performer. Proposal of "Mr. England" not accepted.

1773 Dec.22 Agreement with Duncombe.

1774 c.Jan. WILLIAM DUNCOMBE appointed. C. consistently describe him as organist so it is likely he played himself initially, but probably gave way to THOMAS JONES before 1779.

1779 Dec.22 Mr. Hancock, organ builder, reports organ in bad condition & that he is owed 1½ years for tuning by Mr. Jones. Will cost about £4 to repair damage caused by Abbé Vogler.*

1783 c. Apr. WILLIAM DUNCOMBE retaining annuity but THOMAS JONES definitely acting as organist.

1793 c.Sep. THOMAS JONES died.

1793 c.Sep. Miss CATHERINE JONES appointed by William Duncombe.

1794 May 26 Dissatisfaction "with manner in which organ has been played for a long time". Unless it improves annuity will be discontinued. (Duncombe and Miss Jones attend meeting).

1807 Jan.21 Acceptance of proposal of Catherine Jones as the person entitled to the annuity of £37.16.0, namely receiving for and during the life of Wm. Duncombe the sum of £10 p.a. Moved that annuity now payable to Wm. Duncombe do cease at Lady Day next from which period Catherine Jones to receive £10 p.a. as before mentioned.

1807 c.Jul. Miss CATHERINE JONES vacates.

1807 Jul.23 [ROBERT] TOPLIFF (50) e. u. Wilkins (27), Graday (0). Sal. £30.

1828 Mar.12, June 24 Robert Topliff in dispute with vestry (details in Annotated Index) culminating in

1828 Jul.10 ROBERT TOPLIFF resigns. New appointment to have 40 guineas plus 10 guineas to teach children to sing. Organ blower to be paid out of salary.

1828 Jul.23 17 candidates: Miss Mary Ann Thompson, Miss Ann S. Mounsey, John George Emmett, H.R. Michelmore, W. Rolfe, jun., Mrs. Harriott [sic] Galton, Miss Ann Hill, William Jones, W. Kemp, Henry John Gauntlett (declined), Joshua Done, jun., Thomas Tomlinson, Thomas Severn, Miss S.J. Mountford, T.S. Graday, R. Rutland, J.T. Stiles.

1828 Aug.6 Candidates reduced by ballot to 4: Miss Ann Hill (27), Miss A.S. Mounsey (26), H.R. Michelmore (14) and W. Rolfe (3).

1828 Aug.27 Miss ANN HILL (46) e. u. Miss A.S. Mounsey (27).

1837 Oct.25 Miss ANN HILL resigns.

1837 Nov.7 Miss [ANN SHEPPARD] MOUNSEY (62) e. u. Westley [sic] (16).

* G.J. Vogler (Abbé Vogler), 1749–1814. German pianist, organist and composer.

1853 Mar.31 Annual election Mrs. BARTHOLOMEW (née MOUNSEY).
1891 June 24 Mrs. ANN SHEPPARD BARTHOLOMEW died.

TEMPLE CHURCH

The societies of the Inner Temple and Middle Temple each supplied an organist. The lists, compiled from the Calendar of Inner Temple Records vol. 3, 4, 5[311] and Middle Temple Bench Book, 1937[318] are given below. See also[383 445].

Organ 1683–7 Bernard Smith. 1729–30 swell by Christopher Schreider (and John Byfield, sen. 1741). 1843 enlarged by J.C. Bishop[188 330]. (Destroyed 1941).

78. INNER TEMPLE

1688 May 27 FRANCIS PIGOTT appointed. Sal. £25 (also for Middle Temple).
1704 May 15 FRANCIS PIGOTT died.
1704 May 27 Petition for place by Henry Owen rejected.
1704 May 27 JOHN PIGOTT appointed (also for Middle Temple).
1728/9 Feb.8 JOHN PIGOTT discharged from Lady Day next (continues for Middle Temple).
1729 May 16 OBADIAH SHUTTLEWORTH appointed.
1734 May 2 OBADIAH SHUTTLEWORTH died.
1734 May 13 JOHN STANLEY appointed.
1786 May 19 JOHN STANLEY died.
1786 June 20 RICHARD JOHN SAMUEL STEVENS appointed.
1810 RICHARD JOHN SAMUEL STEVENS resigns.
1810 GEORGE PRICE appointed.
1826 GEORGE PRICE died.
1826 GEORGE WARNE appointed (also for Middle Temple).
1843 GEORGE WARNE resigns.
1843 May 7 EDWARD JOHN HOPKINS appointed (also for Middle Temple).
1898 EDWARD JOHN HOPKINS resigns.

79. MIDDLE TEMPLE

1688 FRANCIS PIGOTT appointed (also for Inner Temple).
1704 May 15 FRANCIS PIGOTT died.
1704 May 27 JOHN PIGOTT appointed (also for Inner Temple).
1736 JOHN PIGOTT vacates.
1737 JAMES VINCENT appointed.
1749 Oct. 6 JAMES VINCENT died.
1749 Nov. 24 JOHN JONES appointed. u. John Stanley.
1796 Feb.17 JOHN JONES died.
1796 Miss EMILY DOWDING appointed.
c.1805 GEORGE EBENEZER WILLIAMS deputy for "Temple Church" in 1805. Period of service not established[182].
1814 Miss EMILY DOWDING dismissed.
1814 GEORGE PRICE appointed (serving Inner Temple since 1810).
1826 GEORGE PRICE died.
1826 Nov.17 GEORGE WARNE appointed (also for Inner Temple).
1843 GEORGE WARNE resigns.
1843 EDWARD JOHN HOPKINS appointed (also for Inner Temple. Installed May 7).
1898 EDWARD JOHN HOPKINS resigns.

80. CHARTERHOUSE

Sources: Charterhouse Assembly orders vol. A–M (1613–1854), with other Charterhouse records[154].

Organ 1626 builder unknown (removed during Commonwealth). 1662 restored and repaired. 1753 new organ cost £190 plus old organ. Sperling says this organ, by Snetzler, removed 18— to Moravian Chapel, Fetter Lane[188]. 1842 new organ by Joseph Walker (rebuilt by J.W. Walker & Sons Ltd. 1924).

1626 Jul.6 Consideration of cost of installing organ in the Chapel and stipend to be paid to an organist also required "to teach the scholars . . . to singe prick songe and to play uppon any Instrument."

1626 Dec.7 [BENJAMIN] COSIN appointed. Sal. £13.6.8 p.a.

[1644 Organ playing in church services prohibited by ordinance of Parliament].

1643/4 Mar.7 BENJAMIN COSIN "removed . . . The stipend belonging to Benjamin Cosin late organist sequestered by the House of Commons . . . No use of our organist . . . Therefore we do remove the said Benjamin Cosin from being organist". Petition "for allowance to be made unto him in recompense of the losse of the organist's place".

1653 Sep. BENJAMIN COSIN died.

1662 June 24 NICHOLAS LOVE e. ("Benjamin Couzens" late organist referred to). Love "to provide an organ" (presumably the old organ, silent and stored since 1644 or before).

1664 June 24 Nicholas Love granted 40/- p.a. to put organ in good order and keep in good repair.

1688 Sep.13 "Indecent behaviour of Mr. Nicholas Love at the Master's table" reported. Love to make public apology otherwise to be removed to the manciples' table.

1710 June 24 Request by Nicholas Love, "now in his extreme age", for his son Thomas to act as assistant. Granted.

1713 NICHOLAS LOVE died.

1713 June 24 THOMAS LOVE appointed. "Place of organist some time void by death of Nicholas Love. Son Thomas has executed office for some years during Father's indisposition and since his death".

1737 THOMAS LOVE died.

1737 Dec.2 JOHN CHRISTOPHER PEPUSCH e. "in room and place of Mr. Love deceased".

1752 Jul.20 JOHN CHRISTOPHER PEPUSCH died.

1753 Jul.2 Scheme for new organ "to cost £190 besides the old organ".

1753 Jul.2 JOHN JONES e. Sal. £4.11.10 a quarter including 10d. for looking after organ.

1765 Nov.22 Petition of Benjamin Cooke organist of Westminster Abbey "to erect at his own charge a monument in the Chapel to the memory of the late J.C. Pepusch . . . who lies buried in the said Chapel". Agreed.

1776 Mar.19 John Jones given additional room after complaining about inadequacy of his apartments.

1787 May 22 Organ to be repaired.

1796 Feb.17 JOHN JONES died.

1796 Mar.4 RICHARD JOHN SAMUEL STEVENS e.

1810 June 19 Organist's apartments to be renovated.

1837 Sep.23 RICHARD JOHN SAMUEL STEVENS died.

1838 Feb.17 Sal. of future organists to be £70 without apartments or other emoluments except for use of a room with a fire when on duty.

1838 Feb.17 WILLIAM HORSLEY e. u. include Edward Hodges[167].

1840 Apr.4 Organ beyond repair. New organ to be purchased for £250 (later raised to £280).
1842 New organ by Joseph Walker (label on present organ, rebuilt J.W. Walker & Sons Ltd. 1924).
1858 June 12 WILLIAM HORSLEY died and succeeded by John Pyke Hullah.

81. CHRIST'S HOSPITAL

Music or singing masters

These are included because they were all organists and many were also organists of the adjoining church of Christ Church, Newgate Street. The holders of the office had to be either bachelors or widowers.

Sources: Christ's Hospital court minute books and committee minute books[156 157]. See also[446].

1659 May 31 Candidates named: "Mr. Robinson, late a child of this house [i.e. Christ's Hospital], Mr. Hopwood, Mr. Price".
1659 Jul.29 RICHARD PRICE chosen. "Richard Price, musician & bachelor presented petition for music master's place".
1675 Dec.17 RICHARD PRICE death reported.
1675 Dec.17 Petitions of John Moss, married (who had been instructing the children for some time), John Curtis, bachelor, and James Cobb, bachelor.
1675/6 Feb.4 JOHN CURTIS appointed. Sal. £20.
1684/5 Mar.18 John Curtis negligent in teaching children. New appointment to be made.
1685 Apr.1 Petition from John Curtis rejected.
1685 Apr.14 Discussion as to successor but John Curtis still there Aug. 1686.
1687 Jul.15 Revelation that Curtis is married. (Samuel) Nicholls to be given a trial, meanwhile Curtis to stay on.
1687 Dec.14 Rules for music master laid down. Name of Richard Browne submitted as possible successor.
1687/8 Feb.8 Complaint against Curtis.
1687/8 Mar.13 John Curtis has frequently used the children with inhumane & barbarous severities. (For his subsequent histrionics see Annotated Index).
1687/8 Mar.13 JOHN CURTIS dismissed.
1687/8 Mar.13 RICHARD BROWNE appointed.
1689 Jul.4 Richard Browne admonished for ill-treatment.
1697 Jul.27 RICHARD BROWNE dismissed for negligence.
1697 Sep.28 JOHN BARRETT e. u. John Mosse, Isaac Blackwell (both music masters) & Richard Browne (disallowed),
1719/20 Jan.28 JOHN BARRETT death reported.
1719/20 Jan.28 PETER HORWOOD e. u. Edward Purcell, John Isham, Charles King (runner-up), all masters of music.
1739/40 Feb.12 PETER HORWOOD death reported (widow to be paid sal. due to him). Died 1739 Dec. bur. Dec.6 at Wandsworth.
1739/40 Feb.12 JOHN YOUNG, jun. e. u. James Worgan, Matthew Hussey, masters of music.
1767 Apr.30 JOHN YOUNG died.
1767 Jul.2 ROBERT HUDSON (57) e. u. Charles Bosseau Burney [i.e. Charles Rousseau Burney] (3), William Riley (8), William Yates (1).
1808 Mar.15 ROBERT HUDSON retires through increasing infirmities and age (77). Awarded pension of £40 p.a.
1808 Mar.25 RICHARD JOHN SAMUEL STEVENS e. unan. u. William Russell.
1810 Feb.16 RICHARD JOHN SAMUEL STEVENS resigns.

1810 Apr.6 ROBERT GLENN e. u. Thomas Everett, Samuel Showell.
1844 Feb.25 ROBERT GLENN died.
1844 May 7 3 candidates selected from 19 unnamed applicants.
1844 May 7 GEORGE COOPER (128) e. u. George French Flowers (54), Thomas Ingram (8).
1876 Oct.2 GEORGE COOPER died.

82. CROSBY HALL

Organ by Henry Cephas Lincoln, 1842. Bought by J.W. & Mrs. E.M. Robins for St. Ann's Church, Stamford Hill, N.15 when built in 1861. No evidence that an organist was ever appointed. See also[447].

83. DUTCH CHURCH AUSTIN FRIARS

Sources: Acta books of the consistory 1671–1923[160], Treasurer's account books 1774–1852[161], Bills and receipts 1791–1805[162].

Organ 1799 William Eveleigh, cost £147. (Destroyed 1940).

1720 Printed forms issued for subscribers to an organ[163]. No evidence found in church records of such an organ or appointment of organist.
1799 Oct.2 F. GOTTSCHALK appointed.
1799 Dec.2 William Eveleigh paid £147 for organ.
1820 Oct.19 F. GOTTSCHALK death reported (Payments in accounts up to 1818 Mar. only).
1821 Mar.2 ROBERT SADLER appointed (Payments in accounts start 1818 Sep.) Sal. £20.
1823 May 15 ROBERT SADLER resigns.
1823 June 19 C.VERDUIN appointed.
1829 Oct.15 C.VERDUIN resigns. Lancelot Sharpe provisionally appointed.
1830 Mar.11 LANCELOT SHARPE appointed. Sal. £20.
1833 June 5 LANCELOT SHARPE resigns.
1833 Jul.11 Miss MARY HALE appointed. Sal. £20 later increased to £25.
1848 June 7 Miss MARY HALE resigns on departure for America.
1848 June 7 H.J. BAKKER appointed. Sal. £25.
1852 H.J. BAKKER vacates.

84. PARISH CLERKS' COMPANY

The Company had an organ in its hall until the nineteenth century.

Sources: the Company's main records no longer exist. The following list has been compiled from James Christie's *Some account of the Parish Clerks*[287], William McMurray's abstracts from the minute books[132] and other scrapbooks in Guildhall Library[133].

before 1684 —— MOSS appointed (?John).
1684 Moss's sal. raised from £7 to £8.
1707 —— MOSS vacates.
1707 CLEMENT MAGNUS appointed.
1732 Apr.17 CLEMENT MAGNUS death reported.
1732 Apr.17 ROGER GETHIN e.
1742 Jan.18 ROGER GETHIN death reported (bur.1741 Dec.27).
1742 Jan.18 MATTHEW HUSSEY e. u. Thomas Moreland, Edward Henry Purcell, "the second of whom found no supporters".
1764 Matthew Hussey paid additional 3 guineas for extraordinary trouble in putting

several new tunes into the Company's psalm books.

1766 c.Apr.1 MATTHEW HUSSEY died.

1766 Jul.14 EDMUND GILDING appointed.

1782 Oct.14 EDMUND GILDING death reported (died Aug.5).

1782 Oct.14 CHARLES BENNETT e. (previously assistant to Gilding).

1790 May 3 CHARLES BENNETT death reported (died before Apr.14 & possibly bur. Mar.21).

1790 May 3 THOMAS LESTER chosen.

1814 Jul.18 THOMAS LESTER resignation reported.

1814 Jul.18 WILLIAM LIGHT e.

1822 Apr.22 WILLIAM LIGHT resigns. Organ to be shut up.

Part Three

ANNOTATED INDEX OF ORGANISTS AND UNSUCCESSFUL CANDIDATES WITH BIOGRAPHICAL NOTES DRAWN FROM ORIGINAL SOURCES.

This is an index to the organists and candidates for organists' posts listed in the second part of this work together with a few organists in neither of these categories who lived in the City or had other connections with it.

Each entry gives first the parishes or other institutions (if any) which the organist served and the dates he held office. This is followed by abbreviated references to his unsuccessful City candidatures prefaced by the letter U. The numbers and years indicate the parishes, according to the numbers allotted to them in part two, and dates of the elections. A "U" entry in italics indicates that the applicant was not accepted as a candidate.

The notes which follow these salient facts are not intended to be fully biographical and are restricted for the most part to documented facts that have emerged from the consultation of primary material. Emphasis is given to information hitherto unknown and to facts that supplement or emend biographical entries in standard works.

The sources of this information are indicated by numbers which refer to the bibliography. The letters V or C following some of these indicate respectively the vestry minute books or churchwardens' accounts of the parishes bearing those numbers. In the case of a few frequently recurring references, numbers have been replaced by letters to be more easily recognisable. Thus B. G and G(5) indicate the *British union-catalogue of early music*[283], *The new Grove dictionary of music and musicians*[302] and the 5th edition of Grove[302a] respectively. The letter L followed by a number indicates that the source of the information is *Lloyd's Evening Post*[234] of the appropriate date. The number is the page number from which the information comes.

Sources are not given for baptisms, marriages and burials as the information supplied is sufficient to identify them. An explanation of this is found in the bibliography following entry 84.

Further economy of space is gained by omitting the page numbers and dates for entries of deaths or other events in contemporary periodicals where the entries can be found readily through the date given or by reference to their indexes.

Under many of the notes, additional symbols and bibliography references give secondary sources of information. Here the B symbol referred to above is indicative of a composer-organist and G or G(5), besides supplying a fuller account and listing additional sources, often gives details of organ posts outside the City of London. For organists who do not appear in Grove, F. Boase's *Modern English biography*[282] is often useful for organists who died after 1850, and Brown and Stratton's *British musical biography*[284] is of great value particularly after 1800.

Only the more recent articles in musical periodicals are included as for the most part older ones are listed in Grove.

ADAMS,
U 25.1826, 20.1836.

ADAMS, James F.
U *75.1825* (J.P. Adams), *45.1826*, 15.1836 (J.F.T. Adams), *74.1844*.
Adams, J. prof. of the organ & pfte. 5 Queen St., Walworth 1828[195]. Adams, James, prof & teacher of music 40 Upper John St., Tottenham Court Rd. 1840[199], of 40 Upper John Street 1844[74V].

ADAMS, Thomas, 1785 – 1858.
St. Dunstan in the West 1832 Oct.25 – 1858 Sep. 15 died. Great tribute by vestry Oct.8.
Son of Edmond & Frances Adams b.1785 Sep.5 bap. St. Katherine Cree. Organist Carlisle Chapel Kennington before 1808 when elected to Roy. Soc. of Musicians on recommendation of B. Jacob. Then living Clarence Row, Camberwell[182]. Died 1858 Sep.15 at his residence Addington Place, Camberwell age 73[232].
G. 282. 284.

ADAMS, W.H.
U *45.1840*.

ADAMS, William, d.1834.
St. Peter Cornhill 1807 Apr.28 – 1834 June 19 death reported.
St. Mary Magdalen Old Fish St. between 1801 & 1815 – 1834 June 18 successor playing.
U 65.1806.
Blind[71V]. Music prof./teacher/prof. of pfte. 2 Walcot Place, Lambeth 1823–34[199].

ALCOCK, John.
Some authorities erroneously ascribe him to All Hallows Bread St. as successor to John Stanley, but he held no City posts.
U 16.1735/6, 37.1736.
St.Paul's choir 1722 under Charles King[342]. Pupil of John Stanley 1729[342].
B. G. 284. 295. 339. 454.

ALLEN, E.F.
U *74.1844*.
Of Guildhall St., Canterbury 1844[74V].

ALLEN, Miss Mary, 1768 – 1851.
St. Andrew Undershaft 1790 Oct.13 – 1836 Apr.7. As an inhabitant of the parish she defeated the professionals at the 1790 election. Her 45 years service punctuated by frequent complaints and dissatisfaction with her playing. Permitted to retire in 1836 on pension of £25 p.a.
Died at Hackney 1851 Jan.12 aged 82, "many years organist at St. Andrew's Undershaft"[232].
282.

ANDREWS, Mrs. Jane Constant *see* Webb, Miss Jane Constant, later Mrs. Andrews.

ANDREWS, Mrs. John Holman *see* Webb, Miss Jane Constant, later Mrs. Andrews.

ANSELL, J.R. i.e. J.K. Ansell?
U 44.1821 (no christian name), *45.1826* (J.R.Ansell).
284? (J.K. Ansell).

ARCHER, Mrs. Marian *see* Hildyard, Miss Marian, later Mrs. Archer?

ARCHER, Miss Mary, later Mrs. Moorcroft.
St. Dionis Backchurch 1849 Nov.22 (after having officiated voluntarily since 1841) – 1862 Aug.8 resigned after marriage in letter from New North Rd. dated June 27.

ARCHER,
U 1.1758.

A Thomas Archer appointed organist St. John Hackney 1727 Jul.29 as successor to John Reading. Gone by 1753 Aug.11[328].

ARNOTT, Miss Hannah Maria, b.1819.
U *12.1842*, *15.1844*, *74.1844*, *63.1844*, 25.1847, 15.1847 (selected by umpire as candidate "though much inferior to other 3". Scored no votes in election).

Born 1819. Daughter of William Arnott, bookbinder & parish clerk of St. Andrew by the Wardrobe[153]. Of 39 St.Andrew's Hill in 1851[153]. Applied for post of organist at her parish church in 1842 and appointed 19 years later, 1861 Nov.28. Resigned 1873 and granted pension of £6 p.a. by Parish Clerks' Company 1885[130].

ARNULL, George William.
St.Michael Cornhill 1810 May 11 – 1849 May 29 retired. At annual election 1825 Apr.7 "not to be re-elected". Apr.26 order rescinded. Re-election postponed 1849 Apr.12 on account of health consequent on age. Retirement letter dated 1849 May 8 from 4 Gloster St., Vauxhall Walk. Granted £30 pension.

——Arnull of 104 Bank Bldngs., Cornhill, oboe player 1794[198]. This was George Arnull probably father of G.W. although his children by his wife Leetitia Adorinia baptised between 1785 & 1795 at St. Margaret Lothbury include no George William.

ATFIELD, John, d.1766
St. Katherine Cree 1753? – 1766 Mar.17 death reported.
St. Bartholomew by the Exchange 1762 June 18 – 1766 Mar.20 death reported.
U 14.1749 (no christian name), 31.1752 (do.), 44.1762 (do.).

John Attfield [sic] musician, of St. Giles Cripplegate took John Hewett as apprentice 1753[149]. Died 1766 Mar.8 John Atwell [sic] organist of St. Catherine Cree church and St. Bartholomew by the Exchange[L246]. John Atfield bur. in the churchyard of St. Michael Cornhill 1766 Mar.13. The same?
B. G(5).

ATKINSON, Mrs. Elizabeth *see* Goadby, Miss Elizabeth, later Mrs. Atkinson.

ATTWOOD, Thomas, 1765 – 1838.
St. Paul's Cathedral 1796–1838 Mar.24 died. No other City posts or candidatures.

Born 1765 Nov.23 bap. St. Martin in the Fields Dec.5. Eldest son of Thomas Attwood, musician, & Ann. Brought up in Chapel Royal. Pfte. & tenor player, composer. Musician to Prince of Wales. Elected Roy. Soc. of Musicians on recommendation of father 1789 Feb.1. Died 1838 Mar.24[182].
B. G. 284. 339. 352. 366. 367.

AUSTIN, Job, d. 1866.
St. Dunstan in the East end of 1828? – end of 1866 (referred to as late organist 1867 Jan.5).

AUSTIN, Miss Sarah Sophia Ann.
Holy Trinity Minories (appointed unanimously) 1846 Mar.19 – 1852+ (still in office).

AYLWARD, Theodore Edward.
St. Lawrence Jewry 1762 May 21 – 1788 June 12 resigned in letter dated Windsor June 7: "appointed to Royal Chapel at Windsor".
St. Michael Cornhill 1768 Apr.29 – 1781 Apr.19 resigned: "going to reside out of town".
U 1.1758 (no christian name).

Elected Roy. Soc. of Musicians 1763[181]. Resigned Oxford Chapel on appointment to St. Michael in 1768[L481]. Elected Gresham Professor of Music 1771 June 5[232].
B. G. 339 etc.

AYRTON, Edmund, d. 1808.
No City appointments but Vicar Choral St. Paul's.
U 10.1766 (no christian name, runner-up).

Elected Roy. Soc. of Musicians 1765. Died 1808[181].
B. G. 284.

BABELL, William, d.1723.
All Hallows Bread Street 1718 Nov. 12 – 1723 Sep.23 died. Death reported Oct.10.

Died 1723 Sep. 23 "William Babell one of the musicians belonging to Chapel Royal & organist of All Hallows Bread St."[233]. Bur. Sep.26 All Hallows "Wm. Babell our organist". Will of William Babell of the parish of St. Andrew Holborn. All his goods, plate, jewels, cloaths, furniture, rings . . . estate to wife Alice, dated 1720 Dec.31 proved 1723[139].
B. G.

BACON, Miss Hannah.
U 68.1806.

BAGLEY,
U 1.1758.
B. has 7 songs c.1756–8 composed by —— Bagley.
B.

BAILDON, Joseph, d.1774.
U 40.1744/5 (runner-up), 48.1745 (runner-up), 34.1747 (no christian name), 22.1747 (runner-up).
Chorister of St. Paul's[342]. Organist of St. Luke, Middlesex and Fulham in 1762[273]. Annually contested John Gates at St. James Garlickhythe 1751–81 [sic] according to V. Purely nominal? As deputy? Elected Roy. Soc. of Musicians 1752[181]. Composer & organist. Contributed psalm tunes to Riley's *Parochial music corrected* 1762[273]. Of Rolls Bldgs., Chancery Lane 1763[211]. Died 1774 May 7 in Great Queen Street[L445].
B.G.

BAILDON, Thomas, d.1762.
No City posts or candidatures found.
Chorister of St. Paul's[342]. Probation as Vicar Choral St. Paul's 1744 Mar.31[99]. Elected Roy. Soc. of Musicians 1747[181]. Died 1762 Oct.1 "Mr. Baildon belonging to the King's Chapel, St. Paul's & Westminster Abbey"[232 242].
G.

BAILEY,
No City posts or candidatures found.
Mr. Bailey, prof. of the organ & pfte., violin & thorough-bass, 90 Leadenhall St., 1828[195].

BAINES, James
U 3.1849.

BAINES, Thomas G.
U 53.1847
Of 15 City Rd., Finsbury 1847[53V]. Organist St. Margaret Westminster 1856[398].

BAKER,
U 25.1847 (declined audition).

BAKKER, H.J.
Dutch Church Austin Friars 1848 June 7 – 1852 vacated.

BALL, Thomas.
St. Bartholomew the Great 1785 Aug.17 – 1793 June 26 discharged for non-attendance. Deserted wife[20V].
U 48.1782 (runner-up).
Thomas Ball, music seller of Islington bankrupt 1793 Apr.9[239]. The same? Thomas Ball, organist, of Gloucester Place, Islington 1794[198].

BALY, William.
U 15.1847 (runner-up).
284.

BAMBER, Walter.
U 18.1766, 7.1767 (no christian name).
B. has one song c.1760.
B.

BANKS, Edward Francis.
U *45.1826*.

BANNER, John.
St. Lawrence Jewry 1805 May 7 – 1821 June 8 resigned. In letter from Vauxhall of June 1 "No longer able to perform to our mutual satisfaction".
St. Michael Wood Street 1818 June 17 – 1828 Nov.26 to resign at Xmas next. 1822 Apr.22 petitioned for increase as he had relinquished St. Lawrence to give all attention to St. Michael.
U 15.1804 (runner-up).
Music prof. or teacher 10 Eden Grove, Holloway 1832–4[199]. "Mr. Banner organist of St. Paul's, Balls Pond, Islington" 1837[256] and 1843[258]. Published collection of sacred music used at St. Michael's Wood St., songs etc.
284.

Bannister,
U 60.1684
Possibly John Banister, jun., violinist and composer. Died 1735/6 Jan.10 "at his house in Bloomsbury, Mr. John Banister about 74 years of age. One of the gentlemen of H.M. Musick and for many years esteem'd a most excellent master of the violin"[228].
G? 325?

Barber, Miss Elizabeth Ann, later Mrs. Smith.
All Hallows London Wall 1825 May 3 – 1837 Mar.28 resigned. 1833 Apr.4 not re-elected but re-elected Apr.11. Before 1834 Mar.27 mar. —— Smith.
Of London Wall in 1825[4V].

Barcas, d.1703.
St. Katherine by the Tower before 1698 Dec.14 (earliest ref.) – 1703 June 16 death reported.
Charles Barkes [sic] mar. Elizabeth Miller at St. Katherine 1700 Oct.22. The same?

Barchard, Mrs. Elizabeth.
U 15.1836 (withdrew).

Barker, Mrs. Ann *see* Blewitt, Miss Ann, later Mrs. Ann Barker?

Barnard, Miss
U 51.1826 (runner-up).

Barnes, John.
St. Botolph Aldgate 1847 Mar.25 – 1866 Aug.23 resigned "in consequence of extreme debility".

Barrett,
U 20.1836.
?William H. Barrett, music prof. or teacher 45 John St., Tottenham Court Rd. in 1840[199].

Barrett, John, d.1719.
St. Mary at Hill 1693 Aug.25 – ?1719 Dec. died. Death reported 1720 Apr. 18.
?Christ Church Newgate Street 1697 Sep.? – 1718 or before? (but see under Christ Church).
Christ's Hospital music master 1697 Sep.28–?1719 Dec. died. Election of "successor to John Barrett deceased" 1719/20 Jan. 28.
John Barrett's death occurred therefore around Dec.1719 – Jan.1719/20. A child of the Chapel Royal of this name until 1691[292]. St. Paul Covent Garden reg. has burial of John Barrett, jun. 1719 Dec.14. The same? This John Barrett in will dated 1718 Apr.16 left all to wife Elizabeth. Proved 1719 Dec.[139].
B. G. 284.

Barron, Edward.
St. Botolph Aldgate? 1681 Mar. – between 1691 and 1702.

Barry,
U 25.1799.
B. has one work by —— Barry c. 1794.
B.

Barry, Miss Mary Ann.
U 34.1797.

Bartholomew, Mrs. Ann Sheppard *see* Mounsey, Miss Ann Sheppard, later Mrs. Bartholomew.

Bartholomew, Thomas, c. 1779 – 1819.
St. Clement Eastcheap 1802 Jan.? – 1819 end of May died. Salary £30. Widow received quarter's sal. for late husband June 30[30aC].
"Thomas Bartholomew of St. Matthew Bethnal Green, 40 years" bur. 1819 June 2 at St. Clement Eastcheap.

Bashan, John.
U 34.1712. One of 2 candidates, polling 33 against Abiell Whichello's 66.

Bates, Joah, d.1799.
No City organ posts or candidatures found. Lived in parish of St. Andrew Holborn bur. St. Andrew 1799 June 15 "from John Street".
G.

Bates, Miss.
U 3.1849, 31.1849.
Miss E. Bates appointed to French Protestant Church St. Martin le Grand 1866 Nov.[243]. The same?

Batt, Charles, 1819 – 1858.
St. Margaret Lothbury 1847 c.May – 1858 May died. Death reported May 27.
U 15.1836 (no christian name), 74.1844

(judged best by umpire), 63.1844 (short list of 6 out of 35), 25.1847 (no christian name).

Son of Thomas Batt, undertaker, & Ann of 20 Walbrook. Thomas, who died 1845 age 52, then of Bucklersbury, parish clerk of St. Mary Woolchurch[130]. Of 19 Bucklersbury 1844[74V]. Mar. 1845 Jul.13 Sarah Ann Cox, dau. of John Cox, lodging house keeper of Bucklersbury, at St. Mary Woolnoth. Register entry describes Charles Batt as organist.

BATTISHILL, Jonathan, d.1801.
St. Clement Eastcheap 1765 Aug.21 – 1801 Dec.10 died.
Christ Church Newgate Street 1767 May 20 – 1801 Dec.10 died.
U 2.1756 (runner-up).

Chorister of St. Paul's[342]. Elected Roy. Soc. of Musicians 1761: expelled for non-payment[181 184]. Jonathan Battishill of St. George the Martyr, prof. of music, took John Hirst as apprentice £47.5.0 in 1761[149]. Composer and teacher on the harpsichord, Orange St., Bloomsbury 1763[211]. Of New Cross 1794[198].
B. G. 284.

BAYLEY, William, 1810 – 1858.
St. Paul's Cathedral music master 1846 – 1858 Nov. 8 died.
No City organ appointments or candidatures found.

Born 1810 Jan. 7 at Tutbury Staffs. bap. Tutbury Apr. 15. Twin son of James & Ann Bayley. Married Catherine Hampson Lloyd 1848 June 2 Bury St. Edmunds. Organist St. John Southwark in 1848. Private teacher. Of 5 Nelson Sq., Blackfriars Rd. 1848. Elected Roy. Soc. of Musicians 1848 Sep.3[182]. Died 1858 Nov.8 at Houghton Place, Ampthill Sq.[232].
282.

BAYLIS, Mrs. Maria *see* Stimson, Miss Maria, later Mrs. Baylis.

BAYNHAM, Thomas.
U 12.1842 (no christian name, disqualified), 59.1843.

Of 10 Marlborough Place, Walworth 1843[59V]. Published collection of psalm & hymn tunes 1860. Compiled some pfte. music.
284.

BEACH,
U 43.1686 (runner-up).

BEALE,
U 25.1847 (short list of 6 out of 63).

BEALE, A.J.S.
U 53.1847.

Of 12 Paradise Place, Stockwell 1847[53V]. Appointed Emmanuel Church Camberwell from 30 candidates 1860 June[243].

BEALE, C.J., d.1882
U 59.1840.

Of 47 Wardour St., Soho 1840[59V]. Later organist St. Paul Covent Garden until 1880 Aug. Died 1882 Mar.19 age 63[243].

BEALE, Robert, b.1792.
St. Mary le Bow deputy in 1817–18 etc.[182].
U 26.1818, 38.1819 (withdrew), 61.1819, 38.1820 (runner-up), 59.1840, 74.1844 (no testimonial, disqualified).

Born 1792 Apr.23 bap. Christ Church Southwark Jul.15. Son of Robert Beale calico glazer & Elizabeth. Chorister Westminster Abbey under Guise and Robert Cooke. Mar. Isabella ——. Flute & pfte. player and teacher. Employed Royalty Theatre. Elected Roy. Soc. of Musicians 1818 on recommendation of William Beale 1817 Oct.5[182]. Of Commercial Rd. 1818[26V], 15 King St. Holborn 1840[59V], 54 Theobalds Rd. Holborn [74V].

BEEDHAM, Thomas.
St. Dunstan in the East c.1680 or 81 – 1683 vacated.

Possibly Thomas Beedham parish clerk of St. Lawrence Jewry 1682 – 1689. He died 1688/9 Feb. 17 and bur. St. Lawrence Jewry. 1684 Apr. 14 "Mr. Beedham to answer complaints for introducing a new sort of psalms into the church"[132]. His eldest son Thomas bap. 1670 Aug.9, succeeded father at St.

Lawrence 1689 – 1715/16 Feb.19 died.

BELL, Francis.
St. George Botolph Lane 1831 Apr.12 – 1848 Jan. 18 resigned.
Son of Richard Bell, parish clerk St. George Botolph Lane 1809 – 1843 died[130].

BELLAMY, Richard, d.1813.
St. Paul's Cathedral almoner 1793–99.
Elected Roy. Soc. of Musicians 1764[181]. Appointed Gent. of Chap. Roy. 1767 Nov.[L437]. Mar. Elizabeth Griffiths of Marsham St. Westminster 1768 Sep.18[L294]. Of 6 Crane Court, Fleet St. 1794[198]. Died 1813[184]. Application for funeral expenses by widow Dorothy [sic] Bellamy to Roy. Soc. of Musicians 1813 Sep.5[184].
B.G. 284.

BENNETT, Charles, d.1790.
St. Edmund, King and Martyr 1782 Aug.21 – 1790 Apr. 14 death reported.
Parish Clerks' Company 1782 Oct.14 – 1790 May 3 successor appointed. (Assistant organist before 1782).
U 3.1780, 37.1785.
Charles Bennet [sic] bur. in south vault of Holy Trinity Minories 1790 Mar.21. The same? Undated will of Charles Bennett of St. John Street, Clerkenwell divided property between brother Joseph and sisters Frances Labrun & Mary Bennett. "Fine musick books of Handels" to Sarah Eastwick dau. of Henrietta Eastwick of Aldersgate, London. (Henrietta Eastwicke goldsmith of 102 Aldersgate Street 1789–93[305]). Execs. brother Joseph & brother in law Richard Labrun. Witn. Henry Eastwick, Joseph Hewitt, John Williams. Proved 1790 Apr.15[139].
B. (12 songs & cantatas c. 1760).

BENNETT, John, d. 1784.
St. Dionis Backchurch (no other post allowed) 1752 Apr.3 – 1784 Sep. died. Death reported Oct.1.
U 40.1744/5 (no christian name), 48.1745, 18.1746 (no christian name) contested Henry Duncalf in annual election.
Elected Roy. Soc. of Musicians 1753[181]. 1763 tenor to the Queen's Band, organist & teacher on the harpsichord, Queen Sq., Bloomsbury[211]. Composer of organ voluntaries. Bur. St. Dionis Backchurch 1784 Sep.24.
B. G. 279.

BENSON,
U 42.1833.

BENSON, Miss Hannah.
U 18.1766, 10.1766 (no christian name), 58.1767 (do.).

BERESFORD, Miss Ann.
U 48.1792 (runner-up).

BERG, George, d.1775.
St. Mary at Hill 1762 Jul.2 – 1775 May 12 death reported.
U 14.1749 (no christian name), 47.1771.
Elected Roy. Soc. of Musicians 1763[181]. Composer & teacher on the harpsichord, Lincoln's Inn Fields 1763[211].
B. G.

BEVERLEY, Mrs. Ann *see* Kitchingman, Miss Ann, later Mrs. Beverley.

BEVERLEY, William.
U 3.1780 (failed to appear).

BEVILL, John.
No City posts or candidatures found.
Elizabeth dau. of John Bevill, organist, bur. St. Giles Cripplegate 1685 Jul.21.

BEXFIELD, William (Richard), d.1853.
St. Helen Bishopsgate 1848 Feb. – 1853 Oct.29 died.[282]
G. 282. 284.

BICKERTON, Miss Mary Worsley, d.1795.
St. Giles Cripplegate 1785 June 29 – 1795 Mar.12 death reported.
Bur. St. Giles Cripplegate 1795 Mar.8 Mary Wosley [sic] Bickerton, a woman, dropsy.

BISSELL,
U *12.1842* ("Bissell from Wednesbury").

BLACKBEARD,
U 1.1758.

BLACKBEE,
U 25.1847 (declined audition).
Robert Felix Blackbee appointed to Emmanuel Church, Forest Gate, Essex 1863 Jul.[243]. The same? And "R.F. Blackbee, sen." to St. Michael & All Angels, Hackney 1864 June[243].

BLACKBOURN, John, 1792–1854.
U 45.1820 (John Blackburn), 70.1838.
Born 1792 Aug. bap. St. Saviour Southwark Sep.7. Son of James Blackburn [sic] fish salesman & Henrietta of Billingsgate[182]. St. Paul's Choir School 1800–08 & continued as assistant instructor & superintendent of the boys until 1811[232]. Then apprenticed to John Sale almoner with fee of £10 from Dean & Chapter[232]. Pfte. player & organist, teaching private & school. Elected Roy. Soc. of Musicians 1818 on recommendation of Thomas Attwood[182]. Organist Wandsworth 1818–21, Clapham 1821 to death at Clapham 1854 Dec.18[232]. Left £150 to Roy. Soc. of Musicians[243].
282. 232 (1855 p.243).

BLACKBURN, A.E.
U *45.1840*.

BLACKBURN, Richard.
U *45.1826*.
Music prof. or teacher 258 High St., Poplar 1832–4, 36 High St., Poplar 1840, 5 St. Ann's Place, Commercial Rd. East 1847[199].

BLACKMAN, William.
U 18.1819, 75.1825, 45.1826 (failed to attend), 25.1827 (no christian name).
Probably music seller & pubr.[310].

BLACKWELL, Isaac, d.1699.
St. Dunstan in the West 1674 Dec. – 1699 May 4 death reported.
St. Michael Cornhill 1684 May 16 – 1699. Death reported Dec.11.
St. Paul's Cathedral 1686/7 Feb.7 – 1699 died.
U 81.1697.
Isaac Blackwell bachelor living in parish of St. Bartholomew by the Exchange c.1695. The same? Is this the Isaac Blackwell whose songs appear in Playford's *Choice ayres* 1675 and is noticed in G? Left widow[60V].
G. 284.

BLEWITT, Miss (Mary) Ann (later Mrs. Ann Barker?), b. 1784.
St. Katherine Coleman in succession to father 1805 May 14 – 1833 Apr. 11 Mrs. Barker not re-elected.
Born 1784 May 29 according to application form of her father Jonas to Roy. Soc. of Musicians[185]. It would appear that she became Mrs. Ann Barker between 1817 Mar. & 1818 Mar.

BLEWITT, Jonas, 1757–1805.
St. Katherine Coleman 1777 Nov.? – 1805 Apr. 16 death reported.
St. Margaret Pattens 1783 Apr.? – 1805 Apr. 10 death reported.
U 20.1777, 3.1780.
Born 1757 Sep. 9 bap. St. George Middlesex Oct.3. Son of John Blewitt, mariner & Mary of Virginia St. Apprenticed to William Godfrey organist of Lambeth[185] in 1769[149]. Composer to Spa Gardens, Bermondsey when applying unsuccessfully for membership of Roy. Soc. of Musicians 1788[185]. Also employed Astley's Theatre, Royal Circus, Apollo Gardens. Of Bermondsey Square 1794[198].
B. G. 284.

BLEWITT, (John) Jonathan, 1779 – 1853.
St. Margaret Pattens deputy to father Jonas Blewitt c.1793 onwards. Sainsbury[325] only authority for this: no confirmation in V. or C.
All Hallows Barking evening lectures (Sainsbury[325] only authority).
U 68.1801, *45.1826*.
Son of Jonas Blewitt. Born 1779 Jul.16 as John Jonathan according to application form of his father to Roy. Soc. of Musicians 1788[185]. (His birth date is usually given as 1782).
G. 282. 284. 325.

BLOCKLEY,
U 25.1827.
Blockley, John, composer, writer & pubr. b. 1800 d. 1882 Dec.24. The same? Blockley, John, teacher of piano, 16 Store St., Bedford Sq. 1823–34[199]. The same? Also John Blockley music

seller 1842–5[310]. J.J. Blockley organist St. Saviour Haverstock Hill 1866, 1867[206, 207].
282. 284.

BLOW, John.
No City organ posts found. Held office at St. Paul's.
Few refs. to him in City parish records but 1686 Sep.30 "passed judgement" on the organ at St. Katherine Cree and assessed organ candidates.
St. Paul's Cathedral almoner 1687 Oct.3 – 1693 resigned[103].
B. G. 360 etc.

BOBBETT, Alfred c. 1819 – c.1865?
All Hallows London Wall 1837 Apr.13 – 1844 Aug.8 dismissed.
St. Stephen Coleman Street 1844 June 20 – 1865 (before May) vacated.
U 48.1834 (age 15), 59.1840, *12.1842*, *59.1843*.
Blind[48V]. Of 1 Meredith St., Clerkenwell 1840[59V], 33 Whiskin St., Clerkenwell 1843 – 1844[59V, 74V].

BOND, F. H.
U 48.1805 (withdrew).

BONSOR, Mrs. Maria.
U 31.1833.

BONWICK, Miss Sarah, d.1819.
St. Bartholomew by the Exchange 1784 Mar.25 – 1819 Aug.10 died.
U 4.1784 (runner-up).
B. has "Sophia", words & music by Miss Bonwick 14 years of age c.1790 [sic]. The same? (or Sophia q.v.) Bonwick, Miss, soprano, organist, Old Jewry 1794[198]. 1819 Aug. 10 died Miss Bonwick in Spital Square, 35 years organist to the parish of St. Bartholomew by the Exchange[232].
B.

BONWICK, Miss Sophia.
U 66.1792 (runner-up).

BOUGHEY, Miss Mary Jane.
U 15.1847, 3.1849 (Mary Ann Boughey), 31.1849.
Deputy before appointment to St. George Botolph Lane in 1861[36V]. Also cand. St. Mary Woolnoth 1851 when address 22 Fish St.[57V].

BOULT, Miss Louisa Augusta.
U 58.1830 (no christian name), *12.1842*.
A canvassing card for the 1830 election reveals that she was a pupil of George Cooper (d.1843), "some years in musical profession" & of 19 Henrietta St., Covent Garden[267].

BOULTON, Miss
U 20.1836.

BOWER, Samuel.
All Hallows Barking by the Tower 1767 Sep. 23 – 1770 Sep. 14 resigned. Both & intervening entries read Bowyer.
U 18.1766.
Undated printed trade card for "Samuel Bower [sic] organist of All Hallows . . . at Mr. Millington's no. 90 Upper Thames St. or at Mr. West's on the Green, Deptford"[268].

BOWLES, Miss Eliza.
U *63.1844*, *74.1844*.
Of 109 Upper Thames Street 1844[63V, 74V].

BOWMAN,
U 33.1713/14.
?Henry or John in G.
B? G?

BOWYER, Samuel *see* Bower, Samuel.

BOYCE, William, 1711–1779.
St. Michael Cornhill 1736 June 2 – 1768 Apr.7 resigned (enforced).
All Hallows the Great 1749 Jul. 28 – 1764 Mar.21 dismissed. Sal. reduced from £30 to £20 1758 Jan.5 when instructed "to change Mr. Bullbrick his deputy".
U 60.1734 (runner-up).
Bap. 1711 Sep.11, St. James Garlickhythe, son of John & Elizabeth Boyce[371]. Mar. 1759 June 9 at St. Dunstan Stepney William Boyce of St. Andrew Holborn gent. and Hannah Nixon of this parish, spinster[183].
B. G. 346. 348. 349. 350. 354. 355. 359. 361. 371. 450. 456.

BOYCE, William, jun. 1764–1823.
St. Matthew Friday Street 1802 Mar.11 – 1812 Oct.21 resigned when Chapman the parish clerk reported to the vestry

that last Sunday afternoon "Mr. Boyce came to him in the Vestry and after giving him the Receipt for his Salary to Michaelmas said to him 'Give my compliments to the Churchwardens and tell them, I am much offended at the Message that was sent me and I give up my Place from this day. There are three weeks since Michaelmas and the Churchwardens may make an allowance if they please for that time' ". Resignation accepted but previous Vs give no indication of what it was all about.

Son of Dr. William Boyce (above) and Hannah (née Nixon) b.1764 Mar.25 bap. Hammersmith Apr.25[182]. Adm. Magdalen College Oxford 1780 Jan.27[295]. Elected Roy. Soc. of Musicians 1792 May on recommendation of John Ashley. Then married but childless, a double-bass player and employed at Haymarket and Covent Garden theatres, Ranelagh and private concerts[182]. No mention in RSM records that he was an organist but Charles Wesley jun. in his notebook wrote "1803 Nov.1: I heard from Mr. Boyce, son of the late worthy Doctor intendg. to become a candidate for ye Vacant Org: at Canterbury . . ."[373]. Living Hungerford Market 1794[198]. Died 1823[181].

G(5.). 284. 372. 373.

BOYER, John, 1823–1902.

Christ Church Newgate Street 1850 Apr.30 – 1866 Apr.5 resigned. No evidence to support Pearce's assertion[323] that "Boyer" organist St. Andrew Holborn up to 1867 (see under St. Andrew Holborn).

U 59.1843 (in top 6 of 43 candidates), 74.1844 (failed to attend audition).

Of Coopers' Hall, Basinghall St. 1843[59V], 93 Newgate St. 1844[74V]. Son of James Boyer (1783–1863) grocer & tea dealer of 93 Newgate St. and clerk to the Coopers' Company 1840–63. John Boyer admitted City of London School 1837[158]. Free of Coopers' Company by patrimony 1844 Jan.[116], assistant clerk in 1851[153] succeeding father as clerk 1863 June. City Press refers to resignation from Christ Church of "John Boyer of Coopers' Hall . . . organist for upwards of 20 years [sic]" and to "the exceptionally able manner in which he discharged his musical duties"[214]. Died 1902 Mar.7 at 29 Highbury Hill age 79[218].

BRACEY, John.

U 59.1840.

Of 11 Maritime Houses, Bow Common 1840[59V].

BRADFIELD, Miss (?) Octavia.

U 4.1837 (runner-up).

BRADFIELD, Miss Sarah Alder.

St. Stephen Coleman Street 1827 Nov.1 – 1844 Apr.19 resigned through ill health. In a letter from London Wall refers to her "severe affliction". Granted pension of £20 p.a. for life.

BRADLEY, William. There are at least two organists of this name who overlap in time. The allocations of candidatures and appointments that follow are the most probable.

BRADLEY, William, c.1783–1819.

St. Bartholomew the Great 1805 Jul.10 – 1819 Sep.3 death reported.

U 48.1805.

William Bradley from Howards Green, City Road age 36 bur. 1819 Sep.8 St. Bartholomew the Great.

BRADLEY, William, 1799–1828?

St. Clement Eastcheap 1819 betw. June & Aug. – 1828 Sep.26 last payment (christian name not given. But Hackett papers give William Bradley appointed 1819 Aug.[166].

U 58.1818 (runner-up), 38.1819, 61.1819 (withdrew), 16.1821, *75.1825*, 45.1826 (in top 4 out of 29).

Born 1799 Mar.20[342]. St. Paul's choir school 1808–15[342]. Bradley, Wm., music teacher, 2 Bell's Yard, Doctors Commons 1823–9[199]. The same?

BRATHETT or BRASHETT, Ezekiel.

St. Martin Ludgate. Sexton of St. Martin Ludgate (evidence of register). Living with wife Anne & children in parish of

St. Martin Ludgate 1695[179]. Annually contested Henry Symonds at St. Martin 1706 – 1721, but almost certainly only as candidate of convenience.

BREWSTER, Henry. c.1748 – 1788.
St. Benet Fink 1765 Aug.22 – 1788 Dec.17 death reported.

Born c.1748[182]. Mar. Elizabeth Glandfield 1785 Mar.2 St. Marylebone (both of that parish). Organist & harpsichord player at Coleman's Theatre[182]. Elected Roy. Soc. of Musicians 1781 on recommendation of Caspar Flack 1780 Aug.6. Petitioned Society for relief on becoming dangerously ill 1788 Oct.5[183] but died before end of year. A Henry Brewster composed set of lessons for the harpsichord or pfte. 1785, Vauxhall & grotto songs 1771. Also author of *Concise method of playing thorough-bass* 1797. The same?
B. 284.

BRIDE, Richard.
U 20.1777.

Possibly Richard Bride music seller & publisher at the Black Lyon in Exeter Change c.1765–75, composer & publisher of songs[310]. His name appears on a flute.
B.

BRIDE, William.
St. Mildred Poultry deputy before 1790 – 1792 Nov.12. Sometimes entered as John Bride.
U 66.1792. 40.1793.

BRIDGE, Mrs. Elizabeth Stirling *see* Stirling, Miss Elizabeth, later Mrs. Bridge.

BRIND, Richard, d.1718.
St. Paul's Cathedral 1707/8 Mar.4 – 1718 Mar. died[104].

Bur. recorded in St. Gregory register 1717/18 Mar. 18: Richard Brind organist in St. Paul's vault. Admon 1718 Apr. "of St. Gregory"[139].
B. G. 284.

BRINE, Albertus *see* Bryne, Albertus.

BROOKES, James.
St. Giles Cripplegate. Sexton James Brookes chosen either to play himself or provide organist 1672/3 Feb.28. Gone by Oct.1673? (see also Baddeley's *St. Giles Cripplegate*[276]).

BROWN, Miss
U 20.1836.

BROWN, Miss Harriet, later Mrs. Oxlee.
Holy Trinity Minories 1840 Mar.20 (or just before) – 1846 Mar.19 resigned. "Mr. Brown stated that he was instructed by his daughter Mrs. Oxlee to resign". Became Mrs. Oxlee between 1844 Apr.9 and 1845 Mar.17.

BROWN, Richard.
U *74.1844*.

Of 5 Borough Rd., Southwark 1844[74V].

BROWN, Thomas.
St. Margaret Pattens 1771 May 24 – 1777 Mar.? vacated.
U 53.1775.

Son of Thomas Brown of St. Gabriel Fenchurch d.1788, parish clerk St. Margaret Pattens 1781–88 for which post he was candidate 20 years earlier[130]. Elizabeth Brown sextoness 1787 – 1813 died. Thomas Brown organist published collection of songs and a cantata for the harpsichord or pfte. 1774.
B. 284.

BROWN, William Bicknell.
U *74.1844*, *63.1844*.

Of 18 Little Knight Rider St.[63V 74V].

BROWNE, Richard, d.1710.
St. Lawrence Jewry 1685 Dec. – 1710 May died. First ref. in V. 1685/6 Mar. 16 "Mr Browne shall continue at St. Lawrence Jewry". Death reported 1710 May 24.
Christ Church Newgate Street (possibly) 1687/8 Mar. – 1697? vacated. This appointment very uncertain, see Christ Church Newgate Street.
Christ's Hospital music master 1687/8 Mar.13 – 1697 Jul.27 dismissed. Name submitted as successor to John Curtis 1687 Dec.14. Admonished for treatment of children 1689 Jul.4. Dismissed for negligence 1697 Jul.27. His subsequent application for post 1697 Sep.28

disallowed.

Organist of Lambeth 1701–10. Living parish of St. Andrew Holborn when married to Temperence Guy of Wimborne, Dorset at Gray's Inn Chapel 1705/6 Mar.14. Bur. Lambeth 1710 May 21.

B. G. 382.

BROWNE, Robert.

U *74.1844*.

Of 204 Blackfriars Rd. 1844[74V].

BRUIN, George.

U 37.1785.

BRYAN, Albertus *see* Bryne, Albertus.

BRYAN, Joseph.

U 2.1756.

Elected organist Asylum of House of Refuge Westminster 1769 Mar.2[L227]. Composer of songs, works for violin, flute, harpsichord c.1756–70. Elected Roy. Soc. of Musicians 1768, withdrew subscription[181].

B.

BRYNE, BRYAN or BRIAN, Albertus (1)

St. Paul's Cathedral 1638 – c.1671? died. Probably still nominal organist after Cathedral's destruction by fire in 1666.

Date of death defies investigation. Barry Cooper says "probably 1670"[374], Pridden Colln. asserts "died 1668 Dec. 2 buried 2 days afterwards"[103]. But a book of Augmentations & salaries 1669–70 in St. Paul's clearly shows Albertus Bryne signing for monies received 1670/1 Jan.14[96]. Disconcertingly there is a nuncupated will of Albertus Brine of Battersea "as he declared it to be underwritten 1668/9 Jan.1" proved 1669 Jul.6[139]. The three children of this Albertus were Albertus (under 21), Elizabeth & Mary (under 17) and the executrix his mother Myldman Buggs [sic]. Further confusion arises from the St. Paul's Vicars Choral void places account[105]: "One other void place by the death of Mr. Brine for 7 years salary due at Michaelmas 1678 the time before paid to his son Albert Brine for his schooling £67.19.7¼". Isaac Blackwell appointed St. Paul's 1686/7 Feb. 1 "vice Albert Bryne deceased"[103].

G. 284. 374.

BRYNE, BRYAN or BRIAN, Albertus (2), d.1713.

All Hallows Barking by the Tower 1676 c. Mar. – 1713 Aug. 21 death reported.

Probably son of Albertus Bryne (1) q.v. Organist of Dulwich College of this name: Archbishop recommended "a young man Albertus Bryan both for his sobriety of Life and good Proficiency in Musick and skill upon ye Organ" 1671 Nov.26. Admitted 1671/2 Jan.10[340] and served until 1677. Mar. St. Marylebone 1676/7 Feb. 8 Albertus Bryan to Sarah Hillyard.

G. 284.

BUCKLAND,

U 12.1842 (failed to supply testimonial).

BUCKLAND, Charles Henry.

St. Michael Bassishaw (temporary Wednesday evenings) 1843 Jan.5.

U 59.1843 (in top 6 of 43), 74.1844 (failed to attend).

Of 12 Bermondsey New Rd. 1843–4[59V 74V].

BUCKLAND, George.

U *63.1844*.

St. Paul's Choir School[342]. Organist St. Michael Queenhithe in 1867[210].

BUCKLAND, Thomas George.

St. Michael Bassishaw 1840 Jan. 31 – 1843 Jan.5 resignation accepted after letter of 1842 Dec.24 stating that health required him to live out of London.

Of Union Rd., Albany Rd. 1840[59V].

BULL, Miss Eliza.

U *74.1844*.

Of 15 Ely Place, Holborn 1844[74V].

BULLBRICK,

All Hallows the Great deputy to William Boyce c.1755 – 1764 Mar.21: not allowed to apply for post when Boyce dismissed. Boyce instructed "to change Mr. Bullbrick his deputy" 1758 Jan.5.

G. Bullbrick playing Drury Lane 1751–57[314]. The same?

BULLOCK, Miss Elizabeth.
U 34.1797.

BURBRIDGE,
U 60.1781.
Burbridge,——, organist St. George Borough, Bagnigge Wells 1794[198]. Burbidge [sic], R. composer of songs, piano works c.1795 – 1800.
B.

BURGESS,
U 53.1730.
New grand concerto for organ by Henry Burgess, composer & organist 1741 June 16 at Cuper's Gardens[399]. Henry Burgess, sen. & jun. original members Roy. Soc. of Musicians 1739[181]. B. has a Henry Burgess, composer of songs c.1720–45 and Henry the younger organ works c.1740–80. Henry Burgess musician in ordinary to King, will P.C.C. 1765 Mar.19[139].
B.

BURNEY, Charles
St. Dionis Backchurch 1749 Oct.26 – 1752 Jan.23 resigned.
The definitive biographies by P.A. Scholes and R.H. Lonsdale could scarcely be fuller or better and there is little to add. The accepted date of 1773 for his appointment to Oxford Chapel is wrong and should be 1768 May [L481]. One of the few City organists to be free of the City and Musicians' Company 1749 Jul.3[128, 129] probably because his wife Esther Sleep (mar.1749 June 25) had become a freeman by patrimony (i.e. because she was a daughter of a freeman) 1747 Aug.7. Esther the dau. of Richard Sleep, City wait, and Frances, bap. St. Vedast Foster Lane 1725 Aug.1 as Hesther unless she was the Esther tantalisingly entered in the bap. reg. of 1723 "Esther dau. of Mr. Sleepe by . . . his wife born 19 May bap. 9 June". The possibility that the first Esther died as a baby is lessened by the fact that her burial is not entered. (See also p.12).
B. G. 313. 326. 451.

BURNEY, Charles Rousseau.
U 74.1775 (runner-up), 81.1767.
Elected Roy. Soc. of Musicians 1769[181].
B. G.

BURNHAM, Miss Ann.
U *75.1825*, 64.1828.

BURROWES, John T.
St. Mary at Hill 1847 Dec. 2 – 1852 June 7 resigned on succeeding late father as organist St. James Westminster.
Son of John Freckleton Burrowes 1787 – 1852. Of 13 Nottingham Place, New Rd. 1847–52[53V].

BUSBY, Thomas, 1754–1838.
St. Mary Woolnoth 1798 Mar. 15 – 1829 May 5 dismissed after postponement of election Apr.1.
U 74.1775, 25.1799 (no christian name).
Born 1754 Dec.26 bap. 1755 Jan.21 St. Margaret Westminster. Son of Thomas & Ann Busby. Organist St. Mary Newington Butts from 1784 Mar. 23 (ves. min. bk.). Unsuccessfully applied for membership Roy. Soc. of Musicians 1787 when living opp. Fountain Court, Strand[185].
B. G. 284. 344. 381.

BYFIELD, John, organ builder, d.1757.
U? Annually opposed Henry Duncalfe St. Bartholomew by the Exchange 1751–56. Presumably nominal only as he built and repaired organ.
G.

BYFIELD, John, the younger, organ builder.
St. Bartholomew the Less? Proposals accepted 1794 Mar.20 that organ be erected by John Byfield the younger age 28 son of John Byfield of Constitution Row, Grays Inn Rd., St. Pancras. To play himself or cause to be played and to be paid £20 p.a. during life & life of sister Mary Frances Byfield now age 24. Last recorded payment 1806 c.Sep. Evidence suggests played himself 1796 – 1800 and in 1806.
U 48.1786 (nil votes out of 91).
G. 396.

CADMAN, John.
U 48.1782.

CAPPAR, James.
U 10.1736 (no christian name). Mr. Capper [sic] in Gen. Ev. Post[229], 3.1737/8.

CAREY, John.
U 20.1740 (no christian name), 40.1744/5 (do.), 22.1747.
Perhaps John Cary elected Roy. Soc. of Musicians 1748[181].

CARREY (sic), Miss.
U 12.1842 (one of 4 selected from about 50 applicants).

CARTER,
U 40.1744/5.
Possibly Richard Carter of St. Giles, London, master of music to whom William Payne was apprenticed £31.10.0 in 1755[149]. B. has 6 sonatas by Richard Carter c.1760. A Richard Carter an original member of the Roy. Soc. of Musicians 1739[181].
B? G?

CARTER, Mrs. Elizabeth *see* Holland, Miss Elizabeth, later Mrs. Carter.

CARTER, John.
U 76.1847 (top 8 out of 57 applicants).

CARY, John *see* Carey, John.

CASH,
U 58.1830.
Blind[58V].

CASH, Andrew.
St. Antholin Budge Row 1821 Sep.12 – 1870 Apr. 21 not re-elected: no money available. Church demolished 1875.
U 44.1821, 26.1822 (runner-up), 44.1823.
Of Globe St., Wapping (same as Joshua Cash) 1822[26V], 17 Union St., Kennington Causeway 1867[210].

CASH, John.
St. Matthew Friday Street (unan. elect.) 1812 Nov.3 – 1815 Mar.22 resigned.
St. Katherine Cree 1815 Mar.28 – 1865 pensioned.
U 6.1811, 3.1812 (runner-up), 17.1812, 58.1835 (disallowed as holder of another post).

CASH, Joshua.
St. Botolph Aldgate 1818 Feb.27 – 1822 Sep.19 death reported.
Of Globe St., St. George's 1818[26V].

CASH, Thomas.
St. Michael Queenhithe 1824 Nov.18 – 1837 Mar.1 resigned. Decision to give him 6 months notice 1831 Apr.5 not proceeded with.

CASSON, John.
U 75.1765 (no christian name), 22.1765.
B. has piano & harpsichord works by John Casson c.1790–4.
B. 284.

CASTELL, William Joseph, b.1789.
St. Katherine Cree deputy c.1814[182].
U *75.1825*.
Born 1789 bap. St. Mary Kilkenny (Eire) May 27. Son of Peter & Sophia Castelli [sic]. Mar. Susanna Elizabeth Mary —— before 1812. Pfte., violin, viola & double bass player. Chorus master Surrey Theatre. Deputy organist St. Mary Lambeth & St. Katherine Cree when elected Roy. Soc. of Musicians .814 on recommendation of George Veale[182]. Son William Jones Castell (born 1812 Apr.18) principal double bass Adelphi & Haymarket Theatres when elected to Roy. Soc. of Musicians in 1834[182].

CHAPMAN, Miss Grace.
St. Bartholomew by the Exchange 1819 Nov.3 – 1841 church demolished. Transferred to St. Margaret Lothbury, the parish to which St. Bartholomew united for weekday services:-
St. Margaret Lothbury (weekdays) 1842 – 1847 Apr. last payment. During her employment became totally blind.

CHELSUM, James.
No City posts or candidatures found.
St. Paul's Choir School[342]. Vicar choral St. Paul's 1737 Mar.15[97].

CHERITON, David.
No City posts or candidatures found.
Vicar choral St. Paul's 1744 Nov.8[98]. Gentleman of Chapel Royal. Organist Dulwich College 1727–31[340].

CHICHELEY, Henry Richard, d.1805.
St. Lawrence Jewry 1788 June 26 – 1805 Apr.18 death reported.
U 1.1758 (—— Chickley), 31.1784 (withdrew), 25.1786 (Henry Chitterly).
Henry son of Richard Chicheley apprenticed to Joseph How, organist, of Precincts, Rochester Cathedral £94.10.0 in 1755[149]. Bur. St. Lawrence Jewry 1805 Apr. 13 "organist of this church".

CHICKLEY, *see* Chicheley, Henry Richard.

CHILD,
U *12.1842* (disallowed).

CHILD, Daniel C.
U *59.1843*, *74.1844*.
Of 10 Chester Place, Old Kent Rd. 1843–4[59V 74V].

CHILD, T.
U *63.1844*.
Of Old Kent Rd. 1844[63V].

CHIPP, Edmund Thomas, b.1823.
No City appointments before 1852.
U 59.1843 (runner-up), 76.1843 (top 3 out of 39)), *63.1844*, 25.1847 (runner-up out of 63).
Born 1823 Dec.25 bap. 1828 Mar.16. Son of Thomas Paul Chipp, professor of music, & Sarah Clara of St. James's. Successor of H.J. Gauntlett as organist St. Olave Southwark 1847 resigning 1852 on appointment at last in the City to St. Mary at Hill[53aV]. Teacher of violin & pfte. Violinist in Queen's Band. Elected Roy. Soc. of Musicians 1848 Feb.6[182]. Of 109 Albany St. Regents Park 1843–4[59V 76V 63V]. 49 Great Portland Street, Portland Place 1847[182]. Died 1886[181].
G(5).

CHITTERLEY, Henry *see* Chicheley, Henry.

CHITTY, George H.
U *12.1842 (—— Chitly)*, *59.1843*.
Of 13 Mill Place, Limehouse 1843[59V].

CHRISTY, Miss Mary, later Mrs. Mary Edmonds.
St. Botolph Aldgate 1790 Oct.6? – 1805 c.Oct. vacated after not playing Sep. – Oct. She appears to have become Mrs. Edmonds late 1791 or early 1792 but marriage not found. Mar. Alexander Edmonds, q.v. who substituted for her St. Botolph Aldgate 1805?
U 34.1790 (runner-up).

CLAPTON,
U 22.1789.

CLARE, Edward, d.1869.
U 45.1841 (runner-up).
Organist & author who died London 1869 Apr.9. Issued *Analysis of practical thorough-bass* (1835) etc. Composed ballads etc. The same? An Edward Clare organist Norwich 1837[256]. Report of proceedings of Professor Clare's candidature for the music professorship of Gresham College [1864?] (BL copy missing).
284.

CLARK,
U 12.1842 (failed to supply testimonial).

CLARK, Miss.
U 53.1826.

CLARK(E), Edward, d.1789.
No City posts or candidatures found.
Edward Clarke son of John Clarke of St. Andrew Holborn apprenticed to John Travers 1745 for £73.10.0[149]. Succeeded John Travers St. Paul Covent Garden on his death 1758 June 21[L594]. Elected Roy. Soc. of Musicians 1775[181]. Died 1789 Jul.27[232].
B.

CLARK, Jeremiah.
St. Paul's Cathedral 1699 June 6 – 1707 Dec.1? died.
St. Paul's Cathedral almoner 1693 – 1707 Dec.1? died.
B.G. etc.

CLAXTON, John.
St. Edmund, King and Martyr 1709 Apr.25 – 1712 Aug.19 vacated.
Deputy before appointment in 1709.
U 48.1706 (no christian name).

CLELAND, George.
U *45.1826*, 20.1827 (no christian name).

Sainsbury (1828) refers to George Cleland late organist St. Mary's Chapel, Queen Sq., Bath, now a teacher of the pfte. in London. "Has published among other music a selection of original chants"[325].
325. 284.

CLEMETSHAW,
U 1.1770.

CLIFTON,
U 25.1799.
Possibly John Clifton 1781 – 1841.
G(5)? 284?

COBB, James.
No City posts found.
U 81.1675 Petition of James Cobb, bachelor, for post of music master, Christ's Hospital, "skilled in playing upon organ only".
Gentleman of the Chapel Royal of this name up to 1679[292].
G.

COLBY, Theodore.
No City posts or candidatures found.
Appointed organist Exeter Cathedral 1665 Mar.25. In April paid £5 towards his charges "in coming from London & ryding upp". Dismissed 1674[316].

COLE, Theophilus, d.1730.
St. Mary at Hill 1720 May 9 – 1730 Apr.20 died. Salary at St. Mary at Hill to be paid to mother 1730 May 7.
Thomas [sic] Cole son of Thomas Cole apprenticed to Dr. J.C. Pepusch £21.10.0 1715[149]. The same? Organist Chelsea Royal Hospital from 1719 Apr.22 and St. Martin in the Fields 1726 until death. "Died under cure for lunacy in the hospital of Bethlem Mr. Cole late organist of St. Martin in the Fields 1730 Apr. 20"[244].

COLLINS, William.
U 3.1737/8.

COOKE, Benjamin (1).
U 60.1736 (no christian name), 48.1740.
Benjamin Cooke of St. Martin in the Fields musician took as apprentice Richard son of John Denson 1736 £25[149]. Probably Benjamin Cooke music seller Golden Harp, New Street, Covent Garden 1726–43[310] which also has John Jones, musical instrument maker, music printer and publisher at the same address c.1716–20. The Golden Harp was insured by the Sun as "the house of the late John Jones at Mr. Arnaudins at the Golden Harp in New St., Covent Garden, St. Martin in the Fields, musical instrument maker". An appended note dated 1723 Jul.2 states that Phillipa Jones relict of John Jones married "Benjamin Cook musician who is now intituled to the interest of this policy & resides in the same house"[194]. His first marriage to Phillipa Jones at Chelsea Hospital 1723, his second, "Benjamino [sic] Cooke of St. Martin in the Fields widower and Eliza Wayet of St. Martin Ludgate, solute" at St. Olave Jewry 1730 Aug.14. Will dated 1742 Dec.15 of St. Martin in the Fields to wife Elizabeth, son Benjamin, dau. Phillipa. Execs. wife and "honoured friend" William Huggins. Witn. G. Barker & James Figg. Proved 1742/3 Feb.17[139].
B. G. 284.

COOKE, Benjamin (2).
U 60.1781 (runner-up to R.J.S. Stevens).
Son of Benjamin (1). Mar. 1758 c.June 24 Mr. Cooke, one of the gentlemen of the Choir and Master of the Singing Boys [at Westminster Abbey] to Miss Jackson of the General Post Office in Lombard St.[L499]. Elected Roy. Soc. of Musicians 1760[181]. Organist of Westminster Abbey 1762–93 etc.
B. G. etc.

COOKE, George Forster, 1779–1849.
U *45.1840*.
Born 1779 Oct.25 bap. St. John Newcastle upon Tyne 1780 May 26. Son of Robert van Cook [sic] & Elisabeth. Mar. Jane —— [182]. Pfte., violin, tenor & flute player "with extensive private teaching & two schools in Hammersmith." Elected Roy. Soc. of Musicians 1807 on recommendation of

John Lord 1806 Dec.7. Died 1849[182].

COOK(E), Thomas Phipson (or Phippen), d.1820.
St. Magnus the Martyr 1795 Aug.24 – 1820 Jul.21 death reported. Widow referred to 1820 Oct.20.

COOPER, Miss.
U 67.1839.
Of Heralds College (Bennet's Hill) in 1839[67V] the address of of George Cooper d.1843 and of George Cooper d.1876 (q.v.)

COOPER, Mrs. Eliza Kingston *see* Probyn, Miss Eliza Kingston, later Mrs. Cooper.

COOPER, George c.1750–1799.
All Hallows Bread Street 1773 Nov.11 – 1799 Sep. Death reported Sep.26.
St. Sepulchre Holborn ("Geo. Cooper, jun.") 1784 Jul.1 – 1799 Sep. Death reported Sep.25.
U 58.1767 (no christian name. The same?), 47.1771.
Bur. under organ loft St. Sepulchre 1799 Sep.25, of Hosea Lane age 49. Cooper, George, music seller, organ, bass etc. 39 Gloucester Place, Islington 1794[198]. The same?

COOPER, George, c.1783–1843.
St. Sepulchre Holborn 1799 Oct. 1 (in succession to George Cooper, d.1799) – 1843 Nov. Death reported Dec.11, "after 45 years service". Succeeded by son. Tribute paid to him by vestry.
St. Paul's Cathedral assistant (up to 1838?).
Son of above. Chorister St. Paul's under Mr. Bellamy[342]. Cooper, George, teacher of music/organ, 12 Bennet's Hill 1832–40[199]. Bur. St. Sepulchre 1843 Dec.1 of Ely Place age 60. As widower perhaps married Miss E.K. Probyn (q.v.) in 1829.
G.284.

COOPER, George, 1820–1876.
St. Benet Paul's Wharf 1833 Dec. 25 (reported 1834 Feb.13) – 1844 Sep.26 successor appointed. Age 13 when elected in 1833.
St. Anne and St. Agnes 1836 Oct.26 – 1844 Jan.12 resigned.
St. Sepulchre Holborn in succession to father 1843 Dec.11 – 1876 Oct.2 died.
St. Paul's Cathedral assistant 1838 Mar. to 1876 Oct.2 died.
Christ's Hospital music master 1844 May 7 – 1876 Oct.2 died.
Son of above. Of Heralds College, Doctors' Commons 1836[167], 25 Ely Place 1840, 1844[199]. Died at residence 14 Heathcote St., Mecklenburg Sq. 1876 Oct.2. Eleanor, his widow d. same address age 44, 1879 Jan. 7[243].
G(5). 282. 284 etc.

COOPER, Joseph Thomas, c.1819–1879.
St. Michael Queenhithe 1837 Mar.8 – 1844 Nov.29 resigned. Variously given as Thomas or J.T. in V. but surely Joseph Thomas [282] [284].
U 58.1835 (J.T. Cooper in top 4 of 28), 20.1836 (no christian name), *15.1836* (J.T. Cooper).
Subsequently 1844 St. Paul, Ball's Pond Rd. and then back to City 1866 Christ Church Newgate Street[243] and Christ's Hospital 1876. Died 1879 Nov.17 at 113 Grosvenor Rd. Highbury age 60[243].
282. 284.

COOPER, Phineas.
U 2.1726/7, 2.1727/8 (one of 12 names submitted by vestry).
Apprenticed to Benjamin Short (q.v.) citizen and master of music £20 1723[149].

COPE, Miss Emily.
U 76.1847 (no christian name, in top 8 out of 57), 15.1847.

COPE, Mrs. Esther Elizabeth *see* Fleet, Miss Esther Elizabeth, later Mrs. Cope.

COPE, Henry.
U 44.1823, 1.1823 (no christian name).

COPE, William.
U 34.1782 & 1790.
Probably W.P.R. Cope, organist St. Saviour Southwark and music & instrument seller[310]. But William Henry Cope, organist Lock Chapel & St. Saviour's Southwark referred to in 1829[159]. B. has 11 works by W.P.R.

Cope c.1790–98 including work in honour of St. Saviour Southwark.
B. 389.

CORPE [sic], i.e. Corfe?
U 27.1815 (runner-up), 39.1838 (withdrew).
Four by name of Corfe (none showing London associations) given by G. and Boase[282].

CORNISH,
U 20.1834 & 1836, 15.1836, 12.1842 (runner-up).

COSIN (or COSYN), Benjamin d.1653.
No City organ posts or candidatures found after 1650.
Organist Dulwich College 1622 Sep.28 – 1624 June 16[341], Charterhouse 1626 Dec.7 – 1643/4 removed (stipend sequestered by Parliament). Sal. £13.6.8[154]. "Benjamin Cossunes or Cosinns, organist" living in St. Botolph precinct of Aldersgate ward with servant Margaret Evans and lodger Sarah Stansmore 1641[148]. Bur. Benjamin Cousins 1653 Sep.14 St. Botolph Aldersgate. The same reg. includes entries for other Cousins or Cozens (e.g. f.148 & 1664 Oct.).
G. 284.

COULDEN,
U 59.1807 (runner-up).

COURTNEY, William, d.1785.
St. Giles Cripplegate 1782 Aug.12 unan. elect. – 1785 June 29 death reported.
U 22.1765, 43.1766, 37.1770.
Elected Roy. Soc. of Musicians 1763: expelled for non-payment[181]. Bur. St. Giles Cripplegate 1785 June 30.

COWTAN, Miss Agatha.
St. Michael Cornhill assistant 10 months 1848 – 1849 Jul.9.
U 15.1847, 3.1849 (no christian name, runner-up), 31.1849.
Of St. Magnus the Martyr London Bridge when candidate St. Mary Woolnoth 1851.

COWTAN, Miss Esther, later Mrs. Henniker.
St. Magnus the Martyr 1841 Jan. 7 – 1861 Apr.18 not unanimously re-elected. When the sextoness Mrs. Mary Cowtan (? her mother) not re-elected because "of age & infirmity", Mrs. Henniker took her place as sextoness. To live with her.
U 59.1840.
Of St. Magnus in 1840[59V]. Mar. licence 1854 Nov.18 for Robert Cowtan [sic] Henniker of St. Magnus, bach. age 21 and Esther Cowtan of St. Magnus spinster age 21 & upwards[177].

COX,
U 44.1762.
Thomas Stokes apprenticed to Hugh Cox of St. Margaret Westminster, musician, £10 in 1754[149]. Sainsbury[325] mentions —— Cox, an organist & composer for his instrument in London c.1780. Hugh Cox died 1763 Dec. 16 one of the Gentlemen of the choir of Westminster Abbey & Chapel Royal [L590]. Hugh Cox one of the Gentlemen of the Chapel Royal, teacher on harpsichord, Bridge St., Westminster 1763[211]. The same? Or John George Cox 3 works in B. c.1730–60?
B.?

CRABB, Thomas.
U 20.1836 (no christian name), 59.1840.
Of 8 Cumberland St., John St., Blackfriars Rd. 1840[59V].

CRANE, Miss.
According to Pearce (quoting Leffler)[323] Miss Crane organist St. Dionis Backchurch in 1800 & possibly as early as 1784. This is incorrect. Sarah Ormes (q.v.) served during this period.

CRATHERN, William. 1793–1861.
St. Magnus the Martyr 1826 Dec. 14 – 1840 Nov.27 resigned in letter dated Nov.19 from 4 Serampore Place, Hammersmith, "appointment offered near my home".
U 37.1818, 38.1819 (runner-up), 61.1819 (runner-up), 53.1826 (withdrew), 25.1826–7 (no christian name).
Born 1793 Feb. 14 bap. St. Leonard Shoreditch Mar. 10. Son of Thomas Anthony & Martha Crathern of Cock

Lane. Pfte. & organ teacher and singing master at several schools[182]. Organ tuner St. Helen Bishopsgate 1820[38V]. Organist St. Paul Deptford in 1826 when elected Roy. Soc. of Musicians[182]. Of 6 Haberdashers Walk Hoxton 1826[195]. Died 1861 Aug. 29 after "severe & lingering illness". Widow Sarah granted assistance by Roy. Soc. of Musicians[182].

CRAWFOOT, John *see* CROFOOT, John.

CREEGER,
U 10.1840.

CRESER, Thomas F.
U 59.1840.
Of 11 Wellington St., Newington Causeway 1840[59V].

CRESWICK, Thomas.
U 58.1830 ("blind", no christian name).
Organist/teacher of music 5 John St., Oxford St. 1837, 1840[256 199].

CRIPPS, Thomas Erard.
U 48.1834, 58.1835 (top 4 out of 28).

CROFOOT, John.
St. Katherine by the Tower deputy 1714 Apr.1 onwards. "Acts as deputy for Mr. Hasletine [i.e. Heseltine q.v.] the organist during his absence [Heseltine also organist Durham Cathedral] allowed of by the Master & to be paid eight pounds per. ann. out of Mr. Hasletine's salary."
U 1.1713 (no christian name), 26.1724 (John Crawfoot).

CROSS,
U 12.1842 (failed to supply testimonials).

CROSS, Charles.
U 3.1780, 27.1784 (runner-up).
Cross, C. *Pastoral anthem* c.1765 in B. Unsuccessfully applied for admission to Roy. Soc. of Musicians 1777 Dec.7 on recommendation of John Jones. Then described as "single, organist to a parish church"[185].
B.

CROSSTHWAITE, Miss Ann.
U *45.1840,12.1842* (no christain name).

CROUCH,
U 76.1809 (withdrew).

CROUCH, William, c.1749 – c.1833.
U 57.1772 (runner-up).
Organist for more than 50 years St. Luke Old Street also organist Clapham. Compiler of psalm tunes as sung at Clapham Church c.1820 and composer of sonatas for pfte. & harpsichord, songs etc. from c.1775. Violinist & viola player & harpsichordist Drury Lane Theatre. Extensive teaching. Age 35 when elected Roy. Soc. of Musicians on recommendation of John Bassett 1784 Apr.4[182]. Mar. second wife Mary Williams, St. Nicholas Deptford 1820 Apr.4[182].
B. G(5). 284.

CROWFOOT, John *see* Crofoot, John.

CRUSE, Edward, d.1879.
U *45.1840*, 74.1844 (failed to attend).
Of 66 Ebury St., Pimlico 1844[74V]. Music teacher 1847 etc.[199]. Self taught organist & composer, author of *Psalms of the church*, 1835. Died 1879 Dec.3.
282. 284.

CULLUM, Henry.
St. Mildred Poultry 1838 c.Aug. – 1840 c.Apr. vacated. No christian name given in church records.
U 15.1836 (runner-up).
Henry Cullum of Chelsea 1837[256].

CUPIT, William.
U 15.1836 (no christian name. In top 4), 59.1843 (top 3 out of 43).
Of 10 Titchbourne St., Edgware Rd. 1843[59V].

CURTIS, John, d.1704.
St. Giles Cripplegate 1676 – 1703/4 Feb. died. Death reported Feb.25.
Christ Church Newgate Street? Proposed by Parish 1682 June 23[156] but organ not installed until 1690. Loss of records obscures possible appointment but *may* have served 1690 until death in 1703/4 Feb.
Christ's Hospital Music master 1675 Dec.17 "John Curtis, bachelor, declaring his skill in playing upon the organ and other instruments of music" petitioned for position of music master.

Elected 1675/6 Feb.4 sal.£20 p.a. Fee granted to provide him with lodgings 1676 Dec.12. Christ's Hospital notified of his appointment to Christ Church 1682 June 23. Negligent in teaching children, new appointment to be made 1684/5 Mar.18. Curtis's petition rejected 1685 Apr.1 followed by discussion as to a fit person to be master Apr.14. Continued to hold position until report of Committee of 1687 June 10 revealed that he was married (post could only be held by bachelor or widower). Mr.[Samuel] Nicholls to be given trial, meanwhile Curtis to stay Jul.15. Name of Richard Browne submitted as successor 1687 Dec.14. Complaint 1687/8 Feb.8. Complaint that "he has frequently used the children with inhumane and barbarous severities": Richard Browne to succeed him 1687/8 Mar. 13. Went off with violins & books and refused to give them to Browne. "Had soe misbehaved himselfe when Mr. Browne now Music Mr. came to receive possession that he utterly refused to give him quiet possession retiring from one roome to another locking himselfe up, till a smith being sent for, broak open all the doores, and out of the last roome he fled and hath not since appeared" 1687/8 Mar.29.

Possibly son of Nathaniel & Mary Curtis of St. Giles Cripplegate[179] and brother of Thomas Curtis "musicioner" of St. Giles Cripplegate who was bur. there 1702/3 Feb.14. John Curtis "organist of this parish – consumption" bur. St. Giles 1703/4 Feb. 19. Will dated 1703/4 Feb.14 proved Feb. 21 everything to George Kidney, John Withers and William Lloyd, joint executors[139].

CURTIS, Thomas, d.1806.
St. Mildred Bread Street 1753 Sep.12 – 1806 May died. Death reported May 21.
U 26.1753, 1.1758 (no christian name), 18.1762, 27.1764, 1.1767, 58.1767 (no christian name), 3.1780, 27.1784.

Son of John, citizen & Weaver and Mary Curtis. Free of Weavers' Company by patrimony 1761 June 1. Apprentices: William Smethergell (q.v.) 1765 Apr.1, John McKerrell (q.v.) 1774 June 20. Lived successively near Hackney Turnpike Bethnal Green, Prescott St., Goodman's Fields, Romford and Stratford Green, Essex (Weavers' Company court minute books etc. Guil. Lib.). Organist of this name St. Mary Whitechapel. Mar. Martha Maynard of Woodford Bridge Essex at St. Matthew Bethnal Green 1760 Nov.20[L493]. *Divine amusement, a selection of psalms and hymns as sung in all the principal churches* by Thomas Curtis. Also *The Jessamine: a collection of six new songs*. B has songs between c.1755 and c.1798. An unidentified Curtis u at Rotherhithe 1765 Dec.17[L594].
B. 284.

CURTIS, William.
U 22.1747, 14.1749 (no christian name).

A Mr. Curtis organist Christ Church Spitalfields until death c. Nov. 1764[L549].

CURZENS, B.
U 25.1826–7.

CUTLER, William Henry. b.1792.
St. Helen Bishopsgate ("Master W.H. Cutler") 1809 May 12 – 1819 Feb.25 resigned.

Son of John & Hannah Cutler born 1792 Jan.14 bap. Feb.5 St. Botolph Bishopsgate. St. Paul's Cathedral School 1803 Jan. – 1807 Dec. – "remarkably fine boy singer"[342].
G(5). 284. 295.

DALE, Henry.
U 60.1810 (runner-up).

DALE, Joseph, c.1750 – 1821.
St. Antholin Budge Row 1777 Feb.28 – 1821 Aug.21 died. Death reported Sep.3.

Importer & publisher of music & manufacturer of musical instruments, 132 Oxford St. (from trade card)[268]. Organist, composer, viola player, Acad. of Anc. Music 1794[198]. Music seller & circulating library, 132 Oxford

St. & Cornhill 1794[198]. Freeman of Merchant Taylors' Company "music seller, Cornhill" 1789 Oct.7, liveryman 1791 Jul.6. (Son Joseph apprenticed to him 1797 Mar.23: "Joseph Dale the younger of Bond Street, music seller" freeman 1804 May 2, liveryman 1804 Jul.11)[123]. Died 1821 Aug.21 age 71. "Long known in musical world as teacher of pfte".[232].
B. G. 284. 310.

DAVIDGE, John, d.1799.
U 1.1758 (no christian name, runner-up), 43.1766, 10.1766 (no christian name), 1.1767 (runner-up), 1.1770 (disqualified as holder of another post).
Organist St. Mary Magdalen Bermondsey 1775 Jan. 19 – 1799 Mar. 26 death reported (ves. min. bk.)

DAVIES, Christopher.
Christ Church Newgate Street 1817 Dec. 16 – 1850 Apr. 30 retired. Increase in sal. turned down 1828 Mar.14, re-elected "pro.tem." at annual elections 1849 Apr.12 & 1850 Apr.4.

DAVIS, Mrs. E.
U 67.1839.
Of 1 Kettesford Place, Hackney 1839[67V].

DAVIS, Edward.
U 1.1758 (—— Daves), 18.1766, 58.1767 (no christian name), 3.1780.
"Mr. Davis chosen St. George the Martyr Southwark" 1766 May 12[L462]. The same?

DAVIS, Henry Christopher
U *74.1844*.
Of 166 Sloane St., Chelsea 1844[74V]. H.C. Davis organist Northfleet 1843[258]. The same?

DAVIS, Henry Edward, d.1860.
St. Edmund, King and Martyr 1797 May 31 ("Master H.E. Davis" polling 79 votes against 4 for 3 other candidates combined) – 1833 end vacated. Paid pension of £5 p.a. until 1859–60 (died).
All Hallows Bread Street 1799 Oct.30 – 1852 June 15 retired. Annual elections give him variously as E.H., H.E., E., Edward or H.Davis. Organist appointed to succeed him in 1852 to have sal. of £60 p.a. during life of Davis and to pay him £25 p.a. until his death.

DAY, Mrs.
U *25.1847*.
Probably identifiable as Ellen Day, pianist, b. London 1828 Mar.3, concert pianist & later organist St. Matthew & Christ Church Westminster[284].
284?

DAY, John.
U 74.1775.
John Day organist St. David's Cathedral 1782–87[339]. John Day composer of sonata for piano or harpsichord c.1789 and songs c.1792 [B]. John Day, composer who flourished around 1800, composer of *Harmonica lyrica* 1820[284]. The same?
B. 284. 339.

DEAN, DEANE or DENE. Owing to inconsistencies in spelling these are grouped together.

DEANE, John Horth, c.1824 – 1881.
U *63.1844*, 68.1845 (for assistant), 25.1847 (no christian name, in top 6 out of 63), 76.1847 (runner-up out of 57), 53.1847, 15.1847 (selected by umpire as greatly superior in all respects to the other candidates but scored no votes in election), 36.1848 (in top 3 out of 18).
Son of Mrs. Deane née Miss Mary Horth (q.v.)? Of 27 Park Street, Islington 1844, 1847[63V 53V]. Died 1881 Apr.20 at Eastbourne age 57, "professor of music, son of the late Henry Deane of Highbury London"[243].

DEAN, Mrs. Mary *see* Horth, Miss Mary, later Mrs. Deane.

DEAN(E), Thomas.
St. Sepulchre Holborn 1705 Mar.27 – 1712 June 12. "Mr. Dean having neglected attendance for ¾ year, place of organist vacant".
B. has various works c.1703–10. Thomas Dean son of William of Notts, cleric b. c. 1687 D.Mus. Oxon 1731, organist Coventry Cathedral 1733–49. The same?
B. G. 284. 295. 339(?)

DEAN, William Philip.
U 4.1825 (Dene, no christian name), *45.1826*.

DENT, Miss Mary.
U 59.1840.
Of 9 Montpelier Rd., Twickenham 1840[59V].

DEPUIS, Charles *see* Dupuis, Charles.

DERAUX, Alfred.
U *45.1840*.

DERMER, T. L.
U *59.1843*.
Of Shad Thames, Southwark 1843[59V].

DEVOY, Thomas.
U 18.1784.

DIGARD, David, d.1745.
St. Martin Ludgate 1740 Apr.25 – 1745 Feb.6 died. Death reported Apr.10.
U 2.1727/8 (no christian name, one of 12 names submitted by vestry).
Son of Charles Digard of St. Bride Fleet St., engraver. Apprenticed to Maurice Greene of St. Clement Danes, organist £20, 1730[149]. Composer of songs [B]. Died 1745 Feb. 6, "organist of Oxford Chapel, St. Martin Ludgate & St. Anne Limehouse"[232].
B.

DOERY(?) or DURY, Miss.
U 4.1825 (Miss Doery).
Dury, Antonia J., music teacher 24 Great Pulteney St. 1823–4[199]. The same?

DOLLER, Henry Lightin *see* Lightin-dollar, Henry.

DOLMAN,
U 2.1727/8 (one of 12 names submitted by vestry).

DONE,
U 51.1826 ("Master Donne"), 25.1827, 58.1830,

DONE, Henry John.
U 53.1826, *45.1826*, 61.1826.

DONE, Joshua.
U *45.1826* (Joshua Don jun.), 77.1828 (Joshua Done jun.), *63.1844* (J. Done).
Of 29 Brook St., Holborn 1828[77V], Tottenham Court Rd. 1844[63V]. Done, Joshua, jun., piano teacher, 5 Staple Inn Bldngs. 1832–4[199]. Done, Joshua, prof. of music, 1 Wellington St., Pentonville, pupil of Cherubini, 1837[256]. Author of many works on organ, pfte. etc. Joshua Done organist St. John Lambeth, Chelsea Old Church etc. d.1848 Nov. 2 in extreme poverty at King's Lynn[284]. The same? Or were there two of same name? Also Joshua Done pianoforte maker, 30 Chancery Lane, 1794[198].
284.

DORRELL, Miss Mary.
St. Martin Ludgate 1786 May 18 – 1792 Feb.28 death reported.

DOUGLAS, Miss Clarissa.
St. Michael Queenhithe 1844 Dec.19 (from 35 applicants) – 1858 Oct. 14 resigned.
U *12.1842* (Miss Douglass), *59.1843* (Miss C. Duglas), 76.1843, 74.1844 (in top 6 of 60 but withdrew), 4.1844 (Miss Duglas).
Of 6 Mount Row, New Kent Rd. 1843–4[59V 74V], 11 Bermondsey Sq. 1844[63V].

DOWDING, Miss Emily.
Temple Church appointed by Middle Temple 1796 – 1814 dismissed for appointing deputy & not personally attending.
Herself a foundling, runner-up at election of organist for Foundling Hospital 1798 May. Organist Magdalen Hospital 1798 – 1841. The statement that she was probably first woman organist in England not correct. At least a dozen earlier ones in City alone.
G(5).

DOWLING, Miss.
U 25.1827, 20.1827.
An Ann Dowling teacher of harp & piano 5 Stonefield Terrace 1832–4[199].

DUNCALF, Henry, d.1762.
St. Mary at Hill 1730 June 24 – 1762 June 10 died. £10 widow's petition granted June 18.
St. Bartholomew by the Exchange 1732

June 21 – 1762 June 10 died. Petition of widow Sarah, as husband died in "very low circumstances" not upheld June 18.
U 57.1727, 2.1727/8 (one of 12 names submitted by vestry), 14.1749 (no christian name, runner-up).

Friend of Abiell Whichello (q.v.) who bequeathed his music to him on his death in 1747. Composer of songs c.1758. Native of St. Bartholomew by the Exchange parish 1732[18V]. Original member Roy. Soc. of Musicians 1739[181]. Contributed psalm tunes to Riley's *Parochial music corrected* 1762[273]. Died 1762 June 10 "organist of St. Bartholomew by the Exchange"[L558]. Bur. St. Bartholomew June 14. Will[141] "of St. Mary at Hill, organist", everything to wife Sarah. Witn. J. Williamson, John Badger.
B.

DUNCOMBE, William, c.1738 – 1819.
St. Dunstan in the West 1764 Dec.24 – 1819 Jan.? died. Death reported Feb.5. Letter to vestry, 76 years old, 49 years at St. Dunstan, state of embarrassment, gratuity of £20 given 1814 May 26.
St. Vedast Foster Lane. Undertook to supply organ for annuity 1773 and to play himself or find substitute. Probably playing 1774 c.Jan. onwards. By 1779 Thomas Jones (q.v.) & later Catherine Jones (q.v.) substituted. W.D. & Miss Jones summoned to meeting of St. Vedast committee 1794 May 26 "much dissatisfied with way organ has been played for a long time. Unless it improves annuity will be discontinued". "Annuity to end Lady Day next" 1807 Jan.21.

Sainsbury[325] includes his name as English composer, published harpsichord lessons c.1770. Also organist Kensington 1794[198]. Living Kensington between 1794[198] and 1815[183]. Elected Roy. Soc. of Musicians 1775 and petitioned the Society for relief 1815 June 3: "borne down with age & infirmities – almost destitute"[183].
B. 325.

DUPUIS, Charles.
U 15.1804 (withdrew).

Son of Thomas Saunders Dupuis, organist, who had no City appointments. Of 4 Park Lane 1794[198].

DURY, Miss *see* Doery, Miss.

EAGLES, *see* Eccles.

ECCLES, jun.
St. Bride Fleet Street 1692/3 Feb. 10 (Organist or candidate?). Mr. Eagles, jun., one of 3 candidates. Either he, Frances Forcer or Philip Hart, jun. organist for 3 years following unrecorded election after 1693 May 11.

Could be one of the 3 sons of Solomon Eccles (or Eagles) in G. viz. John, Henry or Thomas (none described as organist). Significantly however a Henry Eagles with "Ellinor wife & John son" living in parish of St. Bride in 1695[179]. Was this Henry Eagles of St. Martin in the Fields age c.22 bach. who married Elinor Pinings of St. Martin in the Fields age 30 at Chapel of Knightsbridge 1667/8 Mar.23[173]? The age of this Henry precludes possibility of his being son of Solomon. Perhaps "Mr. Eagles, jun." was John, son of Henry & Elinor Eagles.
B? G? 284?

EDMONDS, Alexander, d.1812.
All Hallows Lombard Street 1780 June 2 – 1812 Feb.6 death reported.
St. Botolph Aldgate substitute 1805 Sep. – Oct.
U 4.1784 (withdrew), 27.1784, 31.1784, 25.1786, 44.1788, 22.1789 (no christian name), 34.1790, 14.1790 (withdrew), 45.1795, 27.1805.

EDMONDS, Miss Mary.
U *12.1842* (no christian name), *59.1843*, 15.1844.

Daughter of Alexander, q.v. & Mrs. Mary Edmonds née Christy q.v.? Of 16 Great Guildford St., Southwark 1843[59V].

EDMONDS, Mrs. Mary *see* Christy, Miss Mary, later Mrs. Edmonds.

EGERTON, Medicus.
U *59.1843*.

Of 15 Pilgrim St., Vauxhall 1843[59V].

ELDERTON, Miss.
U 47.1805.

ELISHA,
U 4.1825.

ELSDEN, Miss Eliza.
All Hallows the Great 1833 Apr.10 (asked for vacant post in letter dated Feb.27 from 18 Bush Lane) – 1868 Apr.17 services not required after June 24 next.
18 Bush Lane address of John Elsden, bricklayer. Eliza Elsden blind.

EMMETT, John George.
St. Michael Crooked Lane 1826 Feb.8 – 1830 Mar.8 on appointment to Bermondsey New Church.
U 75.1825 (runner-up), 77.1828.
Of 2 Elizabeth St., Pimlico 1828[77V].

ENGLAND, Mrs. Ann, c.1766 – 1823.
St. Martin Outwich. Described as organist (succeeding G.P. England, q.v.) 1815–23[49C] but as inheritor of G.P. England's annuity probably supplied an unnamed substitute.
Wife of George Pike England, q.v. Bur. St. Andrew Holborn 1823 Mar.5 "from St. Luke Chelsea age 57".
394. 395.

ENGLAND, George Pike, c.1768 – 1815.
St. Martin Outwich. After building organ on annuity basis described as organist 1805–14[49C]. Probably supplied a substitute.
An unchecked trade card is said to assert that he was the "son and successor to John England", organ builder. Bur. St. Andrew Holborn 1815 Feb. 25 "from St. Pancras age 47".
G. 394. 395.

ENGLAND, Miss Jane Ann, later Mrs. Nicholls.
St. Martin Outwich. Mrs. Nicholls described as organist (succeeding Mrs. Ann England, q.v.) 1823 – 1866?[49C] but as inheritor of G.P. England's annuity probably supplied an unnamed substitute.
Daughter of George Pike and Ann England. Mar. William Alfred Nicholls "of St. Martin Outwich" (allegedly G.P. England's foreman) 1812 Aug. 6 St. Martin Outwich.
394. 395.

ENGLAND, Miss Marian, c.1798 – 1819.
St. Martin Outwich. Possibly for a few years before her death 1819 Nov. as substitute for mother Ann England, q.v.
U 18.1819 (runner-up).
Probably daughter of George Pike and Ann England. Bur. St. Andrew Holborn 1819 Dec. 4 "from St. Ann Westminster age 21".
394. 395.

ESSEX, W.H.
St. Botolph Aldersgate substitute. "Mr. Essex jun." or "Mr. W.(?) Essex" substitute for John Monroe during illness 1846.
U 25.1847 (absent from audition through injury), 15.1847.
Appointed to St. Mary Woolnoth 1864[243].

ETHER [sic] Miss *see* Heather, Miss Elizabeth.

EUSTONE, Edward.
No City posts or candidatures found.
Living next door to Mr. Masters on Tower Hill, went to America as organist 1714[391].

EVANCE, James, d.1811.
All Hallows the Great 1764 Apr.6 – 1811 Nov. died. Death reported 1811 Dec. 11.
St. Andrew Holborn 1786 c.June – 1811 Nov. died.
U 75.1765 (—— Evane), 60.1768 (runner-up).
Chorister St. Paul's[342]. Pupil of John Stanley (report of All Hallows election 1764 Apr.)[L343]. Of Kirby St. Hatton Garden[L343]. "Tolerable singer, tenor voice"[342]. Elected Roy. Soc. of Musicians 1765, expelled for non-payment[181]. Burial register St. James Clerkenwell contains entry "1811 Nov. 30 Mr. Evance Clerkenwell Green carried away" (i.e. for burial elsewhere). Will dated 1787 Feb.28 of parish "of either St. James Clerkenwell or St. Andrew Holborn" left £3000 to

mother Mrs. Catherine Evance. Bros. John & William. Sister Sarah £800 and all non-musical books. Brother Richard (q.v.) £150 and all music books, violins. Ruckers harpsichord to Mrs. Ann Arlond. Long list of beneficiaries. Mother and sister Sarah executrixes. Proved 1812 Jan. & Nov. (£5000 null & void)[139].

Evance, Richard.
All Hallows the Great 1811 Dec. 30 (on death of James Evance) – 1817 May 27 resigned.
U 31.1784 (withdrew because of single post clause).
Brother of James, above.

Evans, Peter.
U 48.1782.
Peter Evans organist St. Giles in the Fields 1783 – 1810.

Evans, Richard Tempest.
U 59.1840, 74.1844 (failed to attend audition).
Of 1 Brandon St., Walworth 1840–44[59V] [74V].

Evans, Rowland, d.1739 or 40.
St. Bartholomew the Great 1731 Dec.14 – 1739/40 Jan.13 death reported.
Admon. of Rowland Evans late of parish of St. Giles in the Fields, bachelor, to Samuel Weller (?Woller) principal creditor of deceased[139].

Everett,
U 12.1842 (failed to supply testimonial).

Everett, Thomas.
U 81.1810.
Chorister St. Paul's 1798 – 1804. Organist Tunbridge [sic][342].

Fagg,
U 20.1836.

Fairbridge,
All Hallows Bread Street in 1800 according to Pearce[323]. No contemporary evidence of this.

Fearon,
U 40.1744/5.

Ferry, Hugh (Josiah).
U 71.1800, 20.1805 (Hugh Josiah), 65.1806.

Ferry, Samuel John.
U 15.1804, 1809.
Pianoforte teacher of 9 Northampton St. 1832–4[199].

Ferry, William.
London French Church & St. Matthew Bethnal Green in 1831[159].

Field, James Thomas, c.1759 – 1805.
St. Botolph Bishopsgate 1784 Jul.27 – 1805 June 13 death reported. Left widow.
Buried St. Botolph Bishopsgate 1805 June 5 James Thomas Field organist age 46.

Fieldhouse, George.
St. Michael Bassishaw 1843 Feb.23 (from 43 candidates) – 1856 June 19 dismissed.
Of 53 Red Lion St., Clerkenwell 1843[59V].

Fisher, Miss Sarah, later Mrs. Plummer.
St. Michael Paternoster Royal 1829 Apr.9 (appointed without election) – 1870 Apr.19 resigned in consequence of age & infirmity and succeeded by daughter Sarah until 1880.
Daughter of John Fisher parish clerk of St. Michael Paternoster Royal 1798 – 1830 Oct.29 died (at Streatham). Of 178 Upper Thames St. in 1798. Sarah mar. Thomas Plummer, printer & parish clerk of St. Michael 1836–38 (died). By him she had 4 children between 1831 and 1837[130].

Fitzgerald, George Bentwick.
U 12.1842 (failed to supply testimonial), *74.1844*.
Of Wandsworth 1844[74V].

Fleet, Miss.
U 15.1836.

Fleet, Miss Esther Elizabeth, later Mrs. Cope.
St. Botolph Bishopsgate 1825 Apr.7 – 1839 Apr.4 resigned after being elected to St. Saviour Southwark 1838 Apr.20 on condition that she resigned from St.

Botolph. She supplied W.H. Kearnes as deputy at St. Botolph and he collected Mrs. Cope's pay without authority of vestry. Resultant troubles and result of enquiry 1839 May 2 dealt with in detail in 27V.

U 28.1821 (disqualified after selection in top 4 out of 23 because age found "not to exceed 14"), 44.1823, 1.1823 (tribute paid to "her high abilities").

The youthful Esther and Henry Cope both candidates for All Hallows Barking and St. Lawrence Jewry in 1823. Was this a childhood romance leading to marriage between 1830 Apr. and 1831 Apr. when Miss Fleet became Mrs. Cope[27V].?

FLORIER, Francis.
Pearce's misinterpretation[323] of Francis Forcer (q.v.) copied by other authorities.

FLOWERS, George French.
U 81.1844 (runner-up).

Of 3 Keppel St., Russell Sq. music teacher 1844–7[199].

G(5). 284.

FLUD,
Pearce[323] gives as cand. St. Michael Cornhill 1734 but no evidence in V and presumably a misinterpretation of Froud, Charles (q.v.).

FOORD, William C.
U *74.1844*, 25.1847 (no christian name), 15.1847 (do.).

Of 2 Albany St., Regent's Park 1844[74V].

FORCER, Francis, d.1705.
St. Giles Cripplegate 1673 or 4 – 1676 vacated.
St. Sepulchre Holborn 1676 June ? (entry June 12 that Mr. Forcer the organist be allowed £20 p.a. probably approx. date of appointment) – 1704/5 Feb.1 death reported. Mr. Forcer son & executor referred to.
St. Bride Fleet St. 1692/3 Feb.10 (organist or candidate?). Either he, Mr. Eagles, jun. or Philip Hart, jun. organist for 3 years following unrecorded election after 1693 May 11.

Mr. Forcell [sic] with Dr. Blow, Mr. Mosse and Mr. Purcell passed judgement on organ St. Katherine Cree and assessed candidates 1686 Sep.30. Son Francis born 1676/7 Jan.2 "son of Francis of St. Andrew Holborn" at Merchant Taylors' School 1686/7 – 1696 and then to Oxford[295]. Succeeded father as master of Sadler's Wells, d.1743. Francis Forcer, senior, organist Dulwich College 1669 Oct.25 – 1671 Nov.26 resigned. Appointed Dulwich on recommendation of Archbishop: "I have heard a very good report of . . . Mr. Forcer, both of his skill in Musick, which may render him very fitt to be your organist and of his civill demeanor & sobriety of life"[340]. Bur. St. Andrew Holborn 1704/5 Jan.26 "Francis Forser [sic] from Crosse Street". Will dated 1704/5 Jan.20 to son Francis, sole executor, property in Silver Street, Durham and two houses in Plow Yard, Fetter Lane, Holborn. Daughter Raynton and her son William. Witn. Peter Gelsthorp, Thomas Raynton, Ann Smith. Proved 1705 Apr.[139].

B.G.

FORGE, Miss Hannah, later Mrs. Halley.
St. Mary at Hill 1826 May 30 elected unanimously – 1847 Apr.9 resigned under pressure after complaints about playing. Asked for relief 1848 Mar.9 and granted £6.5.0 p.a.

Daughter of R.S. Forge of 6 Botolph Lane who supplied testimonial 1826[53V]. Richard Forge fish salesman living 6 Botolph Lane 1826[199]. Became Mrs. Halley betw. 1845 Mar.26 & 1846 Apr.29.

FOSTER, d.1714.
St. Dunstan in the West 1699 May 4 – 1713/14 Mar.19 death reported.
U 28.1702.

Bur. St. Dunstan in the West 1713/14 Feb.9 "Thomas Forster [sic] from Bell Yard in Fleet St.". The same? B has 2 songs by —— Fosster c.1720.

B.

FOSTER,
U 33.1713/14.

FOSTER,
U 20.1836.

FOSTER, Samuel J.
St. Mary Somerset 1845 before Apr. – c.1846 successor appointed.
St. Stephen Coleman Street deputy up to 1844.

FOSTER, Samuel P. [sic].
U *74.1844*.
Of 36 Chiswell St., Finsbury 1844[74V]. Probably identical with Samuel J., above.

FOSTER, William.
St. Peter le Poer 1844 Nov.? – 1880 Dec. 25 retired with presentation of £150.
U 53.1826 (the same?), *63.1844*.
Of Upper Park St., Islington 1844[63V], 190 Cornwall Rd., Notting Hill 1880[72V].

FRITH, Edward, c.1771 – 1831.
St. James Garlickhythe 1793 Mar.28 – 1831 June 29 death reported.
U 40.1785–88 possibly deputy.
Bap. St. Saviour Southwark 1771 Jan. 13. Son of Edward Frith, excise officer, & Lydia[182]. Chorister St. Paul's Cathedral[342]. Tenor singer, violinist & viola player[182]. Employed Astley's Theatre 1794[198]. Also organist Whitchurch, Little Stanmore, Middx. Elected Roy. Soc. of Musicians 1796 on recommendation of John Immyns Mar.6[182]. B lists one song c.1800. Suffered from paralysis for nearly 2 years before death 1831 June[182]. Of 183 Upper Thames St. 1794[198], 10 Angel Terrace Clerkenwell 1831, the address given in burial entry St. James Garlickhythe 1831 June 30.
B.

FRITH, Joseph.
U 40.1789 – 1792 possibly deputy or perhaps mistaken entry for Edward Frith (q.v.)

FROUD, Charles, d.1770.
St. Giles Cripplegate 1736 May 25 – 1770 Nov.7 death reported.
U 60.1734 (—— Froude).
Although frequently spelt Frowd, he himself signed the Vestry minute book in 1736 and his will as Charles Froud. Original member Roy. Soc. of Musicians 1739[181]. Frowd, Charles, organist & teacher on the harpsichord, King St., Bloomsbury 1763[211]. Froud in Hawkins[304]. Two songs by —— Froude, c.1760, c.1735 in B. Will dated 1770 June 9 refers to wife Hannah, son Charles, daus. Hannah & Sarah, sister Susannah Froud. "My harpsichord and all my music books to my good friend Edmund Gilding", (q.v.) Proved 1770 Nov.9[139].
B.

FULLER, Miss E.
U 12.1842 ("Fuller" failed to supply testimonial), 59.1843, 76.1843 (no christian name).
Of 122 Sloane St., Chelsea 1843[59V].

GALE, Mrs. Elizabeth *see* Gurry, Miss Elizabeth, later Mrs. Gale.

GALOT,
U 27.1815.
B. has one work by P.A. Galot c.1800.
B.

GALTON, Mrs. Harriott [sic].
U 77.1828.
Of 18 Barnsbury Row, Islington 1828[77V].

GALTON, Mrs. M.A. *see* Pyne, Miss M.A., later Mrs. Galton.

GARDNER, Charles, d.1869.
U 59.1840.
Of 6 Cross St., Bermondsey 1840[59V]. Probably Charles Graham Gardner, organist & pianist. Organist for 36 years St. Margaret's Lee until death 1869 Oct.31[284].
284.

GARRETT, Mrs. Lucy *see* Lindley, Mrs. or Miss Lucy, later Mrs. Garrett?

GATES, John, d.1793.
St. James Garlickhythe 1744/5 Mar.14 – 1793 Mar.21 death reported.
U 34.1747 (no christian name), 14.1749 (do.), 31.1752 (do., withdrew – single post clause), 26.1753, 53.1762 (no christian name).

Perhaps son of Bernard Gates organist and composer d.1773 age 87. Lewis Pearce apprenticed to John Gates of St. George, Middlesex, musician £25.10.0 in 1759[149]. B. has song by John Gates, jun. c.1750. A Thomas Gates elected St. John Wapping 1760 Dec.30[L630].
B.

GAUNTLETT, Henry John.
Christ Church Newgate Street evening organist 1836 – 1846[284] but no confirmation found in church records. However H.J. Gauntlett, "organist of Christ Church Newgate Street & St. Olave's Southwark" in 1837[256].
No other City appointments before 1850 but organist St. Bartholomew the Less 1872 – 1876 Feb.21 died.
U *45.1826*, 74.1827 (no christian name), 77.1828 (withdrew).
Of 15 Serjeants Inn 1828[77V]. Practising solicitor in City. Organist St. Olave Southwark 1827–47 etc.
G. 280. 282. 284.

GAY,
U 59.1807.

GETHIN, Roger, 1703 – 1741.
Parish Clerks' Company 1732 Apr.17 – 1741 Dec. died. Successor appointed 1742 Jan. 18 "Gethin deceased".
Son of Roger Gethin, of the Weavers' Company and Chapel Clerk at Bridewell (died 1722 May 13), admitted to Parish Clerks' Company 1696 Jul.7[130]. Roger sen. mar. Mary Gartrill at Bridewell chapel 1695 Apr.8. Of their ten children bap. Bridewell chapel, Thomas (1696 Dec.30) became an eminent singer[377]. Roger, the organist, bap. 1702/3 Mar.6, mar. Ann Berkley (or Barkley) widow of St. Bride's at St. Antholin Budge Row 1729 Oct.5. Living Fountain Court, St. Bride's 1731[85]. Bur. St. Dunstan in the West near his wife 1741 Dec.27 "from St. Andrew's Holborn". Will[140] disposed of personal effects mostly to Berkley family with remainder to Mother Mary (died 1745 June) but "all my books and papers of musick" to William Withers except "pircels [i.e. Purcell's] book of songs" (destination unrevealed).
377. 378.

GIGLEIR, [sic].
U 31.1752. The name is recorded as Juliere in General Advertiser[227].
Mistaken entry for Gillier? Peter Gillier, violist to H.M. Chapel Royal and original member Roy. Soc. of Musicians 1739[181] Died at his house in Thrift St. Soho 1767 Oct.[L398]. Eight sonatas, or lessons for the harpsichord by Mr. Gillier, jun. (advert. June 1759).
B.?

GILBERT, Edward.
U 59.1843.
Of 1 Ann's Place, East St., Old Kent Rd. 1843[59V].

GILBERT, Miss T.A.
U 59.1843.

GILBERT, Thomas Tyers.
U *74.1844*.
Of 10 Montagu Place, Clapham Rd. 1844[74V].

GILDING, *see* Golding.

GILDING, Edmund, d.1782.
St. Martin Ludgate 1745 Apr.17 – 1782 Aug.5 died. Death reported Aug.14.
St. Edmund, King and Martyr 1753 Nov.23 – 1782 Aug.5 died. Death reported Aug.21.
Parish Clerks' Company 1766 Jul.14 – 1782 Aug.5 died. Death reported Oct.14.
St. Giles Cripplegate (elected "by a great majority") 1770 Nov.14 – 1782 Aug.5 died. Death reported Aug.9.
U 34.1747 (runner-up), 31.1749 (polled 4 votes to Charles Burney's 50).
Contributed psalm tunes to Riley's *Parochial music corrected* 1762[273]. Friend of Charles Frowd (q.v.) who bequeathed him his harpsichord and music books 1770. Died 1782 Aug.5 Mr. Edmund Gilding organist of . . . (as above), a freemason[232]. (Date of death Aug.4 in L134). B. has 6 works c.1740–48.
B.

GILES, Henry.
St. Botolph Aldgate 1822 Oct.5 – 1847 Jan.14 vacated (died?).
U 3.1812, 37.1818, 45.1820.
Of Trinity Square, Tower Hill 1822[26V].

GILLIER, Peter *see* Gigleir (sic).

GLENN, Robert, c.1770 – 1844.
St. Margaret Pattens 1805 May 1 – 1844 Feb.25 died. Reprimanded 1843 Apr.19: "if not more efficient a substitute will be found". (Until 1818 V. & C. wrongly record him as George Glenn).
Christ's Hospital music master 1810 Apr.6 – 1844 Feb.25 died. R.J.S. Stevens (music master 1808–10) says in his recollections[193] that Glenn was deputy to Robert Hudson (music master 1767 – 1808) "before I was appointed".
U 7.1817 (runner-up).
Pupil of Jonathan Battishill[251]. Mar. Rosalind dau. of Samuel Wesley. Rosalind's sister Eliza Wesley (q.v.) deputised for him at St. Margaret Pattens and succeeded him on his death 1844. Robert Glenn died at his residence in Great Ormond Street in 75th year 1844 Feb.25[251].

GLENNY, Alexander.
U 40.1793, 40.1793–1805 annually contested Edward Frith (perhaps his deputy).
Organist Whitechapel in 1794, of Fieldgate St., Whitechapel[198].

GOADBY, Miss Elizabeth, later Mrs. Atkinson.
St. Botolph Aldersgate (jointly with J.C. Pring) 1787 Jan.16 – 1789 Apr.15 last appearance at annual election following dispute.
St. Edmund, King and Martyr 1790 Apr.14 – 1797 May 19 vacated after becoming Mrs. Atkinson about 6 months earlier.
B.?

GODWIN,
U 27.1815.

GODWIN, George.
U 27.1825 (selected by committee as most eligible but runner-up in election), 64.1837.

GOLDING, (?Gilding, q.v.).
U 59.1764 (in top 3 out of 6).

GONDGE (sic), Thomas.
U 74.1844 (failed to attend audition).
Of 7 East Street, Hoxton[74V].

GOODGROOME, William.
St. Andrew Undershaft 1696 Jul.30 – 1697 Oct.? At first he appears to have shared the post with Philip Hart but no evidence that this continued after 1697.
St. Peter Cornhill. No information as to date of appointment but dismissed 1724 Apr.9 after having been acquainted that "the Parishioners have been some time uneasy at his mismanagement of their organ", 1723/4 Feb.12. (Some authorities wrongly assign John Goodgroome to St. Peter).
A child of the Chapel Royal of this name between 1674 and 1679[292]. Possibly mar. Ann Browne St. Marylebone 1689 Oct. 3. Living in parish of St. Edmund, King and Martyr with wife Anne in 1695[179] until c.1700 where their children baptised: Charles 1696 Dec.2, John 1697 Dec.19, Ann 1698 Dec.18, Sarah 1699/1700 Feb.25. Then to St. Dionis Backchurch, the bap. & bur. of Anne 1701 May 5, May 7 revealing her as dau. of Anne & William Goodgroome, "music master, lodger at Dr. Hicks". John Vanomme, "a lodger at Mr. Wm. Goodgroomes" bur. St. Dionis 1703 Dec.1. William Goodgroome of Charterhouse Square (the same?) died 1742/3 Jan.17 of an apoplectic fit[232 242]. This William bur. 1742/3 Jan.23 Christ Church Newgate Street, but admon. granted to *Elizabeth*, his widow 1743[139] suggests he was not the organist or that he had remarried.
G(5) (for other Goodgroomes).

GOODMAN, Joseph c.1782 – 1836.
St. Anne and St. Agnes 1809 Sep.21 – 1836 Sep. died. Death reported Sep.16.
Bur. St. Anne and St. Agnes 1836 Sep.12 from Cloth Fair age 54.

GOODSON,
U 74.1827 (top 6 out of 15).

GOODSON, John, jun.
U 53.1826.

GOODSON, John Edward, b.1808.
U *45.1826*, 25.1827.
The 3 above probably identical with John Goodson, born 1808 March, chorister St. Paul's 1818 Dec. – 1819 Sep.[342].

GOODWIN, Starling, d.1774.
No City posts or candidatures found unless:-
U 34.1747? (no christian name).
Son of Michael Goodwin, citizen and Baker, later Musician (i.e. freeman of Bakers' and Musicians' Companies) to whom apprenticed 1727/8 Jan. 15[165]. Freeman of Musicians' Company 1734/5 Mar.7[165]. U St. Olave Southwark 1736 May 25[94]. Organist St. Mary Magdalen Bermondsey 1738 Apr.4 to death (reported ves. min. bk. 1774 Dec.21). "Succeeded Butler at Ranelagh and there until 1766"[191]. Organist St. Saviour Southwark 1750 Jul.26 to death (reported ves. min. bk. 1774 Dec.20). Author of *Organist's pocket companion*, composer of songs, harpsichord & organ works etc.
B.

GOODWIN, William, d.1784.
St. Bartholomew by the Exchange ("no other post allowed") 1766 Mar.27 (John Goodwin in L305) – 1784 Mar.5 died. Death reported Mar.16.
U 34.1753, 53.1762 ("Goodwin, jun.")
Probably son of Starling Goodwin, above. Expelled from Roy. Soc. of Musicians to which elected 1760[181]. Organist St. Mary Newington until death (reported ves. min. bk. 1784 Mar.23), St. George the Martyr Southwark from before 1764 (ves. min. bk.) until resignation 1766 Apr. [L462]. Succeeded Starling Goodwin at St. Saviour Southwark 1774 Dec.20 defeating Charles Lockhart by 319 votes to 308 (ves. min. bk.). Died 1784 Mar.5 "Mr. Goodwin organist of St. Saviour Southwark and St. Mary Newington Butts and one of the band of musicians belonging to Ranelagh"[232]. Bur. St. Saviour Southwark 1784 Mar.12.
B.

GORTON, William, d.1711.
St. Clement Eastcheap 1702 June? – 1711 Oct. died.
U 28.1702 (no christian name).
Probably identical with William Gorton in the King's (Queen's) band 1694 – c.1711[196 292]. Elizabeth widow & Robert son survived him[30V]. Robert, son of William Gorton late of London, musician, apprenticed to Edward Crank, citizen & Barber Surgeon 1717, £9[149]. Bur. St. Clement Eastcheap 1711 Oct.21 (St. Martin Orgar reg.). Instrumental works & songs c.1701–5. Admon. to widow Elizabeth parish of St. Mary Abchurch 1711[139].
B.G.

GOSS, Sir John.
St. Paul's Cathedral 1838 Apr.26 – 1872.
St. Alban Wood Street 1839 c.Apr. – 1840 Jan.26 resigned. Entered as J.Goss. The same?
Born 1800 Dec.27. Educated choir Chapel Royal and under Thomas Attwood. Organist Stockwell Chapel in 1825 when elected Roy. Soc. of Musicians on recommendation of Attwood, William Horsley & B. Jacob. Married as a minor Lucy Emma New of Chelsea at Christ Church Southwark 1821 Oct.10[182].
G. 282. 284. 339 etc.

GOSS, Walter.
St. Alban Wood Street 1849 betw. Jul. & Oct. – ? End not found from surviving records.
Pearce asserts he was brother of Sir John Goss[323].

GOTTSCHALK, F.
Dutch Church Austin Friars 1799 Oct. 2 – 1820 Oct.19 death reported. (Paid up to 1818 Mar. only).

GRADY, Thomas.
St. Matthew Friday Street 1815 Apr.5 – 1817 Nov.11 resigned, £10 gratuity in

consideration of accident & infirmity. Not referred to by christian name, it is assumed that this was Thomas.
U 42.1805, 48.1805 (withdrew), 68.1806 (runner-up), 59.1807 (no christian name), 77.1807 (do.). Some or all of these candidatures could apply to T.S. Grady, q.v.

GRADY, Thomas Standish.
Holy Trinity Minories 1808 Jul.25 – 1838 Jul.9 dismissed. After annual reelection 1838 Apr.17, "Mr. Evitt laid the subject of poor Izod's daughter before the vestry" on May 10. Grady suspended and banned from church until he clears "his character from the charges made against him". On June 8 vestry takes "further consideration of Mr. Grady & Letitia Izod" following report on the affair by "Mr. Kelly, a very old inhabitant and the treasurer of the parish". The report further considered with Grady present June 25. On Jul.9 "not to be retained in consequence of his conduct not being in accordance with the performance of that sacred duty and that his future services as organist of this church be discontinued". Letter from T.S. Grady of 24 Bread St. Hill pleading innocence and asking for help in his poverty etc. ignored by vestry 1839 Apr.2.
U 77.1828 (T.S. Graday). The candidatures under Thomas Grady could equally well apply to T.S. Grady.
Music teacher of 71 Warren St., Fitzroy Sq. 1823–4[199]. Of 9 Wardrobe Terrace 1828[77V]. Music teacher of 27 Old Change 1833–4[199].

GRANTHAM, William.
U 59.1840.
Of 14 Guildford Place, Spa Fields 1840[59V]. St. Paul's Cathedral chorister of this name 1811 – Dec.1814, born 1804 Apr.25[342].

GRAY, John.
U 2.1756.
Died 1759 Sep.17 Mr. Gray late organist of Shadwell[232 L277]. The same?

GRAY, John.
St. Michael Paternoster Royal 1821 Jul.20 (to continue, so presumably playing for his father William Gray, the nominal organist and organ builder, long before this) – 1829 Apr.9 resigned. Letter of resignation dated Feb.7 from 9 New Road, Fitzroy Sq. "absence from London prevents continuing".

GRAY, Thomas *see* Grey.

GRAY, W.F.
U *63.1844*.

GRAY, William, c.1757 – 1821.
(Organ builder installing annuity organ St. Michael Paternoster Royal 1797). Organist, playing himself or more likely by substitute, St. Michael Paternoster Royal 1797 or 8 – 1821 Jul. 12 died.
Chorister St. Paul's?[342]. Gray, William & Robert, organ builders, 4 New Road, Portland Road 1794[198]. Of New Road, Fitzroy Sq. 1797[62V] until death. Died 1821 Jul.12 in 65th year, Wm. Gray late of the New Road, Fitzroy Sq., organ builder. Mary his wife died 1842 Jul.8 age 79. (Inscription St. James Chapel, Hampstead[286]).
G.

GREEN, George.
U 48.1834.

GREEN, Henry, d.1741.
St. Giles Cripplegate 1703/4 Feb.25 – 1734/5 Mar.10 pensioned. "Organ shall be shut up and he shall be discharged". Recorded as blind on his admission, doubts as to efficiency raised by 1728 & vestry allowed him to continue by 1 vote. Doubts continued & finally awarded pension of £10 p.a. until death which occurred in 1741.
U 40.1722 (no christian name).
A Henry Green an original member Roy. Soc. of Musicians 1739[181]. For his confrontation with the City authorities over the freedom of the City see pp.8–9. Died 1741 Sep.25 Henry Greene, a noted master of music, many years blind[232].

GREENE, Maurice.
St. Dunstan in the West 1713/14 Mar.19 – 1718 Apr.1 resigned.
St. Andrew Holborn 1717/18 Feb.19 –

1718 Apr.3 resigned.
St. Paul's Cathedral 1717/18 Mar.20 – 1755 Dec.1 died.
U 2.1723.
St. Paul's chorister[342]. David Digard (q.v.) apprenticed to Maurice Greene of St. Clement Danes, organist 1730, £20[149]. Original member Roy. Soc. of Musicians 1739[181]. Other apprentices include Edward Salisbury & John Travers (q.v.)[149].
B. G. 284. 358. 368.

GREGG, Mrs. Mary *see* Worgan, Mary, later Mrs. Gregg.

GRESHAM, Mrs. George *see* Harris, Miss, later Mrs. Gresham.

GREY,
U 40.1744/5.
Perhaps Thomas Gray [sic] elected St. Paul Deptford 1759 Oct.19[L398].

GRIFFES, Charles.
U 2.1773.
B. has march & sonata for piano c.1790–5. The same?
B.

GRIFFES, Edward.
St. Dunstan in the East 1753 June 1 – 1811 Aug.? vacated. Died?
U 31.1749, 53.1762 (Griffies, no christian name), 1.1767 (Edward Griffiths, declined to stand), 7.1767 (Griffiths)[L481], 20.1777.
Composer of 2 works c.1755.
B.

GRIFFIN, George, c.1741 – 1809.
St. Mildred Bread Street 1749?–1751 Sep.26. This appointment is not at all clear (see church entry p.60 and pp.13–16 and under Griffin, Thomas). Hardly credible that George was appointed at age of 8. Could the organist have been his father and brother of Thomas?
St. Helen Bishopsgate 1771 May 16 – 1809 Apr. 19 died. Death reported Apr.27.
U 43.1766.
Age 43 with wife & 3 children when recommended for Roy. Soc. of Musicians by Theodore Aylward 1784 May 2 (elected 1785)[182]. Died 1809 Apr.19, "many years organist St. Helen Bishopsgate"[232]. Nephew of Thomas Griffin, q.v.

GRIFFIN, George Eugene, 1781 – 1863.
St. Botolph Bishopsgate 1805 June 20 – 1815 Mar.30 vacated.
Born 1781 Jan.8 bap. St. Botolph Bishopsgate Feb.11. Son of George (above) & Elizabeth Griffin. Organist, pianist, violinist & viola player with extensive private teaching. Elected Roy. Soc. of Musicians 1808 on recommendation of father 1807 Oct.4. Died 1863[182].
G(5). 284.

GRIFFIN, Thomas, d.1771.
Although described as organist in several City church records there is no positive evidence that he played. Installed "annuity" organs in many churches by which in exchange for an annuity he undertook to supply an organ and an organist or to play himself (pp.13–16). He is described as organist in the records of the following churches:-
St. Katherine Coleman (To supply organ 1741 Sep.10). 1742 – 1771 Apr.29 died.
St. Margaret Pattens (To supply organ 1746 June 6, erected 1749). 1749 – 1771 Apr.29 died. Death reported May 15.
St. Helen Bishopsgate (To supply organ 1741/2 Mar.11, contract signed 1742 Apr.22 to be paid £250 & £25 p.a. for life for playing himself or supplying organist). 1744 summer – 1771 Apr.29. Death reported May 16.
St. Mildred Bread Street (To supply organ in conjunction with Richard Hussey? 1744 Oct.11), organ opened 1745 Apr.21. The circumstances are not clear, (see church entry p.60). If he played, as is most unlikely, it could only have been between 1747 and 1751 when vestry agreed that George [sic] Griffin be allowed £8 p.a. during his natural life. Agreed unanimously that church "furnish themselves with an organist". The entries except under 1751 (George) are for "Mr. Griffin".
Also supplied or built organ for St. Michael Bassishaw 1762 June 16, opened 1764 (non-annuity fee of £200).

Son of Richard Griffin, wharfinger of St. Dunstan in the East. Perhaps therefore the Thomas Griffin son of Richard & Anne Griffin born 1703 Oct.18 bap. Oct.24 in that church. Apprenticed to George Dennis, barber, in the Barber Surgeons' Company 1720 Jul.5[109]. Freeman of the Barber Surgeons' Co. 1728/9 Feb.4[111]. Presumably followed trade of barber initially although the 1741 agreement with St. Katherine Coleman describes him as peruke maker[87]. This enigmatic character is also described in the 1746 agreement with St. Margaret Pattens and in a manuscript livery list of the Barber Surgeons' Company[108] as an organ builder of Fenchurch St. which goes some way towards proving that he actually built them. Served on the City's Court of Common Council 1752–63 and as Gresham Professor of Music with apartment at Mercer's Hall from 1763 Jan.11 until his death, defeating the only other candidate John Potter[122]. For this post he would seem to have been unqualified. Died 1771 Apr.29 Mr. Thomas Griffin, Gresham lecturer of Music[232]. See also pp.13–16.
G(5). 351.

GRIFFITHS,
U 76.1843.
Probably George Richard Griffiths born 1816 Jan.18, son of Richard (organist) & Caroline Griffiths of Dover Rd. Newington. Pfte. teacher, contrabasso Princess's Theatre & organist South Lambeth Chapel in 1846 when elected Roy. Soc. of Musicians. Of 23 Clapham Rd. Place, Kennington in 1846. Died 1891[182].

GRIFFITHS, Edward *see* Griffes, Edward.

GROOM, P.T.
U *59.1843*.
Of 39 Mincing Lane 1843[59V].

GROOM, Thomas P.
U *63.1844*, *74.1844*.
Of 9 Liverpool Street, Walworth 1844[63V 74V].

GROOMBRIDGE, John, c.1750 – 1827.
St. Stephen Coleman Street 1775 May 2 – 1827 Aug. died. Death reported Oct.3.
Apprentice of Samuel Jarvis, organist of St. Sepulchre 1760 – 84[189]. Also organist Hackney parish church[198]. Bur. St. Stephen Coleman Street 1827 Aug.8 "late organist of this parish, of Hoxton, age 77". His wife Sophia Campbell Groombridge died "of a decline" age 33 in 1812 and bur. Oct. 27. Flat stone in graveyard St. Stephen Coleman Street now removed. Two works c.1776 in B.
B. 247.

GROSVENOR, John.
St. Andrew Holborn 1811 Dec.? – 1814 vacated? Pearce sole authority[323], church records lost.
U 15.1809 May (no christian name, withdrew), 15.1809 Sep.

GURRY, Miss Elizabeth, later Mrs. Gale.
St. Alban Wood Street 1841 Aug.23 – 1846 betw. Jul. & Aug. vacated as Mrs. Gale (mar. 1846 between Mar.31 & Jul.7).
U 59.1840 (Miss Gurrey).
Of 2 Sion College Gardens, Aldermanbury 1840[59V].

HAINES,
U 43.1702/3.

HAINWORTH,
U 44.1823 (runner-up).

HALE, Miss Mary.
Dutch Church Austin Friars 1833 Jul.11 – 1848 June 7 resigned on departure for America.
U 42.1833 (no christian name).

HALES, Samuel King.
St. James Duke's Place between 1839 Apr. & 1847 Apr. – 1853 Apr. 18 vacated. Sal. £8 later raised to 10 guineas.
U 59.1840, 12.1842 (no christian name, application disallowed), 59.1843, 74.1844 (failed to attend audition), *63.1844* (S. Hailes).
Of 20 Warwick Sq., Newgate St. 1840[59V], 27 Cavendish St., New North Rd., Hoxton 1843[59V], 57 Cavendish St. etc. 1844[74V].

HALL,
U 74.1827.

HALL, William Thomas.
St. Mary Aldermanbury (sole candidate) 1840 Feb.19 – 1855 Nov.1 resigned after refusing to deliver organ keys to incumbent for practice Aug.9 and subsequent complaint from Rev. C.C. Collins.

HALLEY, Douglas William, b.1811.
U *45.1826*.
Born 1811 Feb.12 bap. St. John Wapping Aug.25. Son of Thomas Douglas Halley, professor of music (q.v.) & Isabella Eleanor of Betts St., St. George's Middx. Pianist, violinist, teacher & organist St. John Wapping from 1830. Mar. Mary Ann Priscilla Freeman 1845 Mar.29 All Hallows Barking. Elected Roy. Soc. of Musicians 1847 Apr.4[182]. Of 3 Betts St. 1840[199], 37 Lucas St., Commercial Rd. East 1847[182].

HALLEY, Francis G.
U 47.1844.

HALLEY, Mrs. Hannah *see* Forge, Hannah, later Mrs. Halley.

HALLEY, Thomas Douglas.
U 71.1800.
Organist St. John Wapping prior to his son Douglas William Halley. Published 12 hymns appropriate to charity sermons.
284.

HALLEY, Thomas G.B.
U 59.1840, *74.1844*.
Son of Thomas Douglas and brother of Douglas William (above). Of 3 Betts St., St. George East 1840[59V], 37 Lucas St., Commercial Rd. East 1844[74V].

HALLIDAY, Edward or John.
St. Benet Fink 1834 Apr.3 (John Halliday) – c.1842 church demolished. Organist latterly named as Edward Halliday.
U 35.1827 (no christian name).
Halliday & co., or Edward Halliday or Edward Halliday & co., music sellers & publishers 23 Bishopsgate St. c.1804–49[310]. The same?

HALSEY, Miss M.E.
St. James Duke's Place 1824 Apr.19 – 1838 Apr. 16 resigned (request for increment 1831 Mar.31 refused).
St. Ethelburga Bishopsgate 1827 Feb.1 – 1844 June 20 resigned.
St. Katherine Coleman 1844 c.May – 1869 c.Jan. vacated.
U 4.1825, 42.1837 (runner-up).
Of Jewry St., Aldgate 1825[4V].

HAMMOND, John.
U 20.1805.
John Hammond, music teacher, 7 Polygon, Somerstown 1823–34[199]. Five works c.1795 – 1800 in B.
B.

HANSON, James.
U 68.1806.

HARDIN, Miss (Elizabeth?)
St Peter le Poer 1764 Nov.29 (by a great majority) – no record of termination but possibly 1780, the date of death of Elizabeth Hardin (see below).
Probably dau. of "Joseph Harding [sic] clockmaker and watchmaker in the Old Jewry" died 1778 Aug.19 [L182]. The loss of the V & C of St. Peter obscures her fate. Her appointment to St. Peter le Poer[L525] describes her as "of the Old Jewry". This raises the possibility of her identification as Elizabeth Hardin buried St. Olave Jewry 1780 Jan.28 age 29. Not impossible that she was appointed at age of 14. Elizabeth Hardin composer of 6 lessons for the harpsichord c.1770, Miss Harding [sic] composer of 3 works c.1767 [B]. *Amintor's choice* set to music by Miss Hardin appears in London mag. 1767 p.530[242].
B.

HARDING, William.
U 15.1804.

HARRIS, (1)
U 73.1705, 13.1717/18.

HARRIS, (2)
U 25.1820, 12.1842 (failed to supply testimonial).

HARRIS, Miss, later Mrs. George Gresham?
All Hallows Lombard Street 1849 Aug.10 – 1867 Apr.23 Mrs. George Gresham

resigned. Probably became Mrs. Gresham between 1861 Apr.2 and 1862 Apr.10.

HARRIS, George Frederick, d.1867.
St. Lawrence Jewry 1823 Jan.17 – 1867 Nov.21 died.
U 45.1820 (no christian name, runner-up), 44.1821 (runner-up), 28.1821 (G. Harris in top 4 out of 23).
Music teacher of 73 Lamb's Conduit St. 1832–4[199]. Sometimes known as "Rudolf Normann". Composer of arrangements for piano and organ.
284.

HARRIS, Miss Isabella, later Mrs. Wrightson.
St. George Botolph Lane 1848 Mar.13 – 1861 Apr.26, Mrs. Isabella Wrightson resigned. Became Mrs. Wrightson between 1852 Apr. 14 and 1853 Mar. 30.
U 68.1845 (runner-up for assistant organist).

HARRIS, Joseph John.
U 38.1819, 20.1819.
According to Pearce[323] J.T. [sic] Harris evening organist Christ Church Newgate Street (no date) but no records survive to confirm this.
G(5). 282. 284. 339.

HARRIS, Rees Eldridge.
St. Martin Ludgate 1834 Nov. 20 – 1850 Jan.4 resigned.

HARRIS, Renatus, jun.
All Hallows Lombard Street 1701 Sep.29 – 1737 May 25 death of "Renatus Harris, organist" reported.
U Probably as under Harris, (1), viz. 73.1705, 13.1717/18.
Son of the organ builder. Will dated 1727 Aug.7 proved 1737 June 1[144] "of St. John Hackney". Executrix and sole legatee niece Ann Arundel. But act book[147] probate granted to brother John.
G.

HARRISON, Stephen.
St. Dunstan in the West 1729 May 9 – 1730/31 Mar. 4 resigned.
U 2.1727/8 (—— Harrison one of 12 names submitted by vestry).

HARRISON, William Thomas.
U 74.1844 (failed to attend audition).
Of 2 Charles St., Bridgewater Sq., Barbican[74V].

HARSON, R.A.
U 36.1848 (top 3 out of 18).

HART, Philip, d.1749.
St. Bride Fleet Street 1692/3 Feb.10 (organist or candidate?). "Philip Hart, jun." one of 3 candidates. Either he, Eccles or Francis Forcer organist for 3 years following unrecorded election after 1693 May 11.
St. Andrew Undershaft appointed assistant unanimously to work alternate weeks with William Goodgroome 1696 Jul.30 – 1697 Oct. 19. Combined sal. £20.
St. Andrew Undershaft elected unanimously 1697 Oct. 19 – 1749 Jul.17 died. Death reported Jul.26.
St. Michael Cornhill 1703/4 Feb.25 – 1723/4 Jan.1 resigned.
St. Dionis Backchurch 1724 May 28 – 1749 Jul.17 died. Death reported Jul.27.
U 13.1717/18 (no christian name), 40.1722 (do.) after which "Mr Hart" continued to contest each year at annual elections until 1750 [sic]. Does this mean he served as deputy or was his name used by arrangement as a matter of convenience?
Son of James Hart and Ann. James Hart, gent. of Chapel Royal died 1718 May 8 age 71. "The body of James Hart . . . was carried from Founders' Hall to be buried in Westminster Abbey. Father to the ingenious Mr. Philip Hart who is organist of . . . St. Michael & St. Mary Axe [i.e. St. Andrew Undershaft]"[252]. Organ of St. Peter le Poer opened by Philip Hart 1718 Nov.16[253]. Original member Roy. Soc. of Musicians 1739[181]. Died 1749 Jul.17[242]. Bur. St. Andrew Undershaft 1749 Jul.22 Will dated 1747 Oct.13 witn. John and Catherine Byfield (? the organ builder) leaves all to executor and nephew William Hart son of brother George: proved 1749 Jul.18[139].
B. G. 284. 364. 365. 402.

HART, William.
U 14.1749.
Nephew & executor of Philip Hart.

HARTLEY,
U 63.1779.
Possibly James Hartley, composer of songs & instrumental works c.1755–80.
B.

HARVEY, Miss Eliza.
St. Andrew Undershaft Assistant 1834–1836.

HARVEY, J. jun.
U 37.1818.
Perhaps son of J. Harvey, oboe player at Apollo Gardens, of 7 Green St. Blackfriars 1794[198].

HARWOOD, Peter *see* Horwood, Peter.

HASLETINE, James *see* Heseltine, James.

HAWES, William, 1785 – 1846.
St. Paul's Cathedral almoner 1812 – 1846 died.
Born 1785 June 24 bap. St. George Hanover Sq. Jul.3. Son of John & Ann Hawes. Chorister Chapel Royal under Ayrton. Mar. Elizabeth Mullinex 1805 Mar.12 St. George Hanover Sq. Pianist & violinist. Employed King's Chapel, Covent Garden Orchestra, Antient & vocal concerts. Elected Roy. Soc. of Musicians 1807 on recommendation of Charles Ashley May 3[182]. Of Manchester Buildings 1807. Died 1846 Feb.18[182].
G.

HAWKER, Thomas (Henry).
U 61.1826 (Thomas Henry), 59.1840 (Thomas).
Of 27 Bloomberg Terrace, Vauxhall Bridge Rd., Pimlico 1840[59V]. Thomas Henry Hawker issued *Collection of psalm & hymn tunes, chants etc. as sung at All Saints Church, St. John's Wood* 1854.
284.

HAWKES, Samuel Tanfield, d.1762.
U 2.1727/8 (Tanfield Hawkes one of 12 names submitted by vestry), 3.1737/8 (no christian name, withdrew).
Original member Roy. Soc. of Musicians 1739[181]. Organist Dulwich College 1731–62. Died at Dulwich Village 1762 Dec.18 Mr. Hawkes upwards of 30 years organist of that place[238]. Will dated 1762 Nov.27 bequests to sister Elizabeth Adams, niece Martha Adams, Joseph Allen master of Dulwich College, John Ross of the Bank of England, Mrs. Jane Ross of Dulwich Common. All musical books to College. John Ross executor. Proved 1762 Dec.20[139].

HAYCOCK, Joseph.
U 20.1819.

HAYDEN, George.
U 13.1717/18 (Haydon, no christian name), 13.1718 (runner-up).
"Singing boy in Paul's" 1698[164]. Organist St. Mary Magdalen Bermondsey in 1718[269]. Composer of cantatas & songs.
B.G. 284.

HEATH,
U 43.1686.

HEATHER, Miss Elizabeth.
St. Mary Aldermanbury 1826 Jan.20 – 1829 Jan.8 dismissed for inefficiency.
St. Alban Wood Street 1835 Mar. 24 – 1839 c.Feb. vacated.
U 64.1828, 22.1834 ("Miss Ether").

HELSDING, Adrian van *see* Van Helsding, Adrian.

HENNIKER, Mrs. Esther *see* Cowtan, Miss Esther, later Mrs. Henniker.

HENSHAW, Joseph.
All Hallows London Wall 1784 Jan.21 – 1824 Sep.23 resigned.
Organist St. Marylebone in 1836[257]. Organist, teacher, Edgware Rd. 1794[198]. A William Henry Henshaw apprenticed to John Banks of Kensington, organist 1764[150].

HERON, Henry, d.1795.
St. Magnus the Martyr (unanimously elected) 1762 May 28 – 1795 c.June 20 died. "No charge to be made for funeral of Henry Heron deceased late organist"

June 23. Alleged to have served previously as deputy to John Robinson[385]. Salary increased to £30 1768 Apr.7. In response to extra £10 sent letter of appreciation from 3 York Row, Newington Butts 1792.
U 7.1767 (no christian name)[L481].

Henry Heron, bach. of St. George Hanover Sq. mar. Elizabeth Harrison of St. Andrew Holborn at St. George Hanover Sq. 1756 Feb.2. Henry Sidney (q.v.) son of Henry & Elizabeth Heron of Millman St. bap. St. Andrew Holborn 1757 Feb.20. John Brettell apprenticed to Henry Heron of St. Andrew Holborn musician 1756[149]. "Henry Heron organist of Ewell, Surrey" subscribed & contributed psalm tunes to Riley's *Parochial music corrected* . . . 1762[273]. There seems little doubt that the organist of Ewell is identical with the organist of St. Magnus in that *Parochial music corrected . . . intended for the use of the several charity schools in London* . . . was "adapted, written & composed by H. Heron, organist of St. Magnus 1790". The entry for his burial at St. Magnus 1795 June 21 following the burial of his wife Elizabeth age 60 on 1794 June 8 gives his age as 56 which in view of the date of his marriage suggests an understatement. Many compositions include ten voluntaries for the organ or harpsichord.
B.284. 385.

HERON, Henry Sidney, b.1757.
U 74.1775 (H.S. Heron jun.), 20.1777 (Henry Heron jun.)

Son of Henry (above) and Elizabeth. Bap. St. Andrew Holborn 1757 Feb.20. "Mr. Heron" runner-up St. Mary Newington 1784 Mar.23 (ves. min. bk.)

HERRING,
U 59.1807.

Perhaps John Frederick Herring, organist, viola player, organist Sion Chapel, Whitechapel; of 68 Lemon St. 1794[198].

HERRING, John.
U 68.1781.

See also Herring, above.

HESELTINE, James d.1763.
St. Katherine by the Tower admitted 1709 Sep.22 – 1763 June 20 died. Death not reported until 1763 Nov.17. "John Crofoot acted as deputy for Mr. Hasletine the organist during his absence allowed of by the Master and to be paid eight pounds per ann. to be paid out of Mr. Hasletine's salary" 1714 Apr.1.

Also organist Durham Cathedral from 1711[339].
G. 282. 339.

HEWITT, D.C.
U 25.1827.

Probably Daniel Chandler Hewitt author of several books on music. According to Sainsbury came to London from native Scotland c.1819[325]. Hewett [sic], D.C. prof. of music 14 Soho Sq. 1837[256].
284.

HIGGS, James,
St. Benet Paul's Wharf 1844 Sep.26 – 1852 Apr.15 resigned.
U 59.1843, 76.1843 (no christian name), *74.1844*, 53.1847.

Of 10 Marsham St., Westminster 1843–4[59V 74V]. An organist of this name Mus. Bach. Oxon 1874, organist Eaton Chapel, Pimlico 1843, St. Mark Kennington 1852, St. Michael Stockwell 1864, and to the City again at St. Andrew Holborn 1867 when elected out of 150 candidates. Author of manuals of organ technique.
284. 295

HILBURN,
U 20.1740.

HILDYARD, Miss Marian, later Mrs. Archer.
All Hallows Lombard Street 1842 Mar.30 – 1849 Jul.10 Mrs. Archer died. Death reported 1849 Aug.1 referring to her death on Aug.10 [sic] i.e. Jul.10? Apparently became Mrs. Archer between 1842 Mar.30 & 1844 Apr. 10.

HILL,
U *12.1842*.

HILL, Miss Ann.
St. Vedast Foster Lane 1828 Aug.27 – 1837 Oct.25 resigned.

Of 34 Cheapside 1828[77V], the address of William Hill, hairdresser & perfumer[199].

HILL, William.
U 61.1819, 18.1819.

A William Hill (perhaps his father?) with 2 children aged 4 & 7 admitted to Roy. Soc. of Musicians on recommendation of William Duncombe 1779. He then described himself as violinist & cellist & organist of Trinity Chapel Conduit Street[182]. City wait (i.e. in the Lord Mayor's band) 1777–90 and a freeman of Musicians' Company 1769[128 129].

HILLS, George.
U *45.1840* (George John Hills), 59.1843, 76.1843 (no christian name), *63.1844* (do.).

Of 4 Beaumont Sq., Mile End Rd. 1843[59V], Henley on Thames 1844[63V].

HOAR, Joseph William.
U 51.1826 (no christian name), 61.1826, *45.1826*, 25.1827 (no christian name).

HOBSON, John.
U *45.1840*.
282?

HODGES, Dr. Edward.
U 80.1838.

From Bristol. According to G. left Bristol & went to America 1838.
G. 284.

HODSON, Thomas, c.1799 – 1826.
St. Michael Crooked Lane 1819 Jul. 7 – 1826 Jan. 11 death reported. Bur. St. Michael, 1826 Jan.15 age 26 from Crooked Lane.

HOLDITCH, G.W.
U 59.1843.

Of 12 Greek St., Soho[59V]. G.M. Holdich [sic] organist St. Peter's Croydon in 1867[210].

HOLLAND, Elizabeth, later Mrs. Carter.
St. Augustine Watling Street 1812 Apr.23 until 1831 Easter when as Mrs. Carter suspended after dissatisfaction. St. Faith, a parish united to St. Augustine, thoroughly disunited as regards the organist. While St. Augustine continued to support her, St. Faith elected John Peck in 1832 and continued to support him. An inter-parish feud led to intervention by the Bishop and a case in the Consistory Court. Mrs. Carter and Peck both ostensibly organists until death of Mrs. E. Carter 1842 Oct.31 (date from V.).

Holland, Miss E., teacher of the pianoforte and organ on moderate terms, 9 Elizabeth Place, Ball's Pond 1828[195].

HOLLOCOMBE, George Phineas.
U 44.1823.

HOLMEWOOD,
U *12.1842*.

HOLT, Walter.
St. Michael Cornhill 1699 Dec.11 – 1703/4 Feb.25 discharged.

The identification of the organist with either of the two Walter Holts, father and son who as dancing masters subscribed to Feuillet in 1706[259] remains unproven. Both were well known dancing masters and freemen of the Musicians' Company. The second W.H. (bap. St. Botolph Bishopsgate 1675/6 Jan.27) included among his apprentices Thomas South (1703 June 5)[165] and William Fayling (1722 Aug.21)[165] both distinguished dancing masters. It would appear to be this W.H. who died 1738 Sep.8[245] and whose daughter Frances according to his will[139] was married to Thomas Burney, dancing master and half brother of Dr. Burney. If either W.H. was the organist, W.H. sen. is the more likely. A freeman from 1670 and liveryman of the Musicians' Company[200] his apprentices included Richard Low(e) the organist (q.v.)[165]. He was living in the parish of St. Botolph Bishopsgate with his wife Ann and an expanding family until moving to St. Bartholomew by the Exchange around 1680.

Hook, James.
U 58.1767 (Hooke, no christian name, runner-up), 7.1817.
Possibly James Hook who "came to London about 1763–4" and subsequently organist St. John Horsleydown. Hook, James, composer, organist Vauxhall Gardens, of Charlotte St. Bedford Sq. 1794[198]. Elected Roy. Soc. of Musicians 1767 died 1827[181].
B.? G.?

Hopkins,
U 12.1842 (disqualified).

Hopkins, Edward John.
Temple Church 1843 May 7 – 1898 resigned.
G. 284. 339.

Hopkins, John.
St. Benet Paul's Wharf? No evidence found in V. or C. but according to some authorities appointed 1841 Jul.[282]. Possibly assistant.
U 74.1844 (disallowed – no testimonial).
St. Paul's choir school 1831–8[102]. No other City posts. Of 16 North St., Westminster 1844[74V].
G. 284. 339.

Hopkins, John Larkin, 1819–1873.
U 48.1834 (absent), *45.1840*.
Born 1819 Nov. 25 bap. 1821 Jan.28 St. Margaret Westminster. Son of Edward Larkin Hopkins musician, & Elizabeth of North St. Westminster. Choir of Westminster Abbey under Greatorex & Turle. Organist St. Paul's Chapel Portland St., assistant organist Westminster Abbey, pianist (teacher), flautist when elected Roy. Soc. of Musicians 1841 May 2[182].
G. 284. 339.

Hopwood,
U 81.1659.

Horsley, William, 1774 – 1858.
Charterhouse 1838 Feb.17 – 1858 June 12 died.
Born 1774 Nov.15 bap. St. George Hanover Sq. Dec.11. Son of William & Frances Horsley. Articled to Theodore Smith 5 years. Organist Ely Chapel Holborn in 1797, teaching at school & privately[182]. Engagements as bass chorus singer Covent Garden etc. 1794[198]. Elected Roy. Soc. of Musicians 1797 on recommendation of John Ashley Mar.5[182]. Of 17 New St. Fetter Lane 1794[198], 1 High Row Kensington 1847[199]. Died 1858 June 12.
B. G. 282. 284.

Horth, Miss Mary, later Mrs. Deane.
St. Giles Cripplegate 1818 May 1 – 1832 Jan. resigned. Became Mrs. Deane between 1818 May 1 and 1819 Apr. Mother of John Horth Deane? (q.v.)

Horwood, Peter.
Christ Church Newgate Street before 1718 Nov.[269] – 1739 Dec. died.
Christ's Hospital music master 1719/20 Jan.28 – 1739 Dec. died.
U 73.1705 (Harwood, no christian name), 48.1706 (no christian name).
"Singing boy in Paul's" 1698[164]. Wife Ann (although music masters at Christ's Hospital had to be unmarried). Childen bap. Wandsworth 1724, 1730–36. Died 1739 bur. Wandsworth Dec.6 "Mr. Peter Horwood, organist of Christ's Church and Hospital, London". Admon. to widow Ann 1739 Dec.[139].

Hoskins, J.F.
U *74.1844*, 25.1847 (no christian name, declined audition).
Of Bishopsgate Ward Schools, Peter St. 1844[74V].

Howard, J.H.
U 15.1836.

Howard, Samuel.
St. Bride Fleet Street 1736 Aug.10 – 1782 Jul.13 died. Death reported Jul.26.
Original member Roy. Soc. of Musicians 1739[181]. Contributed psalm tunes to Riley's *Parochial music corrected* 1762[273]. Of Norfolk St., Strand 1763[211]. Also organist St. Clement Danes[273]. Died Norfolk Street 1782 Jul.13[232]. Widow d.1790 Aug.6[232].
B. G. 284. 337.

Howard, Thomas.
St. Mary le Bow. Thomas Howard of Camberwell to erect organ & provide

organist for annuity of £42, St. Mary le Bow. Agreement 1802 Feb.24[93]. Sold interest in organ & annuity to Messrs. Rolfe of Cheapside 1822 Jan.14. No positive evidence that he played himself.
U 18.1784. The same?
Age 33 in 1801[54V]. Of Union Row, Camberwell[54V]. Thomas Howard of 5 Union Row Camberwell music master in 1805[199].

HOWE, James.
U 63.1837 (runner-up).
Probably James Howe born 1820 Oct.24 bap. St. John's Chapel Portsea Hants. Nov.19 Son of James Howe, musician, & Rebecca of Lombard St. Portsmouth. Chorister Westminster Abbey 9 years, later deputy tenor. Piano & organ teacher when elected Roy. Soc. of Musicians 1842 Nov. 6[182]. Mar. Emma Sarah Gray 1857 Jan.23 St. Nicholas Worcester. Of Pilgrim St., Upper Kensington Lane 1864. Died 1864 buried South Metropolitan Cemetery Aug.24 age 43[183].

HOWE, Miss Jane.
U 16.1821, 1.1823 (no christian name), 4.1825 (do.), 75.1825, 61.1826 (no christian name, withdrew).

HOWELL, Charles F.
U 76.1847 (top 8 out of 57), 53.1847 (withdrew).
Of 9 Globe Rd., Mile End 1847[53V].

HUDDEN, Thomas.
U 34.1782 (runner-up), 18.1784, 34.1790.

HUDSON,
U 40.1744/5, 31.1752 (withdrew because of single post clause), 65.1753 (runner-up).
Could be Burton Hudson (below) or William Hudson elected St. Olave Southwark 1736 May 25[94]. The 1752 & 1753 entries could refer to Robert (below). A John Hudson original member Roy. Soc. of Musicians 1739[181].

HUDSON, Burton, d.1765.
St. Benet Fink 1747 Oct.15 – 1765 Aug. died. Death reported Aug.13.
U 48.1745, 31.1749, 34.1753 (runner-up), 2.1756, 18.1762.
Elected Roy. Soc. of Musicians 1747[181]. Bur. St. Benet Fink 1765 Aug. 12 "under the organ loft". Wife predeceased him. Living in parish of St. John Zachary 1765. Admon. 1765 granted to Mary Cooke, wife of Samuel Cooke, sister & next of kin[139].

HUDSON, Miss Mary, c.1758–1801.
St. Olave Hart Street 1781 Dec.20 – 1801 Mar.28 died. Death reported Apr.2. Before election V describes her as "only dau. of Dr. Robert Hudson master of the singing boys of St. Paul's" (q.v.). First organist of St. Olave, she polled 131 votes out of 133 divided between 5 candidates.
St. Mary Magdalen Old Fish Street (no other candidates) 1785 Dec.29 – 1801 Mar.28 died.
Of 1 St. Peter Hill 1794[198]. Buried St. Paul's Cathedral "age 43". Died 1801 Mar.28[232].
G. 284.

HUDSON, Robert.
St. Mildred Bread Street assistant? Not confirmed in church records.
St. Paul's Cathedral almoner 1773 – 1793 resigned.
Christ's Hospital music master 1767 Jul.2 – 1808 Mar.15 retired through increasing infirmities and age (77 years). To retire from London (St. Peter's Hill). Voted pension of £40 p.a. Asked for admission to Christ's Hospital of relative George Edwards age 8 whose family largely dependant on him 1801 Sep.11[155].
One of King's last pupils at St. Paul's. Probation as Vicar Choral 1755 Nov.22, Vicar Choral 1756 Nov.23[342]. Date of birth 1730[342] agrees with age in 1808 (see above) and disagrees with usually quoted date of 1732 Feb.1. Elected Roy. Soc. of Musicians 1757: name struck out by order of wife[181]. Died 1815 Dec.19, bur. St. Paul's Dec. 28 in 85th year, "60 years Vicar Choral".
B. G. 284.

HUGHES, Robert.
U *75.1825*, *45.1826*.

HULL, Miss.
St. Alban Wood Street 1840 Jan.26 – 1841 before Aug.23 vacated.
Probably dau. of William Hull vestry clerk St. Alban in 1840, but an Amelia Matilda, dau. of William Thomas Hull of Exmouth, author of hymns 1850 onwards died 1882[282].

HULL, David.
U 74.1844 (no testimonial, disqualified).
Of Romford, Essex 1844[74V].

HULLATT, Charles.
Christ Church Newgate Street? Possibly deputy after 1773.
R.J.S. Stevens in his *Recollections*[192] describes playing the organ at Christ Church: "I saw the name of Charles Hullatt cut in the desk of the organ. I imagine that he must have been Deputy organist to Battishill [organist 1767 – 1801] at this church when he left Mr. Savage [Almoner & Master of Boys St. Paul's Cathedral until 1773 when succeeded by Hudson]. This is the name of the boy that was contemporary with me in St. Paul's Choir and that secreted a knife to murder me when I was asleep". Maria Hackett lists Joseph Charles Hullatt sometime chorister of St. Paul's, "musician, died in obscurity"[342].

HUSSEY, Matthew, d.1766.
St. Alban Wood Street 1736 Apr.28 – 1766 c.Apr.1 died. Death reported Apr.8.
Parish Clerks' Company 1742 Jan.18 – 1766 c.Apr.1 died.
U 53.1730 (—— Husse), 81.1739/40.
Chorister St. Paul's under Charles King[342]. Original member Roy. Soc. of Musicians 1739[181]. Given additional 3 guineas by Parish Clerks' Company 1764 for "extraordinary trouble in putting several new tunes into the Company's psalm books"[130]. Contributed psalm tunes to Riley's *Parochial music corrected* 1762[273]. "Organist at Newington Butts" 1763[211]. Died 1766 c.Apr.1[L334]. Bur. St. Alban Wood St. Apr.7.
B.

HUSSEY, Richard.
St. Mildred Bread Street. To erect organ and to play for sal. of £20, 1744 Oct. 11. He appears to have been associated in this with Thomas and George Griffin. If Richard Hussey played, as seems likely, it was from 1745 Apr.21 – 1747 end, vacated or died. A Richard Hussey bur. St. Luke Old Street 1746. The same?

HUSSEY, Mrs.
St. Mildred Bread Street (possibly) 1747 Dec. – 1749 vacated or died. Presumably widow of Richard, above (see church lists p.60). If Mrs. Hussey played she would be the earliest recorded woman organist.

IMMYNS, Eliza, b.1788.
U 48.1805.
Daughter of John Immyns (q.v.) born 1788 c.May.

IMMYNS, John, 1764 –
St. Giles Cripplegate 1795 Mar.30 – 1818 Apr.2 resigned. In reply to a letter sent to him by churchwardens asking him to do the whole of his duty he wrote "Mr.Groombridge of St. Stephen Coleman Street attends only every other Sunday morning and the generality of respectable gentlemen in the profession (whose salary is more than mine) only once on Sunday. If I cannot have the same indulgence I must be under the necessity of resigning the situation". Office declared vacant.
U 25.1786.
Born 1764 Oct.26 bap. Congregation of United Brethren in London Oct.28. Son of William & Catharine Immyns[182]. This William Immyns a freeman of Stationers' Company 1760 Mar. after apprenticeship to John Lewis 1752[165]. William's father was John Immyns of St. Bride's, gentleman[165] doubtless identifiable as lutenist of the Chapel Royal in succession to John Shore (died 1752 Nov.20). This John Immyns of Cold Bath Fields "one of the gentlemen of H.M. Band of Music" died 1764 Apr. 17[L375]. John Immyns the organist free of the City of London & Stationers'

Company by patrimony (see p.7) 1788 Mar.[165] and in 1792 as a liveryman of the Company described as "musician, Red Lion St. Clerkenwell"[206]. Mar. ("John Immyns age 22 of Hatton St.") Ann Bickerton, spinster, eldest dau. of Benjamin Bickerton, goldsmith, of Jewin Sq. age 25 St. Dunstan in the West 1787 Jul.4[176 232]. Dau. Eliza (q.v.) born 1788 around May[182]. Harpsichord, violin, viola & 'cello player, organist of St. John Bedford Row & Jewry St. Chapel Aldgate in 1789 when elected to Roy. Soc. of Musicians on recommendation of Richard Huddleston Potter (q.v.)[182]. Described as organist, violoncellist, organist Surrey Chapel of 68 Red Lion St. Clerkenwell in 1794[198]. Later organist Foundling Hospital 1798 May – 1801 Mar. resigned after complaint.
G. (William only). 284. 353.

INGRAM, Mrs. Margaret.
St. Ethelburga Bishopsgate 1844 June 20 – 1853 Apr.4 last recorded entry.
U 59.1843.
Of 11 Canonbury Terrace 1843[59V].

INGRAM, Thomas.
U 20.1836 (no christian name), 81.1844.
Of 4 Denbigh St., Pimlico 1844[156]. Ingram, Thomas, music master & organist, 16A Walcot Place, Lambeth 1847[199]. Thomas Ingram music master & organist Brighton college 1847 to death in 1869. Organist Chapel Royal Brighton[282].
282. 284.

ISAACK, Bartholomew.
U 28.1702 (no christian name), 73.1705 (do.).
A child of the Chapel Royal of this name between 1674 and 1677[292]. Probably Bartholomew Isaack appointed organist St. Saviour Southwark 1705 Jul.26[389].

ISHAM, John, d.1726.
St. Andrew Holborn 1718 Apr.3 – 1726 June died. Successor appointed Aug.
U 73.1705 (no christian name), 13.1717/18 (do.), 81.1719/20.
Bur. St. Margaret Westminster 1726 June 12. Possibly son of Edward & Elizabeth Isham living in Whitefriars Precinct 1695[179]. John Isham Esq. of the Inner Temple bach. mar. Francise Ashfield of Kensington 1705 Jul. 10 St. Edmund, King & Martyr. The same? or (likelier) John Isham mar. Ann Jones, St. Margaret Westminster 1714.
G. 284. 295.

JACKSON,
U 1.1770, 60.1781, 34.1782.

JACKSON, George.
St. Alban Wood Street 1774 Dec.2 – 1790 Oct.7 resigned.
Elected Roy. Soc. of Musicians 1779 on recommendation of Thomas Hogg Sep.5[182]. Composer and author of *First principles, or a treatise on the practical thorough-bass* c.1795.
B. 284.

JACKSON, Thomas.
U? Opposed Henry Duncalf annually St. Bartholomew by the Exchange, 1757 – 62. Nominal only?
B.?

JACKSON, William.
All Hallows Lombard Street 1737/8 Mar.1 – 1780 May 24 death reported.
U 31.1749 (withdrew because of single post clause).
One of this name original member Roy. Soc. of Musicians 1739[181]. William Jackson, Dean St., Westminster, musician 1749[213]. William Jackson teacher of violin Windmill St. 1763[211]. The same? The candidature given above could refer to William Jackson 1730 – 1803 organist of Exeter Cathedral who came to London 1748 to study under John Travers[316].
284?

JAMES, Miss Eliza, later Mrs. Wright.
All Hallows London Wall 1844 Sep.4 – 1858 Apr.6 last recorded entry as Mrs. Wright (mar. between 1857 Apr.14 and 1858 Apr.6).

JAMES,
U 1.1758.

JAMES, John.
U 2.1726/7, 2.1728 (one of 12 names submitted by vestry), 2.1729, 20.1731 (no christian name).

Organist St. Olave Southwark 1729/30 Mar.12 – 1736 Apr.27 resigned[94] and allegedly St. George in the East (Hawkins etc.) but unconfirmed documentarily through loss of records. No doubt identifiable with "John James of St. Bride's, London, musician" to whom "Thomas Harrison son of Thomas Harrison, musician of Southwark" apprenticed 1730 Aug.28[149]. (Thomas Harrison u St. Olave when William Hudson succeeded James 1736 May 25[94]). The problem of James's identification is complicated by the many contemporary Londoners with the same name. His established location in St. Bride parish in 1730 (see above) suggested his common identity with John James, joiner living there from 1727[85 121]. But the joiner, who had a son William b.c.1703 and an unnamed younger son b.c.1709[85], was buried St. Bride 1735 Sep.23. Would the erudition claimed by Hawkins for John be alien to a joiner's younger son? Or is it possible that John James of country origin was living with James the joiner as a London relative? A more cultured background could be expected for John son of George James (son of a Basingstoke vicar), an eminent type founder. Born c.1710 John was apprenticed to William Meares in the Stationers' Company 1724 Nov. 3 and became a freeman 1738 Jul.4[134]. Probably coincidental are the musical associations of a George James and a William Meares who belonged to the Musicians' Company[124] and played in the City waits. (Members of the Musicians' Company sometimes belonged to another company as well). Was William Meares in St. Bride's in 1730? His name appears briefly in the assessments a few years later[85]. In confirmation and elaboration of Hawkins's assertion, John James's son Handel was apprenticed 1750 June 22 to Philip Dale, a Bermondsey waterman, and granted the freedom of the Watermen's Company but not the City in 1757[138]. Analysis of countless John James marriages before 1736 has failed to identify the organist's and his death also remains undiscovered.
B. G. 284.

JARVIS, Samuel, c.1742 – 1784.
St. Sepulchre Holborn (jointly) 1760 Mar.20 (or "Samuel Jarvis jun."[L289]) – 1773 Oct.27.
St. Sepulchre Holborn (sole) 1773 Oct.27 – 1784 June 21 died. Death reported June 24.
St. Botolph Bishopsgate 1764 Nov.7 – 1784 June 21 died. Death reported Jul.22.
U 44.1762 (no christian name, runner-up), 18.1762 (do.), 53.1762 (no christian name), 59.1764 (do.).

Referred to as "Samuel Jarvis, jun." in 1760 & 1773. "A blind youth of great merit" 1764 Nov.[L449]. Elected Roy. Soc. of Musicians 1765, expelled for non-payment[181]. Died 1784 June 21 Mr. Samuel Jervis [sic] organist . . .[232]. Bur. 1784 June 25 St. Sepulchre "under the organ loft from Snow Hill age 42".
B. G(5.) 284.

JEE, John, b.c. 1746.
U 10.1774.

Viola player & organist of Barking Essex when elected to Roy. Soc. of Musicians age 39 on recommendation of William Hudson 1785 [182].

JENKINS, Thomas, d.1726.
No City posts or candidatures found.

Thomas, son of Thomas Jenkins organist & Jane bap. St. Giles Cripplegate 1692 Apr.7. Jane wife of Thomas Jenkins musicioner bur. St. Giles 1701/2 Feb.11. —— [sic] Jenkings, musician bur. St. Giles 1726 Aug.7. Many of the Jenkins family were musicians in the City and some members of the City waits.

JENKINSON, Samuel.
U? Opposed Henry Duncalf annually St. Bartholomew by the Exchange 1747–50. Nominal only?

Samuel Jenkinson parish clerk of St. Bartholomew 1740–74. Died 1777 bur. Aug.26[130].

JEYES, Miss Catherine.
U 71.1786, 66.1792.

JOHNSON, Alexander.
No City posts or candidatures found.
Organist St. John Hackney before death reported 1707/8 Jan.28[328]. Lived in parish of St. Giles Cripplegate where bur. 1707 Dec.3.

JOHNSON, Miss M.A.
U 76.1843 (Miss Johnson), 15.1844.

JOLLY, jun.
St. Bartholomew the Great (by casting vote of chairman) 1834 June 26 – 1836 Apr.7 not re-elected.
U 20 (St. Bartholomew the Great), 1836 (runner-up).
Conceivably Edward Moulton Jolly, son of John Marks Jolly, composer & conductor. Born 1819 Sep.7. Pianist & violinist when elected Roy. Soc. of Musicians 1841[182]. Or Thomas Jolley [sic] U St. Giles Camberwell 1832 Nov.

JOLLY, John?
U 27.1815 (no christian name).
Probably John Jolly born 1794 Feb.11 bap. Rostherne, Cheshire Apr.18. Son of William & Sarah Jolly of Knutsford. Educated "under Mr. White" of Leeds & apprenticed 5 years to Robert Cooke of Westminster Abbey. Pianist, violinist, teacher at 2 schools and privately, organist of Stockwell & deputy organist Westminster Abbey when elected Roy. Soc. of Musicians on recommendation of William Hawes 1816 Jul.7. Of 12 Stafford Place Pimlico 1816[182]. Died 1838 Mar.27 "organist of St. Philip Regent Street"[232]. Widow Sarah Ann[182].

JONES,
U 2.1727/8 (probably John Jones, q.v.).

JONES,
U 51.1829 (runner-up).

JONES,
U 12.1842 (failed to supply testimonial).

JONES, Miss Catherine.
St. Vedast Foster Lane (succeeded Thomas Jones) 1793 c.Sep. – 1807 c.Jul. vacated. Dissatisfaction with playing 1794 May 26.

JONES, Charles.
St. Vedast Foster Lane 1784–98 according to Pearce[323] but no contemporary evidence found. See Jones, Catherine and Jones, Thomas.

JONES, Griffith, b.1757.
U 3.1780.
Born 1757. Son of Griffith Jones, freeman of Stationers' Company from 1741[165]. Apprenticed to K.F. Baumgarten. Performer on violin, clarinet, organ etc. Employed at Covent Garden & Haymarket Theatres[182] and from 1798 to 1836 in City Waits. Elected Roy. Soc. of Musicians on recommendation of W. Dance 1779 Mar.7[182]. Freeman of Stationers' Company by patrimony 1787 Dec.1[165]. Author *Complete instructor for the harpsichord*. Of Devonshire St. 1792[206], 17 Ave Maria Lane 1832–3[208].
B.

JONES, John (1) d.1722.
St. James Garlickhythe 1719 May 14 – 1722 Mar.26 death reported.
Conceivably John Jones, musical instrument maker, printer and publisher at the Golden Harp New Street Covent Garden[310]. This John Jones's widow, Phillipa, married 1723 Benjamin Cooke (1) (q.v.).

JONES, John (2).
U 2.1718 (referred to also as William Jones, q.v.), 2.1727/8 ("Jones" one of 12 names submitted by vestry. The same?).
An undated electioneering broadside in support of John Jones refers to the 1718 election. "Whereas it has been Industriously and Maliciously reported, that Mr. John Jones (now a Candidate for the Place of ORGANIST to the United Parishes of Allhallows Breadstreet, and St. John the Evangelist) is a BUNGLER etc." This "false report" was repudiated by 9 leading London

organists: "that the said Mr. Jones is a Person fitly Qualified, and Capable of playing on any Organ, being very well recommended and approv'd . . . We . . . do certifie That Mr. John Jones, brought up in the Cathedral Church of St. Paul's, is Capable of Playing (in any Parish-Church in England) on the Organ . . ."[269]. A John Jones original member of Roy. Soc. of Musicians 1739[181]. *See frontis.*

JONES, John (3) d.1796.
Temple Church (elected by Middle Temple) 1749 Nov.24 – 1796 Feb.17 died.
Charterhouse 1753 Jul. – 1796 Feb.17 died.
St. Paul's Cathedral 1755 Dec.25 – 1796 Feb.17 died.

Elected Roy. Soc. of Musicians 1750[181]. Vicar Choral St. Paul's Cathedral 1757 Jan.26[101]. Mar. Sarah Chawner at Sudbury, Derbyshire (recorded in Charterhouse Chapel reg.). Their children bap. Charterhouse from 1758. Thomas Jones apprenticed to him 1764[150]. Sarah his wife d.1792 Oct.8 age 62. He died 1796 Feb.17 age 67. Both bur. Charterhouse Chapel (inscription).
B. G.

JONES, John Jeremiah.
St. Andrew by the Wardrobe 1811. Only evidence from his *Six fugues with introductions for the organ*, 1811, by John Jeremiah Jones "organist of St. Andrew by the Wardrobe and St. Anne Blackfriars" (the amalgamated parish with no separate church). Church records do not in fact refer to an organist until 1815 although faculty for organ granted 1808 May 20.

Presumably J.J. Jones acted voluntarily before going to Oxford matric 1812 Feb.14 age 23, "son of John Jones of St. Andrew, London, gent."[295]. This identification of his father strongly suggests the relevancy of the entry in the register of St. Andrew Holborn: 1789 Feb. 14 bap. John Jeremiah son of John & Tabitha Jones, Leather Lane, Holborn.

JONES, Joseph.
U 2.1726/7, 33.1729 & 1731.

JONES, Miss Margaret.
St. Mildred Bread Street 1806 May 21 – 1809 June 6 resigned after suspension 1809 May 17.
U 2.1799, 42.1805, 48.1805, 17.1812.

JONES, Thomas.
St. Vedast Foster Lane c.1779 – 1793 c.Sep. died. Appointed by William Duncombe, holder of annuity.

Thomas Jones apprenticed to Samuel Long (q.v.) of St. Andrew Holborn, organist £30 in 1764[150]. After Long's death in Aug. Thomas Jones apprenticed to John Jones of Charterhouse organist £24.16.0 in 1764[150]. The same? Harp, harpsichord or piano works 1788–9 by Thomas Jones reviewed in European Mag. 1793[225].
B.?

JONES, William.
U 2.1718 (referred to also as John Jones, q.v.).

JONES, William.
U 77.1828, 33.1832 (runner-up).

Of Ormes's Distillery, Borough 1828[77V].

JONES, William.
U 59.1843, 74.1844 (failed to attend audition).

Of 3 John St., Cambridge Heath, Hackney 1843–4[59V 74V].

JOPP, John Alexander, d.1885.
St. Clement Eastcheap 1847 Dec. 16 – 1885 Mar.24 death reported. Assistant c.1845 – 1847. Election without opposition.
U 53.1847.

Of 8 Lawrence Pountney Lane 1847[53V]. Son of James & Marriann Jopp, relieving officer[153].

JULIERE *see* Gigleir.

JUNNINGS [sic], John.
U 37.1785.

KAHLMAN (?), Mrs.
U 4.1825.

KEARN(E)S, W. H.
St. Botolph Bishopsgate. Filled gap without authority 1838–9. (see Fleet, E.E.)
Possibly William Henry Kearns, 1794 – 1846, Irish violinist, conductor & composer who came to London 1817.
G? 284?

KEARNS (or KEARN), Miss.
St. Alphage London Wall 1845 June 27 – 1854 Mar.30 resigned.

KEEBLE, John.
U 28.1736 (no christian name).
Apprentices: 1746 John Burton of St. George Hanover Sq. to John Keeble of St. James Westminster & 1752 Charles Stephen Philpot to John Keeble of St. George Hanover Sq.[149]. Of Hanover St., St. George's Westminster 1749[213], Maddox St. Hanover Sq. 1763[211].
B. G. 284.

KEENE, John, c.1723 – 1800.
U 22.1747.
Elected (jointly) organist St. Leonard Shoreditch 1757 c.Nov.15[L404]. A fulsome inscription in St. Leonard indicating that he died 1800 Mar.3 age 77[300]. Bur. Mar. 11 "of Union Crescent, organist of this church for 42 years".

KEITH, Cornelius, c.1759 – 1800.
St. Peter Cornhill 1786 May 18 – 1800 Aug.7 died. Death reported Aug.22.
St. Dionis Backchurch substitute 1784 Jan. – Oct.
U 3.1780 (withdrew), 68.1781, 18.1784, 31.1784 (runner-up).
Born 1758 June 20 bap. St. Dunstan Stepney June 24. Son of William Keith, musician (q.v.), & Mary of Mile End Old Town. Studied music under father. Mar. Sarah Langford 1784 Aug.5 St. Leonard Shoreditch. Children included Robert William b.1787 Mar.20, Mary Ann b. 1789 Feb.25, John Langford & Sarah b.1794 Dec.22, Cornelius b.1797 Oct.11, Henry Frederick b.1800 June 20. Violin & guitar player & organist. Private teaching. Organist St. Peter Cornhill, Danish Church Well Close Sq. & City of London Lying-in Hospital in 1788 when recommended for election to Roy. Soc. of Musicians by S. Arnold Nov.1 (elected 1789)[182]. Died Mile End Old Town 1800 Aug.7 buried Bunhill Fields[151]. Sarah Keith, widow, married Josiah Wood 1801 Sep.22 St. Martin in the Fields[183]. Of the children mentioned above Robert William free of Musicians' Co. by redemption 1809 Dec.4 described as professor of music, 91 Aldersgate St.[125]. He was a pianist, author of books on music, music seller & publisher. Moved from Aldersgate St. c.1822 to succeed Longman & Herron at 131 Cheapside and the firm became Keith, Prowse & Co. c.1829. He died 1846 June 19[284]. His brothers John Langford Keith & Cornelius apprenticed 1809 & 1811 to William Reading musical instrument maker of Warwick Sq., Golden Sq. in 1809 & 3 Upper John St. Golden Sq. in 1811[182].

KEITH, William.
U 59.1764 (no christian name), 57.1764 (do.), 16.1777 (do.). No proof that these are William, indeed the 1777 entry could be for Cornelius, q.v.
Father of Cornelius Keith q.v. William Keith cand. St. Paul Deptford 1759 Oct.19[L398]. Published *Hymns and airs sung at the Jewish Synagogue*. Died 1800 Apr.9 at Mile End, William Keith, many years organist West Ham[232].
B.

KELLY, C.
U 74.1844 (failed to attend audition),
Of 7 Bretten Terrace, King's Rd., Chelsea 1844[74V].

KELWAY, Joseph.
St. Michael Cornhill 1734 June 20 – 1736 June 2 resigned.
Resignation because 1736 May 12 "chosen by great majority St. Martin in the Fields"[230]. Original member Roy. Soc. of Musicians 1739[181]. Living "near Depuis's Coffee House in Conduit St." 1739 & King's Row, Upper Grosvenor St. 1747 (imprints on his music).
B. G.

KEMM, Samuel, c.1770 – 1828.
St. Paul's Cathedral deputy[342].
U 25.1799 (no christian name).

Kemm, Samuel, organist, alto Oratorio, Drury Lane, Westminster Abbey. Holiday Yard, Creed Lane 1794[198]. Chorister of St. Paul's Cathedral[342]. Bur. St. Paul's Cathedral 1828 Sep.19 Samuel Kemm late of Greenfield St., Whitechapel age 58.

KEMP, W.
U 4.1825 (no christian name), 77.1828.
Of 16 Euston St. 1828[77]V.

KEWELL, John.
St. Margaret Pattens 1777 Mar.? – 1783 Apr.? vacated.
U 43.1766 (runner-up).

KING,
U 1.1758 (declined playing), 53.1762.

KING, Charles.
St. Benet Fink 1714/15 Jan.6 – 1747 Sep.9 dismissed after reduction in salary from £20 to £15 p.a. 1746 Jul.3.
St. Paul's Cathedral almoner 1707 – 1748 Mar.17 died.
U 57.1705/6 (no christian name), 44.1710 (do.), 34.1712, 81.1719/20 (runner-up).

"Singing boy in Paul's"[164]. Apprenticed to Jeremiah Clarke & mar. his sister[342]. Vicar Choral St. Paul's. Living London House Yard near St. Paul's 1711 (from printer's imprint). Left valuable collection of mss. to St. Paul's Cathedral[342].
B. G. 284.

KINGSBURY, Frederick.
U *74.1844*, *63.1844*.

Of 35 Dean St., Soho 1844[74]V, Liverpool Rd. 1844[63]V. A professor at Guildhall School of Music of this name, conductor Strand Music Hall, founder of London Vocal Academy d.1892 Feb.26.
282? 284?

KINKEE, Frederick, 1826–1899.
U 59.1843.

Born 1826 Mar.27 bap. St. Mary Lambeth Apr.30. Son of Ralph Kinkee, musician (q.v.), and Elizabeth of Carlisle Place. Professor of organ & pfte. & organist of St. Paul Knightsbridge when elected to Roy. Soc. of Musicians 1852 Feb.1[182]. Organist St. Mary Lambeth 1868–79[298]. Of 47 Albany St. Regent's Park 1843[59]V, 4 Graham St. Eaton Sq. 1851[182]. Died 1899[182].

KINKEE, Ralph, b.1792.
St. Olave Jewry 1814 Aug.9 (jointly) – 1834 Aug.28. The appointment an annuity arrangement until 1834 Aug.28 when his playing being disapproved of, Kinkee willing to forego his contract for annuity of £20 which still continuing 1860.

Father of Frederick Kinkee (q.v.). Age 22 in Nov.1814[69]V. Of Carlisle Place Lambeth 1826.

KIRBY, Miss Caroline.
U 4.1825 (Miss Kerby or Kirby), 53.1826, *45.1826*.

KIRKSHAW, (also Kirshaw).
U 10.1766.

KITCHINGMAN, Miss Ann, later Mrs. Beverley.
St. Mildred Poultry 1778 Feb.24 – 1792 Nov.12 successor appointed. A stormy tenure with frequent trouble shown by entries in V. Some relate to her deputy but 1790 Feb.8 "Mrs. Ann Beverley, formerly Ann Kitchingman, has for many years neglected to play". "Confined at Hull by indisposition" 1790 Apr.21. Mrs. Beverley's continued absence and failure to apply for salary for considerable time led to an advertisement for her which produced no result. Salary of her deputy, William Bride, increased from £10 to £15, 1791 Dec.23 and new election held 1792 Nov.12.

KNOWLES, William.
U 18.1819, 16.1821 (runner-up).

KNYVETT, Charles, d.1822.
All Hallows Barking by the Tower (joint) 1770 Nov.22 – between 1782 Apr.4 & 1783 Apr.24 vacated.

Pupil of Dr. Cooke[182]. Elected Roy. Soc. of Musicians 1778 on recommen-

dation of John Ashley 1777 Jul.6[182]. Died 1822.
B.G. 284. 339.

LAHEE, Henry.
St. Swithin London Stone 1843 Nov.29 – 1847 Sep.1 resigned on election to Holy Trinity Brompton.
U *12.1842* (no christian name), 59.1843.
Of 32 Cheyne Walk, Chelsea 1843[59V], 16 Manor Place, Chelsea 1843–47[76V 199].
G.(5). 284.

LAMPE, Charles James Frederick, d.1767.
All Hallows Barking by the Tower 1758 Dec.29 – 1767 Sep.10 died. Death reported Sep.15. Entries in V. & C. contain wide variety of christian names usually giving 2 of his 3 but with all 3 in later entries.
Succeeded his grandfather Charles Young at All Hallows 1758[L6] when living in parish of St. Martin in the Fields. Charles Young bequeathed to him "my harpsichord, all my papers, my watch and my books" (will). Mar. 1763 May 7 Miss Smith singer at Marylebone Gardens[L453]. Elected Roy. Soc. of Musicians 1762[181]. Also of Covent Garden Theatre[L453]. Died 1767 Sep.10[L277]. Bur. All Hallows Barking 1767 Sep.15.
B. G.

LANDERGAN, William Henry.
St. Mary Somerset 1843? – 1845 vacated.
U 59.1840 & 1843.
Of 30 Great Ormond St., Queen's Sq. 1840[59V], 2 Wellington St., Pentonville 1843[59V].

LARKIN or Larken, Edmund.
U 31.1749 (polled 1 vote against Dr. Burney's 50).
"For the benefit of Mr. Edmund Larken [sic]. 1744/5 Feb. at Stationers' Hall . . . will be perform'd the Masque of Acis and Galatea"[237]. Songs by —— Larken c.1740–50.
B.

LEA, Miss.
St. Matthew Friday Street 1830 Nov.10 – 1835 May 14 resigned following complaints 1835 Apr.23.

LE CREN, Miss Mary.
U 74.1844 June 20. One of 60 applicants but not selected as candidate. Despite this, voted for by vestry & topped poll. "Election disallowed" and the incident followed by much strife fully recorded in V with letter from her father of 26 Moorgate Street (address of James Le Cren, painter & plumber). A law suit followed[270].

LEFFLER, Henry.
St. Katherine by the Tower 1819 – 1848 (Church records not available). Source is Pearce[323] who asserts that he succeeded father J.H. Leffler.

LEFFLER, James Henry, c.1764 – 1819.
St. Katherine by the Tower 1788 Mar.27 – 1819 died. Proposed by Chapter of St. Katherine 1788 Feb.14, patent executed by Chapter & ordered to be registered Mar.27.
Born c.1764 (age 21 in Jan.1785). Violin, viola, clarinet & oboe player[182] and in 1794 bassoon player[198]. Employed Covent Garden Theatre. Elected Roy. Soc. of Musicians 1785 on recommendation of James Sarjant[182]. Probably author of the ms. *Account of organs and organ builders collected by Henry Leffler* (c.1800 – c.1819) on which Pearce based his work[323]. Mar. Elizabeth Shiel of Lambeth 1791 Jul.21. Eleven children surviving at time of death in 1819 fully justifying claim by widow Elizabeth for assistance from Roy. Soc. of Musicians[183]. Of Green St. Leicester Sq. 1794[198], Hercules Buildings Lambeth 1819[183].
G(5). 362.

LE MARE (or LEMARE), F.
U 58.1818 (after "very improper letter" from Mr. LeMare senr. & junr. to churchwardens, payment usually given to unsuccessful candidates withheld), 20.1819 (Fr. LeMare runner-up), 18.1819 (F. Lemare).
Mr. Lemare, teacher of music on organ & pfte. St. Mary Charity School Hammersmith 1828[195]. Lemare, Frederick Handel, jun. Godalming 1837[256]. Lemare, Frederick Handel

organist Godalming Church 1843[258]. Frederick Lemare & Son music sellers Guildford & Godalming c.1845[310].

LESTER, Thomas.
Parish Clerks' Company 1790 May 3 – 1814 Jul.18 (before) resigned.
U 10.1790 (runner-up), 40.1793.

LESTRANGE, John.
U 10.1736 (—— L'Estrange in V, Le Strange in Gen. Ev. Post[229]), 3.1737/8 (runner-up).
Original member Roy. Soc. of Musicians 1739[181]. John Lestrange free by redemption Musicians' Company 1741 June 3[124]. John Lestrange, householder, bur. St. Mary le Bow 1742 Oct.15 (wife Mary). The same?

LEVINGSTONE, George Scott, c.1749 – 1808.
St. Augustine Watling Street 1767 Feb.12 – 1808 Apr.22 death reported.
U 7.1767 (no christian name).
Bur. St. Augustine 1808 Apr.24 Livingstone [sic], George Scott aged 59, organist.

LEWIS, Peter.
U 2.1729.

LEWIS, William.
St. Peter Cornhill c.1780 – 1786 Apr.20 retired "incapacitated by infirmities". £15 for remainder of life.
U 1.1767.

L'HEUREUX, David.
U 34.1753 (no christian name), 1.1758 (do.).
Candidate St. John Hackney 1753 Sep.22 where elected 1765 Oct.5[328]. Also candidate St. Leonard Shoreditch 1757 c.Nov.15[L404].

LIGHT, William.
Parish Clerks' Company 1814 Jul.18 – 1822 Apr.22 resigned.
St. Margaret Lothbury 1831 Mar.25 – 1847 Apr.26 resigned. "He has been organist for about 41 years". Untrue, unless he served as deputy before 1831. Awarded annuity £20, last payment 1853 Apr.16.

LIGHTENDOLLER (or Lightindollar, Lighten Doller etc.), Henry, d.1702.
St. Bride Fleet Street 1696 Mar.27 – 1702 June 3 death reported.
St. Clement Eastcheap 1696? – 1702 May (end) died. Appointment at least as early as 1698 so probably first organist after completion of organ by Harris 1696.
Son of Abraham Lichtenthaller of Sulzbach, Bavaria[139]. Lodging with Mrs. Reames, Ave Maria Lane, Ludgate 1702. Bur. St. Bride 1702 June 3. Will dated 1702 Apr.27 proved Jul.[139]. To be buried St. Bride with a funeral sermon and two anthems at cost not exceeding £60. Bequests to father, brother John Jacob Lichtenthaller, godfather and other relatives. Bequests to various City friends including "my harpsicon made by Mr. Player and all my music books" to William Hobday of Bucklersbury, best violin to Mr. Heath of Quality Court, Chancery Lane, three other violins, a spinet and two tenor violins to Mr. Shuttleworth of Aldermanbury. Execs. Mr. Lente of Mincing Lane and William Hobday.

LIMMING,
U 1.1823.

LIMPUS, Richard, d.1875.
St. Andrew Undershaft 1847 Apr.8 – Jul.8 resigned on appointment as organist of Philanthropic Society.
St. Michael Cornhill 1849 Jul.9 – 1875 Mar.15 died. Appointed from many applicants without election on umpire's recommendation. Resigned and re-elected in 1861[243].
U 74.1844 ("Richard Limpus junr." Disallowed, failed to supply testimonial).
Founder with others of Royal College of Organists. Later City appointment at St. Ethelburga Bishopsgate. Of 23 Hampton St. Walworth 1844[75V].
G(5). 282. 284.

LINDLEY, Mrs. or Miss Lucy, later Mrs. Garrett?
St. Botolph Aldersgate 1847 Mar.27 – 1864 Aug.11 resigned as Lucy Garrett. Elected in 1847 from 63 applicants.
U 74.1844 (runner-up out of 60 applicants).

Of 5 Langthorne Place, Stratford, Essex 1844[74V]. Of 4 Colet Place, E. 1864[25V].

LING, William.
St. Dunstan in the West 1819 Feb.5 – 1829 Apr.22 not re-appointed on rebuilding of church, given gratuity £30. Request for increase in salary 1824 Apr. 20 granted.

Of 4 Moore Place Lambeth 1824[33V]. Ling, Wm. jun. composer, organist, Helmet Court, Strand 1794[198]. Same address as Thomas Ling, violin, bassoon, oboe 1794[198]. Sainsbury in 1828 describes William Ling as "musician in London about 1790, published several pieces"[325].
B. 284.

LINLEY, Francis.
No City posts or candidatures found.

Blind organist of Pentonville Chapel also composer, music seller & publisher of 45 Holborn 1797–8[284 310]. Bankrupt 1797 Feb.4[239]. Went to America as organist 1796–9?[333].
B. G. 284. 310. 333.

LINTON, Miss Catherine Frances.
St. Mildred Poultry 1792 Nov.12 – 1838 Jul. retired & granted pension.

LINTON, Miss Louisa.
St. Olave Hart Street 1801 Apr.9 – 1805 Dec.12 resigned.

LINTOTT [sic], Miss.
St. Mary Abchurch (jointly) 1823 Feb.20 – 1823 Apr.24. A trial period of 2 months with Emma Smith at the end of which Miss Lintott narrowly defeated by Emma Smith in a straight fight.

LISSANT, George.
U 59.1843 (top 8 out of 43), *74.1844*, 63.1844 (runner-up out of 35).

Of 2 York St., Hans Place, Chelsea 1843–4[59V 74V 63V].

LITTLE,
U *12.1842*.

LITTLE, James Hyatt.
U 9.1808.

Possibly James Little in St. Paul's Cathedral school to 1793[342]. James Little, piano teacher, 14 Goswell Rd. 1832–4[199].

LIVINGSTONE, George Scott *see* Levingstone, George Scott.

LLOYD, John.
U 76.1847 (withdrew on appointment to another post. In first 8 out of 57).

LOCK, Mary.
U 3.1780.

LOCKHART, Charles, c.1739 – 1815.
St. Katherine Cree 1766 Mar.24 – 1815 Feb.9 died. "Having been 47 years organist" to be paid annual gratuity of £15, 1813 Apr.20.
U 22.1765 (runner-up).

Thomas Castlelow apprenticed to Charles Lockhart of St. Mary Lambeth, musician 1766[150]. Mar. 1769 Nov.11 at Lambeth Charles Lockhart organist to Miss Henrietta Truman of Jermyn St., St. James's[L463]. Runner-up (308 votes) to William Goodwin (319) St. Saviour Southwark 1774 Dec.20 (ves. min. bk.) Organist Lock Chapel, St. Mary Lambeth, Orange St. Chapel. Blind from birth. Also composer & tenor singer. Of 20 Stangate St. Lambeth 1794[198]. Died 1815 Feb.9 bur. Lambeth Feb.18 age 76.
B. 284. 298.

LOCKHART, Miss Henrietta.
U 44.1788 (runner-up. Supported by letter from her father Charles Lockhart, q.v.).

Organist Magdalen Hospital 1794 – 1798 resigned on marriage, being forbidden by husband "to play at all in public". Miss Lockhart, soprano & organist of 20 Stangate St., Lambeth 1794, same address as Mrs. Lockhart, canto, & Charles Lockhart[198].

LONG, Samuel, d. 1764.
St. Peter le Poer 1745? – 1764 Aug.7 died[L142]. As the records of St. Peter have been destroyed not possible to confirm date of appointment which may have been much later. Pearce gives 1745[323].

Chorister at St. Paul's under Charles King[342]. Elected Roy. Soc. of Musi-

cians 1757: 2 years in arrears with subscription at death in 1764[181]. Organist & teacher on the harpsichord, Cross St., Hatton Garden 1763[211]. Contributed to Riley's *Parochial music corrected* 1762 (psalm tunes)[273]. Mr. Long organist of St. Peter le Poer mar. 1763 Feb.22 to Miss Whitefoot of Hatton Garden[L198]. This marriage by licence 1763 Feb.21[175]: Samuel Long of St. Ethelburga bach. age over 21 and Sarah Whitefoot of St. Andrew Holborn, spinster, a minor, dau. of Edward Whitefoot. Witness of marriage in St. Ethelburga, Dorothy Lawson & John Hamond. Thomas Jones apprenticed to Samuel Long of St. Andrew Holborn, organist 1764[150]. Awarded Catch Club premium for best English glee 1764 May[L469]. Died 1764 Aug.7 Samuel Long at Mr. Whitefoot's in Hatton Garden, organist of St. Peter le Poer[L142]. Bur. St. Andrew Holborn Aug.12, "of High Holborn". Admon. to widow Sarah 1764 Apr.[139].
B. G(5).

LORD, Walter Augustus, b.1784.
All Hallows the Great 1817 June 3 – 1833 Mar.26 resigned on appointment as parish clerk in succession to his late father.
Son of William Loveday Lord and Ann (née Goodwin). Born 1784 Dec.24 and bap. St. Benet Paul's Wharf. Appointed parish clerk 1833 on death of father and served until 1866? when address 3 Little Bush Lane[130].

LOVE, Nicholas, d.1713.
Charterhouse 1662 June 24 – 1713 died.
At Charterhouse charged with indecent behaviour at the Master's table. To make public apology or be removed to the manciples' table[154]. Petitioned for his son Thames to act as assistant 1710 June 24: "now in his extreme age"[154].

LOVE, Thomas, d.1737.
Charterhouse 1713 June 24 – 1737 died. Elected after acting as substitute for father Nicholas from 1710 June 24[154].

LOWE,
U 28.1736 (runner-up).

LOWE,
St. Andrew Undershaft. "Mr. Lowe (formerly deputy of Mr. Worgan) interferes with the present deputy" 1756 Apr.19.

LOWE, Mrs. Johanna.
U 37.1785.

LOW(E), Richard (1).
St. Martin Ludgate in succession to his father Thomas Low 1690 Oct.31 – 1703 Apr.7 successor elected. Churchwardens to speak to Mr. Low about his playing on the organ 1702 Apr.6.
Son of Thomas Low(e), q.v., freeman of City and Musicians' Company to whom apprenticed 1688 June 7. On father's death in 1690 turned over to Walter Holt (q.v.). Free of City and Musicians' Company 1695 Oct.[165]. Wife Susanna. Richard Low died before 1705 according to freedom certificate of his apprentice Richard Shirley Jan. 1705/6[165].

LOW(E), Richard (2).
U 40.1722 (no christian name), 2.1726/7 & 1729, 33.1729, 53.1730 (no christian name).

LOWE, Richard (3), d.1793.
St. Stephen Walbrook 1765 June 26 – 1793 Mar.1 death reported.
U 26.1753 (runner-up).

LOWE, Richard (4), d.1798.
St. Mary Woolnoth (Richard Lowe jun.) 1772 Jan.3 – 1798 Mar.6 death reported.
U 75.1793 (—— Lowe, jun. son of Richard Lowe late organist).

LOW(E), Thomas, d.1690.
St. Martin Ludgate 1685 Apr.21 – 1690 Oct.31 death reported.
Freeman of the City of London and of the Musicians' Company (see Richard Low (1) above). Succeeded by son Richard Low(e) (1) above. Bur. St. Bride Fleet Street 1690 Oct. 14 Thomas Low from Wine Office Court. Admon Oct.29 to Sarah Lowe [sic] relict of Thomas Lowe late of St. Bride[145].
B.?

LOWES, J.W.
U 15.1836 (withdrew).

LOWNDES,
U 28.1782.
Thomas Lowndes bookseller & publisher, Fleet St. 1756–84. "Did not generally publish music but issued & sold a number of libretti, some in conjunction with W. Lowndes"[310].

LOWNDES, W.
U 2.1799 (no christian name), 73.1799.

LOWNDES, William.
U 20.1819.

LUDDINGTON or LUDINGTON, William, d.1724.
St. Botolph Aldgate 1702 Oct. 22 – 1724 June 30 death reported.
U 43.1713/14 (declined invitation by vestry for candidature).
Perhaps William Luddington, child of the Chapel Royal up to 1697[292].

LUMLEY, Algernon Sidney.
U 15.1844.
Possibly A.S. Lumby (sic) given in 1867 as organist Holy Trinity Grays Inn Rd.[210].

MACKENSIE,
U 25.1827.

MCKERRELL, John.
U 18.1784, 14.1790 (John McKerroll).
Son of John McKerrell, baker, of Welbeck St., Marylebone. Apprenticed to Thomas Curtis (q.v.) citizen & Weaver consideration £63 1774 June 20. Freeman & liveryman Weavers Company 1801 Jul.14. Then of 7 Red Lion St. Clerkenwell, later Islington. (Weavers Co. records, Guil. Lib.). Author of *Familiar introduction to the first principles of music* c.1800. Songs & other compositions[284].
B.284.

MACKIE *see* Markie.

MCMURDIE, Joseph, 1793–1878.
No City posts or candidatures found.
Born 1793 Mar.19 bap. St. Bride Fleet St. Apr.14. Son of John & Sarah Macmurdie [sic] of 110 Half Paved Court. Pianist, violinist & organist of Christ Church Southwark when elected to Roy. Soc. of Musicians on recommendation of B. Jacob 1815[182]. B. Mus. 1814 Nov.24[295]. Glee writer etc. Died 1878 Dec.23[182].
284. 295.

MACQUISTIN, George, c.1773–1836.
Christ Church Newgate Street 1801 Dec. or 1802 Jan.? – 1817 Nov.21 resigned on "coming into a fortune". The date of appointment not definitely established. Could be as late as 1814.
St. Bartholomew the Less (no christian name) 1806 c.Sep. – 1822 Mar.25 last payment to Mr. McQuistin. The same?
Of 34 Burton St., Burton Crescent 1817[7aV]. "Died 1836 Apr.30 George Macquistin Esq., age 63." "Died Hammersmith 1828 Sep.29 Mary March Macquistin age 14 only child of George & Ann." (Tablet in Christ Church Newgate Street)[169].

MAGNUS, Clement, d.1732.
Parish Clerks' Company 1707 – 1732 Apr.17 death reported.
Mar. Flowers Motts St. James Duke's Place 1695 Apr.17. Living with wife ("Flora") in parish of St. Gregory by St. Paul's 1695[179]. Admon. dated 1732 Apr.8 "of St. Giles in the Fields"[146].

MAGNUS, William Edmund.
U 33.1718 (petitioned by father Clement Magnus).
Sainsbury mentions "—— Magnus, organist St. Giles in the Fields in first half of 18th century. Esteemed a great master of harmony. Became insane and died a young man"[325].

MAJOR, J.S.
U 76.1843 (no christian name), 53.1847 (withdrew candidature).
Of 3 Percy Circus, Pentonville 1847[53V].

MAJOR, Joseph, 1771–1828.
U 45.1795 (runner-up), 25.1799 (no christian name), 2.1799 (runner-up), 15.1804 (withdrew), 20.1805 (runner-up).
Born 1771 Nov.23. Son of Samuel Major, bookseller & Amy (dau. of Joseph Stenson of Derby) of St. Martin

le Grand. Viola player. Organist Knightsbridge Chapel in 1794 and teacher at 2 schools. Elected Roy. Soc. of Musicians 1794 on recommendation of John Francis Wood May 4[182]. Issued *A collection of psalm & hymn tunes* c.1825, *A collection of sacred music*, etc. Song composer. Of 35 Duke St. West Smithfield 1794[198], the same address as Samuel Major (presumably his father) described as 'cellist, tenor singer & music seller[198]. Died 1828.
B. 284.

MANWARING, Samuel, d.1780.
St. George Botolph Lane deputy 1739 Sep.26 – 1745 Oct.31.
St. George Botolph Lane 1745 Oct.31 – 1780 Jul.19 death reported.
U 2.1726/7, 57.1727, 2.1727/8 (one of 12 names submitted by vestry), 2.1729, 53.1730 (no christian name), 60.1736 (do.).

MARKHAM,
U 40.1722, 20.1731, 40.1744/5.

MARKHAM, Philip, d.1764.
U 31.1749 (withdrew because of single post clause).

Son of William Markham (q.v.) Apprenticed to Joseph Jennings, citizen & Dyer 1733 May 2 afterwards turned over to Mary Richardson, citizen & Mercer[117,118]. Freeman of City 1740 May 7 "son of William Markham of All Hallows the Less, schoolmaster"[165]. Liveryman Dyer's Company described in 1750 as "Musician, St. John's Clerkenwell"[204]. Singing master of the school of the Society of Ancient Britons Clerkenwell Green[L153] (1764). Organist St. John Clerkenwell 1754–64. Died 1764 Jan.27 Philip Markham, organist of Highgate Chapel & St. John Clerkenwell[L109].

MARKHAM, William, d.1749.
St. Michael Crooked Lane 1731 Jul.29 – 1749 Jul.6 died.
U 2.1729.

Father of Philip Markham, above. "Many years organist of St. Michael Crooked Lane. Master of the Charity School of Bridge & Candlewick Wards and author of several books [L242] (1749). Wife Ann bur. St. Martin Orgar 1726 Apr.13. Remarried 1726/7 Feb.6 at Lamb's Chapel to Sarah Barker James, widow, of Clerkenwell. Author of a spelling book which passed through many editions up to mid-19th century. Died 1749 Jul.6[242].

MARKIE, (Mackie?).
U *63.1844*

Of New North Rd. 1844[63V].

MARSHALL, Samuel, c.1687–1714.
St. Katherine Cree 1702/3 Mar.9 – 1713/14 Mar.11 died. Death reported Mar.18.

Interred under organ in St. Katherine Cree with an informative inscription: "Died Mar.11, 1713/14 . . . [in 27th year of his age]. Samuel Marshall was scholar to Dr. Blow, choir of St. Paul's. Above eleven years the exquisite organist of this church and master to other good organists". The inscription mentions that he composed music[171,329].
B.

MARTIN, George William, c.1828–1881.
U 12.1842 (application disallowed), 59.1843.

St. Paul's chorister?[102]. Of 8 Ernest St., Regents Park 1843[59V]. Died 1881 Apr.16 in 54th year[243].
G. 284.

MARTIN, Mrs. Thomasine *see* Wesley, Miss Thomasine, later Mrs. Martin.

MARTINDALE, Miss.
U 25.1847 (in top 22 out of 63).

MASON, Miss (or Mrs.)
U *12.1842*.

MATHER, George, d.1854.
St. Bride Fleet Street 1821 Aug.28 – 1854 Jul.20 death reported.
U 37.1818, 20.1819, 44.1821 (no christian name).

Music teacher, 21 Great New St., Fetter Lane 1832–4[199]. Composer, compiled *The Calcutta melodies, comprising 36 original psalm and hymn tunes* 1844 etc. Blind. Mus.D.
284. 388.

MAY, Edward.
U 75.1825 (failed to attend audition).
Probably Edward Collett May, organist Greenwich Hospital 1837 to 1869.
G. 282.

MAY, Henry S.
U 12.1842 (no christian name. In top 4 out of 40), 59.1843, 63.1844 (top 6 out of 35).
Of 61 Nelson Sq., Blackfriars Rd. 1843–4[59V 63V]. Brother of Edward according to G(5).
G(5).

MEACO,
U 48.1707 (at annual election).

MELLISH, Thomas.
U 25.1847 (no christian name), 26.1847.

MERRETT, Charles.
U *45.1826*.

MERRITT, William.
U *75.1825*.

MEYER, W.H.
U 48.1805 (failed to attend audition).

MICHELMORE, Frederick, 1814–1834.
St. Mary Magdalen Old Fish Street (temporary) 1834 June 18 – 1834 Sep. successor appointed.
Born 1814 Mar.11, St. Paul's Choir School 1822 Mar. – 1831 Jan.[342]. Bur. St. Paul's Cathedral 1834 Oct.14, of Addle Hill age 21 [sic].

MICHELMORE, Horatio Rowland, 1799–1840.
St. Mary Aldermanbury 1829 Jan.8 – 1840 Feb.19 death reported. (Although referred to in V as Henry or H.R. Michelmore, date of death etc. confirms identification as Horatio).
U *45.1826* (no christian name), 20.1827 (do.), 74.1827 (do. runner-up), 77.1828 (3rd out of 17).
Born 1799 Mar.2 bap. St. Margaret Westminster Mar.31. Son of William & Mary Michelmore[182]. St. Paul's Choir School 1805–14[342]. Mar. (i) 1824 Feb.15 Mary Ann Sutton, St. George the Martyr Middx. (ii) 1827 Feb.5 Ann Maria Browne St. Andrew Undershaft (iii) 1832 May 15 Caroline Browne St. Luke Middx. St. Paul's Choir "deputy for Mr. Vaughan" c.1828. Pfte. teacher. Member of Concert of Antient Music. Elected Roy. Soc. of Musicians 1828[182]. Of St. Mary Axe 1828–9[77V], 16 Clare St. 1824[182], 83 White Lion St. 1834[182]. Ill with diseased lungs 1837, petitioned Roy. Soc. of Musicians for relief[183]. Died 1840.

MIDDLEBROOK,
U 20.1731.
A William Middlebrook chorister of Lincoln Cathedral 1719, organist Lincoln 1741 to death in 1756[339].
339?

MILBORNE or MILBOURNE,
St. Katherine Cree 1714 Mar.25 – 1743 end.
U 1.1713.
Conceivably Gordon Milbourn of Watford, friend of Abiell Whichello (q.v.) who bequeathed him all his scores of Corelli's concertos and sonatas. Or Luke Milbourne author of *The psalms of David* 1698.

MILLER,
U 48.1706, 33.1713/14, 2.1727/8 (one of 12 names submitted by vestry).
Perhaps William Miller (1), q.v.

MILLER, M.B.
U 75.1825 (failed to attend audition).

MILLER, Thomas.
U 59.1843.
Of 71 Pearson St., Kingsland 1843[59V].

MILLER, William (1).
U 53.1720 (having played for 3 weeks since previous organist's death).

MILLER, William (2), d.1873.
St. Giles Cripplegate 1832 Feb.17 – 1873 when son William, assistant for some years, became joint organist with father. Applied for salary increase 1841 Apr.12.
Probably identical with William Miller of the India Office author of *London before the fire of 1666 with an*

historical account of St. Giles without Cripplegate, 1867 and *Jottings of Kent*, 1871. First organist of Sacred Harmonic Society. Of 171 Bishopsgate St. 1841[37]V. Active in raising funds for restoration of St. Giles. Died London 1873 June 25.
284.

MILLS, John.
U 58.1830 (no christian name), 48.1834, 59.1840, 74.1844 (no testimonial supplied).
Blind [48]V. Of 62 King St., Borough 1844[74]V, the address of Richard Mills, locksmith & bell ringer.

MILWARD, Mrs. *see* Smallshawe, Miss, later Mrs. Milward.

MILWARD, John Frederick.
U 15.1804, 47.1804 (—— Melward).

MINTON. Miss Elizabeth, later Mrs. Weatherhead, b.c.1812.
St. James Duke's Place 1838 Apr.16 – between 1839 Apr.1 and 1847 Apr. vacated.
Daughter of Samuel Minton woollen draper and parish clerk of St. James 1833–55. Elizabeth mar. William Weatherhead, clerk, 1841 Jul.20[130].

MITCHELL,
U *12.1842*.

MITCHINSON,
U *12.1842*.

MOLSON, Alfred, d.1900.
Holy Trinity Gough Square until death 1900 Jan.7. Date of appointment obscure but between opening of church in 1838 and 1852 (vote of sympathy on death of wife 1883 Apr.19: Alfred Molson "organist for more than 30 years"). Death reported 1900 Apr.26, "organist of Holy Trinity for 48 years".
Of 8 Brownlow St. W.C. 1889, the address of Molson Brothers, law stationers.

MONK, William Henry.
U 59.1840, 74.1844 (failed to attend audition), 63.1844 (top 3 out of 35).
Of 8 Lower Grosvenor St., Grosvenor Sq. 1844[74]V [63]V.
G. 282. 284.

MONRO, George.
St. Peter Cornhill 1724 Jul.15 or Sep.30 – 1731 c.Mar. died?
B. G(5). 284.

MONRO, John.
St. Bartholomew the Great 1819 Oct.27 – 1827 Jan.26 resigned.
St. Botolph Aldersgate 1827 Jan.18 – 1847 Mar. vacated. Letter to St. Botolph from 11 Holborn Bars stating he is very ill 1846 Apr.14.
U 25.1820 (runner-up).
Composer, organist, pianist & music seller. In partnership with H. May at 11 Holborn Bars. A cruel but amusing anonymous broadsheet issued on the occasion of his appointment to St. Botolph comprises 64 lines of doggerel. Entitled *The "wonder", respectfully inscribed to the inhabitants of St. Botolph* it is scathing both about Monro himself and his skill as an organist, also involving his partner-in-business Harry May[274].

MOORCROFT, Mrs. Mary *see* Archer, Miss Mary, later Mrs. Moorcroft.

MOORE,
U 40.1722.
Perhaps William Moore, organist St. Mary Magdalen Bermondsey until death (reported ves. min. bk. 1737/8 Mar.22).

MOORE, James.
U 58.1767 (no christian name), 1.1767, 37.1770, 1.1770 (no christian name), 57.1772, 25.1773 (no christian name).

MORELAND, Thomas.
U 84.1742.

MORGAN,
St. Michael Bassishaw temporary 1764.
U 59.1764 (runner-up after serving as temporary organist).

MORPHETI,
U 25.1827.

MORREL, Miss Elizabeth, later Mrs. Stiles, d.1843.
St. Swithin London Stone 1809 Jul.4 – 1843 Oct.3 died. Death reported Oct.13. Became Mrs. Stiles between

Dec. 1825 & June 1826.
A blind organist [76V].

MORRICE, Miss Mary.
St. Ethelburga Bishopsgate 1812 Nov.12 – 1823 June 23 resigned.
All Hallows Barking by the Tower 1823 June 10 – 1840 vacated. At 1823 election polled 117 votes, her 7 rivals each nil.
U 3.1812.
Daughter of James Morrice (1757 – 1834) of 22 Seething Lane, parish clerk of All Hallows Barking 1798 – 1834[130].

MORRICE, Miss Sarah, later Mrs. Wood.
St. Olave Hart Street 1806 Jan.24 – 1857 Apr.16 death reported. Became Mrs. Wood between 1810 Apr.8 & 1811 Apr. Perhaps sister of Mary Morrice?

MORRIS, Miss Ann.
U 76.1843 (no christian name), *74.1844*, *63.1844*, 25.1847 (no christian name, top 6 out of 63), 48.1850 (no christian name, runner-up. Her own parish!).
Of 35 Ludgate St. 1844–50[74V 63V 48V] address of Morris & Co. bookbinders' tool cutters[199]. St. Martin Ludgate has many baps. after 1825 of children of Joseph & Lydia Morris of Ludgate St., engravers, but no entry for Ann.

MOSS, John.
St. Mary Woolnoth 1678 Dec.? – 1705/6 Mar.1 resigned. Date of appointment doubtful. £6 allowed organist from Xmas 1678 but not named until 1681/2 Jan.10 "Mr. Moss should be paid for his attendance as to the organ what shall be justly due to him and afterwards to be paid quarterly". (There had been difficulties about paying organist 1681 June 7).
St. Dunstan in the East 1683 Mar.? – 1696 vacated.
Parish Clerks' Company before 1684 – 1707 vacated. (No christian name given but assumed to be John Moss).
Christ's Hospital music master 1675 Dec.17 "John Moss, a married man, declaring his skill in playing upon the organ and other instruments of musick" petitioned Court of Christ's Hospital for post of music master. Disallowed as only bachelors & widowers eligible. John Moss however had been instructing children since death of Richard Price (in 1675). Election of new master postponed and Moss continued until appointment of John Curtis 1675/6 Feb.4.
U 81.1697 (Christ's Hospital: perhaps a widower by that date?)
Possibly identical with John Moss, musician for the King's private music between 1669 and 1684[292].
B. G.?

MOUNSEY, Miss Ann Sheppard, later Mrs. Bartholomew, d.1891.
St. Michael Wood Street 1828 Nov.26 – 1837 Nov.22 resigned. Salary reduced 1834 June 5 for reasons of economy: accepted without complaint.
St. Vedast Foster Lane 1837 Nov.7 – 1891 June 24 died.
U 77.1828 (runner-up).
Of Basing Lane, Bread Street 1828[77V], 31 Brunswick Place, City Rd. 1834–37[64V]. Mar. William Bartholomew 1853.
G. 284.

MOUNSEY, Miss Elizabeth, c.1820–1905.
St. Peter Cornhill 1834 June 19 – 1882 May 26 retired. Elected at age of 14 she admitted "increasing infirmity" 1882 Apr.11. Rector's letter paying tribute to 48 years' service 1882 Jul.12. To be paid $\frac{2}{3}$ of late salary of £35. Shall have use of organ for pupils and opportunity of playing entrance voluntaries on Sundays. Died 1905 Oct.3.
G. 284.

MOUNTAIN, William.
U 71.1800.

MOUNTFORD, Miss S.J.
U 77.1828.
Of 45 Gloucester St., Queen's Square 1828[77V].

MOZE, John Henry, d.1787.
St. Katherine by the Tower 1763 Nov.17 – 1787 Dec.21 or 27 died. Death reported 1788 Feb.14. Unanimously appointed by Chapter 1763 Nov.17,

patent of appointment read & executed 1763 Nov.29.
U 34.1753.
Appointed organist St. Ann Soho 1774 Nov.24 [L514]. Died 1787 Dec.27 in Wardour St., Soho, Mr. John Henry Moze, organist of St. Anne Soho, the collegiate church of St. Katherine by the Tower and the German church in the Savoy[232]. Date of death also given as Dec.21[222]. B. contains more than 30 entries c.1755–70.
B.

Munro, John *see* Monro, John.

Naish, Miss Maria.
St. Benet Fink 1818 Apr.3 (only candidate) – 1834 Apr.3 resigned.
U 17.1808 (runner-up), 38.1809 (no christian name), 76.1809 ("Miss Nash" withdrew), 15.1809, 17.1812.
Probably daughter of Thomas Naish, q.v. whom she succeeded at St. Benet Fink.

Naish, Thomas.
St. Benet Fink 1789 Feb.11 – 1818 Mar.26 resigned. "Long & faithful service" rewarded with £10 gratuity.
Thomas Naish apprenticed to Isaac Rimington citizen & Musician £105 1768[150]. Does not appear to have become free although Thomas Naish, toll collector of 107 Whitechapel free of Musicians' Company 1802 Feb.23[125].

Nash,
U 42.1805.

Neale, Captain.
U 2.1727/8 (one of 12 names submitted by vestry; runner-up).
Possibly Richard Neale, below, or John Neale of St. James Westminster, musician, to whom Joseph Abington apprenticed 1737[149]. Both John Neale and Abington appear to have been violinists. John Neale original member Roy. Soc. of Musicians 1739[181].

Neale, Richard, d.c. 1745.
St. James Garlickhythe 1722 Mar.26 – 1744/5 Jan.16 death reported.
U 33.1731.
Original member Roy. Soc. of Musicians 1739[181]. In list of subscribers to Handel's *Rodelinda* 1725[263]. Author of *A pocket companion for gentlemen and ladies being a collection of the finest opera songs . . . also figur'd for the organ harpsicord* [sic] *and spinet* by Mr. Ri[d] Neale organist of St. James's Garlick-hith. (1726).
B. 284.

Neeves, Timothy.
St. Martin Ludgate 1782 Aug.21 – 1786 Apr.21 vacated (no reason).
Anne Neeves bur. St. Martin 1781 Dec.9 but nil Timothy. The name of Neeves recurs in musical circles in the City. Corbett Neeves, a City wait, master & professor of the bassoon d.1761 and his father William at the Violin beyond Fleet Bridge.

Negus (?),
U 20.1785.
A St. Paul's chorister of this name "died very poor"[342]. John Negus age 62 bur. Bunhill Fields 1791. The same?

Niccolls,
U 43.1686 after audition by Dr. Blow, Mr. Purcell, Mr. Mosse & Mr. Forcell [sic i.e. Forcer] who judged him to play next best to Mr. Snow. However he polled only one vote out of the 15 cast.
Probably Samuel Nicholls, q.v.

Nicholls(1) (probably more than one, including Archibald, below).
U 2.1799, 47.1805 (Nichols), 60.1810, 27.1815, 4.1825, 21.1825 (Nichols), 74.1827 (top 6 out of 15).

Nicholls (2),
U *63.1844*.
Of Kingsland Rd. 1844[63].

Nicholls, Archibald.
U 42.1805 (Archibald Nichols), *75.1825*.
See also Nicholls (1) above.

Nicholls, Mrs. Jane Ann *see* England, Miss Jane Ann, later Mrs. Nicholls.

Nicholls, Samuel.
Christ's Hospital music master probationer 1687 Jul.15 for 3 months. Claim for payment 1689 Jul.4.

Probably identical with Niccolls above.

NICKINSON, John.
U 59.1840.
Of 8 Coleman St. 1840[59V], address of David Nickinson, solicitor[199].

NIGHTINGALE,
U 60.1810, 27.1815.

NIGHTINGALE, John Charles, 1790–1833.
U 3.1812.
Born 1790 May 29 bap. St. Leonard Shoreditch June 27. Son of Thomas & Sarah Nightingale of Cumberland St. 'Cellist, organist of Holywell Mount Chapel, teacher at 2 schools, private teacher & composer when elected to Roy. Soc. of Musicians 1812 on recommendation of William Russell 1811 Sep.18[182]. Deputised for William Russell at Foundling Hospital before own appointment there 1813–33. Mar. Amelia Wilmshurst 1817 Oct.14 St. Mary Islington. Died 1833[182]. Widow remarried in 1837 to Francis Ripley[183]. 284.

NIGHTINGALE, Joseph, 1778–1847.
St. Helen Bishopsgate 1820 Sep.20 – between 1842 & 1847 when died after long illness (uncertainty through gap in records).
U 15.1809 (runner-up), 38.1819.
Brother of above. Born 1778 Jul.8 bap. St. Botolph Bishopsgate Aug.2. Son of Thomas & Sarah Nightingale. Pianist & double bass player & teacher. Employed as pianist at the Royal Circus[182]. Elected Roy. Soc. of Musicians 1807 on recommendation of William Russell June 4[182]. Mar. Sarah Jane Peterson 1824 Feb.14 St. Mary Newington. Petitioned R.S.M. for relief 1837 due to ruptured bladder & paralysed wife. Only income then £30 p.a. as organist of St. Helen Bishopsgate[183]. Wife Sarah Jane from Bethnal Green age 44 buried St. Helen 1842 Sep.25. Joseph died 1847[182] burial untraced.

NORMAN,
U 22.1834, 10.1840, 76.1843.

NORMAN, John.
U 75.1793, 40.1793.
Probably John Norman, organist St. John Wapping who had an address in the City "at Sir J. Marriott's, Doctors' Commons" 1794[198].

NORMANN, Rudolf *see* Harris, George Frederick.

NUNN, Miss Rachel.
U 59.1840, 12.1842 ("Nunn" failed to supply testimonial), 59.1843.
At Mr. Wheelwright's, 1 South Place, Finsbury 1840[59V], of 32 Clifton St., Finsbury 1843[59V].

OAKEY,
U 12.1842 (disallowed).
?John Oakey, music teacher, 33 Manor Place, Walworth 1840[199].

OLIVE, Joseph, d.1786.
St. Botolph Aldersgate 1773 Jan. 14 – 1786 Nov.8 died. Death reported Nov.14.
U 63.1779 (no christian name, runner-up).
Chorister St. Paul's. "Composer to Sadler's Wells where he played the harpsichord. Mr. S thinks he married one of the dancers"[342]. Died 1786 Nov.8 Mr. Olive, organist of St. Botolph Aldersgate[232]. Bur. Nov.13 St. Botolph Aldersgate.
B.284.

ORBELL, d.1754.
St. Michael Queenhithe 1748? – 1754 Dec.13 death reported.
Succeeded his father Isaac Orbell.

ORBELL, Isaac, d.1748.
St. Bartholomew the Great 1721 Aug.16 – 1731 autumn? vacated.
St. Michael Queenhithe 1731 – 1748 Apr.3 death reported.
U 1.1713 (no christian name, runner-up).
Bur. St. Andrew Holborn 1747/8 Mar.6 "of Grays Inn Passage". Admon. to widow Jane 1748 Apr.7[139].

ORGER, Miss Caroline, later Mrs. Reinagle.
U *45.1840*.
284.

Ormes, Miss Sarah, d.1842.
St. Dionis Backchurch 1784 Oct.7 – 1832 Dec.13 to resign from next Easter.
U 73.1784 (no christian name), 18.1784.

Inscription in St. Dionis recording benefactors to the church includes "Mrs. [sic] Sarah Ormes many years organist of this parish gave £100 consols for gift of £1 each to 3 aged needy respectable widows or single women of this parish". Will dated 1842 Nov.22 proved Dec.14[294]. Of Islington 1832[31V], of 3 Terrace, Islington, organist & teacher 1794[198].

Owen, Henry.
U 78.1704.

Oxlee, Mrs. Harriet *see* Brown, Miss Harriet, later Mrs. Oxlee.

Page, Mrs. Harriet.
U 7.1817 (withdrew).

?Page, Mrs. pianoforte, Guildford St., Grays Inn Lane, or at Windsor 1794[198], same address as John Page, principal tenor[198].

Paice,
U *12.1842*.

Pain, Miss? Harriet.
U 48.1805.

Pallet,
St. Bartholomew Moor Lane 1850 Apr.? – 1851 successor appointed.

Palmer, John.
St. Martin Ludgate 1684 Mar.31 – 1685 Apr.21 death reported.

Parker,
U 1.1758.

Parker, Benvici (?).
U 4.1837.

Parker, Septimus.
U 59.1843, 76.1843 (runner-up), 74.1844 (failed to attend audition).

Of 19 North Bank, Regent's Park 1843[59V 76V], 1 Bedford St., Strand 1844[74V]. Composer and organist of Ashtead 1844–59 & 1874–77, Epsom 1859–61, Godalming 1864–74 etc.[284].
284.

Patch,
U 1.1758.

Pawsey, Mrs. Alice *see* Soward, Miss Alice, later Mrs. Pawsey.

Paxton, Miss Frances.
U 2.1773 (twice).

Possibly dau. of Stephen Paxton, composer (Gent's mag. 1787 p. 837[232] and Grove (5)).

Payton, Miss Sarah Day.
U 10.1840 (no christian name), 45.1841 (top 4 out of 17).

Pearce, Lewis.
U 20.1777, 3.1780 (Lewis Pearse).

Apprenticed to John Gates (q.v.) of St. George Middlesex, musician 1759[149]. *Bermondsey Spa, a song* c.1782 in European mag. vol. 2 p. 217.
B.

Pearce, Thomas *see* Peirce, Thomas.

Peck, John, d.1851.
St. Augustine Watling Street 1832 Apr.27 – 1851 Feb.26 death reported. For details of somewhat chequered tenure see under St. Augustine.

Probably John Peck, music engraver, music seller & publisher of 44 Newgate St. John Peck, son of George Peck, apprenticed to Daniel Gadene, machine ruler, of Maidenhead Court, Moor Lane 1820 Sep.5. The same? John Peck, music teacher, at 44 Newgate St. 1840[199].
310.

Peirce, Pierce or Pearce, Thomas, d.1776.
St. Peter Cornhill (Thomas Pierce or Peirce) 1731 – 1776 died. No reference to death in V. when no organist elected as "the money by which the [organist] is paid is seized by Dr. Thomas the Rector" 1776 Apr.10.
U 14.1749 (—— Peirce).

Listed as organist in livery lists of Barber Surgeons' Company, of Crosby Square 1747–54 and of Hackney Rd. 1765–76 "died"[108]. As there are 2 freemen of the Barber Surgeons of this name, impossible to identify which of (1) Thomas Peirce, son of Richard, yeoman of Kingsland, co. Hereford, apprenticed to William Hemmings 1733 Nov.6, free 1740 Dec.2[110], or (2) Thomas Peirce, son of Thomas of Christ Church Spitalfields, victualler, apprenticed first to John Morrell, Barber, 1737 May 17 then to John Hawkins, Barber, 1738 Sep.13 and lastly to Edward Cawson, Barber[110]. Free 1740/1 Feb. 3[112].

PEPUSCH, Johann Christoph, (John Christopher) d.1752.
Charterhouse 1737 Dec.2 – 1752 Jul.20 died.

Original member Roy. Soc. of Musicians 1739[181]. Apprentices: Thomas Cole 1715[149] (q.v.), John Oliver 1730[149]. Of St. Clement, Middlesex 1730[149]. Of Fetter Lane (City of London) 1735–7[172]. Died 1752 Jul.20[232 242]. Wife died 1746 Aug.[242]. Will dated 1752 Jul.9 exec. Nicholas Mann (renounced) admin. by John Travers & Ephraim Kellner, residuary legatees 1753 May 21[139].
B. G. 353. 357.

PERKINS, Jonathan.
St. Alban Wood Street 1790 Nov.4 – 1835 Mar.24 resigned.
St. Margaret Lothbury 1801 c.Mar. – 1831 Mar.25 vacated. Petition for increase of salary 1816 Apr.19 with comparative rates at other parishes (details under St. Margaret Lothbury). Salary increased from £25 to £35.
U 73.1799 (Jonathan Perkins, jun. runner-up. The same?).

Jonathan Perkins, junr., organist, alto singer, Choral Fund, Handelian Soc., Oratorio Drury Lane, Oxford Meeting 1793, Westminster Abbey, 16 Hosier Lane, West Smithfield 1794[198].

PERKIS, John *see* Purkis, John.

PERKS, (see also Purkis).
U 25.1799.

PERRY,
St. Botolph Aldersgate substitute 1826 Mar. – Oct.
U 1.1823, 4.1825, 20.1836.

Probably George Frederick Perry, violinist, organist and composer who, according to G., settled in London 1822. but could be H.W. Perry, below, or Edward Perry born 1811 June 24 Maldon Essex, performer on violin, harp, pfte. & organ & employed Covent Garden Theatre & Vauxhall Gardens. Elected Roy. Soc. of Musicians 1835[182].

PERRY, H.W.
U *75.1825*.

PESCOTT, Miss.
U 20.1836.

PETERS, Miss Jane.
U 59.1843.

Of Windsor Terrace, City Rd. 1843[59V].

PETERSON,
U 42.1833.

PHILLIPS, Miss Matilda.
U 59.1843, 63.1844.

Of 86 West Smithfield 1843–4[59V 63V] address of Thomas Phillips, pewterer[199].

PHILLIPS, William Lovell, 1814 – 1860.
St. Katherine by the Tower 1848 – 1860 Mar. 19 died.

Born 1814 Dec.26 bap. St. Augustine the Less Bristol 1826 Feb.13. Son of William Phillips, accountant, & Ann of College Green. In 1838 principal 'cello Theatre Royal & English Opera House, organist Brunswick Chapel. Pianist & teacher. Elected Roy. Soc. of Musicians 1838 Sep.2. Died 1860 leaving widow Mary & 2 children who applied for relief on failure of "music business". She died age 69 1892 June 21[182 183].
G(5). 284.

PICKERING,
U 25.1847 (declined audition).

PICKERSGILL, Miss Sophia.
U 59.1840.

Of 16 Henrietta St., Covent Garden 1840[59V].

PIERCE *see* Pearce and Peirce.

PIGOTT, Francis, c.1666 – 1704.
Temple Church (for Inner & Middle Temples) 1688 May 27 – 1704 May 15 died.

Death reported Inner Temple May 19. A child of the Chapel Royal of this name between 1679 and 1683[292]. Mar. 1688 Dec.5 St. Benet Paul's Wharf, Anne Pelling dau. of City apothecary John Pelling of Mark Lane. Age 22 in 1688 (mar. banns St. Benet Paul's Wharf).
B. G. 284.

PIGOTT, John.
St. Edmund, King and Martyr 1702 Dec. – 1709 Apr.25 vacated.
Temple Church (for Inner & Middle Temples) 1704 May 27 – 1728/9 Feb.8 discharged by Inner Temple from Lady Day next. Continued until 1736 for Middle Temple.
U 48.1704 (no christian name).
G.

PITTMAN, Josiah.
U 15.1836 (withdrew).
Organist Lincolns Inn 1852–64.
G. 282. 284.

PLATTS,
U 22.1789.

PLATTS, jun.
St. Martin Orgar c.1800? Pearce the only authority[323]. St. Martin Orgar (French church in the City) not included in this survey.

PLATTS, Charles George.
St. Mary Aldermary in 1834. Pearce the only authority[323]. No evidence in church records but the organ an "annuity organ" so that he could have been paid by the annuitant.
C. G. Platts organist St. Paul, Marylebone 1837[256].

PLATTS, Thomas Martin, 1791–1845.
St. Michael Paternoster Royal "evening organist" 1810 May 9 – 1820 Dec.25. Vacated on appointment of new (full) organist. Canvassed for the office but failed to secure it.
U 17.1808, 28.1821 (Thomas Platts runner-up out of 23), 62.1821, 63.1824 (Thomas Attwood, organist of St. Paul's as umpire, considered Platts a better player than Thomas Cash the successful candidate).
Born 1791 May 5 bap. St. Clement Danes May 29. Son of Martin & Sarah Platts. (Martin Platts born c.1763, a violinist, horn player & minor composer married Sarah Vanhagen 1789[182], became freeman of Musicians' Company 1784 after apprenticeship to William Burnitt[125] & in same year elected Roy. Soc. of Musicians). Thomas Martin apprenticed to father 1805 Oct.[125]. Pfte., harp & double bass player, organist & full time teacher. Elected Roy. Soc. of Musicians 1813 on recommendation of Edward Frith 1812 Dec.6. Died 1845[182]. A younger brother of Martin, James Platts born 1770 Jul.9, a minor composer & teacher of harp, violin & viola, free of Musicians' Company 1803 June 13[125].

PLUMMER, Mrs. Sarah *see* Fisher, Miss Sarah, later Mrs. Plummer.

PLUMSTEAD,
U *63.1844*.
Probably William Henry Plumstead music teacher in the City at 119 Fore St. 1832–4, 66 Fore St. 1840[199]. Published *Beauties of melody* 1827, *Church of England music* 1846, *Observations on the present state of congregational singing* 1846.
284.

POLE,
U 20.1836.
Probably William Pole, organist St. Mark's North Audley St. 1836–66.
G. 284.

POOL(E), Francis.
U 15.1782 (no christian name), 31.1784 (withdrew because of single post clause).

POOLE, Miss Sophia.
St. Michael Bassishaw 1807 June 22 – 1840 Jan.11 resigned.

PORTER,
U 42.1833 & 1837.

POTTER, Richard Huddleston, 1755 – 1821.
St. Bride Fleet Street 1782 Jul.30 – 1821 June 13 death reported.
Born 1755 Dec. 10 bap. St. Olave

Silver St. Dec.15. Son of Richard Potter, flute maker, & Mary Frances Potter of Silver St. 1770 Feb.7 apprenticed to father in Turners' Company for 7 years[135]. 1789 Jan.14 freeman & liveryman of Turners' Company[136]. Played oboe[198], organ, harpsichord, flute ("at Mr. Crosdale's & other public concerts") & had "a great many scholars"[182]. Married with 1 child when elected to Roy. Soc. of Musicians in 1785[182]. Of 2 Pemberton Row Gough Sq. before 1789[137], 39 Margaret St. Cavendish Sq. up to c.1800 then 2 Foley Place, Portland Place[137].
G. 388

POWERS, Arnold.
U 20.1731 (no christian name), 18.1732–45 (opposed Henry Duncalf every year in annual officers' election. Nominal only?).

POWIS, C.E.
U 37.1818.

PRELLEUR, Peter, d.1741.
St. Alban Wood Street 1728? – 1735 or 1736. Surviving records provide no confirmation. Hawkins gives 1728 and the date of resignation seems reasonable as appointed Christ Church Spitalfields 1736 Mar.
U 20.1731 (—— Preluer).
Perhaps Pierre Preleur son of Jacque Preleur, weaver, and Francoise "over against Crispin St. Stepney" bap. Threadneedle St. church 1705 Dec.16[343]. First organist of Christ Church Spitalfields 1736 Mar. at sal. of £30 polling 99 votes to John Worgan's 62[236]. Died 1741 June bur. Christ Church Spitalfields June 27 "from Corbet's Court". Will dated 1741 June 19 ". . . of the parish of Christ Church organist. Debts to be paid. Residue and all such sums of money as I am or shall be entitled unto by vertue of the orders or resolutions of the Society of Schoolmasters whereof I am a member" to brother James Prelleur the younger (executor) and Magdalen wife of Gilbert Stephens clerk equally. Witn. Turley Hawkins & Hannah Yomanson[139].
B. G.

PRICE,
U 25.1847 (disqualified as blindness not considered compatible with teaching).

PRICE, Alfred.
U 74.1844 (failed to attend audition).
Of 21 Windsor Terrace, City Rd. 1844[74V]. Same address as H. Price, below.

PRICE, George, d.1826.
St. Augustine Watling Street 1808 May 5 – 1812 Apr.? vacated.
Temple Church (for Inner Temple) 1810 – 1826 died.
Temple Church (for Middle Temple) 1814 – 1826 died.
Born 1789 Mar.7 bap. St. Giles in the Fields Apr.5. Son of George & Sarah Price[182]. Chorister St. Paul's Cathedral 1799 – 1804[342]. Apprenticed 7 years to John Sale. Violinist, organist & pfte. teacher. Employed Theatre Royal, Drury Lane. Elected Roy. Soc. of Musicians on recommendation of Thomas Attwood 1813 Jan.3. Mar. Mary Andrew 1809 Aug.20 St. George Hanover Sq. Of 5 Stanhope St. Strand 1813, Hyde St. Bloomsbury 1814, Gordon Row Bloomsbury 1820, York Cottage Battersea Fields 1822. Died 1826[182].

PRICE, H.
U *63.1844*.
Of 21 Windsor Terrace, City Rd. 1844[63V]. Same address as A. Price, above.

PRICE, Richard, d.1675.
Christ's Hospital music master 1659 Jul.29 – 1675 Dec.17 death reported. Described as musician & bachelor on appointment in 1659. Richard Price "Arts Mr. in Song" appointed parish clerk Christ Church Newgate Street 1661 May 13 & licensed 1662/3 Mar.1[130]. Presumably not Richard Price petticannon [sic i.e. minor Canon of St. Paul's] bur. St. Gregory 1674 Dec.26.

PRINCE, John, d.1834.
St. Martin Ludgate 1805 May 16 – 1834 Nov.13 death reported.

Died 1834 Oct.14 age 63 John Prince Esq., eldest son of late Rev. John Prince of the Magdalen Charity[232]. The same?

PRING, Joseph Cubitt, 1770–1799.
St. Botolph Aldersgate (joint organist) 1787 Jan.16 – 1799 Jul.10 death reported (sole organist from 1790). At election 1786 Nov.23 Miss Elizabeth Goadby polled 117 against Pring's 116. Bitter dispute as a result of which, nearly 2 months later, the post was shared, Goadby afternoon & evng., Pring morning and to teach children.

Born 1770 bap. Lewisham Nov.3. Son of Jacob & Martha Pring[182]. Chorister St. Paul's Cathedral[342]. Mar. Mary Shuckburgh, widow, 1790 Dec.16 St. Andrew Holborn. Organist, teacher of singing & harpsichord. Elected Roy. Soc. of Musicians on recommendation of John Sale 1793 June 2[182]. Of 9 Cross Keys Sq. Little Britain 1794[198]. Died 1799[182].
B. G(5). 284.

PRING, Joseph.
U 48.1792.
Chorister St. Paul's 1785–92[342]. Brother of Jacob Cubitt Pring.
B. G(5). 284. 339. 376.

PRINTER, John, b.1756.
St. Katherine Coleman 1772 – 1777 Nov.? resigned to devote whole Sunday time to Foundling Hospital.

Born 1756, admitted to Foundling Hospital Nov.27. One of first 3 blind foundlings to be taught music. Organ lessons from 1768 Feb. from Mr. Cook. Engaged to sing morning & evening in Foundling Hospital for salary 1777 June. Later lodged at Hospital & 1800 May presented organ value £60. Retired 1807 June[321]. Also performer Vauxhall Gardens 1794[198].
B.

PRITCHARD, Mrs.
U 39.1838.

PROBYN, Miss Eliza Kingston, later Mrs. Cooper.
St. Bartholomew the Less 1825 May 4 – 1863 retired.
St. Stephen Walbrook 1825 Dec.16 – 1868 retired.
U 27.1825 (second choice, but doubts that a female organist would have command over the boys while teaching them to sing).

Mar. St. Michael Cornhill 1829 June 9 George Cooper, "widower of this parish & Eliza Kingston Probyn spinster of this parish". Was he George Cooper d.1843 (q.v.)? "Eliza Cooper, music teacher "at Bennet's Hill (his address) 1832 etc.[199].

PURCELL, Daniel.
St. Dunstan in the East between 1696 & 1698 – 1717 Nov. died. In C. first entry 1698 Nov.3 "Mr. Purcell (from 1700 entered as Daniel) ½ years salary £10". For the 2 years before this there was no payment for an organist (previously John Moss, vacated 1696). Daniel Purcell is believed to have come to London 1695 May. Did he in fact play for no reward in 1696, 1697 and the first part of 1698 as he did at St. Andrew Holborn shortly before 1717? Last payment St. Dunstan 1717 Nov.11.
St. Andrew Holborn c.1713 – 1717 Nov. died. (Bur. St. Andrew Nov.26 "from Fetter Lane"). Date of appointment not ascertainable from church records. But an undated case regarding the office of organist at St. Andrew Holborn in cases submitted to Sgt. Pengelly 1719 & later[308] throws some light: "About 27 years ago organ erected but no organist appointed for many years. About 1715 Dr. Sacheverell being then rector . . . raised money sufficient to pay debt. At that time one Mr. Purcell played said organ without being elected or appointed or without any fixed salary and he died some 10 years since . . ." Daniel Purcell played at the instigation of Dr. Sacheverell according to Bloxam[281]. As Henry Sacheverell was appointed to the living of St. Andrew 1713 Apr.17 it is unlikely that Daniel played voluntarily before this.
U 28.1702 (no christian name. Daniel Purcell?)
B. G. 284.

PURCELL, Edward, d.1740.
St. Clement Eastcheap 1711 end of year – 1740 Jul.1 died. Bur. St. Clement Eastcheap 1740 Jul.4 near the organ gallery door.
U 13.1717/18 (He lost no time in advertising for himself as candidate[219]: "Edward Purcell only son to the late famous Henry Purcell" in room of his uncle Daniel Purcell), 13.1718, 40.1719 (entered as Edward Henry Purcell but presumably Edward Purcell), 81.1719/20.
Organist St. Margaret Westminster 1726 Jul.8 until death. Referred to in testimonial for John Jones (2) (q.v.) 1718[269] as Edward Henry Purcell organist of St. Martin Orgars (church destroyed in 1666 & parish amalgamated with St. Clement Eastcheap). Original member Roy. Soc. of Musicians 1739[181].
B. G. 284.

PURCELL, Edward Henry, d.1765.
St. Clement Eastcheap 1740 c.Jul. – 1765 c.Aug.1 died. Bur. St. Clement Aug.5 "by the organ galary".
St. Edmund, King and Martyr 1747 Sep.10 – 1753 Oct.10 resigned.
U 84.1742 (he "found no supporters"), 65.1751 (no christian name. Edward Henry?). Edward Henry also entered as candidate 40.1719 but presumably this was Edward Purcell, q.v.
Organist St. John Hackney 1753 Sep.22 – 1765 died. Death reported Aug.3[328].
G. 284.

PURKIS, John, 1781–1849.
U 48.1792 (John Perkis age 10), 75.1793 (runner-up), 45.1795.
A blind prodigy. Born 1781 June 21 bap. St. Dunstan in the West Aug.12. Son of John & Jemima Purkis of Bell Yard. Performer on pfte., harp & organ, organist St. Clement Danes & St. Olave Southwark from 1793 May 20[94]. Elected Roy. Soc. of Musicians on recommendation of J.H. Leffler 1806 Jul.29. Died 1849[182].
B. G(5). 284. 325.

PYNE,
U 47. 1805.

PYNE,
U 20.1827.
Probably James Kendrick Pyne, 1810–93.
G. 282. 284.

PYNE, Miss M.A., later Mrs. Galton.
St. Michael Wood Street 1837 Dec.7 – 1859 May 11 resigned as Mrs. Galton after postponement of election following dissatisfaction.
Daughter of George Pyne of 1 Field Terrace, Battle Bridge, parish clerk of St. Michael Wood Street 1834–54[130]. Marriage c.1840.

RACKSTRAW, William Smith *see* Rockstro, William Smith.

RAYMOND, John, d.1807.
St. Michael Bassishaw 1764 Apr.12 – 1807 June 9 death reported.
U 1.1758 (no christian name).
Elected Christ Church Spitalfields 1764 Dec.5 in room of Curtis deceased. Chosen by a great majority. "This young gentleman is a pupil of Mr. Worgan and a few months ago was chosen for St. Michael Bassishaw"[L549]. Of Brick Lane, Spitalfields 1794[198]. Will dated 1807 Mar.6, of the parish of Christ Church Spitalfields, leaving whole of money to the poor of the parish. Proved 1807 June 4[139].
B.?

REA, William.
St. Andrew Undershaft (only candidate) 1847 Jul.8 – 1858 Aug.12 resigned because of "more advantageous appointment".
U 74.1844 (in top 6 out of 60), *63.1844* (no christian name).
Of Nelson Street, Commercial Rd. East 1844[74V 63V].
G(5). 284.

READING, John, d.1764.
St. Mary Woolnoth 1727 June 30 – 1764 Sep.2 died. Death reported Sep.14.
St. Dunstan in the West 1731 Apr.9 – 1764 Sep.2 died. Death reported Nov.8.

A child of the Chapel Royal of this name up to 1699[292]. Mar. St. Mary Magdalen Old Fish St. 1703 Apr. 13 John Reading of St. Margarets in Lincoln and Ann Corbet of St. Andrew Holborn. Organist St. John Hackney 1707/8 Jan.28 to 1727 Apr.4 when "to provide himself with another place" within 3 months[328]. Original member Roy. Soc. of Musicians 1739[181]. Died 1764 Sep.2 age 87 . . . organist of St. Dunstan in the West and St. Mary Woolnoth[232]. Curiously, death prematurely reported as 1762 June 23[L605], correctly entered 1764 Sep.[L221].
B. G. 284.

READY (sic)
U *12.1842*.
Of Newcastle on Tyne 1842[12V] so possibly Samuel Reay 1822–1905 of Newcastle who held several London posts outside City (see G.).
G. 284.

REDHEAD,
St. Katherine Coleman 1771 May? – 1772 vacated.

REEVE, William.
St. Martin Ludgate 1792 Mar.15 – 1805 Apr.17 resigned.
U 48.1786 (runner-up).
Born 1757 Mar.4. Elected Roy. Soc. of Musicians 1786[181]. Composer, organist, alto singer. Employed Covent Garden Theatre, Sadler's Wells Theatre 1794[198]. Of 6 Charles St., Covent Garden 1794[198].
B. G.

REILLY, Mrs. Ann *see* Russell, Miss Ann, later Mrs. Reilly.

REINAGLE, Mrs. Caroline *see* Orger, Miss Caroline, later Mrs. Reinagle.

RELFE, Lupton, d.1805.
U 14.1749 (no christian name), 31.1749.
Organist of Greenwich Hospital. Mar. Miss Coleman 1758 Oct.14[L375]. Elected Roy. Soc. of Musicians 1765: expelled for non-payment[181]. Died 1805 bur. Greenwich Hospital. Members of Relfe family including other Luptons bur. Bunhill Fields. They include Lupton Relfe's son and pupil John, a composer, who died 1843 Nov.25 age 83 of Southampton Place, Camberwell. Bur. Nov.28[152].
B. G(5). 284.

RENNOLDSON, Martin, c.1739–1802.
St. Matthew Friday Street 1767 May 21 – 1802 Jan. died. Bur. Jan.20 "Mr. Martin Reynoldson late organist of the united parishes aged 62 in the church yard. Organist 33 years".
Chorister St. Paul's, chorus singer. Also engraver[342] perhaps identifiable as ——Rennoldson referred to by Thieme und Becker[332] & Bénézit[278]. Alto Drury Lane Theatre, Oxford Meeting, Westminster Abbey, 6 East St., Red Lion Sq. 1794[198].

REYNOLDS, Joshua.
St. Andrew Holborn c.1828 – 1867 Jul. pensioned[215 216]. Approximate date of election deduced from City Press[216]. Although referred to only as "J. Reynolds", identification as Joshua Reynolds seems likely.
U 51.1829 (no christian name), 10.1835 (J. Reynolds), 15.1836.
Possibly J. Reynolds, 21 Powell St. East, King Sq. music teacher 1847[199] and Joshua Reynolds, music teacher 42 King Square, Goswell Rd., E.C. 1864[199].

REYNOLDSON, Martin *see* Rennoldson, Martin.

RIBBLE, Mrs.
U 4.1825.
Of 8 High St., Aldgate 1825[4V].

RICHARDSON,
U 27.1815.

RICHARDSON, Miss Lucy.
U 58.1835 (runner-up out of 28), 64.1837 (runner-up).
Miss Richardson organist Chelsea Old Church 1840[264]. The same?

RIDLEY,
U *12.1842* (Ridley from Newark).
Probably William Ridley b. Newark, Nottingham 1820 who held many posts

in the north, d. Liverpool 1886.
284.

RILEY, William, c.1725–1784.
U 81.1767 (runner-up).
William Riley of Bedford Row appointed by Society of Ancient Britons to be singing master to their school in Clerkenwell Green in room of late Mr. Markham 1764 Feb.[L153]. Died 1784 June 22 William Riley age 59 music & singing master. In Little James St., Bedford Row, singing master to most of the charity schools . . . in London & Westminster. For many years conducted their singing at Christ Church[232]. Writer of many books on church music including *Parochial music corrected*, 1762[273] and *Psalms and hymns for the use of the Chapel of the Asylum for Female Orphans*, 1773. Also compiler of church music.
B. 284.

RIST, Miss Lisetta.
All Hallows Barking 1840 – 1880 vacated (date of appointment unconfirmed owing to gap in records).
U 42.1833 (no christian name), 71.1834.
While at All Hallows Lisetta Rist often seen scattering ashes on Tower Hill to help the horses[312].

ROBINSON,
U 81.1659.

ROBINSON,
U 1.1823, 20.1827 (runner-up).

ROBINSON, John, d.1762.
St. Lawrence Jewry 1710 May 24 – 1762 Apr.30 died. Death reported May 12.
St. Magnus the Martyr c.1712 – 1762 Apr.30 died. Death reported May 3.
U 57.1705/6 (no christian name).
Original member Roy. Soc. of Musicians 1739[181]. Died 1762 Apr. 30 aged upwards of 80 in North St., Westminster, 35 years organist of Westminster Abbey, likewise organist of St. Lawrence near Guildhall & of St. Magnus, London Bridge[L422]. Daughter, a dancer, d. Jan.1741[242].
B.? G. 284. 339.

ROBINSON, W.F.
St. Olave Jewry 1834 Oct.30 – 1874 Jul.? vacated.
U 15.1836.
Organist Eaton Chapel, Eaton Sq., Pimlico in 1834[159].

ROCKSTRO alias RACKSTRAW, William Smith.
U 59.1840, 45.1841 (top 4 out of 17), *12.1842*, 59.1843 (top 6 out of 43), 74.1844 (failed to attend audition), 25.1847 (top 6 out of 63).
Of 20 Great Dover St., Southwark 1840 – 43[59V], at Mr. W.S. Smith's 49 Francis St., Newington 1844[74V].
G. 282. 284.

RODD, Miss Elizabeth.
All Hallows Lombard Street 1812 Feb.13 – 1842 Mar.30 retired.
U 38.1809 (no christian name, runner-up), 15.1809 (runner-up), 60.1810, 6.1811.

ROE,
U 20.1836.

ROGERS, Miss Catherine.
U 33.1832, *12.1842* (no christian name).

ROGERS, Charles.
St. Katherine by the Tower 1703 June 16 – 1709 before Sep. vacated. Successor appointed Sep.22.
Charles Rogers, a musician from St. Clement Danes parish, bur. in Fetter Lane churchyard 1709 May 10 (St. Dunstan in the West). The same?

ROLFE family.
St. Mary le Bow. Messrs. Rolfe of Cheapside purchased from Thomas Howard, (q.v.), interest in organ and his annuity arising therefrom amounting to £42 p.a. 1822 Jan.14.
St. Mary le Bow. 1822–1838 Dec. Rolfe & son, Rolfe & co. appear in C. as organists. Various members of the family played, probably mostly Thomas Hall Rolfe (q.v.) and William Rolfe, jun. (q.v.).
The firm of Rolfe, founded when William Rolfe dissolved partnership with Culliford & Barrow 1797 Sep.29[239]. William, son of Robert Rolfe

of Eltham, Kent, joiner and Mary (Humphreys), free of City and Glovers' Company 1795 described as "music vendor"[119]. Continued as music sellers & publishers & pfte. makers at the same address, 112 Cheapside. Joined in partnership by his sons Thomas Hall Rolfe (q.v.) died 1847, Nicholas Rolfe died 1858 Apr.21 and James Longman Rolfe resigned 1844 Mar.25, died 1857, who continued after William's death in 1829 (will proved 1830 Jan.22)[139]. Firm carried on at 112 Cheapside until 1841 (later by James Rolfe, q.v.) then opposite at no.61 until 1862, 12 Great Marylebone St. up to 1871 and 11 Orchard St. until 1879. Piano patents taken out by William 1797 Jan.31 and Thomas Hall Rolfe 1829 Aug.11[322].
G.

ROLFE, James, b.1826 or 7.
St. Mildred Bread Street 1847 Jul.1 – 1869 Apr.1 not re-elected through lack of funds.
U *12.1842?* (no christian name. James Rolfe?).
Son of Nicholas Rolfe, patent self acting piano manufr. of 112 Cheapside. At City of London School 1837–41[158]. Mar. Ellen Elizabeth Pilcher at St. Pancras 1858 Dec.7. (She died Haywards Heath 1929 Jan.24 age 92). Pfte. maker of Cheapside. Eldest son Frederick William born 61 Cheapside 1860 Jul.22, died Venice 1913 age 53, was famous Baron Corvo.

ROLFE, Thomas, b.1820.
No City posts or candidatures found before 1850.
Brother of James & William, q.v. Elected St. Mary Woolnoth 1851 May 14. Of 61 Cheapside[57V].

ROLFE, Thomas Hall, 1785–1847.
St. Mildred Bread Street 1809 June 6 – 1847 died. Death reported Jul.1, succeeded by James Rolfe, q.v.
St. Mary le Bow 1822–38. He and other members of the Rolfe family organists during this period.
St. Botolph Aldgate relief 1805 Nov. (no christian name. T.H. Rolfe?).
U 65.1806.
Born 1785 Sep.14 bap. St. John Zachary Nov.8. Son of William Rolfe, pfte. maker of Cheapside, & Ann[182]. In father's business with brother Nicholas after joint apprenticeship to him 1799 Aug.30[119]. Both free of City and Glovers' Company 1806 Sep.13[120]. Viola player. Elected Roy. Soc. of Musicians on recommendation of William Russell 1812 Jan.4. Died 1847[182].

ROLFE, William, jun., b.1811.
St. Mary le Bow (probably) c.1822–38 under Rolfe & Co.
U 77.1828 (4th out of 17).
Of 112 Cheapside 1828[77V]. Born 1811 Mar.27 bap. All Hallows Honey Lane, son of Nicholas, music seller, and Elizabeth of 112 Cheapside. Brother of James (above). At Merchant Taylors' School[317]. Mar. Julia Hannah Lance 1834 Jul.31 at St. Marylebone (she died Reading 1869 Apr.2). Went to U.S.A.
Some of this information kindly supplied by Mr. A.W. Rolfe.

ROST, John Matthew, b.1805.
U 74.1844 (failed to attend audition).
Born 1805 June 29 bap. St. Margaret Westminster Jul.21. Son of John Christian & Esther Rost. Performer on harp & pfte. Teaching at several schools in Hammersmith & privately. Organist Berkeley Chapel when elected Roy. Soc. of Musicians 1834 Feb.1[182]. Of Frith St. 1835, High St. Camden Town 1837, & Hawley Terrace Camden Town 1840–44[199, 74V].

ROUTH, G.
U *12.1842* (no christian name), 59.1843.
Of 8 Temple St., Dalston 1843[59V].

ROWE, Robert.
U 6.1764, 59.1764 (no christian name), 10.1766 (do.).

ROWLANDS, Edward, 1802–44.
U *45.1826* (Edward Rowland).
Although entered as Edward Rowland in 45v, doubtless Edward Rowlands, organist of Bedford Chapel in 1829[182]. Born 1802 Feb.25 bap. St. Paul Covent Garden Mar.25. Son of Edward & Catherine Rowlands. Also performed on pfte., 'cello & double

bass & employed Drury Lane Theatre. Elected Roy. Soc. of Musicians 1829. Died 1844[182].

RUSH, Jonathan, d.1849.
St. Botolph Aldgate relief 1805 Sep. – Oct. (no christian name).
St. Dionis Backchurch deputy c.1810 – 1833 Apr.23.
St. Dionis Backchurch 1833 Apr.23 – 1849 Nov.8 death reported.
U 44.1805 (runner-up), 59.1807, 15.1809, 3.1812.
Jonathan Rush, music teacher, 28 Little Bell Alley, City 1832–4[199].

RUSSELL,
U 4.1825.
Of Hadden St., Bloomsbury 1825[4V].

RUSSELL, Miss Ann, later Mrs. Reilly, 1779–1854.
St. Mary Aldermary 1825? Entered in C. as organist but unlikely to have played having inherited organ annuity on death of father 1825.
Dau. of Hugh Russell, q.v. Mar. Philip Reilly, surgeon, of St. George Bloomsbury at that church 1828 Aug.2[91]. Died age 74 at 17 Brunswick Place, Islington 1854 June 17[92].

RUSSELL, Hugh, c.1738–1825.
St. Mary Aldermary c.1783 Jan.2 – 1825 Oct.10 died. Built and installed organ & found "proper person to play" for annuity of £46.4.0 p.a.[88 89] during his life & lives of children William (q.v.) age 6 & Ann (q.v) age 4. No positive evidence of his playing but son William (q.v.) almost certainly played subsequently.
Organ builder of Theobalds Rd., Holborn 1781 – 1825. Died in 88th year 1825 Oct.10, bur. St. Andrew Holborn Grays Inn burial ground Oct.18[187]. Will proved 1825 Nov.12 naming surviving children Timothy, Ann (q.v.) and Elizabeth. Elizabeth, wife of Hugh Russell, d.1824 Oct.19 age 77[187]. Son Timothy succeeded him in business of organ builder. Maintained organ of St. Mary Aldermary after death of father from "Organ manufactory", 2 Grays Inn Terrace. No evidence that he played organ.

RUSSELL, William, 1777–1813.
St. Mary Aldermary deputy 1789 – 1793 and 1798. Originated by Sainsbury[325] with church wrongly given as St. Mary Aldermanbury, this is probably correct despite lack of evidence in C. or V.
U 81.1808.
Born 1777 Oct.6 bap. St. Andrew Holborn Oct.26. Son of Hugh (above) & Elizabeth Russell. Pianist Covent Garden Theatre & pfte. teacher. Organist St. Anne Limehouse & Foundling Hospital until death. Elected Roy. Soc. of Musicians on recommendation of John Immyns 1802 Oct.3[182]. Died Clerkenwell 1813 Nov.21 bur. St. Andrew Holborn Grays Inn Rd. burial ground Nov.28 age 36.
B. G. 284. 295. 384.

RUTLAND, Robert.
U *45.1826*, 74.1827 (no christian name, in top 6 out of 15), 77.1828.
Of 20 Old Burlington St., Bond St. 1828[77V] address of James Rutland, baker[199]. Organist St. James Chapel 1834[159].

SADLER, Robert.
Dutch Church Austin Friars 1821 Mar.2 (although paid from 1818 Sep.) – 1823 May 15 resigned.
U 59.1840.
Of 4 Gloucester St., Cambridge Heath, Hackney Rd. 1840[59V]. Described as music teacher[199].

SALE, John.
St. Paul's Cathedral almoner 1799 – 1812 resigned.
Born c.1759. Gentleman of Chapel Royal & Vicar Choral of Windsor & Eton when elected Roy. Soc. of Musicians on recommendation of Thomas Barrow 1785 Apr.3[182]. Of 227 Piccadilly in 1794[198].
G(5). 284.

SALISBURY, Edward.
All Hallows Bread Street 1726/7 Mar.15 – 1727/8 Mar.22 vacated.
Son of Edward Salisbury of London, victualler. Apprenticed to "Maurice Green [sic] of London, gent. £81" 1718[149]. Edward Salisbury organist

York 1727–34 & afterwards Trinity College, Cambridge[339]. The same?

SALISBURY, J.
St. Michael Bassishaw temporary 1843.

SALMON, John.
St. Andrew Undershaft deputy up to 1749 June 8.
U 14.1749, 31.1749 (stand-in since death of previous organist).
John Salmon free by redemption Musicians' Company 1734 Jul.17. Son of William Salmon of Calton, Leics., yeoman[165]. The same?

SALTER, John.
St. Dunstan in the West 1718 Apr.8 – 1729 Apr.25 "gone beyond the seas". Called to vestry to answer complaints 1724/5 Jan.15.
U 33.1713/14 (Mr. Solter).

SANDFORD,
U 26.1732.
John Sandford u St. Olave Southwark 1736 May 25[94].

SAVAGE, George.
U 26.1818 (runner-up).
Of Bethnal Green 1818[26V].

SAVAGE, William, d.1789.
No City organ posts or candidatures found.
St. Paul's Cathedral almoner 1748 – 1773 removed.
Elected Roy. Soc. of Musicians 1740, withdrew subscription[181]. An organist of this name at Finchley in 1743[260]. Probation as Vicar Choral St. Paul's 1748 Apr.5[100]. Thomas Selves apprenticed to William Savage of Doctors' Commons 1763[211]. Died 1789 Jul.27 in East St., Red Lion Square[222, 232].
B. G. 284.

SCHMIDT, Bernhard *see* Smith, Bernard.

SCHNEEGANS, Miss.
U 74.1844 (failed to attend audition).
Of 93 Upper Seymour St., Euston Sq. 1844[74V].

SCHNERGANT, Miss R.
U 15.1844.

SCOTT,
U 26.1732.

SCOTT,
U 31.1752 (withdrew because of single post clause), 10.1766.
Probably John Scott (q.v.) but conceivably Thomas Scott, Musician, Old Change, free Musicians' Company 1765 Feb.10, son of Bennet Scott, citizen & Blacksmith admitted 1733–34 by apprenticeship[165].

SCOTT,
U 25.1799.

SCOTT, James, d.1738.
St. Dunstan in the East 1718 c.Jan. – 1738 Dec. died.
Organist Lambeth parish church 1725 – 1738[298]. Survived by widow Mary[32V].

SCOTT, John, d.1792.
St. Michael Crooked Lane 1749 Jul. – 1792 Jan. died. Bur. St. Michael Jan. 25. Death reported Jan.31.
U 18.1762, 20.1777. (See also under Scott, above).
James Bird apprenticed to John Scott "of St. Michael, London" [sic] organist, £1 1753[149]. John Scott "blind gentleman", chosen without opposition St. Olave Southwark, 1764 Mar. 19[L273], death reported 1792 Jan.27[94].

SCRIVEN,
U 4.1825.

SCRIVENER, George.
U 33.1764.

SECOND, F.
U 74.1844 (disallowed, no testimonial).
Of 6 Victoria Rd., Pimlico 1844[74V].

SELBY,
U 1.1758 ("declined playing"), 53.1762.
Could be either John or William below. B. has Mr. Selby, jun. *A new Medley*, c.1780.
B.?

SELBY, John.
St. Mary Woolnoth 1764 Sep.14 – 1772 Jan.3 resigned.
U 18.1762, 33.1764 (runner-up).

SELBY, William.
All Hallows Bread Street 1756 May – 1773 Oct.14 resigned.
St. Sepulchre Holborn joint organist 1760 Mar.20 – 1773 Oct.27 resigned. "To quit this Kingdom the 10th instant".
U 34.1753.

Elected Roy. Soc. of Musicians 1762: expelled for non-payment[181]. Contributed psalm tunes to Riley's *Parochial music corrected*, 1762[273]. Free by patrimony of Musicians' Company 1766 Feb.20, of Wood Street, son of Joseph Selby, citizen & Fishmonger[165]. The same? Included in the Dict. of American Biography as "musician & composer probably born in England, little is known of early life". Holder of organist's post in America 1772 (op.cit.). Assertions in biographical sources that he went to America 1771 disproved by above entries. Organist Magdalen Hospital 1766–1769.
B, G.

SEL(L)MAN, Miss.
U *25.1847*, 76.1847 (in top 8 out of 57), 15.1847.

SENIOR (?or Simon), Miss.
U 15.1847 (withdrew).

SEVERN, Thomas Henry, 1801–1881.
German Church, Trinity Lane (City of London) in 1838. (This Lutheran church not included in the lists in part 2).
U 77.1828 ("Thomas Severn").

Born 1801 Nov.5 bap. St. Leonard Shoreditch 1802 Aug. 1. Son of James & Elisabeth Severn of Masons Court. Mar.(i) Caroline Plumstead 1825 Nov.12 St. Mary Islington, (ii) (as a widower) Emma Cawthorn 1839 Oct.1 St. Paul Covent Garden. Performer on organ, pfte., violin, viola, 'cello & double bass. Teacher. Elected Roy. Soc. of Musicians 1839 Dec.2[182]. Of St. Mary Haggerston 1828[77V], 7 James St. Covent Garden 1838[182]. Petitioned R.S.M. for relief 1873 Apr.: incapacitated 4 years by rheumatism[183]. Died 1881 Apr.15 at 5 Birdhurst Rd., Wandsworth[243].
G(5). 282. 284.

SHACKLETON,
U 26.1732.

SHARPE, Lancelot.
Dutch Church Austin Friars 1830 Mar.11 – 1833 June 5 resigned.
St. Katherine Coleman 1833 May 21 – 1837 Dec.6 resigned.

SHICKELWORTH (sic) *see* Shuttleworth.

SHIELDS, Charles.
U 59.1840.

Of 19 Bridge Rd., Lambeth 1840[59V], address of John & Sarah Shields, wire workers.

SHORT,
U *12.1842*.

SHORT, Benjamin, c.1674–1760.
St. Sepulchre Holborn 1712 June 20 – 1760 Mar.12 died. Death reported Mar.20.
U 73.1705 (no christian name), 43.1713/14 (—— Short declined invitation for candidature), 13.1717/18 & 1726.

Phineas Cooper, q.v., apprenticed to Benjamin Short citizen & master of music £20 1723[149]. William Ingram apprenticed to Benjamin Short of St. Andrew Holborn organist £30 1742[149]. Also organist St. Dunstan Stepney[260] and "at the Playhouse"[241]. Original member Roy. Soc. of Musicians 1739[181]. Died 1760 Mar.12 ——Short, musician & many years organist of parish churches of St. Sepulchre & St. Dunstan Stepney, in James St., Bedford Row in 87th year[L253]. Will dated 1759 Oct.17 "Of St. Andrew Holborn" left money in trust for dau. Elizabeth Blamire, widow & her dau. Elizabeth. Children of late brother Thomas referred to. Spinet made by Hitchcock to Miss Colley dau. of Rev. Colley (i.e. Cawley, rector of Stepney). Harpsichord made by Thomas Hancock, violin and books to dau. Elizabeth. Harpsichord to granddau. Elizabeth. Execs. William Crutchfield of Holborn Bridge, colourman, and Charles Alexander of Doctors' Commons, gent. Proved 1760 Mar.18[139].
B.

SHORT, John.
U 40.1782 (contested John Gates at annual election. Probably a mistake in V. for Richard Short q.v.).

SHORT, Richard.
St. Michael Queenhithe 1779 Mar.30 – 1824 Sep.15 resigned. Annual re-election of organist postponed 1817 Apr.19 till the sentiments of the vestry were conveyed to him "concerning his methods of playing the psalm tunes".
U 53.1775, 40.1783–4 (contested John Gates at annual election).

SHOWELL, Samuel, d.1825.
St. Stephen Walbrook 1793 Mar.8 – 1825 Nov.16 death reported. By 1804 Apr.25 accused of great neglect of duties. Requested increase of salary 1812 Apr.17, 1813 Apr.22 & May 6. Refused on grounds of inattention to duty. Salary raised to £42 1814 Apr. 12 with stipulation as to future conduct.
U 18.1784, 27.1784 ("on occasion of election at St. Botolph Bishopsgate, Mr. Deputy Bullock acquainted the vestry that Mr. Showell, one of the candidates . . . as he was coming to church on the day of election was thrown down by a horse in Bishopsgate St. and received a wound on his head and was obliged to be carried to the Hospital where he now is with very little hopes of recovery". Suggested vestry pays him £10 if and when recovered. If he failed to survive, £10 to be paid to his father for and towards his son's expenses "he was at during the election and in the hospital". Agreed), 25.1786, 22.1789 (no christian name), 10.1790, 48.1792, 81.1810.

The circumstances of the election at St. Botolph Bishopsgate and his behaviour at St. Stephen suggest the dishonesty which appears to be characteristic. Following his death in 1825 his wife and family almost destitute. Subscription raised in parish for their relief 1826 Mar.26.
379.

SHOWELL, Theodore.
U 75.1825.

SHOWERS, Miss Hannah.
U 4.1825 (runner-up), *75.1825*, 61.1826 (runner-up).

Of Globe Court, Fish St. Hill 1825[4]V.

SHRUBSOLE, William, d.1806.
St. Bartholomew the Less 1800 Oct. – 1806 Jan.18 died. V. & C. do not supply christian name nor specific dates. Known to be playing 1800 Oct. and last mention 1805 but evidence suggests still there at beginning of 1806 Jan. This tallies with date of death of William Shrubsole.
U 68.1781.

Of 13 Great Sq., Gray's Inn, organist Spa Fields Chapel, pfte. teacher etc. 1794[198]. Tombstone inscription Bunhill Fields "In memory of William Shrubsole who died 18 Jan. 1806 age 46 years. Composer of Miles's Lane".
B. G. 284. 339.

SHUCKFORD, John.
U 53.1775, 3.1780.

SHUTE (?), Elizabeth Anne.
U 25.1786.

SHUTE, John.
U 3.1780 (failed to attend audition).

SHUTTLEWORTH, John, d.1730.
No City organ posts found but the first three U under Obadiah Shuttleworth, below, could apply.

Organist St. Olave Southwark until death reported 1729/30 Feb.4[94].

SHUTTLEWORTH, Obadiah, d.1734.
St. Michael Cornhill 1723/4 Jan.1 – 1734 May 2 died. Death reported June 20.
Temple Church (for Inner Temple) 1729 May 16 – 1734 May 2 died. Death reported May 13. Sal. £25.
U 73.1705 (no christian name), 44.1710 (Shickelworth), 43.1713/14 (no christian name, runner-up), 2.1723 (The first three of these U could apply equally to John Shuttleworth, above).

"We hear there will shortly be publish'd Twelve Sonatas, Twelve Concertos, and Twelve Solos for a Violin and a Bass, with a Book of Cantatas for One and Two Voices with Symphonies; some of which were compos'd at Thir-

teen Years of Age by the ingenious Mr. Obadiah Shuttleworth, whose judicious Performances on the Harpsichord and Violin are sufficiently Known"[240]. Living in parish of St. Botolph Bishopsgate with wife Ann Ailay (or Aishlay) Shuttleworth where children Thomas & Katherina bap. 1724 Oct.18 and 1726/7 Jan.3 (Thomas bur. 1725 Dec.22). "Mr. Shuttleworth . . . gave fine performance on new organ at St. Bartholomew's behind the Royal Exchange" 1732[221]. Died 1734 May 2[232 242]. Admon. . . . of all Hallows London Wall: goods etc. to Joseph Maisters principal creditor of deceased and Anne Shuttleworth widow. To Catherine S., a minor & Elizabeth S., infant, daus. & only children of deceased[143].
B. G. 284.

SILVERLOCK, Miss Eliza Ann, b.c.1821.
St. Olave Hart Street assistant 1845 Apr.28 – 1857 Apr.16.
St. Olave Hart Street 1857 Apr. 16 – 1885 vacated.
U *12.1842*, 59.1843, 76.1843 (no christian name), 74.1844 (in top 6 out of 60), *63.1844* (no christian name), 47.1844 (runner-up).
Dau. of John Silverlock, clerk to a wharfinger, and Ann. Eliza Ann, music teacher and her sister Emily ran a school at 7 Black Raven Court. Age 30 in 1851[153]. Of Seething Lane 1867[210].

SILVESTER, John.
All Hallows Bread Street 1728 Apr.17 – 1729 Nov. or Dec. vacated.
U 2.1727/8 (one of 12 names submitted by vestry).
Chorister of this name St. Paul's under Charles King[342]. John Silvester organist Exeter Cathedral (1741–53 died) constantly in trouble and in prison[316]. The same?
339.

SIMMONDS, Henry *see* Symonds, Henry.

SIMON, Miss *see* Senior (or Simon), Miss.

SIMPSON,
U 25.1799, 4.1825.
Possibly Henry Purver Simpson (B) or John Simpson, as under.
B.?

SIMPSON, John.
U 71.1800 (St. Peter Cornhill).
Possibly John C. Simpson, music seller, of Sweetings Alley Cornhill, bankrupt 1797 Apr. 11[239]. Or John Simpson who flourished late 18th century & composed 12 voluntaries for the organ or pfte. c. 1800[284].
284? 310?

SINDERBY, Miss.
U 58.1830, 20.1834 (one of 4 selected by umpire), 58.1835.

SLATER,
U 58.1835.

SLYFIELD, George.
U 12.1842 (no christian name, failed to supply testimonial), *74.1844*, *63.1844* (no christian name).
Of 5 Norfolk St., Strand 1844[74V 63V], address of George Slyfield, boarding house.

SMALLSHAW, Frederick Augustus.
U 10.1790.
Frederick Smallshaw organist Silver St. Chapel in 1794 also tenor singer Covent Garden, Westminster Abbey etc.[198].

SMALLSHAWE, Miss, later Mrs. Milward.
St. Anne and St. Agnes 1782 Oct.29 – 1804 Oct.17 vacated as Mrs. Milward. Mar. before 1783 Apr.24.

SMART, Timothy, d.1781.
U 22.1765, 17.1766, 58.1767 (no christian name).
A City wait of this name 1769 May 30 – 1781 May 15. Son of Richard Smart of Richmond, Surrey, shoemaker, he was apprenticed to John Ward the elder, citizen & Musician of Foster Lane (himself a City wait) 1752, and free of Musicians' Company 1761 Apr. 15[165]. Living near St. Clement's Church in the Strand 1772 when Francis Phillips apprenticed to him. Advertised himself as candidate for St. Augustine 1766 Nov. " . . . Your votes and interest are most humbly desired for Timothy

Smart, musician, to be your organist . . . Having no other organ, and serving my apprenticeship in one of the parishes [i.e. St. Augustine or united parish of St. Faith], I am extremely sorry I must lay myself under the necessity of acquainting my friends that one of the candidates has been mean enough to insinuate I had declined standing a candidate any longer, though he knew well to the contrary . . ."[226]. Elected Roy. Soc. of Musicians 1769. Died 1781[181].

SMETHERGELL, William.
All Hallows Barking by the Tower joint organist 1770 Nov.22 – 1783 Apr.24.
All Hallows Barking by the Tower 1783 Apr.24 – 1823 May 1 superannuated.
St. Mary at Hill 1775 May 26 – 1826 Mar.30 "advanced age" and long service pensioned £36 p.a. Pension continued to Christmas 1835 (no payment Mar. 1836).

Son of William Smethergell of Tower St., citizen & Poulter (i.e. a freeman of the Poulters' Company). Apprenticed to Thomas Curtis (q.v.) citizen & Weaver consideration £52.10 1765 Apr.1. Free of Weavers' Company (later a liveryman) 1772 May 4 then described as musician, Tower Dock. (Weavers' Company records Guil. Lib.). Mar. Ann Moore of Bridgewater Square 1772 May 14 St. Giles Cripplegate. First viola at Vauxhall & teacher when elected to Roy. Soc. of Musicians on recommendation of Jacob Neilson 1779 Jul.4[182]. Living 55 Aldermanbury 1790. Described as composer & violinist of 7 Bull's Head Court, Newgate St. 1794[198]. Took Peter Wilcox (son of William Wilcox of 9, Clerkenwell Close, musician) as apprentice 1795 Oct.6 (Weavers' Co. records). After various changes of address lived 71 Bishopsgate Without (do.). Work reviewed European Magazine vol. 6, 1784 p.136. Died probably end of 1835 or before March 1836.
B. G. 284.

SMITH, d.1706.
St. Martin Ludgate 1703 Apr.7 – 1706 Oct.8 death reported.

SMITH,
U 20.1740.

SMITH,
U 43.1713/14.

SMITH,
U 60.1781.

SMITH, Miss.
St. Mary Somerset 1846 Mar.? – 1847 vacated.

SMITH, Anthony.
U 42.1805 (joint runner-up).

SMITH, Bernard.
St. Peter Cornhill ?c.1683–4. Only evidence in C from Easter 1683 to Easter 1684 "Pd. Mr. Smith the organist £30". Doubt is cast by entry in 71V (1683 Nov.21) authorising payment of £30 due for the organ. However, as he was an organist (notably at St. Margaret Westminster from 1675 until death) as well as an organ builder[296], Smith could have played at St. Peter.
G. 448. 457.

SMITH, C.
U 61.1819, 20.1819 (withdrew).

Perhaps Charles Smith, organist Welbeck Chapel & "composer to the theatre" when elected Roy. Soc. of Musicians 1812 on recommendation of Thomas Attwood. Born 1786 Sep.8 bap. St. James Westminster Oct.5. Son of Felton & Elizabeth Smith. Chorister in Chapel Royal before 5 year apprenticeship to John James Ashley[182].

SMITH, Miss Elizabeth.
U 74.1775, 53.1775, 25.1786 (no christian name).

Also u St. Mary Magdalen Bermondsey 1775 Jan. 19 (ves. min. bk.)

SMITH, Mrs. Elizabeth Ann *see* Barber, Miss Elizabeth Ann, later Mrs. Smith.

SMITH, Miss Emma, later Mrs. Thomas.
St. Mary Abchurch 1823 Apr.24 (from Feb.20 jointly) – 1858 Apr.30 resigned as Mrs. Emma Thomas "through failing health, . . . having served these last 30 years".

Alleged to be dau. of parish clerk: not confirmed.

SMITH, Frank A. *see* Smith, John.

SMITH, George.
St. Peter Cornhill deputy up to 1834 June 19 when runner-up at election. Letter from George Smith of 51 Lothbury 1834 Aug.14 having "served so long as deputy" & not now elected asks for gratuity. Granted £10 1834 Aug.22.
U 71.1834 (runner-up).

SMITH, George.
U *63.1844*, *74.1844*.
Of 9 Surrey Sq. 1844[63V 74V].

SMITH, Henry.
St. Botolph Aldgate 1805 Nov.22 – 1818 Jan.2 resigned.
U 44.1805.
Henry Smith St. Paul's choir 1786[342]. The same? Also "alto, late of St. Paul's choir, singer Academy of Ancient Music, Oratorio Drury Lane, Westminster Abbey, 75 St. Paul's Churchyard" 1794[198].

SMITH, John or Frank A.
St. Andrew Undershaft (unopposed) 1836 May 26 – 1847 before Apr.8 vacated.
A list of subscribers 1843 gives organist as Frank A. Smith[258].

SMITH, Miss Louisa.
U 10.1835.

SMITH, R.
St. Mary Somerset 1847? – 1853 vacated.

SNELL,
U 20.1827.
Mr. Snell, professor of the pfte., terms moderate, 48 Red Lion St., Holborn 1828[195]. The same?

SNOW, Moses, d.1702.
St. Katherine Cree 1686 Sep.30 – 1702/3 Mar.9 death reported. Elected after audition by "Dr. Blow, Mr. Purcell, Mr. Mosse & Mr. Forcell (i.e. Forcer)": "Mr. Snow played best and most skilfully". Salary reduced from £20 to £16 (it would appear through irregular appearances) 1700 June 19. (Christian name appears only once, in C., and not at election or death).
Moses Snow appointed musician for the King's private music 1689 Jul.11[292]. Probably Moses Snow, gentleman of the Chapel Royal etc., d.1702 Dec.20 and bur. Westminster Abbey Dec.24. Will dated 1702 Dec.12 proved 1702/3 Feb.11 by brother George and sister Sarah Gibbons[139]. *The second book of the Divine Companion set by several eminent masters viz. Moses Snow etc.* (B).
B. G. 337.

SOAPER, John, c.1740–1794.
No City organ posts or candidatures found.
Chorister of St. Paul's[342]. Succeeded Robert Wass as Vicar Choral St. Paul's 1764 c.Mar.26 – 28[L301]. Appointed Gentleman of Chapel Royal 1764 May 3[L435]. "Good composer and admirable organ player: retained treble voice till 18 then bass singer"[342]. Died 1794 June 5 in Sion Gardens, Aldermanbury, Mr. John Soaper, one of the gentlemen of the Chapel Royal and one of the lay vicars of St. Paul's Cathedral[232]. The European Magazine gives the date of death as June 15 " . . . at his apartments in Sion College, Mr. John Soaper . . . Celebrated while under Mr. Savage (at St. Paul's) for the uncommon excellence of his voice & ear . . . When his vocal powers declined he still retained a very respectable rank in the musical profession as a composer and a performer on the organ. His compositions are but few, but they are such as must ever cause the lovers of harmony and especially of church music, to regret that his abilities in that line were not more frequently exerted"[222].
B. 284.

SOWARD, Miss Alice, later Mrs. Pawsey.
St. Mildred Poultry 1840 c.May – 1872 vacated on demolition of church.
Mar. late 1847 or early 1848.

SPENCER,
U 4.1825.

STANLEY, John d.1786.
All Hallows Bread Street 1723 Oct.23 – 1726/7 Mar.8 resigned.
St. Andrew Holborn 1726 Aug. 17 – 1786 May 19 died.

Temple Church (for Inner Temple) 1734 May 13 – 1786 May 19 died.
U 79.1749 (Temple Church: for Middle Temple).

Married 1738 Jul.21 "Dr. Stanley, a blind young gentleman skilled in musick and organist of St. Andrews Holborn and the Temple, to Miss Arnold with £7000"[232]. Living parish of St. Stephen Walbrook 1738–51[172]. Benjamin Skinner son of Benj. Skinner apprenticed to John Stanley of St. Stephen Walbrook musician etc. £120, 1745[149]. Original member Roy. Soc. of Musicians 1739[181]. Living in Hatton Garden described as composer, organist and teacher on harpsichord 1763[211]. "On Thursday [i.e. 1783 Jul.31] . . . the gentlemen of His Majesty's Chapels Royal held their annual feast at the Queen Arms Tavern St. Paul's Churchyard . . . The next regale proceeded from the "flying fingers" of the incomparable Stanley, who is yet able to "kiss the strings" at the age of eighty, with the devotion of an enthusiast, and the vivacity of five and twenty"[L116]. Died "at his house in Hatton Garden" 1786 May 19[L478].
B. G. 293. 345. 347. 401. 453. 458.

STANTON,
U 43.1713/14.

Perhaps Richard Stanton, son of Thomas Stanton of St. James Westminster, farrier, apprenticed to John Wade of Musicians' Company 1697 Nov.3. Free of City and Musicians' Company 1704/5 Feb.[165]. Of Limehouse 1750[204]. Thomas Eyres apprenticed to him 1719[149].

STAPLES,
U 76.1809 (withdrew).

STEELE(?), Miss.
U 25.1786.

STEELE, Nicholas, d.1785.
St. Bartholomew the Great 1777 Feb.14 – 1785 Aug.17 death reported.

Married Margaret Judith Claridge of Bushey, Herts. 1770 Mar.17 St. Marylebone. Member of Westminster Abbey Choir & Vicar Choral St. George's Chapel Windsor. Elected Roy. Soc. of Musicians on recommendation of Redmond Simpson & Thomas Barrow 1780 Jan.2[182]. Died 1785 Aug. Will dated 1784 June 15 "of St. Margaret's Churchyard Westminster". Wife Margaret Judith legatee & executrix. Proved 1785 Aug.19[139].

STEPHENS,
U *12.1842*.

Possibly Charles Edward Stephens holding organ posts outside the City 1843 onwards. Born 1821 Mar.18 bap. St. Marylebone Apr.14. Son of Samuel John & Charlotte Ann Stephens. Pianist, violinist & composer. Elected Roy. Soc. of Musicians 1843 Jul.2[182]. Of 24 Portman Place Edgware Rd. 1843. Died 1892[182].
G? 282? 284?

STEVENS, Richard John Samuel, d.1837.
St. Michael Cornhill 1781 May 21 – 1810 Feb.20 resigned.
Temple Church (for Inner Temple) 1786 June 20 – 1810 resigned.
Charterhouse 1796 Mar.4 – 1837 Sep.23 died.
Christ's Hospital music master 1808 Mar.25 (unanimous) – 1810 Feb.16 resigned.
U 42.1777 (Canvassing by his friends for this post alluded to in his diary)[190].

St. Paul's Cathedral school 1766 – 1773[342]. Of Lambeth Walk 1794[198]. Elected Roy. Soc. of Musicians on recommendation of Thomas Smart 1776 Jul.7[182].
B. G. 284. 363. 369.

STEWARDSON, William.
U 59.1843.

Of 10 John St., Cambridge Heath, Hackney 1843[59]V.

STILES, Mrs. Elizabeth *see* Morrel, Miss Elizabeth, later Mrs. Stiles.

STILES or Styles, James T.
U 45.1826 (James T. Styles failed to attend audition), 77.1828 (J.T. Stiles).

Of 3 Poland St. 1828[77]V. Stiles, James, music master 110 Hatton Garden 1832–4[199].

STIMSON, Miss Maria, later Mrs. Baylis.
St. Dunstan in the East 1811 Aug.29 – 1830 Dec.15 last payment.
Dau. of Thomas Stimson of 5 St. Dunstan's Hill in 1796, parish clerk of St. Dunstan 1794 – 1820 (died)[130]. Maria Stimson mar. Thomas Baylis of St. Mary Whitechapel at St. Dunstan 1821 Feb.14.

STIRLING, Miss Elizabeth, later Mrs. Elizabeth Stirling Bridge, d.1895.
No City posts or candidatures found before 1850.
A review of a recital by Miss Stirling age 17 in St. Sepulchre's church appears in Times of 1837[249] "of whom as yet the world has heard little or nothing. She must rise to a distinguished place in her profession. A pupil of Mr. W. Holmes". Organist All Saints Poplar from 1839 and later in the City at St. Andrew Undershaft 1858 – 1880. Composer of part songs and organ works. Mar. F.A. Bridge 1863 May 16, died 1895 Mar.25.
284.

STONE,
The various Stones are not easily distinguished and overlaps probably occur in the following entries.

STONE,
U 25.1827, *12.1842*.

STONE, John.
St. Mary Woolnoth (previously deputy) 1829 May 5 – 1851 Apr. resigned.
U *75.1825*.

STONE, Joseph.
U 75.1825 (failed to attend audition), 45.1826 (in top 4 out of 29), *45.1840*.
Stone, Joseph, piano teacher 47 Lower Belgrave Place, Pimlico 1832–4[199]. The same?

STONE, Joseph Thomas.
U *74.1844*, *63.1844*, 48.1850 (no christian name).
Of 4 High St., Stoke Newington 1844–50[74V 63V 48V].

STONE, Joshua.
St. Alban Wood Street 1846 (between Jul. & Oct.) – 1849 (between Jul. & Oct.) vacated.

STONE, Samuel.
U *74.1844*.
Of 8 Hawley Crescent, Camden Town 1844[74V].

STRICKLAND, John (Joseph).
St. Mary le Bow 1838 Dec.? – 1866 vacated.
U 15.1836, 15.1844 (runner-up).

STROLGER, William.
St. Botolph Aldgate 1724 June 30 – 1732 Nov. 10 resigned: "gone to reside into the country".

STUBL(E)Y, Simon.
U 36.1739 (for deputy), 48.1745.
Organist St. John Clerkenwell c.1740–54 died. Composer of vocal music in Gentlemans Magazine.
B. 284.

STURGES, Edward, 1808–1848.
U 1.1823 (no christian name), 75.1825, 53.1826, 45.1826 (top 4 out of 29).
Born 1808 Feb.24, St. Paul's Cathedral school 1814 Mar. – 1821 Xmas[342]. Organist Foundling Hospital 1833 – 1848 Feb. 15 died[232].
284.

STYLES, James T. *see* Stiles, James T.

SWIFT, Hopsen (?).
U 48.1690.

SYMONDS, Henry, d.1740.
St. Martin Ludgate 1706 Oct.8 – 1739/40 Jan.6 died. Death reported 1740 Apr.7. At annual re-election 1707 Apr.7 "Mr. Symonds chosen so [long] as he plays on holly dayes & behaves himself like a christian".
Original member Roy. Soc. of Musicians 1739[181]. Died 1739/40 Jan.6 "at his house in Princes St., Bedford Row, Mr. John [sic] Symonds, a musick master, organist of West Ham & of St. John's Chapel in St. John's Square"[246]. Sainsbury wrongly gives date of death as 1730, asserts that he was in the King's Band, organist of St. Martin Ludgate and a celebrated master of the harpsichord. Composed six sets of

lessons for the harpsichord.
B. 284. 325.

TAPLEY,
U 48.1703, 48.1704 (annual election).

TAYLOR,
U 25.1799.

TAYLOR, Miss Elizabeth Mary.
U 26.1822.
Of Jubilee Place, Stepney 1822[26V].

TAYLOR, Rayner.
U 37.1785, 14.1790 (runner-up).
Chorister in King's Chapel under Gates & Nares. Engaged Marylebone Gardens as singer & organist "when Tom Lowe was proprietor". Later associations at Chelmsford where organist and teacher at schools throughout the county[223].
B. G.

TAYLOR, William.
St. Anne and St. Agnes 1804 Nov. 1 – 1809 Apr. 19 vacated after suspension at annual re-election. Elected again St. Anne and St. Agnes with a big majority 1809 May 5 – 1809 Sep.14 vacated (no reason given).

TEMPLE,
U 25.1847 (being blind considered unsuitable for teaching and disqualified).

TERRYLL,
U 42.1805 (joint runner-up).

THATCHER, William.
St. Dunstan in the East 1669 or 1669/70 Jan. – 1680 Oct.? vacated (?died). C. the only source[32C] in which the last ref. is dated 1680 Oct.18.
Admon. of William Thatcher of St. Mary Magdalen, Old Fish Street 1680 Oct.12 to Mary Thatcher widow[142]. The same? but burial not at St. Mary or St. Dunstan. Perhaps William Thatcher who, according to Hawkins[303], was born Dublin, came to England & taught on virginals, died London 1678 [sic].

THOMAS, Mrs. Emma *see* Smith, Miss Emma, later Mrs. Thomas.

THOMPSON,
U 34.1753.

THOMPSON, Miss Mary Ann.
U 7.1817, 25.1820 (no christian name), 77.1828.
Of 8 Christopher Court, St. Martins le Grand 1828[77V].

THOMPSON, or Thomson, William.
U 28.1782 (Thomson, no christian name), 44.1788 (William Thompson, also Thomson).
B.?

TIDMARSH,
U 20.1836.

TILBURY, George Hayward.
St. Martin Ludgate 1850 Apr. 4 – 1852 June resigned in letter written from Derby.
Of 18 Ernest St., Regents Park 1850[48V].

TOLKIEN, George.
U 75.1825, 59.1843.
Of 28 King William St., London Bridge 1843[59V], address of Henry Tolkien, music seller & pfte. maker. *Note* John Benjamin Tolkien age 66 bur. 1819 Jan.27 & Mary his wife age 91 bur. 1837 Mar.16 in family grave of William Shrubsole, organist (q.v.) in Bunhill Fields[152].

TOLPUTT, W.B.
U 74.1844 (failed to attend audition).
Of 28 St. Thomas's St. East, near Guy's Hospital 1844[74V].

TOMLINSON, Thomas.
U 77.1828.
Of 17 Queen St., Lower Rd., Islington 1828[77V].

TOOKEY, Miss.
U 53.1826, *45.1826*, 25.1827, 20.1827.

TOOKEY, Miss Ann Eliza.
U 64.1837, 59.1843, *74.1844*.
Of 15 Skinner St., Snow Hill 1837[64V], 86 Snow Hill 1843–4[59V 74V].

TOOTH, W.E.
U 59.1840.
Of 37 Monkwell St. 1840[59V].

TOPLIFF, Robert.
St. Vedast Foster Lane 1807 Jul.23 – 1828 Jul.10 resigned. Salary raised from

£31.10.0 to £52.10.0 in addition to £10.10.0 for teaching children to sing 1817. Told to play more regularly: if "his more lucrative engagements elsewhere" do not permit this there will have to be another election 1828 Mar.12. Letter from 12 Great Queen St., Lincoln's Inn Fields: unable to come to town because giving recitals Hemel Hempstead and other places for charity; will continue to do duty at St. Vedast. Vestry not satisfied, re-election suspended until Sep.29, 1828 June 12. Letter of resignation dated Jul.3: "sees no justification for vestry's attitude".
U *75.1825*, 25.1827 (no christian name).

A blind organist. Mr. Topliff, professor of singing and the pfte., 12 Great Queen St., Lincoln's Inn Fields 1828[195]. Subsequently organist Holy Trinity, Southwark[256 210]. Composed church music and songs. Of 51 Trinity Sq., Southwark 1837[256], 1847[199].
284.

TOWNSEND, Miss Carolina.
St. Mary Magdalen Old Fish Street 1834 Sep. – 1855 Apr.13 retired on account of severe illness.

TRAVERS, John, d.1758.
St. Paul's Cathedral sub-organist c.1727[262].
No other City appointments or candidatures found.

Son of Joseph Travers of Windsor, shoemaker. Apprenticed to Maurice Greene, citizen & gent. [sic] £70, 1719[149]. While organist St. Paul Covent Garden took as apprentices Thomas Barrow 1737 and Edward Clarke (q.v.) 1745[149]. Original member Roy. Soc. of Musicians 1739[181]. Died 1758 c.June 9 —— Travers, musician and organist to King's Chapel and St. Paul's Covent Garden[L556].
B. G. 284.

TREMAIN,
U 75.1765.

Possibly Thomas Tremaine apprenticed to Thomas Capell organist of Chichester Cathedral £59, 1752[149]. Thomas Tremaine deputy Chichester Cathedral 1771[339].
B. 284. 339.

TRIPCONY, Thomas.
U 34.1797, 71.1800 (no christian name), 48.1805 (failed to attend audition).

TRUFLEY (or Tufley), Miss E.
U 15.1847.

TUCKER, Edward, 1805–33.
U *45.1826*.

Born 1805 Oct.28 bap. Bathwick, Somerset Nov.17. Son of Edward & Ann Tucker. Performer & teacher on organ, pfte. & harp. Organist Christ Church Southwark when elected Roy. Soc. of Musicians 1832 Aug.3[182]. Of 20 College St. Westminster[182]. Died 1833.

TURENE, John.
U 60.1781, 68.1781.

TURLE, Robert, d.1877.
St. Lawrence Jewry 1821 June 26 – 1822 Dec.31 resigned on appointment to Armagh Cathedral in letter written from 21 Great Waterloo St., Lambeth.

Organist Armagh Cathedral 1823–72[339]. Died 1877 Mar.26 at The Close, Salisbury age 73[243].
G. 284. 339.

TURNER, John.
U 6.1764 (declined to stand).

John Turner elected Roy. Soc. of Musicians 1759: died 1776[181]. The same? John Turner organist Woolwich and appointed Charlotte St. Chapel, Pimlico at opening 1768 Jan.[L87]. The same?

UNONIUS, Miss (or Mrs.)
U *12.1842*.

URLING, George.
St. Peter Cornhill 1800 Aug.22 – 1807 Apr.10 resigned because "business at the Bank makes it impossible to attend in morning".

VAN HELSDING, Adrian.
St. Bartholomew the Great 1715 Dec.7 – 1721 c.June vacated. Name subject to

several variations in church records. On appointment entered as Venallson and at departure Vanghelsden. C. entries also include Vanhelsding and, once, Adrian Vanhelsden.

Probably identifiable with Adrian van Helsdingen bur. Dutch Church, Austin Friars 1721 Nov. 3.

VERDUIN, C.
Dutch Church Austin Friars 1823 June 19 – 1829 Oct.15 resigned.

VINCENT, James, d.1749.
Temple Church (for Middle Temple) 1737 – 1749 Oct.6 died.
U 26.1732 (no christian name).

James Vincent bound apprentice in Musicians' Company 1731/2 Mar.6[124], but not free of City of London. The same? Thomas Vincent a City wait 1726–43, in King's band and composer (see G.). James Vincent, organist, d.1749 Oct.6[242]. James, Richard & Thomas Vincent original members Roy. Soc. of Musicians 1739[181].
B. G.

VINNICOMBE, John (?)
St. Ethelburga Bishopsgate 1823 Jul.9 – 1827 Feb.1 resigned. Described as J. Vinnicombe, jun.
U 44.1823 (not described as junior).

Probably John Pewtner Vinnicombe born 1807 Aug.20 bap. Oct.4 St. Ethelburga. Eldest son of John Pewtner Vinnicombe & Ann. The elder J.P. Vinnicombe parish clerk St. Ethelburga 1818–34 Apr.9 died[130]. Of 4 Cavendish St., Houndsditch 1822[130].

VINNECOMB, J.H.
U 75.1825, *45.1826* (T.H. Vinnicombe), 25.1827 (no christian name).

Probably identical with J. Vinnicombe, above, as no baptism of J.H. or T.H. Vinnicombe found in bap. reg. of St. Ethelburga among 8 children of J.P. Vinnicombe.

VOKES, Henry, d.1820.
St. Botolph Aldersgate 1799 Jul.25 – 1820 Jul.26 death reported. Also instructed charity children of Aldersgate ward in singing.
U 66.1792.

Compiler of *Psalms and hymns with select sentences of scripture sung at the parish church of St. Botolph Aldersgate*, c.1820. Died 1820 Jul.17 in Gloucester St., Queen Sq., Bloomsbury age 44 Mr. Henry Vokes[232]. The same?
284.

WADE, James.
St. George Botolph Lane 1780 Jul. 19 – 1831 Apr.12 superannuated.
U 3.1780 (runner-up).

WADE, James.
U *45.1826*.

WAFFORNE, Miss.
St. Bartholomew the Great 1827 Apr.19 – 1834 Apr.3 "retired to the country – not to seek re-election".

Either Mary (b.1803 Mar.13), Amelia (b.1804 Dec.22) or Clara (b.1808 Mar.21) daus. of Mary & Joseph Wafforne, oilman, of 43 Cloth Fair. Her move to country coincided with death of father bur. 1834 Mar.5 in 60th year St. Bartholomew.

WAFFORNE, Miss Elizabeth Ellen, later Mrs. Williams, b.1815.
St. Bartholomew the Great 1836 May 25 – 1849 Apr.12 resigned as Mrs. Williams "after 13 years service". Mar. between 1842 Mar.31 and 1843 Apr.20.
U 20.1834 (St. Bartholomew the Great after sister's resignation. Lost by casting vote of chairman. One of 4 selected by umpire).

Sister of Wafforne, Miss, above. Born 1815 Mar.28 bap. 1816 Oct.27 St. Bartholomew.

WAFLER,
U 65.1753.

WALLER, Miss S.
U 15.1844 (4 selected by umpire collected equal votes. Miss Waller lost by casting vote).

WARBOYS, Thomas.
U *63.1844*.

Of Putney 1844[63V].

WARD, Miss Eliza.
U *74.1844*.

Of 41 Grosvenor Row, Pimlico 1844[74V].

WARD, Richard, d.1777.
St. Antholin Budge Row 1735/6 Feb.25 – 1777 Feb.13 death reported.
St. Bartholomew the Great 1740 Mar.26 – 1777 Feb.12 death reported.

Chorister St. Paul's under Charles King[342]. Original member Roy. Soc. of Musicians 1739[181]. Organist and teacher on the harpsichord Budge Row, Cheapside 1763[211].

WARING,
U 4.1825.

WARNE, Miss.
U 25.1827 (runner-up), 20.1827.

WARNE, George.
St. Helen Bishopsgate 1819 Mar.18 – 1820 Jul.17 resigned "on appointment to another parish".
St. Magnus the Martyr 1820 Aug.7 – 1826 Nov.20 resigned in letter dated Nov.17 from 57 Aldermanbury "I have today been elected organist of Temple Church". Signed by mark because of blindness.
Temple Church (for Inner & Middle Temples) 1826 Nov.17 – 1843 resigned.
U 27.1815 (no christian name).

Of 57 Aldermanbury 1823–4, 1826[199 45V], 73 St. Paul's Churchyard 1828[195], 47 Edgware Rd. 1832–4, 191 Sloane St. 1840[199]. Works include *Set of psalm tunes as sung at the Temple Church, London*, 1838, songs, dances, pfte. works.
B. 284. 383.

WARNE, Miss Mary, d.1826.
St. Botolph Aldersgate 1820 Sep.7 – 1826 Oct.18 death reported. "Very ill from diseased state of lungs" 1826 Mar.23. Then living with father G. Warne of 8 Cockey Lane, Norwich. To have £10 gratuity.

WARNER, John.
U 48.1805.

WARRELL,
U 28.1782 (runner-up).

WARRELL, William.
St. Olave Jewry. Proposal to provide organ for annuity 1814 Aug.9. Proposals adopted Aug.24 & shared by Ralph Kinkee, q.v. who was probably the organist in fact until 1834.

Of 53 Carlisle Place, Lambeth 1814[69V]. William Warrell (the same? or Warrell above?) author of *Warrell's companion for the German flute* c.1785(B). William Warrell had installed annuity organ in same manner St. Mary le Strand 1790 (see 69V under 1814 Aug.12). —— Warrell, music seller and organ builder of 17 Bridge St. Lambeth 1794[198].

WATERHOUSE, William.
U 53.1775.

A William Waterhouse elected Roy. Soc. of Musicians 1769 died 1822[181]. Violoncellist of this name of Mount St., Grosvenor Sq. 1794[198]. Also William Waterhouse music seller of Blackmoor St., Southampton Bldngs. bankrupt 1790 Apr.24[239].

WATTS, Thomas, d.1680.
No City organ posts or candidatures found.

Thomas Watts, organist, bur. St. Giles Cripplegate 1680 Dec.15.

WAYNE, Benjamin, d.1774.
St. Alban Wood Street 1766 Apr. 15 – 1774 Dec.2 death reported.
U 25.1773 ("Benjamin Wayn" runner-up).

Organist of this name appointed St. Mary, Stratford le Bow 1762[307].

WEATHERHEAD, Mrs. Elizabeth *see* Minton, Miss Elizabeth, later Mrs. Weatherhead.

WEBB,
U 16.1777.

Probably John, q.v. but possibly Samuel Webbe (1) (see G.).

WEBB, C.J.
U 58.1830 (runner-up).

?G.J. Webb (b.1803) organist Falmouth 1830 then to U.S.A.[232].
232? 234?

WEBB, Miss Jane Constant, later Mrs. Andrews, c.1817 – 1878.
St. Matthew Friday Street 1835 June 16 – 1878 Apr.24 last appearance at annual election. Between 1835 and 1836 Apr. mar. John Holman Andrews.
U 58.1830 (no christian name), 48.1834 (runner-up).
Jane Constant Webb, music teacher, 4 Great Distaff Lane 1840[199]. Described as teacher of the pfte. etc. at this address on undated trade card in Guildhall collection. Published two part exercises 1860, songs and instrumental music. Died 1878 Apr.29 at 60 Baker St. Portman Sq. age 61[243].
284.

WEBB, John.
U 53.1775, 3.1780.
John Webb u St. Mary Magdalen Bermondsey 1775 (Ves. min. bk.)
B.?

WEBB, John Charles, c.1778–1830.
St. Matthew Friday Street 1818 Mar.6 – 1830 Oct.12 death reported. Bur. St. Matthew 1830 Oct.7 John Charles Webb, organist of the united parishes, of 6 Knightsbridge age 52.
Teacher or organ, pfte., thorough-bass etc., pianofortes tuned & schools attended, 90 Leadenhall St. 1828[195]. Same address as Bailey, —, q.v.

WEIBER (?),
U *63.1844*.
Of Grafton St. East 1844[63V].

WELCH, Miss Ann.
St. Nicholas Cole Abbey 1824 or 5? – 1850 Oct.10 resigned. Evidence suggests appointment 1824 or 5 but not definite until 1838 May 31 when situation far from secure. An election held 1839 Jan.25 when appointment regularised.
Of 20 Crutched Friars 1839[67V].

WELDON, John, d.1736.
St. Bride Fleet Street 1702 June 18 – 1736 May 7 died. Death reported Aug.10.
Premature announcement of death 1735/6 Jan.4 of "Mr. Weldon, organist to His Majesty & of St. Bride's in Fleet St."[228] precedes the correct one: 1736 May 7 "died at his house in Downing St., Westminster Mr. John Weldon organist of St. Martin in the Fields and St. Brides Fleet St."[230]. Will dated 1735 Nov.27 "of parish of St. John the Evangelist, Westminster" all to widow Susanna, sole executrix. Proved 1736 May 10[139].
B. G. 284. 297.

WESLAKE, John.
U *74.1844*, *63.1844* (T. Westlake), 25.1847 (Mr. Westlake), 76.1847 (one of 3 cands. selected by John Goss), 53.1847 (J. Westlake).
Of 28 Bridge St. Southwark 1844[74V] (address of John Westlake, watch & clock maker), of Southwark 1844[63V], 21 Bridge St. Southwark 1847 [53V]. Organist of this name St. Saviour Southwark 1866, 1867[209, 210].

WESLEY,
U 63.1844 (top 6 out of 35).
Conceivably Samuel Sebastian Wesley, q.v.

WESLEY, Miss.
U 35.1823 (withdrew).

WESLEY, Miss Eliza.
St. Katherine Coleman 1837 Dec.13 – 1844 c.Apr. resigned. Never referred to by christian name but doubtless Eliza as Eliza appointed St. Margaret Pattens 1844, the date of her resignation from St. Katherine.
St. Margaret Pattens 1844 Mar.27 (in succession to Robert Glenn her brother-in-law who died 1844 Feb.25) – 1887 Apr. last appearance at annual re-election. Said to have acted for Glenn at St. Margaret's during latter part of his life[324].
U 64.1837, 77.1837 ("Westley". The date of this application and the fact that Miss Mounsey is entered as "Mounsey" suggests that this was Miss Eliza Wesley).
Of 8 King's Rd., Pentonville 1837[64V]. Daughter of Samuel Wesley 1766 – 1837 and sister of Thomasine and Samuel Sebastian.

WESLEY, Samuel (Sebastian).
U 44.1823, *75.1823* (Samuel Westley,

jun.), 53.1826 (Samuel Wesley, jun.), 74. 1827 (Samuel Westley, jun. in top 6 out of 15).

Presumably Samuel Sebastian Wesley, son of Samuel Wesley, 1766–1837. G. 284. 339. 356. 449. 452. 455.

WESLEY, Miss Thomasine, later Mrs. Martin.
St. Andrew by the Wardrobe 1842 Nov.11 – 1858 May 6 resigned as Mrs. Martin (wife of Richard Alfred Martin).

Daughter of Samuel Wesley 1766 – 1837 and sister of Eliza, q.v. After resignation from St. Andrew organist of St. Bride Fleet Street until death 1882.

WEST, (1).
U 53.1730.

Possibly Benjamin West, organist & composer of *Sacra concerto, or the voice of melody* 1769 & other works[284].
B.? 284?

WEST, (2).
U 21.1825.

WEST, Edward.
U 15.1836, *12.1842* (no christian name), 74.1844 (failed to attend audition), *63.1844* (no christian name).

Of 3 Robert St., Chelsea 1844[74V] address of Edward West, organ & piano teacher 1832 – 1847 etc.[199].

WESTLAKE, John *see* Weslake, John.

WESTLEY, Samuel *see* Wesley, Samuel (Sebastian).

WESTROP, East John, d.1856.
St. Anne and St. Agnes 1847 Dec.2 – 1856 Oct.27 died. Death reported Nov.13. One of 4 candidates selected by umpire but not considered the best.

Older brother of Henry & Thomas, son of John & Anne Westrop. Music teacher, published *Musical services of the Church of England*, 1845 etc.[282].
G(5). 282. 284.

WESTROP, Henry, 1812 – 1879.
St. Edmund, King and Martyr 1833 end – 1879 Sep.23 died[243].

Born 1812 Jul.22 bap. Lavenham Suffolk Jul.26. Son of John & Anne Westrop (formerly East). Married Maria Holmes 1833 Aug.22 St. Pancras. Pianist, violinist, organist & private teacher. Elected Roy. Soc. of Musicians 1837 Aug.6[182]. Of 65 Judd St., Brunswick Sq. 1837[182], 8 Lloyd St. Lloyd Sq. W.C. 1867[210]. Application for relief to RSM because of paralysis granted 1875 Oct.[183]. Daughter then acting as deputy at St. Edmund until his death 1879 Sep.23[243].
G(5.) 282. 284.

WESTROP, Thomas, 1821–1881.
St. Swithin London Stone 1847 Oct.14 – 1881 Dec.17 died. Death reported Dec.28. Elected out of 57 candidates.
U 74.1844 (failed to attend audition).

Born 1821 Dec.15 bap. Lavenham Dec.31. Son of John Westrop, yarnmaker & Anne. Brother of East John & Henry. Organist, pianist, violinist, teacher of harmony. Elected Roy. Soc. of Musicians 1845 May 4[182]. Of 27 Henrietta St. Brunswick Sq. in 1844–5[74V]. Died 1881 Dec.17.
G(5). 282. 284.

WHEATLEY,
U 34.1747.

Jonathan Wheatley elected organist Greenwich 1763 June 10[L561] and elected Roy. Soc. of Musicians 1764[181]. The same? Or perhaps William Wheatley, pupil of William Savage and organist of Lewisham.

WHICHELLO, Abiell, 1683–1747.
St. Edmund, King and Martyr 1712 Aug.28 – 1747 Aug. died. Successor appointed Sep. 10.
St. Andrew Undershaft deputy "for some years to Philip Hart at St. Andrew and St. Michael Cornhill" according to Sainsbury[325] but no documentary evidence found.

Eldest son of Potter Whichello, glover and liveryman of the Glovers' Company[200 201] and Hopestill Whichello, born 1682/3 Mar.1 bap. Mar.4 St. Giles Cripplegate. Three other children born between 1685 and 1688 and, following the death of the fourth child Thomas, Potter Whichello and Hope-

still are found in the Fore St. precinct of St. Giles Cripplegate in 1695 with 3 surviving children, Abiell, John and Sarah[179]. Mrs. Hopestill Whichello buried Bunhill Fields 1716. Abiell Whichello apprenticed 1698 Dec.5 to Erasmus Micklewright 7 years in Clockmakers' Company[114]. Abiell Whichello taught harpsichord "to some of the first families in the City"[325]. Original member Roy. Soc. of Musicians 1739[181]. Died 1747 Aug. by reason of "age" and buried Aug.16 St. Giles Cripplegate. Will dated 1743/4 Feb.23 indicative of considerable wealth and many bequests but no children mentioned. Of his music "all my scores of Corelli's concertos and sonatas" given to his friend Gordon Milbourn (see Milborne, ——) of Watford and "all the rest of my musick to my friend Mr. Duncalf organist of St. Mary at Hill". (i.e. Henry Duncalf, q.v.)[139].
B. G. 284.

WHITAKER and WHITTAKER.
Owing to alternative spelling and the number of instances when christian names are not given, both surnames are given in one sequence. The groupings in each entry are arbitrary but appear to be the most probable.

WHITAKER, (1)
U 25.1799.
Possibly John Whitaker, composer & organist, b.1776[284].

WHITTAKER, (2)
U 58.1818.

WHITTAKER, James.
U 22.1834 (no christian name), 15.1836, 4.1837 (James Whitaker), 12.1842 (no christian name, failed to supply testimonial), 59.1843.
Of 36 Ann's Place, Hackney Rd. 1843[59V].

WHITAKER, John, d.1847.
St. Bartholomew the Great (after playing during absence of predecessor) 1793 Jul.3 – 1805 June 25 discharged for neglect of duty. Rector brought charge against him for gross neglect of duty on Sunday mornings & festivals: re-election suspended "until he apologises" 1805 Apr.18 which he failed to do.
St. Clement Eastcheap 1828 end – 1847 Dec. died. Death reported Dec.16.
A St. Paul's Cathedral chorister of this name[342]. In 1817 John Whitaker charged with refusal to serve office of constable in parish of St. Bartholomew the Great. Case tried in Court of King's Bench where stated he was one time organist of the church, lives in parish and has successful music shop in St. Paul's Churchyard. Pleaded unfit for office having lost an eye and being subject to spitting of blood and maintained that his election designed merely to extract £10 fine from him for not serving. Jury's verdict in favour of parish[338]. The successful music shop referred to was Button & Whitaker, 75 St. Paul's Churchyard[310]. It cannot be proved that the organists of St. Bartholomew and St. Clement were identical. The latter died 1847 and buried St. Clement Dec. 17 "of Thavies Inn, Holborn age 71". The directories describe him as piano and organ teacher of 21 (or 24) Thavies Inn[199].
G. 284.

WHITCOMB, Adolphus Corelli.
U *75.1825*, 25.1827.
Organist St. Leonard Bromley 1834[159].

WHITE, Edward, jun.
U 76.1847 wrote to vestry offering service without salary until Easter. Had been organist at early Thurs. morning service without fee. Also did full duty from May last to closing of church in Jul. Although one of 8 on short list out of 57, not one of 3 selected for election.
Of 27 Cannon St. 1847[76V] address of Edward White, basket & brush maker.

WHITE, Mrs. M.C.
U 74.1844 (failed to attend audition).
Of 2 Frederick St., Portland Town 1844[74V].

WHITE, William, d.1825.
St. Botolph Bishopsgate 1815 Apr.27 – 1825 Feb.24 death reported. Dissatisfaction over deputy caused postpone-

ment of re-election 1821 Apr.25.

Possibly W.J. White composer and editor. Issued *Sacred melodies suitable for public and private devotion* c.1820 and *New sacred melodies*.
284?

WHITE, William.
U 59.1843, 15.1844 (one of 4 applicants selected by umpire for election. Lost by casting vote in tie by all four).
Of 64 Lambeth Walk 1843[59V].

WHITTAKER *see* Whitaker.

WHITTELL or WHITTLE, John.
U 22.1747 (John Whittell), 14.1749 (Whittle, no christian name).
William Bradstock apprenticed to John Whittell of West Smithfield, London, musician £30.6.0, 1753[149]. Robert Whittle free Musicians' Company 1734 Sep.30, son of James Whittle late of Chorley Lancs. yeoman deceased[165].

WIGAN,
U *12.1842*.
Of Brighton 1842[12V]. Possibly Arthur Cleveland Wigan, writer and composer b.1815, author of *Modulating dictionary* 1852 and *Miscellaneous music, vocal and instrumental*, 1839.
284?

WILD, W.
U *75.1825*.

WILKINS,
U 77.1807 (runner-up).

WILKINS, possibly Mrs.
U *25.1820*.

WILKINS, John.
U 68.1801 (runner-up).
B.?

WILKINSON,
U 15.1836.
James Wilkinson, music teacher, 92 Upper Seymour St. 1840[199]. The same?

WILLIAMS, Miss.
U 64.1837.
Organist of this name St. Ann Limehouse 1837[256].

WILLIAMS, Mrs Elizabeth Ellen *see* Wafforne, Miss Elizabeth Ellen later Mrs. Williams.

WILLIAMS, George Ebenezer, 1783–1819.
Temple Church deputy in 1805[182]. Period of service not established.
U 25.1799 (no christian name so not necessarily G.E.)
Born 1783 Aug.30 at Clerkenwell Green. Son of Thomas & Sara (dau. of Elizabeth Kingley) Williams of Clerkenwell Green. St. Paul's chorister. Deputy organist Temple Church and teacher in Hammersmith school when elected Roy. Soc. of Musicians 1805[182]. Later organist Westminster Abbey etc. Died 1819 Apr.17.
B. G. 284. 339.

WILLIAMS, James.
St. George Botolph Lane 1723 Oct.17 – 1745 Oct.31 discontinued. Father presented petition to vestry on question as to whether he should continue as organist. Vestry decided by 14–10 that he should on condition that deputy be chosen. Williams to be paid £8 p.a. during lifetime, Samuel Manwaring chosen deputy £12, 1739 Aug.29. Vestry decided he should no longer continue 1745 Oct.31.

WILLIAMS, Miss Mary Ann.
St. Bartholomew the Great 1849 June 13 – 1867 Apr.24 office of organist abolished until church reopens.
Daughter of Rev. D. Williams, lecturer of the parish[20V].

WILLIAMS, Robert, b.1794.
St. Andrew by the Wardrobe 1816 Apr.17 – 1842 Oct.6 resigned.
Born 1794 Oct.14 bap. Walcot, Somerset Nov.16. Son of Henry & Charlotte Williams. Organist, pianist, performer on harp & violin & teacher. Elected Roy. Soc. of Musicians 1818 on recommendation of V. Novello. Of 15 Hatfield St., Blackfriars Rd. 1818. Resigned from R.S.M. 1847[182].

WILLSDON, Miss Matilda Ann, 1806–1844.
St. Peter le Poer ? – 1844 Oct.28 died

having "served for several years"[130].
U 4.1825, 42.1837 (no christian name).
Born 1806 Feb.16, bap. 1807 Apr.26 St. Peter le Poer. Dau. of Michael & Sarah Willsdon. Michael parish clerk of St. Peter 1814–46 succeeding his father, also Michael, parish clerk 1793–1814[130]. Matilda died 1844 Oct. 28 bur. St. Peter Nov.5, of Providence Row, Finsbury age 38. Bodies of family later re-interred Ilford cemetery.

WILSON,
U 25.1799.

WILSON,
U 25.1847.

WILSON, William.
St. James Garlickhythe 1831 Jul.6 – 1867 Apr.24 pensioned.
Chorister of St. Paul's 1791–8, "belongs to one of the theatres"[342]. The same? Of 4 Oxford Rd., Islington 1867[40V]. *New dictionary of music* by W. Wilson 1835. The organist?
284?

WILSON, William Brand.
U *45.1840*.
William B. Wilson organist St. Mary Greenwich 1837[256]. W.B. Wilson organist St. Thomas, St. Pancras 1866, 1867[209 210]. Willson [sic], Wm. B. 18 Stepney Causeway, music teacher 1847[199].

WINDSOR or WINSOR,
St. Mary Woolnoth 1705/6 Mar.1 – 1716 vacated on demolition of church prior to rebuilding.

WISE, Michael.
St. Paul's Cathedral almoner 1686/7 Jan.24 – 1687 Aug.23 killed by a watchman in Salisbury[103]. These dates given as 1686/7 Jan.27 & 1687 Aug.24 by M.J. Smith[375].
B. G. 375.

WOOD, Miss Caroline.
U *12.1842* (no christian name), 59.1843 (in top 8 out of 43), 15.1844 (Miss Caroline Mary Wood).
Of 204 Bermondsey St. 1843[59V], address of Mrs. Sarah Wood, undertaker.

WOOD, Richard.
U 59.1840.
Of 21 Minerva St., Hackney Rd. 1840[59V].

WOOD, Mrs. Sarah *see* Morrice, Miss Sarah, later Mrs. Wood.

WOOD, Thomas.
U 37.1736.
Impossible to differentiate between two Thomas Woods both of Brownlow St. Long Acre described in 1763 as (Thomas) first violin at Covent Garden Theatre and (Thomas, jun.) organist and violin teacher[211]. Probable that the 1736 candidate was the first of these, elected to Roy. Soc. of Musicians 1743[181]. "Thomas, jun." is more likely to be identifiable as the Thomas Wood "of Brownlow St., musician by trade" free by redemption of Musicians' Company and City 1771 June[128 129 165]. A Thomas Wood contributed psalm tunes to Riley 1762[273] and served as organist Chelsea Royal Hospital from 1767 and St. Giles in the Fields until his death in 1783.
B.

WOODTHORPE,
U 22.1789 (runner-up), 59.1807, 33.1819.
Possibly Vincent Woodthorpe, chorister of St. Paul's described by Miss Hackett as an engraver with no musical career[166]. Engraver of frontispieces & bookplates of this name 29 Fetter Lane, c.1780 – 1803[199 278 332].

WORGAN, James, 1713–1753.
St. Botolph Aldgate 1732 Nov.10 – 1753 May died. Death reported May 7.
St. Dunstan in the East 1738 Dec.22? – 1753 died before May 10 when next election held. Date of appointment according to G. which is compatible with entries in C. Loss of V. makes confirmation impossible.
U 60.1734 (no christian name), 3.1737/8 (do. withdrew), 81.1739/40, 20.1740 (no christian name), 31.1752 (do. withdrew because of single post clause). Some of these without christian

names could be candidatures of John Worgan, q.v.

Bap. 1713 Nov.15 St. Botolph Bishopsgate, son of John, carpenter, and Mary Worgan. Original member Roy. Soc. of Musicians 1739[181]. Free of City and Musicians' Company by patrimony 1740/1 Mar.13[124 165]. John Worgan, his father, free of City and Carpenters' Company 1710 June 6 after completion of apprenticeship to John Freeman, citizen and Carpenter[113]. John Worgan died 1741 and bur. St. Botolph Bishopsgate 1740/1 Mar.13 age 51. Will dated 1740/1 Mar.7 everything to wife Mary[139]. James Worgan living in parish of St. Clement Danes at time of death 1753 c.May but not buried there. Died unmarried and admon. granted to Mary Worgan, his mother, 1753 May 16[139].

B. G. 284.

WORGAN, John, 1724–1790.

St. Katherine Cree 1743 end – 1753?

St. Andrew Undershaft 1749 Sep. 14 – 1790 Aug.24 died. Death reported Sep.8. Re-election postponed 1752 Mar.30. Called to vestry & undertook to provide a proper deputy and to play himself at least every other Sunday etc. Apr.8. Complaint about interference by previous deputy (Lowe, q.v.) with present deputy who was not qualified. Worgan to find a well qualified person 1756 Apr.19. Further complaints about deputy's "bad behaviour & indifferent performance" 1759 Apr.16, Dr. Worgan's infrequent attendance and indifferent performance by deputies 1785 Mar.28. Re-elected 1787 Apr.9 after "alleging cause" for non-attendance.

St. Botolph Aldgate 1753 May 14 – 1790 Aug.24 died.

U 36.1739 (for deputy), 20.1740 (no christian name – John or James?), 31.1752 (do. do. withdrew because of single post clause). See also under candidatures of James Worgan.

Second surviving son of John Worgan and Mary of St. Botolph Bishopsgate bap. 1724 Nov.2. Younger brother of James Worgan (q.v. for details of parentage. An earlier John born 1715 died age one). 1736 Mar. "The ingenious Mr. Worgan" (then aged 11) lost election at Christ Church Spitalfields to Peter Prelleur, q.v., by 62 votes to 99[236]. Allegedly married thrice (i) Sarah Mackelcan 1753 Sep.1 (divorced 1768), (ii) Eieanor d. Rathbone Place 1777 Jan.11[L46] bur. Jan.20 Westminster Abbey age 36, (iii) Martha Cooke, widow, of St. Thomas Apostle at St. Mary Aldermary 1779 June 12. Organist of St. John's Chapel Bedford Row in 1762[273]. Of St. John's Sq., Clerkenwell 1763[211]. Died 1790 Aug.24 in Gower St.[222 232]. Tablet to his memory in south aisle of St. Andrew Undershaft erected by Incorporated Society of Musicians 1906: "Buried near this spot"[170]. Will dated 1783 Apr.11 proved 1790 Aug.31 by relict Martha & son-in-law William Parsons, Doctor of Music[139].

B. G. 257. 284.

WORGAN, Miss Mary, later Mrs. Gregg, b.1717.

St. Dunstan in the East 1753 May 10? – 1753 May? resigned. No evidence from C. or V. (lost) but "1753 May 19 Mr. Gregg of Tower Street mar. to Miss Mary Worgan who was lately chosen organist of St. Dunstan in the East. Since her marriage she has resigned"[232]. (Mar. 1753 May 19 Liell Gregg & Mary Worgan of St. Botolph Bishopsgate at St. Dunstan in the East). Next election at St. Dunstan June 1.

Daughter of John Worgan, carpenter, and Mary of St. Botolph Bishopsgate bap.1717 Apr.23, brother of James and John (q.v. for details of parentage). (An earlier Mary died infant 1712). The earliest woman organist in the City of London and probably in England.

B.

WORGAN, Richard.

U 14.1790 (Declined invitation to be candidate after death of father Dr. John Worgan but polled one vote at election).

Richard Worgan published a *Sett of Sonnets* etc. in 1810. The same? 284?

WREDE, W.
U 15.1836.

WRIGHT, Charles.
St. Botolph Bishopsgate 1839 May 2 – 1863 Dec.30 retired: "unable to perform duties of organist".

WRIGHT, Mrs. Eliza *see* James, Miss Eliza, later Mrs. Wright.

WRIGHTSON, Mrs. Isabella *see* Harris, Miss Isabella, later Mrs. Wrightson.

WYLDE, Henry.
St. Anne and St. Agnes 1844 Feb.23 – 1847 Oct.14 resigned in letter dated Oct.7 describing him as Professor of the Royal Academy of Music, 65 Westbourne Terrace, Hyde Park. (In 1844 elected by chairman's casting vote).
U 12.1842 (Wyld, no christian name. The same?).
G. 284.

YARNALD (also entered as Yarnold & Yarnell), Benjamin.
St. Mildred Bread Street 1751 Sep.26 – 1753 Aug.8 vacated.

YARNOLD,
U 1.1770.

YARROW,
U 27.1815, *45.1840*.

YATES, William, d.1769.
U 7.1767 (no christian name), 1.1767 (William Yeates), 81.1767.

Organist and teacher on the harpsichord. At Spring Gardens Vauxhall 1763[211]. Died at Lambeth, William Yates, an ingenious organist of this City 1769 Jan.3[L23]. Probably identifiable with the composer who appeared in London at concert given by himself 1764.
B. G(5). 284.

YEATES, William *see* Yates, William.

YOUNG,
U 60.1734 & 1736 (runner-up), 3.1737/8 withdrew.

YOUNG, Anthony.
U Probably some or all of those listed under Young, above.

A child of the Chapel Royal of this name up to 1700[292]. Original member Roy. Soc. of Musicians 1739[181]. Organist St. Clement Danes in 1743[260] but never of St. Katherine Cree as stated by Burney[285]. G. suggests he was son of William Young, violinist in King's band, and brother of Charles, below.
B. G.

YOUNG, Charles, d.1758.
All Hallows Barking by the Tower 1713 Aug.21 – 1758 Dec.12 died. Bur. All Hallows Dec.16, death reported Dec.22.
U 13.1717/18 & 1718.

Possibly brother of Anthony, above, St. Paul's chorister of this name 1698[164]. Possibly Charles Young of St. Martin in the Fields mar. to Elizabeth Nash of St. James Clerkenwell at St. Benet Paul's Wharf 1706 Mar.30. Later living in City in parish of St. Lawrence Jewry where children of Charles Young, "music master" and Elizabeth bap: William 1713 Jul.12, Elizabeth 1714 May 8 and Hester 1716/17 Feb.17. Another bap., of Isabella 1715/16 Jan.3, seems to fit into this pattern despite the fact that she is entered as daughter of John [sic] and Elizabeth Young. No other John entries so this probably an error in register. Hawkins says Charles had 3 daughters all good singers: Cecilia, Isabella and Hester. Cecilia's bap. not found but presumably pre-dating William before Charles moved to St. Lawrence (not found at St. Martin in the Fields). Cecilia mar. Thomas Arne, the composer, at Lincoln's Inn Chapel 1736/7 Mar.13. Isabella mar. John Frederick Lampe, the composer, at St. Benet Paul's Wharf 1737/8 Jan.31. Charles Young's wife Elizabeth predeceased him. He died 1758 Dec.12[L573] and his will dated Dec.11[139] gives his address as Precinct of the Savoy. Only legatee his "grandson Charles Lampe" (his successor at All Hallows Barking) who was given

"my harpsichord and all my papers and my watch and my books in general". No executor having been named, admon. granted to Esther Young, spinster, his daughter 1759 Jan.23.
B.G.

YOUNG, John, 1718–1767.
St. Matthew Friday Street 1735 Aug.29? – 1767 Apr.30 died. Death reported May 6.
Christ Church Newgate Street 1739/40 c.Feb. – 1767 Apr.30 died.
Christ's Hospital music master 1739/40 Feb.12 ("John Young, jun.") – 1767 Apr. 30 died. Death reported Jul.2.

One of the famous Young family of St. Paul's Churchyard (parish of St. Gregory) which produced violin makers, violinists and organists. The parish registers of St. Gregory clarify many family details. Four consecutive John Youngs in the same line can be considered. The first of these, described as "of the City of London, gent" 1693[165], probably identifiable as John Young in King's band from 1673[292]. His son John, born in or just before 1672[165] apprenticed to music seller & publisher John Clarke of St. Paul's Churchyard, citizen and Leatherseller, 1686. Free of the City and Leathersellers' Company 1693 Apr.27[165]. Age "above 21" when mar. to Mary Clark of St. Sepulchre age 18 at St. Martin Ludgate 1692/3 Jan.13[275]. As violin maker etc. St. Paul's Churchyard later joined in partnership by his sons John, violinist etc. born 1694 Aug.23, (father of organist John) and Talbot born 1699 June 25 q.v. All these Youngs associated with the St. Paul's Churchyard business which Peter Thompson, son of Samuel Thompson, hair merchant of St. Martin in the Fields, appears to have joined on becoming free of the City and Shipwrights Company 1731 Nov.30 describing himself as musical instrument maker of St. Paul's Churchyard[327] (Peter Thompson, violinist and oboeist at St. Paul's Cathedral – the same?). Thompson took over from Youngs c.1741[172] paying annuity from the business to Talbot Young's aunt Ann Clark (see his will).

John Young, organist, son of John Young violinist and partner in family firm, born 1717/18 Mar.1. Original member Roy. Soc. of Musicians 1739[181]. Violinist in King's band from c.1750 to death[196 197] and teacher of violin[211]. Living Red Lion Street Clerkenwell 1763[211]. Free of City and Musicians' Company 1748 Mar.2 "son of John Young of St. Paul's Churchyard musical instrument maker"[165]. Liveryman of Musicians' Company 1752, steward 1757[128 129]. Died 1767 Apr.30 "at his house in Red Lion Street Clerkenwell . . . one of H.M. band of music, music master to Christ's Hospital and organist of Christ Church Newgate Street"[L415]. Buried St. James Clerkenwell 1767 May 6 "Mr. John Young age 49 of Red Lion Street; in church". Admon. to widow Sarah 1767 Jul.2[139].
G.

YOUNG, Talbot, 1699–1758.
St James Garlickhythe 1719 Mar.25 – 1719 May 14.
All Hallows Bread Street 1729 Dec.31 – 1756 Mar.30 resigned.
U 40.1719.

Born parish of St. Gregory 1699 June 25, son of John and Mary Young of St. Paul's Churchyard and uncle of organist John Young (q.v. for family background). In family business. Violinist in King's band c.1717 to death[196 197]. "Of St. Gregory age upwards of 23 years" in 1722[174] when mar. to Elizabeth Longford age 21 of Highgate at St. Nicholas Cole Abbey 1722 Jul.24. In St. Paul's choir under Greene (i.e. after 1718) and choirs of Chapel Royal and Westminster Abbey[L180(1758)]. Member Roy. Soc. of Musicians 1747[181]. Living parish of St. Andrew by the Wardrobe and, by 1749, Richmond, Surrey (will). Wife Elizabeth d.1756 bur. Richmond May 15. He d.1758 c.Feb.20[L180], bur. Richmond Feb.24. Long and complex will dated 1749 Jan.6 with 12 codicils proved 1758 Mar.3[139]. Legacies to poor of St. Gregory, "parish I was born in", All Hallows Bread St. (where organist) etc. His friend Francis Wollaston (i.e. Woolaston) one of executors.
G.

BIBLIOGRAPHY

The textual references to the bibliography are mostly numbered. For a few more frequently quoted references, however, letters have been adopted: B British union-catalogue of early music printed before 1801, 2 vol., 1957. G The new Grove dictionary of music and musicians ed. S. Sadie, 20 vol., 1980. G(5) Grove, Sir G., Dictionary of music and musicians, 5th ed., 10 vol., 1954–61. L Lloyd's evening post. Here the number following L is the page number in the volume for the appropriate date.

Primary Sources: Manuscript

(Except where otherwise stated all manuscripts listed are in Guildhall Library).

PARISH RECORDS: VESTRY MINUTE BOOKS (V), CHURCHWARDENS' ACCOUNTS (C) ETC.

Vestry minute books and churchwardens' accounts provide the main sources for the first 77 lists in part 2 of this work. Entries 1–77 in the bibliography correspond to these numbers and give the Guildhall manuscript numbers of the vestry minute books (V), churchwardens' accounts (C) and other manuscripts. Parishes differentiated by the letter "a" are parishes without churches which were united to the parishes listed next above them.

1. All Hallows Barking by the Tower V & C at church.
2. All Hallows Bread Street V 5039/1–3 C 5038/3–8.
3. All Hallows Lombard Street V 4049/2–9 C 4051/2–3.
4. All Hallows London Wall V 5342/2–4 C 5090/4–5.
5. All Hallows Staining V 1705, 4957/1–3 C 1704.
6. All Hallows the Great V 819/2–5.
7. Christ Church Newgate Street (records destroyed in 1940).

7a. St. Leonard Foster Lane V 9132.

8. Holy Trinity Gough Square V 6572, New church building minutes 1836–8, 14829.
9. Holy Trinity Minories V at Tower Hamlets Central Library.
10. St. Alban Wood Street V 1264/1–2 C 1265/1–3.

10a. St. Olave Silver Street V 1255/1–5.

11. St. Alphage London Wall V 1431/6,8.
12. St. Andrew by the Wardrobe C 9133.

12a. St. Anne Blackfriars V 4511/5–7 C 1061.

13. St. Andrew Holborn V 4251/1–3.
14. St. Andrew Undershaft V 4118/1–4 C 4117/1–5.
15. St. Anne and St. Agnes V 1604/3–9 C 587/4–5.

15a. St. John Zachary V 591/2–3.

16. St. Antholin Budge Row V 1045/2–5 C 1046/2–4.
17. St. Augustine Watling Street V 635/2, 635A.

17a. St. Faith under St. Paul V 613/1–4.

18. St. Bartholomew by the Exchange V 4384/4–8.
19. St. Bartholomew Moor Lane (cash book only) 6200.
20. St. Bartholomew the Great V 3990/2–6 C 3989.
21. St. Bartholomew the Less V, C & records of Governors at St. Bartholomew's Hospital.
22. St. Benet Fink V 1304/1–3 C 1303/2–4.
23. St. Benet Gracechurch V 4214A C 1568A.
23a. St. Leonard Eastcheap V 2946/2 C 4058/4.
24. St. Benet Paul's Wharf V 877/3–4 C 878/6.
25. St. Botolph Aldersgate V 3863/1–4, 3864/1–6.
26. St. Botolph Aldgate V 2644/2 (Renter Wardens accounts) 2626, 2627.
27. St. Botolph Bishopsgate V 4526/4–7.
28. St. Bride Fleet Street V 6554/2–11.
29. St. Christopher le Stocks. (no organ).
30. St. Clement Eastcheap (V & C uninformative).
30a. St. Martin Orgar V 959/3–7 C 959/1–2, 958/1–2 also 963, 976.
31. St. Dionis Backchurch V 4216/3–6.
32. St. Dunstan in the East V 4886/1–3 C 7882/2–11.
33. St. Dunstan in the West V 3016/2–12 C 2968/5–10.
34. St. Edmund, King and Martyr V 4266/1–2 C 4266/1–2.
34a. St. Nicholas Acons V 4060/1–4 C 4291/1–2.
35. St. Ethelburga Bishopsgate V 4242/2–4 C 4241/5–7.
36. St. George Botolph Lane V 952/2–3 C 951/2–4.
37. St. Giles Cripplegate V 6048/2–5, 6049 C 6047/2–6.
38. St. Helen Bishopsgate V 6846/2–4 C 6844/2–4.
39. St. James Dukes Place V 1218/2 C 1218/1.
40. St. James Garlickhythe V 4813/3–10.
41. St. Katherine by the Tower, Chapter minutes 6963/1–6, 9694–8 Accounts 9603/1–10.
42. St. Katherine Coleman V 1123/1–2, C 1124/3–6 also 1125.
43. St. Katherine Cree V 1196/1–3, 7704 C 1198/1–4. Annual accounts 7897/1–17.
44. St. Lawrence Jewry V 2590/2–7.
45. St. Magnus the Martyr V 2791/1–2, 1180, 1181, 1183 C 1179/1–4.
46. St. Margaret Lothbury V 4352/5–6, Trustees mins. 4359.
46a. St. Christopher le Stocks V 4425/2, 3061.
47. St. Margaret Pattens V 4571/2–3, 2947 C 4570/3–4. Churchwarden's instructions 6488.
47a. St. Gabriel Fenchurch Street V 4583/1–3 C 4582/1–3.
48. St. Martin Ludgate V 1311/1–4 C 1313/1–5.
49. St. Martin Outwich C 11394/2–3.
50. St. Mary Abchurch V 3892/3.
50a. St. Lawrence Pountney joint V 3894, 3895.
51. St. Mary Aldermanbury V 3570/3–5.
52. St. Mary Aldermary V 4864/1–2 C 4863/3–6.
53. St. Mary at Hill V 1240/1–4 C 1239/3–6, 3885/23–43 (parish accounts).
53a. St. Andrew Hubbard V 1278/2–5.
54. St. Mary le Bow V 5006/1–3.
54a. St. Pancras Soper Lane V 5019/2–4.
55. St. Mary Magdalen Old Fish Street V 1340.
55a. St. Gregory by St. Paul C 1337/4–7.
56. St. Mary Somerset C 5714/3–4.
57. St. Mary Woolnoth V 1001/1–4 C 1002/204.
57a. St. Mary Woolchurch Haw V 1012/1–3 C 1013/2–3.
58. St. Matthew Friday Street V 3579, 1014/1–3 C 1016/2–5.
58a. St. Peter Westcheap V 642/2–4 C 645/3–5.
59. St. Michael Bassishaw V 2598/3, 2599, 2504 C 2601/3–5.
60. St. Michael Cornhill V 4072/1–7 C 4071/2–6.

61. St. Michael Crooked Lane V 2769/1–2, 1187 C 1188/2–8.
62. St. Michael Paternoster Royal V 601/2–3 C 605.
62a. St. Martin Vintry joint C 2851.
63. St. Michael Queenhithe V 4827/1–2 C 4825/2–3.
64. St. Michael Wood Street V 526/4, 2261.
65. St. Mildred Bread Street V 3469/1–4 C 3470/2–3.
65a. St. Margaret Moses V 3478/1–3 C 3476/1–2.
66. St. Mildred Poultry V 4436/2.
66a. St. Mary Colechurch V 65, 4441 C 4440/1–2.
67. St. Nicholas Cole Abbey V 5693.
67a. St. Nicholas Olave V 5701.
68. St. Olave Hart Street V 858/1–4.
69. St. Olave Jewry V 4415/3, 4416 C 4410/2, 4412.
70. St. Paul's Cathedral see nos. 96–105.
71. St. Peter Cornhill V 4165/1–9 C 4164/1–6 also C for 1664–90 in Bodleian Lib.
72. St. Peter le Poer V 2423/1–2.
72a. St. Benet Fink V 1304/2–3.
73. St. Sepulchre Holborn V 3149/2–9 C 3146/2–10.
74. St. Stephen Coleman Street V 4458/4–9.
75. St. Stephen Walbrook V 594/4–5.
75a. St. Benet Sherehog V 838/2–4.
76. St. Swithin London Stone V 560/3–4.
77. St. Vedast Foster Lane V 779/1–4 C 778/4–9.
77a. St. Michael le Querne joint V 779A.
78. Temple Church: Inner Temple see no. 311.
79. Temple Church: Middle Temple see no. 318.
80. Charterhouse see no. 154.
81. Christ's Hospital see nos. 155–157.
82. Crosby Hall see no. 159.
83. Dutch Church Austin Friars see nos. 160–163.
84. Parish Clerks' Company see nos. 130–133.

PARISH RECORDS: REGISTERS OF BAPTISMS, MARRIAGES AND BURIALS

Baptisms, marriages and burials which feature constantly throughout this work are not accorded reference numbers as they would unduly bulk the bibliography. Most of them are to be found in the registers of City of London churches and the information given in the Annotated Index together with the *Handlists of parish registers* published by Guildhall Library will readily provide the key to the entries. For London parishes outside the City of London the Greater London Council's *Survey of the parish registers of the dioceses of London and Southwark*, will likewise give the location of the registers.

PARISH RECORDS: OTHER

85. St. Bride. Tithe rate account books 1719 – MS.3437/1–
86. St. Dionis Backchurch. Subscribers to new organ 1722 with assignment 1723 June 24 by Renatus Harris of Bristol. MS. 11276.
87. St. Katherine Coleman. Articles of agreement with Thomas Griffin 1741 Sep. 10. MS.7730

St. Mary Aldermary. London parochial charity deeds no. 10, 12, 15, 17, 18:-

88. Articles of agreement with Hugh Russell 1781 Mar.26 (no. 10).
89. Grant of annuity to Hugh Russell 1783 (no. 12).
90. Certificate of death of William Russell 1813 Nov. 28 (no. 15).
91. Certificate of marriage P. Reilly & A. Russell 1828 (no. 17).
92. Certificate of death of Anne Reilly 1854 June 17 (no. 18).
93. St. Mary le Bow. Papers relating to the erection of an organ etc. 1802 – 1908. MS.7813.
94. St. Olave Southwark. Vestry

minute book 1725–1808. Newington Library.

95. St. Stephen Walbrook. Report by the joint vestry committee appointed to consider the building of a new organ 1767. MS.7629.

ST. PAUL'S CATHEDRAL RECORDS (transferred from St. Paul's Cathedral Library to Guildhall 1980)

96. Book of augmentations and salaries 1669–70.
97. Dean and Chapter minute book 1733–60 fo.23V.
98. fo.84V, 89V.
99. fo.89.
100. fo.116.
101. fo.197V.
102. Hackett, Maria. Papers.
103. Pridden collection vol. 2.
104. Subscription book.
105. Vicars Choral void places account.
106. Cathedral School pupils admitted Dec. 1812 – Sep.1829 (ref.1/2).

CITY OF LONDON LIVERY COMPANY RECORDS

107. Bakers. Court minute book 1705–33. MS.5177/7.
108. Barber Surgeons. Lists of Courts and Livery 1711. MS.5276.
109. Register of apprentices 1707–25. MS.5266/3.
110. 1725–42. MS.5266/4.
111. Register of freemen 1707–32. MS.5265/4.
112. 1732–57. MS.5265/5.
113. Carpenters. Freedom admission book 1700–14. MS.4335/2.
114. Clockmakers. Court minute book 1681–99. MS.2710/2.
115. 1729–78. MS.2710/4.
116. Coopers. List of freemen 1765–1815. MS.5636/2.
117. Dyers. Freedom admissions 1735–1826. MS.8167/3.
118. Apprenticeship bindings 1706–46. MS.8169.
119. Glovers. Court minute book 1790–1804. MS.4591/4.
120. Freedom admissions 1785–1851. MS.4592/3.
121. Joiners. Court minute books and quarterage books. MS.8046, 8055/1.
122. Mercers. Court minute book 1763. Mercers' Company.
123. Merchant Taylors. Court minute book. Merchant Taylors' Company.
124. Musicians. Renter warden's accounts 1712–54. MS.3091.
125. Court minute books 1772–1839. 4 vol. MS.3087/1–3,5.
126. Quarterage books 1770–91. MS.3093.
127. Apprentices 1765–1832. 2 vol. MS.3094/1–2.
128. Freemen index 1743–69. MS.3097.
129. Freemen chronological list 1743–1831. MS.3098.

Parish Clerks (All 17th to 19th century minutes, accounts, registers etc. perished in 1940 but the following secondary MS material survives):-

130. McMurray, W. London parish clerks 1500–1940. MS.3704.
131. List of admissions 1660–1926. MS.3705.
132. Extracts from minutes 1610–1926. MS.3706.
133. Ebblewhite, E.A. Scrapbooks 1701–1890. MS.4894/2.

Shipwrights see no. 327.

134. Stationers. Court minute books and apprenticeship registers. Stationers' Company.
135. Turners. Court minute book 1752–83. MS.3295/4.
136. 1783–1825. MS.3295/5.
137. Quarterage books. MS.3299.
138. Watermen and Lightermen. Apprenticeship bindings 1745–56. MS.6289/9.

WILLS

139. Prerogative Court of Canterbury (P.C.C.) in the Public Record Office. The full citations are not given as the information supplied in the Annotated Index is sufficient to find the wills by referring to the calendars in the Public Record Office.

. Archdeaconry Court of London:-

140. Register of wills 17 p.285–290 (1741). MS.9051/17.

141. 19 p.249(1762). MS.9051/19.

142. Act book 12 p.61A (1680). MS.9050/12.

143. 23 p.45A (1734). MS.9050/23.

Commissary Court of London:-

144. Original wills 1737 (Admon. with will). MS.9172 box 142.

145. Act book 1690 Oct.29. MS.9168/26.

146. 1732 Apr.8 MS.9168/36.

147. 1734–7. MS.9168/37.

OTHER MANUSCRIPT SOURCES (INCLUDING TYPESCRIPTS)

(B British Library, G.R.O. Guildhall Records Office, P.R.O. Public Record Office).

148. Aldersgate Ward 4th precinct (St. Botolph) poll tax 1641 p.64. E 179/252/1 P.R.O.

149. Apprentices of Great Britain 1710–62. 33 vol. 1929–36 (Index of returns in P.R.O.). Typescript.

150. Apprentices of Great Britain 1763–74. 7 vol. 1937–41 (Index of returns in P.R.O.). Typescript.

151. Bunhill Fields register of interments 1800. MS.1092/3.

152. Inscriptions on gravestones 1869. Ref.19/2 in MS. 897/6.

153. Census returns 1851. P.R.O.

154. Charterhouse. Assembly orders A–M, 1613–1854; muniments PS 1/5, 1/7, 1/9. Charterhouse, London.

155. Christ's Hospital. Children's registers 1657–1827. 11 vol. MS.12818/4–14.

156. Court minute books 1677–1843. 9 vol. MS.12806/7–15.

157. General committee minute books 1654–1897. 30 vol. MS.12811/1–30.

158. City of London School register. Typescript.

159. Crosby Hall. Letters and papers relating to its preservation 1832–41. MS.10189/5.

160. Dutch Church Austin Friars. Acta books of the consistory 1671–1815. MS.7397/9–10.

161. Treasurer's accounts 1774–1852. MS.7389/3.

162. Bills and receipts 1791–1805. MS.7396/15.

163. Bills and receipts 1706–25. MS.7396/9 no.540.

164. Farringdon Ward precinct of St. Faith assessment 1698. Assess. 69.3 G.R.O.

165. Freedom certificates of City of London. Chamberlain of London.

166. Hackett, Maria. Letters and papers 9 vol. MS.10189.

167. Hawes, W., Vicar Choral of St. Paul's. Letters in his possession. MS.10189/1.

168. Jewers, A.J. Monumental inscriptions in the churches within the City of London, 1910–19. vol.1 p.59. MS.2480/1.

169. vol.1 p.93 & 97. MS.2480/1.

170. vol.1 p.183. MS.2480/1.

171. vol.2 p.598. MS.2480/2.

172. Land tax assessments (City of London) 1692–4 and 1703 onwards arranged by wards. MS.11316, 522 vol.

173. London Diocese marriage allegations 1667/8 Mar.23. MS.10091/27.

174. 1722 Jul.4 MS.10091/61.

175. 1763 Feb. MS.10091/109.

176. 1787 Jul. MS.10091/157.

177. 1854 Nov.18. MS.10091/231.
178. London Diocese Faculty register 1806–26. MS.9532/10.
179. London inhabitants 1695. Index based on assessments in Guildhall Records office. 4 vol. Typescript.
180. Organographia (anon). Collection of notes relating to organs. Early 19th century. Royal College of Music.
181. Royal Society of Musicians. Register of members. (At Society).
182. Files relating to members (from 1776).
183. Files of petitions.
184. Minute books.
185. Unaccepted applications.
186. St. Andrew Holborn. Monumental inscriptions in Gray's Inn burial ground, 1884, p.3. MS.5866.
187. p.105. MS.5866.
188. Sperling, J.H. Notes on organs vol.1, 19th century. Royal College of organists.
189. Stevens, R.J.S. Recollections, vol.1 p.39 Pendlebury Library, Cambridge.
190. p.55.
191. p.60.
192. p.438.
193. p.475.
194. Sun Insurance Company registers entry 9019 in MS. 11936/7.

Primary Sources: Printed

DIRECTORIES

195. Boarding School and London Masters' Directory, 1828.
196. Chamberlayne, E. Angliae notitia & Magnae Britanniae notitia, 1669–1755.
197. Court and city register from 1746.
198. Doane, J. Musicial directory, 1794. Roy. Coll. of Music.
199. London directories from 1734.
London poll books (livery lists):-
200. 1700.
201. 1710.
202. 1722.
203. 1727.
204. 1750.
205. 1768.
206. 1792.
207. 1796.
208. 1832–3.
209. Mackeson, C. Guide to the churches of London, 1866.
210. 1867.
211. Mortimer's universal director, 1763.
212. Royal Kalendar from 1767.
213. Westminster poll book, 1749.

NEWSPAPERS AND PERIODICALS

214. City Press 1866 Feb.17 p.5.
215. City Press 1867 Jul.20 p.4.
216. Aug. 31 p.3.
217. Oct.12 p.2.
218. 1902 Mar. 12 p.5.
219. Daily Courant 1717 Dec.11.
220. Daily Journal 1731 Oct.30.
221. 1732 Apr.26.
222. European Magazine from vol.1 1782. References to the European Magazine, Gentleman's Magazine, London Magazine and contemporary entries in the Musical Times are not generally accorded volume and page numbers as most bound sets of these periodicals carry annual name indexes. In the case of the Musical Times where used for appointments and deaths, the dates given in the Annotated Index are adequate for finding the relevant entries.
223. European Magazine vol. 7 1785 p.352.

224. vol.7 1785 p.39 & 283.
225. vol.24 1793 p.327.
226. Gazetteer & New Daily Advertiser 1766 Nov.3.
227. General Advertiser 1752 Feb.17.
228. General Evening Post 1735/6 Jan. 3–6, Jan. 10–13.
229. 1736 Apr. 22–24.
230. 1736 May 8–11.
231. 1736 May 11–13.
232. Gentleman's Magazine from vol.1 1731. See note under European Magazine, no.222 above.
233. Historical Register Chronicle 1723 p.41.
234. Lloyd's Evening Post from 1757. Each reference in the text to Lloyd's Evening Post (L) is followed by a page number. This, together with the given date, is sufficient to identify the entry cited.
235. London Chronicle from 1757.
236. London Daily Post 1736 Mar. 27.
237. 1744/5 Feb.9.
238. London Evening Post 1762 Dec. 18–21.
239. London Gazette. The date given in the Annotated Index is sufficient to identify the entry.
240. London Journal 1722 Apr.28.
241. 1726 Aug. 13, Flying Post 1726 Aug. 16–18, St. James's Evening Post 1726 Aug. 16–18.
242. London Magazine vol.1 1752–1783. See note under European Magazine. no.222 above.
243. Musical Times vol. 1 1841– (Contemporary references to appointments and deaths only. For articles in Musical Times see nos.357 et seq.) See note under European Magazine, no.222 above.
244. Political State of Great Britain vol.39 1730 p.449.
245. 56 1739 p.282.
246. 57 1740 p.87.
247. Quarterly Musical Magazine vol.9 1827 p.225–9.
248. Spectator 1712 Feb. 8 (advert by Abraham Jordan).
249. Times 1837 Oct. 13 p.2f.
250. 1842 Nov.12 p.7c.
251. 1844 Feb.27 p.7d, Feb.28 p.16.
252. Weekly Journal 1718 May 17.
253. 1718 Nov.22.
254. 1724 Jul.11 p.2913.
255. 1724 Jul.18 p.2920.

SUBSCRIBERS' LISTS IN THE FOLLOWING WORKS

Most are in the Gresham Music Library (GML) in Guildhall Library.

256. Cherubini, M.L.C.Z.S. A course of counterpoint and fugue transl. by J.A. Hamilton, 2 vol. 1837. GML 243.
257. Cruse, E. Psalms of the church, 3rd edit. 1836? GML 28.
258. Dowland, J. The first set of songs, 1844 containing a list of members of the Musical Antiquarian Society, 1843. GML 207/2.
259. Feuillet, R.A. Orchesography, or, the art of dancing. Transl. by John Weaver, 1706. B.L. 558*C.39.
260. Greene, M. Forty select anthems, 1743. GML 138.
261. Hall, W.J. Collection of psalm and hymn tunes arranged by J. McMurdie, 1854? GML 246.
262. Handel, G.F. Admetus, 1727. GML 259.
263. Rodelinda, 1725. GML 11.
264. Warne, G. A set of psalm tunes, 2nd edit. 1840? GML 150.

OTHER PRINTED SOURCES (PRIMARY)

265. Bankrupts. Lists transcribed from London Gazette 1772–93, 1794.
266. 1786–1806, 1806.
267. Boult, Miss L.A. Canvassing card for organist's post 1830. Guil. Lib. Trade Card collection.
268. Bower, S. Trade card (undated). Item 22 in Stone collection, Guil. Lib.

269. Jones, John. Election broadside beginning "Whereas it has been industriously and maliciously reported . . ." 1718. B.L. 1855 C.4 (58).
270. Law reports. 14 Law journal Queen's Bench 1844 p.34.
271. 88 English reports p.152.
272. 8 Modern reports p.211.
273. Riley, W. Parochial music corrected, 1762.
274. The "wonder" respectfully inscribed to the inhabitants of St. Botolph. S. sh. Guil. Lib. Bs.6.92.

Secondary Sources: Books

275. Archbishop of Canterbury Vicar general marriage allegations (Harl. Soc. vol.31), p.244.
276. Baddeley, Sir J.J. St. Giles Cripplegate, 1888.
277. Baildon, W.P. Baildon and the Baildons, 3 vol., 1912–27.
278. Bénézit, E. Dictionnaire des peintres, 8 vol., 1948–55.
279. Bennett, J. Voluntaries IX & X ed. H.D. Johnstone with biographical notes. (Novello Early organ music no.15).
280. Bishop, J. A frustrated revolutionary: H.J. Gauntlett. (Roy. Coll. of Organists lecture), 1971.
281. Bloxam, J.R. Register of St. Mary Magdalen College, vol. 2, 1852 p.203.
282. Boase, F. Modern English biography, 6 vol., 1892–1921.
283. British union-catalogue of early music printed before 1801, 2 vol., 1957.
284. Brown, J.D. & Stratton, S.S. British musical biography, 1897.
285. Burney, C. General history of music, vol.4, 1789 p.663.
286. Cansick, F.T. Epitaphs of Middlesex, vol.1, 1869 p.222.
287. Christie, J. Some account of the Parish Clerks, 1893.
288. Clarke, A.W.H. The monumental inscriptions of St. Peter le Poer, 1909.
289. Clutton, C. & Niland, A. The British organ, 1963.
290. Compston, H.F.B. The Magdalen Hospital, 1917 p.215 etc.
291. Crewdson, H.A.F. A short history of the Worshipful Company of Musicians, 1971.
292. De Lafontaine, H.C. The King's musick 1460–1700, 1909.
293. Dictionary of national biography, 22 vol., 1967–8 (reprint).
294. Endowed charities County of London, vol.6, 1904 p.51.
295. Foster, J. Alumni Oxonienses, 8 vol., 1887–92.
296. Freeman, A. Father Smith, 1926 p.18, 55.
297. Organs and organists of St. Martin in the Fields, 1922.
298. Organs of Lambeth parish church, 1922.
299. Godwin, G. Churches of London, 2 vol., 1838–9.
300. Greater London Council Survey of London, vol.8: The parish of St. Leonard Shoreditch, 1922 p.111.
301. Greater London Council Survey of London, vol.27: Spitalfields, 1957 p.162.
302. The New Grove dictionary of music and musicians ed. Stanley Sadie, 20 vol., 1980.
302a. Grove, Sir G. Grove's dictionary of music and musicians, 5th edit. 9 vol., 1954, supplement 1961.
303. Hawkins, Sir J. A general history of music, vol.2, 1875 p.771.
304. vol.2, 1875 p.807.
305. Heal, Sir A. The London goldsmiths 1200–1800, 1935.
306. Herbert, W. St. Michael Crooked Lane, 1833.

307. Hill, O.C. St. Mary Stratford Bow (London survey committee monograph vol.2), 1900 p.27.
308. Historical Manuscripts Commission 7th report appendix, 1879 p.689b.
309. Hopkins, E.J. & Rimbault, E.F. The organ: its history and construction, 1877.
310. Humphries, C. & Smith, W.C. Music publishing in the British Isles, 1970.
311. Inner Temple. Calendar of records, vol.3,4,5, 1901–36.
312. Jackson, T. Our dumb companions, 1865.
313. Lonsdale, R.H. Dr. Charles Burney, 1965.
314. MacMillan, D. Drury Lane calendar 1747–76, 1938.
315. Maskell, J. All Hallows Barking, 1864.
316. Matthews, B. The organs and organists of Exeter Cathedral, 1965.
317. Merchant Taylors' School register 1561–1934, 2 vol., 1936.
318. Middle Temple bench book, 1937.
319. Milbourn, T. History of St. Mildred Poultry, 1872 p.88.
320. Miller, W. London before the fire of 1666 . . . with an historical account of . . . St. Giles without Cripplegate, 1867.
321. Nichols, R.H. & Wray, F.A. History of the Foundling Hospital, 1935.
322. Patent Office. Abridgments of specifications vol.26 (musical instruments), 1871 p.29 & 110.
323. Pearce, C.W. Notes on old London City churches and their musical associations, 1908.
324. Pitman, K.W. History of the organ and organists of St. Margaret Pattens, 1958.
325. Sainsbury, J.H. Dictionary of musicians, 1824.
326. Scholes, P.A. The great Dr. Burney, 2 vol., 1948.
327. Shipwrights' Company records vol. 1 1428–1780, 1939.
328. Simpson, R. Memorials of St. John at Hackney pt. 3, 1882 (includes extracts from vestry minutes).
329. Strype, J. Survey of London, vol.1, 1768 p.315.
330. Sumner, W.L. The organ; its evolution, principles of construction and use, 1962.
331. Sumner, W.L. Organs of St. Paul's Cathedral, 1931.
332. Thieme, U. & Becker, F. Allgemeines Lexikon der bildenden Künstler, 37 vol., 1907–50.
333. Thompson, O. International cyclopedia of music, 1964.
334. Tilmouth, M. Calendar of references to music 1660–1719 (Royal Mus. Assn. research chron. no.1 1961 reprinted 1968), cf. index.
335. Van der Straeton, E.S.J. The romance of the fiddle, 1911.
336. Van der Straeton, E.S.J. The history of the violin, vol.1, 1933.
337. Venn, J.A. Alumni Cantabrigienses, 10 vol., 1922–54.
338. Webb, E.A. Records of St. Bartholomew's Smithfield, vol.2, 1921 p.349–50.
339. West, J.E. Cathedral organists, 1921.
340. Young, W. History of Dulwich College, vol.1, 1899 p.163, 429.
341. p.61.

Secondary Sources: Periodicals

342. Guildhall Studies in London History vol.1, 1974 p.82–93 K.I. Garrett on St. Paul's Cathedral choristers.
343. Huguenot Society publications vol.16, 1906 p.268q.
344. Music and Letters vol.37, 1956 p.141–53 K.G.F. Spence on Busby.

345. 39, 1958 p.359–62 J. Wilson on Stanley.
346. 41, 1960 p.136–45 C. Cudworth on Boyce & Arne.
347. 53, 1972 p.284–92 T. Frost on Stanley's cantatas.
348. 55, 1974 p.437–43 R.J. Bruce on Boyce manuscript recoveries.
349. 56, 1975 p.26–40 H.D. Johnstone on Boyce's *Cathedral music*.
350. Music Review vol.14, 1953 p. 275–87 E. Taylor on Boyce & the theatre.
351. Musical Opinion vol.76, Oct.1953 p.51 T. White on Griffin.
352. vol.89, 1965–6 p.97–8 E.O. Wilshere on Attwood.
353. Musical Quarterly vol.31, 1945 p.54–70 C.W. Hughes on Pepusch (with note on Immyns p.65).
354. vol.46, 1960 p.425–36 S. Sadie on Boyce & Arne chamber music.
355. vol.57, 1971 p.87–106 G. Beechey on Boyce.
356. vol.59, 1973 p.190–206 J.I. Schwarz on S. & S.S. Wesley.
357. Musical Times. vol.93, 1952 p.209–10 A.J.E. Lello on Pepusch.
358. 96,1955 p.634–5 R. Graves on M. Greene.
359. 97,1956 p.133–5 L.G.D. Sanders on the Festival of the Sons of the Clergy.
360. 99,1958 p.542–4 Watkins Shaw on the music of John Blow.
361. 101, 1960 p.479–82 Watkins Shaw on the music of William Boyce.
362. 103, 1962 p.564–5 P.W. Williams on Leffler.
363. 103, 1962 p.754–6, 834–5 C. Cudworth on R.J.S. Stevens.
364. 106, 1965 p.510–15 F. Dawes on Hart.
365. 106, 1965 p.685 Letter H.D. Johnstone re Hart.
366. 106, 1965 p.844–5 C.B. Oldman on Attwood.
367. 107, 1966 p.23–7 (do.)
368. 108, 1967 p.36–9 H.D. Johnstone on Greene.
369. 108, 1967 p.602–4 C. Cudworth on R.J.S. Stevens.
370. 108, 1967 p.1006 H.D. Johnstone on an unknown book of organ voluntaries.
371. 109, 1968 p.802–7 D. Dawe on Boyce.
372. 109, 1968 p.1019 Letter A. Cruft on Boyce jun.
373. 112, 1971 p.1009 B.Matthews on C. Wesley.
374. 113, 1972 p.142 B. Cooper on Bryne.
375. 114, 1973 p.69–73 M.J. Smith on Wise.
376. 114, 1973 p.529–31 O.W. Jones on Joseph Pring.
377. 116, 1975 p.1003–6 D. Burrows on T. Gethin.
378. 117, 1975 p.34–5 Letter D.Dawe on Gethin.
379. The Organ. vol.1, 1922 p.167 A. Freeman on St. Stephen Walbrook.
380. 2, 1922 p.125 Organ specification Christ Church.
381. 2, 1923 p.184– A. Freeman on Busby.
382. 3, 1923 p.54–6 do. on Browne.
383. 3, 1923 p.74 do. on Temple Church.
384. 3, 1924 p.199 do. on Foundling Hospital.
385. 5, 1925 p.1–8 do. on St. Magnus the Martyr.
386. 6, 1926 p.1–8 do. on St. Mary Woolnoth.
387. 7, 1927 p.1–9 do. on St. Bride (1).
388. 7, 1927 p.9 do. on St. Bride (2).
389. 7, 1928 p.201 do. on Southwark Cathedral.
390. 7, 1928 p.220 C.W. Pearce on Vanished City churches.
391. 7, 1928 p.252 S. Salter on Early organs in America.
392. 10, 1931 p.178 C.W. Pearce on Vanished City churches.
393. 10, 1931 p.242–6 A. Freeman on St. Botolph Aldersgate.

394. 20, 1941 p.47 do. on the Englands(1).
395. 20, 1941 p.141 do. on the Englands(2).
396. 25, 1946 p.112– do. on Harris & Byfields(1).
397. 25, 1946 p.145– do. on Harris & Byfields(2).
398. 45, 1966 p.112 W.L. Sumner on St. Margaret Westminster.
399. 48, 1968 p.35–40 B. Matthews on London pleasure gardens.
400. 53, 1974 p.73–7 C.M. Houghton on St. Botolph Aldgate.
401. Royal Musical Association proceedings 1950–1 p.66–75 G. Finzi on Stanley.
402. 1967–8 p.63–75 F.Dawes on Hart.

(See also addenda p.174).

Secondary Sources: Miscellaneous

ADDITIONAL ITEMS RELATING TO CITY OF LONDON ORGANS AND ORGANISTS

In addition to the books and articles cited above further items relating to the lists forming pt.2 of this work are given below. The articles in *The Organ* (0) are mostly by Andrew Freeman (F) or C.W. Pearce (P).

403. All Hallows Barking by the Tower. 0.8.86–92 (F); 0.48.71–7 (W.L. Sumner).
404. All Hallows Bread Street. 0.7. 178–9 (P).
405. All Hallows the Great. 0.7. 180–1 (P).
406. St. Alphage London Wall. 0.7. 181–2 (P).
407. St. Andrew Holborn. The parish church of St. Andrew Holborn: the organ, 1905; 0.44.153–61 (W.L. Sumner).
408. St. Andrew Undershaft. Cruden, R.J. St. Andrew Undershaft: Renatus Harris organ, 1969; Wait, W.M. Organ and organists at St. Andrew Undershaft, 1889.
409. St. Antholin Budge Row. 0.7. 216–8 (P).
410. St. Bartholomew by the Exchange. 0.7.218 (P).
411. St. Bartholomew the Great. Mus. Times 114.941–3 (A. Morris).
412. St. Bartholomew Moor Lane. 0.7.218–9 (P).
413. St. Benet Fink. 0.7.219–20 (P).
414. St. Benet Gracechurch. 0.7.221 (P).
415. St. Botolph Bishopsgate. 0.10.112–5 (G. Benham).
416. St. Bride Fleet Street. Reynolds, G. The organ in St. Bride's, 1961; 0.39.178–88 (G. Reynolds).
417. St. Dionis Backchurch. 0.8.47–50 (P).
418. St. Edmund, King and Martyr. John Compton Organ Co. Ltd. The organ in St. Edmund, 1932.
419. St. George Botolph Lane. 0.8.50–2 (P).
420. St. Giles Cripplegate. Notes on the organs (Occasional paper no. 2, 1971?).
421. St. Helen Bishopsgate. 0.37.152–6 (J. White).
422. St. James Duke's Place. 0.8.115–20 (P).
423. St. Katherine Coleman. 0.1.31–5 (F); 0.8.244–6 (P).
424. St. Lawrence Jewry. Freeman, A. St. Lawrence Jewry, a history of the organs, revised N.P. Mander, 1963; 0.4.65–76 (F).
425. St. Magnus the Martyr. Lightwood, J.L. Church of St. Magnus the Martyr: the story of the organ, 1964; 0.9.119 (P).
426. St. Martin Ludgate. 0.9.36–41 (F).
427. St. Martin Outwich. 0.10.116 (P).

428. St. Mary at Hill. 0.23.118–22 (R.S. Gilbert).
429. St. Mary Magdalen Old Fish Street. 0.10.117–8 (P).
430. St. Mary Somerset. 0.10.117 (P).
431. St. Matthew Friday Street. 0.10.178–9 (P).
432. St. Michael Bassishaw. 0.10.179 (P).
433. St. Michael Cornhill. 0.8.193–8 (G. Benham).
434. St. Michael Paternoster Royal. 0.7.65–71 (F).
435. St. Michael Queenhithe. 0.11.54–5 (P).
436. St. Michael Wood Street. 0.11.55–6 (P).
437. St. Mildred Poultry. 0.11.186–7 (P).
438. St. Olave Hart Street. 0.35.113–24 (R.Illing).
439. St. Paul's Cathedral. Bumpus, J.S. The organists and composers of St. Paul's, 1891; 0.2.1–15 (F); 0.2.105–8 (Somers Clarke); 0.27.97–107 (W.L. Sumner); Clutton, C. The organ in St. Paul's, 1977; Musical Opinion 101, 1977 p.93–99 (A.Nyland).
440. St. Peter le Poer. 0.11.241–2 (P).
441. St. Sepulchre Holborn. 0.13.116–8 (G. Benham).
442. St. Stephen Coleman Street. 0.14.53–7 (F. Burgess).
443. St. Stephen Walbrook. 0.11.177–80 (G. Benham).
444. St. Vedast Foster Lane. Mander, N.P. A short account of the organs of St. Vedast, 1962.
445. Temple Church. Macroy, E. A few notes on the Temple organ, 1859; 0.34.65–91 (G. Benham).
446. Christ's Hospital. Jeans, S. The Easter psalms of Christ's Hospital (Roy. Mus. Assn. procs. 1961–2 p.45–60).
447. Crosby Hall. Mus. Times 114.641–3 (B. Matthews).

(See also addenda p.174).

A SELECTION OF OTHER WORKS CONSULTED

Barrett, W.A. English church composers, 1882.
English glees and part songs, 1886.
Blom, E. Everyman's dictionary of music revised by Sir. J. Westrup, 1972.
Boyd, P. Index of London and Middlesex burials 1538 – 1853 (microfilm).
Boyd, P. Index to London and Middlesex marriages 1538 – 1837, 73 vol., 1927–36 typescript.
British Museum. Catalogue of the King's Music Library, 3 vol., 1927–9.
British Museum. Catalogue of manuscript music, 3 vol., 1906–9.
Bumpus, J.S. A history of English cathedral music 1549 – 1889, 1972 (reprint).
Champlin, J.D. & Apthorp, W.F. Cyclopedia of music and musicians, 3 vol., 1889–90.
Cobb, G. London City churches, a brief guide, 1971.
Dearnley, C.H. English church music 1650 – 1750, 1970.
Deutsch, O.E. Handel: a documentary biography, 1955.
Dictionary of American biography, 21 vol., 1928–36.
Elkington, G. The Coopers: Company and craft, 1933.
Fellowes, E.H. English cathedral music revised by Sir. J.A. Westrup, 1969.
Fellowes, E.H. Organists of St. George's Chapel Windsor Castle, 1969.
Guildhall Library. Gresham music library catalogue, 1965.
Hackett, M. A brief account of cathedral and collegiate schools, 1827.
Hackett, M. Correspondence and evidences respecting the ancient collegiate school attached to St. Paul's Cathedral, 1832.

Harben, H.A. A dictionary of London, 1918.
Long, K.R. The music of the English church, 1972.
MacDermott, K.H. The old church gallery minstrels 1660 to 1860, 1948.
Matthews, B. The organ: a complete index 1921–70, 1970.
Musgrave, Sir W. Obituary prior to 1800, 6 vol., 1899–1901.
Routley, E. The musical Wesleys, 1968.
Scholes, P.A. The mirror of music 1844 – 1944, 2 vol., 1947.
Scholes, P.A. The Oxford companion to music, 1970.
Stevenson, G.J. Memorials of the Wesley family, 1876.
Wilkes, R. English cathedrals and collegiate churches and chapels, 1967.
Young, P.M. A history of British music, 1967.
Zimmerman, F.B. Henry Purcell 1659 – 1695, 1967.

ADDENDA

Secondary Sources: Periodicals (continued from p.171)

448. British Inst. of Organ Studies jnl. vol.2, 1978, p.10–23. J. Rowntree on B. Smith.

449. Musical Opinion vol.100, 1976 p.140–1 B.Matthews on S.S. Wesley.

450. vol.102, 1979 p.429–30 G.Beechey on Boyce.

451. Musical Quarterly vol.65, 1979 p.313–45 H.Brofsky on Dr. Burney and Padre Martini.

452. Musical Times vol.117, 1976 p.303–5 Watkins Shaw on S.S. Wesley.

453. vol.117, 1976 p.810–15 Glyn Williams, H.D. Johnstone and M. Boyd on Stanley.

454. vol.118, 1977 p.118–20 P.Marr on John Alcock and Fanny Brown.

455. vol.119, 1978 p.443–5 Watkins Shaw on S.S. Wesley.

456. vol.120, 1979 p.293–7, 385–91 I.Bartlett on Boyce and early English oratorio.

457. vol.120, 1979 p.764–6 J. Rowntree on B. Smith.

458. Royal Musical Association proceedings 1974–5 vol.101 p.101–6 B. Cooper on Stanley's organ music.

Secondary Sources: Miscellaneous

ADDITIONAL ITEMS RELATING TO CITY OF LONDON ORGANS (continued from p.172).

459. St. Bartholomew the Less. Detailed account in pamphlet entitled *View day, 1979: festival of flowers*.

460. St. Botolph Aldgate. Padgham, C. The organ of St. Botolph's. 1975.

461. St. Lawrence Jewry. The bells and the organ (anon). 1978?.

Subsidiary Index of Musicians and Musical Instrument Makers excluding City Organists

a. apprentice; d. dancing master; m. musician; m.i.m. musical instrument maker; m.s. music seller or publisher; o. organist; o.b. organ builder; p.c. parish clerk; v. vocalist